NO LONGER LADIES AND GENTLEMEN

STANFORD STUDIES IN JEWISH HISTORY AND CULTURE
Edited by David Biale and Sarah Abrevaya Stein

No Longer Ladies and Gentlemen

Gender and the German-Jewish Migration to Mandatory Palestine

VIOLA ALIANOV-RAUTENBERG

STANFORD UNIVERSITY PRESS
Stanford, California

Stanford University Press
Stanford, California

© 2023 by Viola Alianov-Rautenberg. All rights reserved.

This book has been partially underwritten by the Susan Groag Bell Publication Fund in Women's History. For more information on the fund, please see www.sup.org/bellfund.

No part of this book may be reproduced or transmitted in any form or by any means, electronic or mechanical, including photocopying and recording, or in any information storage or retrieval system, without the prior written permission of Stanford University Press.

Printed in the United States of America on acid-free, archival-quality paper

Library of Congress Cataloging-in-Publication Data
Names: Alianov-Rautenberg, Viola, author.
Title: No longer ladies and gentlemen : gender and the German-Jewish migration to Mandatory Palestine / Viola Alianov-Rautenberg.
Other titles: Gender and the German-Jewish migration to Mandatory Palestine | Stanford studies in Jewish history and culture.
Description: Stanford, California : Stanford University Press, [2024] | Series: Stanford Studies in Jewish history and culture | Includes bibliographical references and index.
Identifiers: LCCN 2023016820 (print) | LCCN 2023016821 (ebook) | ISBN 9781503636330 (cloth) | ISBN 9781503637238 (ebook)
Subjects: LCSH: Jews, German—Palestine—History—20th century. | Sex Role—Palestine—History—20th century. | Palestine—Emigration and immigration—Social aspects. | Palestine—Social conditions—20th century. | Palestine—History—1917–1948.
Classification: LCC DS113.8.G4 A45 2024 (print) | LCC DS113.8.G4 (ebook) | DDC 305.3089/924056940904—dc23/eng/20230419
LC record available at https://lccn.loc.gov/2023016820
LC ebook record available at https://lccn.loc.gov/2023016821

Cover design: Jason Anscomb
Cover photograph: Andreas Meyer, *Press Conference in Nahariya*, May 30, 1935

Contents

Acknowledgments — vii

Introduction — 1
Migration, Gender, and Change

1 *Liftmenschen* in the Levant — 27
Voyage, Arrival, and Absorption

2 We Are the West in the East — 68
Gendered Encounters in Mandatory Palestine

3 Capable Women and Men in Crisis? — 114
German Jews in the Yishuv Labor Market

4 How to Cook in Palestine? — 160
Homemaking in Times of Transition

5 Qualities That the Present Age Demands — 198
Gender and the Immigrant Family

Conclusion — 242

Notes — 251
Bibliography — 283
Index — 301

Acknowledgments

YEARS AGO, WHEN I FIRST started the research for this book, I began to formulate these acknowledgments in my head. Envisioning this moment, when I would finally be able to write them at the beginning of my book, was a way to keep myself going through the more difficult periods of this project. I drafted them during my drives to archives and interview partners all over Israel, over the course of long days in the library, and while walking up and down the steep and winding roads of Mount Carmel on breaks from my research. It is deeply gratifying to arrive at this moment. Over the years, researching, writing, and revising this book has taken me through different cities and countries and to countless conferences, meetings, archives, interviews, and lectures. On this long journey, in all of these places, I have been incredibly lucky to receive support, criticism, and encouragement from many people and institutions.

The origins of this book began at the Technical University of Berlin. I researched and wrote it in Haifa, but I was supervised by a joint team of "PhD mothers," as the Germans call it. Stefanie Schüler-Springorum and Deborah Bernstein, both eminent scholars in their respective fields, deeply affected the ways in which I think about questions near and dear to my heart: gender, migration, German Jewry, and the Yishuv. Both of them "mothered" this project continuously over many years, from both near and far. Both provided invaluable insights, critique, support, and encouragement—academic as well as in all other aspects of life. They steered me back on track when I started to lose myself in details, and they cheered me on for all my small and large successes along the way. I am deeply grateful to both of them for their commitment, dedication, and friendship.

Financially and intellectually, I am honored to have been supported by a range of prestigious organizations. Without them, this research would not have been possible. The Leo Baeck Fellowship Programme and Studienstiftung des deutschen Volkes provided crucial support throughout the initial research. The Center for Research on Antisemitism and the office for the advancement of women at the Technical University of Berlin, as well as the Fritz Halbers Award of the Leo Baeck Institute New York and the Carlebach Award of the University of Hamburg, provided further substantial financial support. Fellowships at the Herbert D. Katz Center for Advanced Judaic Studies at the University of Pennsylvania and the Minerva Post-Doctoral Fellowship enabled me to write this book while managing the distractions of a pandemic, a school-aged daughter, and a baby. In addition, travel grants from the Association of Israel Studies, the Association of Jewish Studies, and the Deutscher Akademischer Austauschdienst allowed me to present my ideas at multiple conferences and scientific meetings and to receive valuable feedback.

The foundation of this book is the archival research I conducted in multiple archives. Without the assistance and access granted to me by these archives, this book could not have been written. First and foremost, I have to thank the staff of the Archives of the German-Speaking Jewry Heritage Museum in Tefen/Galilee from the bottom of my heart. Nili Davidson of blessed memory and Ruthi Ofek allowed me to move from the formal reading room right into the archive itself, where I excitedly opened box after box, for months. Not only did they try to answer all of my never-ending questions, they went above and beyond in hosting me at the archives (which were at that time located in a pastoral location in the Galilee that was difficult to reach), including organizing rides for me to and from the archives and treating me to lunch at the archive cafeteria. The Central Zionist Archives in Jerusalem hold an unbelievable wealth of materials, and their archivists patiently helped me to obtain a variety of materials from within their holdings. Thanks are also due to a variety of small archives of German-Jewish immigrants in Israel: although I did not end up using all of them for this book, their hospitality was much appreciated. Special thanks to the archives of Kfar Shmaryahu, Bet Yizhak, and Sde Warburg. Special thanks as well to Shimon (Moni) Goren, the grandson of Leni Grünstein, to whom I owe the song that I quote in the introduction. Finally, the library of the University of Haifa, the National Library in Jerusalem, the library of the Institut für die Geschichte der deutschen Juden in Hamburg, and the library of the Herbert D. Katz Center for Advanced Judaic Studies at the University of Pennsylvania enabled me to acquire even the most obscure books.

I am deeply grateful to the interviewees who were willing to answer my questions and invite me into their homes and lives. This was often an anthropological experience, as I sat in apartments with furniture brought from Germany, being treated to *Kaffee und Kuchen*. In addition, many members of the second generation provided me with additional insights about their parents' generation. Many thanks also to the Irgun Yozey Merkas Europa. At the Jewish Museum Berlin, I am incredibly grateful to Mrs. Maurer-Porat for her quick and insightful help regarding photographs and permissions. I am further grateful to Jacob Barnai for allowing me to use his mother's recipes, as well as to the United States Holocaust Memorial Museum for allowing me to use a photograph from their collection.

Over the course of this project, I was lucky to have three academic homes on three different continents: each provided unique and invigorating intellectual opportunities in addition to substantial material support. The Institut für die Geschichte der deutschen Juden in Hamburg, where I worked first as a student assistant and later as a research fellow, provided me with formative intellectual academic experiences. I have benefited tremendously from the insights, collegiality, mentoring, and friendship of my colleagues there, and I am greatly indebted to them, especially to Stefanie Schüler-Springorum, Andreas Brämer, Björn Siegel, Miriam Rürup, Karen Körber, Kirsten Heinsohn, and Beate Meyer.

My fellowship at the Herbert D. Katz Center for Advanced Judaic Studies at the University of Pennsylvania was the most amazing intellectual experience, and although my year there was cut short due to the pandemic,

I benefited immensely from the intellectual comradery, critique, support, and friendship of its staff and of my entire cohort, "The Jewish Home." My deepest gratitude to Steven Weitzmann and Nathalie Dohrmann for their ongoing support and advice, as well as to Anne Albers, Esther Lassmann, and Karen Schnitker. In addition, I am deeply grateful to the Society Hill Synagogue of Philadelphia and its community for making that year so significant, even in spite of the pandemic. Particular thanks to Sahar Oz, Rabbi Nathan Kamesar, Ally Kaplan, and Micah Hart.

The Bucerius Institute for the Research of Contemporary German History and Society has been my academic home during various stages of my career. My heartfelt gratitude goes to Cedric Cohen-Skalli and Amir Bar-On for their intellectual, financial, and emotional support, especially during a time complicated by the Covid-19 pandemic in conjunction with my being pregnant and having a baby. I am deeply thankful to Cedric and Amir for their unwavering optimism and friendship. They provided a sanctuary, special permissions, cookies and coffee, and company during the lonely time of finishing a manuscript during a pandemic. During the last stages of finalizing this book, they accommodated my challenging reality of working while having a newborn, meeting me at playgrounds and for walks with the stroller, or holding my baby while I delivered talks.

I am indebted to many colleagues who have supported me constantly throughout the last years. First and foremost, I am incredibly grateful to a group of much-appreciated colleagues who patiently read chapters of this book (and much more), and provided feedback and critique that greatly improved it: Ofer Ashkenazy, Cedric Cohen-Skalli, Yotam Hotam, Guy Miron, Moshe Naor, Danna Piroyansky, Joachim Schlör, and Björn Siegel. I am grateful to all of them for the invaluable advice they always provided on short notice and at all times of the day and night, sharing materials, wisdom, and, in general, a positive outlook.

Many colleagues have provided support and shared insights with me over the years, whether in person, at conferences, or through email: Gur Alroey, Leora Auslander, Eitan Bar-Yosef, Ela Bauer, Yossi Ben-Artzi, Melissa Cradic, Sigal Davidi, Lea Dror, Gabriela Fenyes, Sylvie Fogel-Bijaoui, Federica Francesconi, the late Sharon Gillerman, Atina Grossmann, Esther Carmel Hakim, Aviva Halamish, Katharina Hoba, Marion Kaplan, Bat-

Zion Eraqi Klorman, Mihal Kofman, Jan Kühne, Hagit Lavsky, Marjorie Lehman, Laura Levitt, Micha Limor, Sharon Livne, the late Gilad Margalit, Amos Morris-Reich, Sharon Musher, Jannis Pannagiotidis, Talia Pfefferman, Marcos Silber, Sabrina Spatari, Bat-Sheva Margalit Stern, Joshua Teplitsky, Marc Volovici, and Orit Yaali. During the early years of this research project, my PhD study group with Deborah Bernstein ("Debbie's PhD students") patiently read through many different drafts of my chapters and papers. I am thankful to Vardit Garber, Hadas Fischer-Rosenberg, Yahel Ash Kurlander, and Naomi Levenkron. Our meetings were all about spending long hours around tables full of food—along with rigorous debate and feedback. Parts of this book were presented at the Migration Forum and the Forum for the Research of Mandatory Palestine, and I received many helpful comments during those meetings. The Association for Jewish Studies summer writing group proved to be essential for writing the proposal and rewriting the introduction, and I have to earnestly thank my small writing group, Laura Leibmann and Anastasia Badder, for their close reading. I also sincerely thank Marie Deer for saving me from many errors.

I am grateful to Stanford University Press, specifically David Biale, Margo Irvin, Sarah Abrevaya Stein, and Cindy Lim, for their enthusiastic support for this book. I also want to thank Catherine Mallon for copyediting. It has been a delight to work with all of them.

I am blessed with many wonderful friends who have patiently listened to the ups and downs of my research for years. Most especially, I must mention Mihal Kofman, Rotem Moadav, Tammy Noth, Nina Pauer, Danna Piroyansky, Yael Segev, Lara Yasnogorodskiy, and Aviva Zimbris. A very special thanks is due to Shlomit Paz.

My family in Germany and in Israel has supported this project over its entirety in many ways. My mother, Marike, has patiently listened to myriad variations of my openings, endings, and transitions, only for them all to be completely rewritten again afterwards. She is not only genuinely interested in my research but also fascinated by the possible implications as well as by the difficult minutiae of archival work, grant writing, and combining all of that with motherhood. She has been my number one cheerleader these last years. Joachim Krauter of blessed memory was very invested in this book and never failed to lift my spirit with his witty jokes and optimism when I struggled. From the beginning, my parents-in-law, Emma and Boris, as well as Ernst Gross of blessed memory, have been intrigued by my research and all the stories of my small adventures in the archives and the larger adventures of my journeys and relocations. They have remained a warm, steadfast, and generous source of support through the years. My brother, Boris, and my sister-in-law Mieke, have provided encouragement and optimism, along with desk space, food, and company when needed during my work in Hamburg, and Boris has also provided constant design advice, from business cards to PowerPoint presentations.

This book is dedicated to the loves of my life: Yevgeny, Kinneret, and Carmel. My husband, Yevgeny, has been through the ups and downs of this research with me from the very beginning: through its exhilarating highs and frustrating lows, he never left my side, joining me for research and conference trips near and far and providing child support, food, and technical assistance as well as unwavering love, calm, and humor. Our two daughters, Kinneret and Carmel, were born into this research at different stages. Kinneret was born while I was doing the research for my dissertation and had to be very patient with me while I finished this project. Carmel was born during the final stage of revising this manuscript. Both have been dragged to conferences and talks, mostly very patiently, since before they were two months old. Most importantly, both of them always bring me back to thinking about things that are even more important than German-Jewish migration to Mandatory Palestine: going to the playground, building pillow forts, dancing, singing, and laughing. I could not ask for anyone better than you three, ever. This book is dedicated to you with love and gratitude.

NO LONGER LADIES AND GENTLEMEN

INTRODUCTION

Migration, Gender, and Change

THE DUSTY STORAGE BOX IN the little archive in central Israel was filled to the brim with materials from the late 1930s and 1940s. The letters, pictures, and protocols of official meetings bore witness to the early community life of Bet Yitzhak, a small village established in 1939 by new immigrants from Germany. In with the other documents, the box also included an unexpected find: the lyrics to a song written in 1940 by the recent immigrant Leni Grünstein. In this song, written for a celebration with her fellow community members, the author reflects on the new realities they had all faced since their immigration:

Als wir einst ins Land herkamen—   *When we first came to the country,*
waren Herren wir und Damen   *we were ladies and gentlemen*
Anders ist es heut'   *Today it is different.*

Arbeitsanzug—unsre Mode—   *Work clothes are our fashion now*
Primus—unsre Kochmethode   *Primus is the way we cook*
Haben niemals Zeit.   *We never have time.*

Arbeitstag währt 15 Stunden—   *The working day lasts 15 hours—*
Bäuche sind dahin geschwunden   *our bellies are gone*
Anzug ward zu weit.   *Our clothes become too big.*

Mit Turiah und Spaten—   *Armed with turiah and spade,*
sind als Beth Jizhaks Soldaten   *we are always ready to fight*
Wir stets kampfbereit.   *As Bet Yitzhak's soldiers.*

Fort mit Lippenstift und Smoking—   *Away with lipstick and tuxedoes*
Fort mit Frack, denn das ist shocking   *Away with tailcoats, they are shocking*
Fort das Abendkleid.   *Away with evening gowns.*
Weil ab jetzt dem Hühnerzüchten—   *Because from now on, raising chickens—*
Kühe melken, Felder richten   *Milking cows, and working the fields*
Wir uns ganz geweiht.[1]   *Is what we are entirely devoted to.*

Leni Grünstein was part of the mass Jewish emigration from Nazi Germany: between 1933, when Hitler came to power, and 1941, when emigration became illegal, two hundred and fifty thousand German Jews left the National Socialist state. While the largest group went to the United States, about sixty thousand German Jews migrated to Mandatory Palestine, then a small, poor, underdeveloped country that was not yet a sovereign state. Before the beginning of Nazi rule, German Jews had been a heterogeneous group, yet with a distinct shared socioeconomic profile: predominantly middle class, educated, urban, secularized, and assimilated. Immigration to Palestine brought about radical change, transforming their professional and social lives in almost every way. Crucial to these all-encompassing shifts were the changing gender relations within the immigrating group.

Grünstein's song speaks directly to these changes. As she writes, she and her peers arrived as ladies and gentlemen—terms that are deeply connected with both class and gender roles. And while in pre-Nazi Germany before Nazi rule, Jewish men and women of the middle class had primarily lived and worked in separate spheres and according to different norms, this changed after immigration. As Grünstein vividly sums it up, there was a transformation from lipstick and evening gowns for the ladies and tailcoats and tuxedoes for the gentlemen to uniform work clothes for both sexes. Those who settled in agricultural villages, both men and women, now worked together, doing physical labor in agriculture and poultry farming, without leisure time or creature comforts, which brought changes to their bodies, relations, and self-perceptions.

The majority of the immigrants from Germany eventually settled in the cities of Mandatory Palestine, rather than the countryside. However, they, too, experienced the same dramatic changes that Grünstein describes for her little village: downward social mobility, accompanied by a loss of former profession, status, and class affiliation.

For almost all of the German immigrants to Mandatory Palestine, new employment patterns led to immediate changes in their gender relations and family dynamics. In the cities, husbands and fathers, who had formerly been their families' breadwinners and providers, often became unemployed and had to depend on the incomes of their spouses and former homemakers. At the same time, families that had once lived according to middle-class gender norms now needed to dwell in small apartments, often shared with other families, while simultaneously coping with a new climate and language, as well as an emergent society engaged in an intensive nation-building process, characterized by a socialist pioneering ethos, which emphatically penetrated all aspects of the immigrants' lives and produced relentless demands to change. As this book argues, both the absorbing bodies and a majority of the immigrants themselves experienced this situation as a crisis—and this crisis was gendered. While the migration led to radical transformations in the lives of all of the immigrants, the experience and outcome of the migration process differed for men and women. These crucial differences in the immigration experience, along with the consequences of a highly gendered absorption policy, have not yet been explored in the research literature.

This book analyzes the German-Jewish migration to Mandatory Palestine through a close examination of the first decade of absorption in order to shed light precisely on the critical role that gender played in this time of turmoil. Employing a great variety of sources that have not previously been focused on, I look here at gender in a broad array of different spheres (from private to public), scenes (from the ship to the workplace to the kitchen), and perspectives (of the immigrants, the absorbing apparatus, the veteran society). This multiplicity of sources and perspectives makes it possible to juxtapose the levels of discourse, policy, and experience and to demonstrate, in the process, that gender differences in policies of migration, absorption, and support caused gendered changes in the most intimate aspects of the individual immigrant's life: from how they cooked and cleaned, through how they worked and lived their family lives, to their apparel and their bodies.

Methodologically, this combination of micro and macro perspective brings to the fore a new understanding of migration. By bringing such diverse sources as cookbooks and statistics, social welfare reports and songs, letters of complaint and newspaper articles into dialogue with each other, this approach demonstrates the relational quality of gender not only between men and women but also between everyday life and policies, between public and private, between center and margins. Integrating these extremely varied perspectives allows us to gain a deeper understanding of the complexity of the migration process, its historic actors, and their decisions more generally.

Ultimately, considering the impact of gender on this unique historical migration can help us in thinking more broadly about the timely phenomenon of large migration movements. How do normative ideologies from their countries of origin influence migrants' absorption processes? How do gendered and ethnic hierarchies in the absorbing societies affect the migrants? And how do societies, after absorbing large migration movements, transform and reorganize around questions of power, privilege, and access to resources?

GENDER AND MIGRATION

Immigration brings about radical change: migrants leave their old homes and homelands, families and friends, professions, and mother tongues. While these aspects of migration affect all migrants, migration is not by any means a gender-neutral process. The term *gender*, the social construction of differences between men and women (as opposed to *sex*, the biological differences), refers to a category defined by the historian Joan W. Scott as a constitutive element of social relationships. It includes symbols, normative concepts, social organizations, and subjective identity.[2] As such, gender is a crucial aspect of immigration processes: from a macro perspective, the migration policies of both sending and receiving countries influence and provide differing migration opportunities for men and for women.[3] For example, immigration laws can generate gendered disadvantages by giving women a derivative status.[4] Simultaneously, from a micro perspective, migration challenges and often transforms individual immigrants' gender relations and gendered self-perceptions. While under sedentary conditions, such change usually takes many years, immigration tends to propel processes that had begun long before, causing drastic and immediate transformations in the allocation of tasks within the family, concepts of masculinity and femininity, and participation in the labor market.

Located at the intersection of German-Jewish and Israeli history, this book tells the gender history of the "German Aliyah" to Mandatory Palestine / Eretz Israel. It argues that this Jewish migration from Nazi Germany was shaped and structured by gendered policies and ideologies and experienced in a gendered form by men and women who found refuge in Mandatory Palestine between 1933 and 1940. It uses gender as a relational category, discussing not only women or men but their relation to one another, as well as the relation between different kinds of women and different kinds of men. Therefore, gender is used here neither as an equivalent for women nor as an essential and stable category but as a historical category and, consequently, subject to change. Relating both to the immigrants' lives in Germany before migration and to the complex reality of their new homeland, this book analyzes where such change occurred and how it was perceived by the immigrants, on the one hand, and the absorbing society, on the other.

These issues are crucial for understanding not only this specific immigration wave, but also the involuntary Jewish exodus from Germany more broadly. The respective conditions of the host countries across the globe led to a wide variety of different experiences among the immigrants. What was shared, however, was the experience of a gender role reversal for the immigrants, in conjunction with downward social mobility.

Employing gender as a methodological tool also enables a more comprehensive discussion of the character of the organized Jewish community in Mandatory Palestine, the Yishuv. Using the case of German Jews in this society, this book discusses their interactions with the receiving society on the cultural, social, political, and economic levels. In so doing, it reveals the ideologically charged discourse of these years and the demands of the absorbing society toward newcomers more generally. Further, it brings to the fore the question of interactions among different groups in Mandatory Palestine, both Jewish and non-Jewish, arguing that gender was crucial to these encounters and to the self-perception of the immigrants vis-à-vis the other groups. Lastly, this book also makes a methodological claim about the historical study of migration in general, asking how we study migrants and migration: do we choose the perspective of the immigrants or of the absorbing society, and do we base our analysis on contemporary documents or those conducted in hindsight? This study makes a case for bringing together both macro and micro viewpoints, as well as a multiplicity of sources.

REFUGE, ALIYAH, AND MIGRATION

The migration movement at the center of this book is part of two historical processes: on the one hand, the Jewish exodus from Nazi Germany and the subsequent development of a worldwide German-Jewish diaspora, and on the other, the history of Jewish immigration to Mandatory Palestine in the crucial decade before the founding of the state of Israel. This migration can hence be understood as both an epilogue to Jewish life in Germany before the Holocaust and a chapter in the history of the Yishuv at the height of its nation-building period, and has accordingly been researched from two different disciplinary standpoints: that of exile studies and that of Israeli migration history. In exile studies, the German Jews on the move are generally understood as emigrants and refugees rather than immigrants. Their history is considered mainly in the context of the Holocaust, since—as Debórah Dwork and Robert Jan van Pelt have pointed out—if they had not managed to leave Germany in time, they would have been murdered, too.[5] Given this focus, the terminology used to describe them highlights their forced emigration and flight. Research on the mass Jewish emigration from Nazi Germany to the various countries of absorption initially concentrated on famous émigrés, such as scientists, intellectuals, and authors, most of whom were men. In the 1980s and 1990s, the research turned to simple rank-and-file immigrants and their immigration experiences.[6] As interest shifted in this way, the studies also began to include female émigrées and, later, gender.

In Israeli research, the focus is different. The history of the Yishuv and of the modern state of Israel are inextricably linked with immigration; indeed, as the historian Aviva Halamish has put it, "Immigration *is* Israel's history."[7] Until recently, the historiography was dominated by a Zionist narrative in which immigration to Israel was perceived as a unique and incomparable form of migration, expressed in the terminology of *Aliyah* (Hebrew: ascent) and *Yerida* (Hebrew: descent) for immigration and emigration, respectively, with all the positive and negative connotations of each of those terms.[8] From the Zionist point of view, once Jews had entered Palestine, it was assumed that they automatically became members of the society and, thus, they were no longer considered refugees, even if they had fled from their country of origin.[9] *Immigrant* was also the legal category that the British Mandate power applied to Jews arriving in Palestine with the intention of staying. The German-Jewish migrants, therefore, are also called immigrants in this field of research and considered mainly as a memorable part of the last and largest immigration wave to arrive in Palestine before the establishment of the state of Israel.

In this book, I will address the German Jews in Mandatory Palestine as migrants and immigrants, rather than as emigrants. Firstly, this is for historical reasons. While emigrating from Germany did take place under conditions of persecution and discrimination, it was not generally characterized as a refugee movement: from 1933 until late 1938, as Hagit Lavsky and others have pointed out, migrants did have the choice to emigrate and therefore the opportunity to plan and prepare for that process, even though that choice became increasingly limited as time went on.[10] After the November pogrom, the situation changed: German Jews now tried to leave Germany at all costs, turning emigrants into refugees who were fleeing with not much more than their lives. But by that time, most of the emigrants who would eventually settle in Palestine had already arrived there, and the United States and the United Kingdom had become the central absorption countries.

The second reason for this terminological choice in this book is conceptual. Researching these immigrants using the methods of historic migration studies, rather than treating them as a refugee movement, means taking into consideration the different stages of the migration process: the developments leading to their emigration, the process of decision-making, their preparations, the journey itself, and the immigration policies and conditions in the country of absorption. This book is interested primarily in migration and absorption and the interaction with the receiving society. But by the same token, while the focus is on the immigrants' lives in Palestine, I do also consider their pre-migration life in Germany, because I am precisely interested in the change from the gender relations and gendered perceptions that were rooted in their old life. For these women and men, neither emigrants longingly looking back to their old homeland nor ideologically motivated *olim* (Hebrew: immigrants), the words *migrants* and *immigrants* encompassed their many different experiences on the move and the ways in which they were absorbed into their new homeland.

INTEGRATION, IDENTITY, AND MEMORY

The research literature on German-Jewish immigration to Mandatory Palestine has hitherto largely concentrated on two issues. Firstly, it has assessed the eventual level of the integration of these immigrants into society. Secondly, it has pointed out their manifold contributions to the emerging state of Israel. These two focal points already emerged in early historiographic works in the 1960s, which were almost entirely penned by the immigrants themselves.[11] With these two focal points, the early research set the tone for much of the later literature; the topics of contribution and integration have remained the main topics of interest in the research literature on the German-Jewish immigration to Palestine. A plethora of studies has since researched this population's contributions to industry and production, commerce and consumer culture, banking and finance, architecture, the tourist industry, medicine and medical services, science and academia, the judicial system, technology, and high culture.[12] Collectively, these contributions have been referred to as impulses toward the modernization, professionalization, and Westernization of the culture, economy, and society of the Yishuv and later the state of Israel. Since the 1990s, the research has begun using different methodologies, including oral history and autobiography-based research. As a result, questions of experience, identity, and the memory of the immigrants have been brought to the fore.[13] As a part of this shift, and due to more general interest in gender as a discipline, the research has also begun to address questions of femininities and masculinities as well as most recently sexuality.[14] Gender as a relational category, however, considering both men and women, has not yet been systematically utilized.

How can we historicize these shifting focal points of the research literature? The argument about contributions originates in the initial dominance of the immigrants' own perspectives and can be read as their desire to become part of the master narrative of Israeli historiography, as well as a reaction to the criticism on the part of the receiving society in the 1930s and 1940s that the immigrants allegedly refused to merge into the Yishuv melting pot.[15] In his analysis of memoir literature, Guy Miron has characterized these German-Jewish migrants as an "interpretive community" whose members grappled extensively with both their individual and their collective past in an effort to shape their legacy for future generations.[16] In recent decades, this attempt has been continued, through exhibitions, conferences, and publications, by members of the second and third generations of German immigrants. Such initiatives "demand the integration of the German story within the heroic national narrative, to emphasize its importance in the Zionist epic and promote its potential for the general society, present, and future," as Hagit Lavsky has put it.[17] Methodologically, this concentration on contributions is not analytical, as it automatically concentrates on positively connoted features and limits the research perspective. For example, what was crucial to the immigrants' self-perception was the Orientalist lens through which they observed the absorbing society. This book is interested precisely in this self-perception of the newcomers in the context of the absorbing society, as well as the intersecting categories of power, class, ethnicity, and gender that such a perspective entails.

The focus on integration must also be understood as an attempt by the immigrants-turned-historians to pinpoint the success of their extensive attempts at "self-absorption" through their organizations. In an immigration country such as Israel, the question of integration appears straightforward from the perspective of the absorbing society; after all, the society is interested in successfully integrating the newcomers. Studies agree on the eventual economic integration, but the degree of cultural and social integration has been more disputed. The assessments range from slow but thorough integration to assertions of alienation and cultural incompatibility. The latter position claims that a distinction between German Jews and the receiving society based on the former group's adherence to its own language, cultural heritage, and habits hindered or even prevented its complete integration. This narrative of distinction, in the research literature as well as in popular memory, has strengthened a stereotypical and folkloristic characterization of the immigrants. Rakefet Sela-Sheffy, for one, has challenged this notion, criticizing the uncritical perpetuation of this narrative of cultural alienation—a narrative, she claims, that helped the immigrants to achieve what she calls "integration through distinction."[18] The standard narrative about well-to-do immigrants with cultural integration problems may well have contributed to the under-studied status of difficult economic integration and social distress. Studies that explicitly concentrate on the ultimate integration of the German Jews, along with research that uses mainly sources composed in hindsight, run the risk of omitting the struggles of early absorption. It is precisely these challenges, and the place that gender had in them, that this book is interested in.

Because the migrants are part of two national histories—the histories of Germany and Israel—most of the research has been conducted in those two countries. The shift in interest away from the former focal points of research, both in Germany and in Israel, has different reasons in the different places: the two national historiographies have addressed the topic not only from different vantage points but often also using different terminologies and methodologies. The concentration on identity and experience in the newer Israeli studies can be seen as a reaction to the dominant historiography of Israeli academia: looking at the perspective of the immigrants themselves rather than using a viewpoint from above can be understood as a reaction to the traditional Israeli narrative that made German-Jewish contributions to the state-in-the-making and its institutions, along with successful integration, the main factor, rather than focusing on experiences.[19] Meanwhile, on the side of German scholars, the emphasis on experience and memory may have different reasons behind it. Here, since the 1990s, studies have increasingly been based on either oral history or research into autobiographies.[20] Because most autobiographies were published in German, and the interviewees still spoke German, this research focus bypassed any need for German scholars to read Hebrew sources and research literature. This may have amplified the perspective that treats German Jews in Palestine more as isolated emigrants looking back on their lost life in Germany than as immigrants who were a part of Yishuv society. The extensive use, in Germany, of oral history in place of, rather than in addition to, contemporary sources may also have helped perpetuate the stereotype of culturally alienated and isolated immigrants who did not manage to properly integrate into the host society. As Anja Siegemund has suggested, such a research approach understands the German Jews as part of German history rather than Israeli history.[21] The historical research itself thus reflects how the German-Jewish migrants are remembered by the two societies, for different reasons and with different ramifications.

GENDER AND THE GERMAN-JEWISH EMIGRATION

Gender has so far not been used as a systematic tool in researching this migration movement. However, rich historical studies, most notably Marion Kaplan's work, have proven gender to be a crucial category for understanding modern German-Jewish history. In 1933, the Jewish minority made up less than 1 percent of the total German population, about five hundred thousand people. Before Nazi rule began, most understood themselves as Jewish Germans and identified with the ideals of German culture. Despite an ever-present anti-Semitism, German Jewry had been a successful group with a quick social upward mobility. Between the end of the eighteenth century and the beginning of World War I, they had undergone a process of modernization, assimilation, and emancipation. Marion Kaplan argues that women, by preserving Jewishness within the family while enabling the process of acculturation, were instrumental in this "making of the Jewish middle class."[22] While the primary responsibilities of German-Jewish women were toward the home and the family, from the beginning of the twentieth century there had been more possibilities provided for female education. The number of female students at the universities as well as that of female professionals rose, and alternative female role models, such as the *Neue Frau* (New Woman), appeared in Weimar.[23]

With the National Socialist rise to power in 1933, the emancipation of German Jewry was set back. Over the course of thirteen years, from 1933 through 1945, German Jews were first subjected to legal disenfranchisement, then social ostracism, discriminatory legislation, economic expulsion, Aryanization, and finally forced emigration, violence, deportation, and murder. The destruction of Jewish businesses and the limitation of Jewish participation in the economy started as early as April 1933, with the nationwide boycott. The introduction of the so-called Aryan Paragraph then led to the dismissal or early retirement of "non-Aryan" civil servants, lawyers, judges, and physicians, causing increasing unemployment and privation. The formal deprivation of Jews' rights as citizens and the establishment of racial segregation were finalized in the September 1935 Nuremberg Laws. In 1938, a period of increasing brutality in the National Socialist persecution began. In November of that year, the pogrom night escalated the violence, with the burning of synagogues, the demolishing of flats and businesses, the murder of hundreds, and the imprisonment of thirty thousand Jews in concentration camps. In 1941, emigration was banned, and the deportations to the extermination camps began. And of the millions of Jews murdered in the Shoah, 165,000 were German Jews, including those who fled to other countries that were later conquered by the Nazis.[24]

Gender was a decisive factor in Jewish life under National Socialism. As Kaplan and others have demonstrated, both Nazi persecution and the survival strategies of the victims were gendered. Jews were attacked first and foremost as Jews, but while Jewish women were ultimately targeted too, it was men who were in the direct line of fire of Nazi politics at first: their careers were destroyed, they became incapable of providing for their families, and they also, initially, faced the more immediate physical danger. As a result, Jewish women in Nazi Germany had to take on new roles as breadwinners when their husbands lost their sources of livelihood, while simultaneously continuing to fulfill their old roles, such as homemaking and child-rearing, under worsened conditions. Emotional support was especially needed for those men who now felt worthless because they were no longer able to provide for their families, and even more so for those who were traumatized after having been imprisoned in the camps. Many women also became active defenders of their families and their businesses and interceded with the authorities on behalf of their arrested husbands.[25]

Nazi rule radically transformed the lives of German Jews, increasingly eroding their socioeconomic position. This meant a wearing away of what Guy Miron and others have described as the bourgeois habitus that had characterized German-Jewish life in pre-1933 Germany, including gender roles and female participation in the labor market.[26] The slow changes that had been taking place in gender roles over the previous decades were hence involuntarily accelerated through the National Socialist persecution, even before German Jews emigrated.

The approximately two hundred and fifty thousand German Jews who did manage to emigrate found shelter in about ninety countries around the world. Roughly a hundred thousand of them emigrated to the United States, sixty thousand to Palestine, and forty thousand to England. Other main countries of refuge included South American states such as Brazil and Argentina, as well as South Africa, Australia, and Shanghai.

German-Jewish women and men in all countries of exile experienced gendered crisis and role reversal. The specific manifestations differed from country to country, however, due to the ranges of gender relations and ideals of masculinity and femininity in each place.[27] These manifestations also depended on the timing of their migration. Many of the challenges that emigration posed to their former middle-class status, such as male unemployment, female participation in the labor market, and downward socioeconomic mobility, had already increasingly been part of Jewish life in Nazi Germany. Most of the German Jews who immigrated to Palestine, however, left Nazi Germany relatively early. Therefore, in comparison with the majority of German-Jewish emigrants, who left after 1938, and mainly to other countries, the migrants to Palestine had been subjected to less Nazi persecution and less of the concomitant erosion of their middle-class identity while they were still in Germany. This is why, for German-Jewish immigrants to Palestine, the socioeconomic changes in immigration were perceived as bringing such radical change, as described in Leni Grünstein's song above.

For emigrants from Nazi Germany in general, the picture that has been drawn in the research literature is that, at least in the first decade, men suffered more from the deterioration of their status, the loss of their career, the loss of the fatherland, and the breakdown of their old culture. As a result, many became depressed or ill or even collapsed. The female immigrants, by contrast, appear from the research to have shouldered the overall immigration situation and their new lives much better.[28] However, most of these scholarly works did not engage with gender relations per so but focused instead on women or, in a few cases, men.[29]

The same narrative appears in the research on German Jews in Palestine. Guy Miron and Dorit Yosef have dealt with female immigrants and their features in autobiographies and memoir literature.[30] Patrick Farges has recently examined oral history interviews conducted in the 1990s regarding expressions of masculinity in this material.[31] These studies point out that gender did matter for the experience and memories of the individual immigrants; however, they do not apply gender as a relational category. In other words, they do not consider both men and women, nor do they examine gender as a structural element in migration and absorption policies. The same is true for other Israeli studies that have recently touched upon German immigrants in the framework of professional women in medicine, social work, education, and architecture in Mandatory Palestine.[32] Aiming to highlight the contributions of women in all these fields (and, ultimately, in the establishment of the state of Israel), these historical works tend to engage with a small professional elite and not the experience of the majority of immigrants. In addition, few of these studies discuss how these professional women perceived themselves in contrast with other groups of women in Mandatory Palestine, namely those Jews of Middle Eastern and North African origin who were referred to as "Oriental" Jews at the time. In other words, they do not explore gender as a relational category with multiple dimensions, where groups of women are studied in relation not only to men but also to other groups of women in different categories of class and ethnicity. As this book argues, however, such perceptions and related questions of power, superiority, and inferiority were crucial to the immigrants' efforts to find their place in their new society.

This book discusses men and women as gendered actors in relation to each other in the immigration process. Moreover, it relates to gender on both micro and macro levels, bringing to the fore gender as a factor in individual experiences and memory and as a structural category in immigration and absorption policies. Furthermore, instead of researching this immigrant group in isolation from the rest of society, I investigate the gendered interaction between this group and the receiving society on the cultural, social, political, and economic levels. In using gender as a relational category, I critically examine the paradigm of women being able to cope better than men in Jewish migration by questioning the social circumstances of the contemporary debates and the underlying normative ideas of femininity and masculinity.

How did gender matter in Jewish emigration from Nazi Germany? Being able to leave Germany depended both on Nazi politics and on the immigration policies of the countries of refuge. At first, it was the objective of Nazi policy, using economic pressure, discrimination, and isolation, to prompt as many Jews as possible to leave Germany. At the same time, the Nazis restricted the amount of currency and property that Jews could take with them. With each year of Nazi persecution, these conditions worsened, and the German Jews were increasingly expropriated. The Nazi policies were unpredictable and deceptive. In the 1930s, therefore, it was not possible to predict the deportations and mass murder of the "final solution" or to know

FIGURE 1. A train carrying German-Jewish emigrants from Berlin to Marseille leaving the Anhalter train station in Berlin, September 1, 1936. Photographer: Herbert Sonnenfeld. Source: Jewish Museum Berlin, FOT 88/500/106/034, purchased with funds provided by the Stiftung Deutsche Klassenlotterie Berlin. Reprinted with permission.

that emigration would be the only way to survive. Even Jewish organizations concerned with emigration initially thought that they would have much more time for the emigration process. So rather than hurrying the process, they worked to ensure that German Jews were well prepared for their emigration.[33] Only in the wake of the 1938 pogrom did emigration became mass flight. By this point, the conditions for leaving had become even more desperate, mainly because most Jews still in Germany were destitute by then.

Meanwhile, most countries of absorption had restrictive immigration policies. Already suffering from massive unemployment due to the Great Depression, they did not want impoverished immigrants who would become indigent. This was even more the case when these immigrants were old and when their professions did not suit the demands of the host country—in most countries of refuge, different occupations were asked for than those prevailing among German Jewry. The most attractive countries of immigration, namely the United States and England, both had restrictive immigration policies until 1938 and only eased those restrictions after the November pogrom. Then, with the outbreak of World War II in September of 1939, the belligerent nations halted immigration from Germany almost completely, while the neutral states strictly restricted it. In the autumn of 1941, Nazi Germany banned emigration entirely. Shortly after that, the deportations to the extermination camps began.

Trying to start a new life abroad, therefore, required not only courage but also money, skills, knowledge, and networks. In deciding to emigrate, gender was a crucial factor, in addition to age, political affiliation, and marital and socioeconomic status. As Marion Kaplan argues, women were more willing than men to leave Germany and start a new life abroad because women were less integrated into the public world but more family-oriented. Therefore, she continues, women sensed hostility in everyday encounters earlier than men, causing them to favor emigration.[34] And yet, ultimately, fewer women than men emigrated from Nazi Germany. The research literature suggests several possible reasons for this. Despite the changes in gender roles discussed above, in married couples it was still mainly the husband who made the emigration decision for the couple. Another reason for the unequal emigration ratio was that women, unlike most men, were still able to find employment in commercial jobs and as household personnel within the Jewish sector in Germany for a while.[35] Men, on the other hand, had more business connections abroad—a fact that helped them leave Germany. However, as Stefanie Schüler-Springorum has argued, there were also women who did not want to leave, whether for fear of the unknown or because of responsibilities for family members who were unable to leave and needed to be taken care of. And at the same time, there were also many men who were not willing to leave their life's work behind. As Schüler-Springorum suggests, it is therefore impossible to reach a definitive answer to the question of whether it was men or women who pushed harder for emigration.[36] Furthermore, there was the structural factor that Jewish community welfare organizations provided more support for emigrating men than for women, leading to greater emigration by young men.[37] Lastly, there were also gendered restrictions in migration policies from the absorbing countries, as in the case of Palestine.

GERMAN-JEWISH IMMIGRATION TO MANDATORY PALESTINE

Palestine was one of the main destinations for German Jewry: between 1933 and 1940, it absorbed almost a quarter of the total emigration. Palestine had been a relatively neglected part of the Ottoman Empire until it was conquered by the British during World War I, after four hundred years of Ottoman rule, and subsequently became subject to British colonial rule from 1918 to 1948. Entrusted in 1922 by the League of Nations to serve as the Mandatory Power for Palestine, the British had full legislative and administrative power over the region's clashing inhabitants: the majority Arab population and the Jewish community of pre-state Israel. Between the end of the nineteenth and the early twentieth century, championed by the Zionist movement, five "Aliyot" or immigration waves arrived in Palestine, mainly from Russia and Eastern Europe, leading to the establishment of the so-called New Yishuv. The "Fifth Aliyah" (ca. 1929–1939), larger than all previous immigration waves, brought nearly a quarter of a million people to Palestine and doubled the population of the Yishuv. The majority of this Aliyah was from Poland, but the sixty thousand immigrants from Germany and another thirty thousand from German-speaking central Europe (Austria, Czechoslovakia, and the Free City of Danzig) figured prominently and led to a common perception of this wave as the "German Aliyah."

The German Jews arrived during a period of intensive nation-building efforts by the organized Jewish community. In the 1930s, the Yishuv was a state-in-the-making, striving for autonomy. It had formed an infrastructure with political, military, cultural, and health institutions and a rudimentary parliament recognized by the British Mandate. A unique cultural life emerged in the Yishuv, characterized by a socialist pioneering ethos and centered on the renewal of the Hebrew language and its use in developing a Hebrew culture.[38] While women were part of all these developments in the Yishuv, and despite its proclaimed goal of creating a new society, traditional gender inequality continued to exist in the political and private life of the Yishuv.[39]

Despite the economic depression, the Yishuv retained its great interest in large-scale immigration and continued to support that immigration, against the wishes of the majority Arab population. It was the British Mandate, though, that ultimately decided on immigration policy.[40] British immigration regulations divided the immigrants into four groups and allocated certificates accordingly: category A certificates for "capitalists," persons of independent means who could prove the ownership of 1,000 Palestine pounds; category B certificates for students, pupils, and persons of religious occupations whose maintenance was assured; category C certificates for persons with a definite prospect of employment, labeled "labor," or pioneering immigrants; and category D certificates for dependents of permanent residents of Palestine or of immigrants in other categories. In the first years of the German immigration, between 1933 and 1937, the British policy was conducted under the "economic absorptive capacity," an estimate of the country's ability to absorb immigrants without harming the economy. Only category C (labor) immigrants were subject to the economic absorptive capacity principle in this period; immigrants in the A, B, and D categories were not expected to join the labor market and hence not regulated in this way. In 1937, though, this policy was replaced with the "political high level." The immigration policy became restrictive, causing a decrease in German-Jewish immigration to Palestine. Britain now aimed to maintain the existing demographic composition of Palestine (one-third Jewish and two-thirds Arab) by limiting Jewish immigration of all types. In May of 1939, the total number of Jewish immigrants was limited to 75,000 for the following five years (i.e., only 15,000 per year).

Now persons of independent means were also restricted by a quota and had to wait for a certificate. While the British had sole control over immigration in the categories A, B, and D, they granted partial authority for the allocation of labor certificates (category C) to the Zionist Organization (which had to guarantee the maintenance of the immigrants during their first year in Palestine).[41] The Zionist Organization dispensed these certificates among its members primarily according to party affiliation and according to the needs of the country; preference was given to young and mainly male pioneers.

A crucial gendered difference in migration to Palestine was that women were disadvantaged in the allocation of visas by both the British and the Jewish Agency.[42] They were not, for instance, entitled to obtain category A (capitalist) certificates, for owners of private means, even if they possessed such means. Nor could they be considered heads of families; hence, they could not bring dependent husbands or children of their own, and female residents of Palestine could not request certificates for their family members. Instead, married women could only immigrate as dependents. Single women without relatives could come as dependents or could obtain labor certificates, but these were limited.[43] Divorced women and widows, as opposed to still-married women with living husbands, could get their own certificates, but in the labor category (category C) they could do so only if they immigrated without children. The ratio of men to women among German Jews migrating to Palestine was 51.9 (men) to 47.4 percent (women). Within Germany in 1933, however, the German-Jewish population was 52.4 percent women.[44] In other words, women and men eager to leave Nazi Germany did not have the same chance to enter Palestine.

Two organizations were central to the absorption of German Jewry in Palestine: the immigrant self-help organization Hitahdut Oley Germania (Association of Immigrants from Germany) and the German Department of the Jewish Agency. The Hitahdut Oley Germania (HOG) was founded in 1932 from within the small community of early German-Jewish immigrants. It turned into a self-help organization when the mass immigration began, and it became the backbone of the absorption process, representing the immigrants before both the Palestine government and the national Yishuv institutions. Meanwhile, in the autumn of 1933, under the lead of the Zionist Federation of Germany (Zionistische Vereinigung für Deutschland), a new body was established to organize the sudden mass immigration of German Jews: the Central Office for the Settlement of German Jews. It was divided into three branches, based in Jerusalem, London, and Berlin, respectively, with the London headquarters headed by Chaim Weizmann. The office in Jerusalem, colloquially referred to within the Jewish Agency as the German Department, was headed by Arthur Ruppin and led by the German Zionists David Werner Senator and Georg Landauer. Both the German Department and the HOG were staffed by German or Central European veteran Zionists. The German Department administered the funds that were collected internationally for the German Jews and coordinated the measures for their integration, while the HOG perceived itself as the executor of the German Department and as a bridge builder between the immigrants and the Yishuv, with financial support from the latter. Together, the two organizations provided information for those still in Germany and organized the absorption of those already in Palestine: from admitting the immigrants at the ports and seeing to their preliminary arrangements; through finding housing, vocational training, employment, loans, and education for children and adults; to arranging Hebrew classes, social and cultural acclimatization, and financial support and establishing mutual aid organizations.[45] As Irith Cherniavsky and others have pointed out, German Jews were treated favorably, in some ways, when compared to the other main group of immigrants at the time, Polish Jews. For one thing, the British determined a specific number of certificates that had to be given to German Jews, but without increasing the overall number of certificates. This led to a de facto decrease in certificates for immigrants from other countries. In addition, the special funds that were collected to help with the absorption of German Jews were to be used only for them and not for any other migrants. And lastly, German Jews were given more flexibility in fulfilling some of the criteria for obtaining certificates.[46]

German-Jewish immigration to Palestine occurred in waves that were related both to National Socialist politics and to British immigration policy.

FIGURE 2. Emigrants boarding a ship to Palestine from Marseille, September 1936. Photographer: Herbert Sonnenfeld. Source: Jewish Museum Berlin, 2003/229/27. Reprinted with permission.

The very first immigrants arrived in the direct wake of the shock of January 1933. Because they had left Nazi Germany in haste, they were inadequately equipped and organized, and the number of capitalists among them was small. After these first months, however, the character of the immigration changed. From 1933 to 1936, the immigrants included a large proportion of "capitalists." Almost thirty-five thousand immigrants—the majority of this migration movement—arrived in these first years of mass immigration. These were prevailingly prosperous years, and the positive economic climate was an incentive for German Jews to invest in the Yishuv. Another incentive for immigration to Palestine was the *Ha'avara* agreement (Hebrew: transfer). This agreement, reached in August 1933 between German Zionists, the Jewish Agency, and the *Reichswirtschaftsministerium* (German Ministry of Economics), enabled German Jews to transfer money and property in more significant proportions to Palestine than to other countries.[47] However, after 1936, the character of immigration changed again. Economic crisis, the so-called Arab Revolt from 1936 to 1939 (which violently opposed British rule and the Jewish presence in Palestine), and the more restrictive policy of the British combined to produce a severe decline in the number of German immigrants. Then, with the outbreak of the war, immigration dwindled even further due to the problems of reaching Palestine, both because of restrictions within Nazi Germany and because of the British restrictions on immigration from an enemy country. Throughout World War II, only a few thousand immigrants came from Germany, most of those arriving before 1941, and the majority of them young students who were part of the Youth Aliyah. Finally, when there was no longer any legal way to enter, the last option for getting to Palestine was through risky voyages across the Mediterranean (dubbed "Sonder-Hahshara" or "Aliyah Bet").[48] The several thousand German Jews who managed to save their lives in this way constituted the last chapter of German-Jewish immigration to Palestine before the end of the war.

This book focuses primarily on immigration in the years from 1933 through 1940. Hence, immigrants before 1933 and survivors of the Shoah after 1945 are not the subject of this study. With the beginning of World War II in September 1939, as already noted above, immigration to Palestine largely came to a halt. In addition, the political and social situation in Palestine drastically changed in the war years, as it did later, once again, with the fight for national independence. Further, this book investigates only German Jews who immigrated to Mandatory Palestine. It does not include immigrants from other German-speaking countries, such as Austria. The element of a shared language, while meaningful, does not justify treating these diverse groups as one. There were crucial differences between these countries in terms of cultural and geographic experiences, as well as in terms of the experience of Nazi rule. Moreover, the conditions of emigration varied widely given the immigrants' country of origin, leading to very different migration experiences.

This book is attentive to the place of gender in a multidimensional way. It asks what impact gender had on the processes of immigration and absorption of the immigrants, how immigration affected the gender relations of the immigrating group, and how it shaped interactions with the receiving society. In understanding gender as a central axis of social relations, this study considers both the macro and the micro levels of migration. Such a focus means incorporating sources in such a way as to enable an analysis of migration policies, guidelines, and the implementation of absorption, as well as individual experiences, family dynamics, and self-perceptions. To integrate these multifold perspectives, my research draws on a wide variety of archival material in German, English, and Hebrew, including administrative records, personal documents, contemporary newspapers, and oral history interviews.

The administrative perspective on the German immigrants is expressed in immigration statistics, surveys, and reports on the absorption of the German Jews into the Yishuv, as well as the minutes of the discussions of various committees. These materials document all aspects of the work of the absorption apparatus and provide pivotal insights into social, political, economic, and legal questions regarding mass immigration from an administrative perspective. Most members of these bodies were themselves part of the German-Jewish community. In this book, I not only read these materials as documentation of the activities of the apparatus, but I also analyze discussions of potential absorption policies with an eye to the inherent questions of normative ideologies and expectations expressed in them. The same is true for the analysis of information material, running the gamut of daily life, that was provided for the immigrants in the form of leaflets, booklets, newsletters, and guidebooks. On the one hand, these materials were intended to offer valuable information to the new immigrants. On the other hand, they also aimed to boost immigration to Palestine, foster occupational change, and encourage settlement in agricultural villages.

This book also uses contemporary newspapers and periodicals, especially the two most prominent and widely circulated publications for the new immigrants: the *Mitteilungsblatt* and the *Jüdische Rundschau*. The *Mitteilungsblatt* (German: Bulletin) was the newsletter of the Hitahdut Oley Germania (Association of Immigrants from Germany). Published bimonthly and for the most part in German, it provided new immigrants from Germany with much practical information regarding life in Palestine and information about the activities of the Hitahdut Oley Germania. The *Jüdische Rundschau* (German: Jewish Review), the official mouthpiece of the Zionist Federation of Germany, covered immigration to Palestine extensively. Correspondents in Palestine covered political, social, economic, and cultural developments in the Yishuv and the state of German immigration. In this, the *Jüdische Rundschau* had a double task: it provided information both for Jews who were still in Germany and were seen as potential immigrants, and for those who had already immigrated to Palestine. Thus, the correspondents were under pressure to report in a way that did not underestimate the hardships of those settling in Palestine, but at the same time encouraged additional immigration. The contents of both of these periodicals are used in this book to shed light on contemporary events and how these were communicated to the immigrants. In addition, they are used to explore debates and controversies, which can be traced not only through the articles but also through readers' letters, advertisements, and personal ads.

While the administrative documents provide a perspective from above, ego-documents shed light on the absorption from the standpoint of individual immigrants. To this end, this book uses contemporary letters, diaries, songs, poems, and plays, as well as sources written in hindsight, such as unpublished autobiographical manuscripts and published memoirs. An additional source group consists of oral history interviews. I interviewed close to forty individuals who had emigrated from Germany to Palestine as children, youth, or young adults between 1933 and 1939.

This book focuses on the perspective of German Jews in Mandatory Palestine. Hence, the sources used here are mainly German-Jewish sources, written from the perspective either of the immigrants themselves or of the responsible absorbing bodies—which themselves also consisted mainly of German Jews. The various source groups analyzed in this book were created at different points in time. They also differ significantly in their purposes and perspectives. Unlike contemporary documents, the autobiographies and interviews look back at experiences that took place many decades earlier and express selective memories of these events, memories that have likely changed over time.[49] Memoirs hence always also (and sometimes even mostly) reflect the present situation of the authors, as Miron demonstrates in his analysis of the autobiographies of German-Jewish immigrants.[50] The same is true for oral history, in which the historian, as interviewer, is also part of the creation of the source.[51] While an understanding of these limitations needs to be incorporated into any analysis of documents conducted in hindsight, it is crucial to be aware of the limitations of contemporary documents as well:

letters written to family members are phrased differently than those to authorities; reports by social workers differ in purpose from published articles on the same subject. Hence, all of these sources, not only those composed in hindsight, are closely analyzed regarding their respective intentions, expectations, and omissions. By utilizing a broad basis of different sources, this book is able to include various aspects of the respective materials while critically interpreting and linking them with each other and thus can shed light specifically on the struggles of early absorption and the conflictual encounter with the absorbing society.

BOOK OUTLINE

Gender mattered in different ways at different stages of the migration process. The first chapter of this book considers the place of gender in the preparations and the physical journey from the old to the new homeland, as well as in the experiences of the new immigrants during their arrival and first absorption in Palestine. It argues that while the shock of arrival was experienced by both men and women, they felt it in different ways, as different roles were prescribed to them by the immigration apparatus as well as by the immigrant community itself.

From the moment they set foot on the shore of Palestine, the immigrants engaged with the absorbing society, both Jewish and non-Jewish. The second chapter takes a close look at these interactions and discusses encounters with the British and Arabs in Palestine as well as interactions with Mizrahim and Eastern European Jews within the Jewish community. The chapter demonstrates how gender contributed to the dynamics of these encounters and how the respective interactions were framed in gendered terms. It argues that being a German immigrant—in terms of both the perception from outside and self-perception—was different for men and women.

One of the most crucial challenges the immigrants faced was finding a way to earn an income. The third chapter investigates the integration of immigrants into the labor market in two different ways. First, it discusses the attempts of the absorbing apparatus to monitor and support the immigrants. Gender, intersecting with class, age, and the body, played a crucial role in this process. And second, the chapter turns to the perspective of the immigrants themselves and explores how they coped with occupational change, unemployment, and loss of former status. Women and men featured differently in this process: they worked in different jobs, under different conditions, and for different wages.

As the immigrants rebuilt their lives in Palestine, their homes were in no way shelters of privacy from the all-encompassing demands of immigration. The immigrants' housework was not an invisible and private practice but was, rather, highly visible and publicly discussed, exposed to demands from the absorbing society, the community, and the family. Immigrant cuisine, in particular, was a focus of attention. The fourth chapter discusses the various ways in which homemaking practices changed due to immigration and how they were examined by social workers, the authorities, and the immigrant community.

Relationships between family members—whether between spouses, or between parents and children—were one of the most intimate realms in which migration forced decisive changes. Responsibilities within the family that had been distributed according to the sex of the family members changed over the course of the immigration process, as did the responsibilities that had been distributed to parents and children. The final chapter of this book turns a gendered lens on the immigrant family. It discusses the myriad challenges to which families were subjected through the immigration process—such as chain migration, different marriage strategies, pressure on marriages, and new forms of parenting—as well as the consequences of those challenges.

In writing gender into the history of this migration, this book questions historical assumptions about the German-Jewish migration to Palestine and its place in the emerging society, as well as about German-Jewish emigration in general. Rather than following the dominant approaches in the research literature, focusing on long-term contributions to the emerging state or questions of memory and identity, this book uses gender as a novel approach to conflict and crisis in the immigrants' first decade in the country. As Leni Grünstein wrote in the song with which I began this introduction, migration changed how the migrants worked, cooked, looked, dressed, lived, loved, and related to one another. As this book ultimately argues, gender was a crucial element in each of these all-encompassing shifts.

ONE

Liftmenschen in the Levant

VOYAGE, ARRIVAL, AND ABSORPTION

IN NOVEMBER 1933, THE NEWSPAPER *Jüdische Rundschau* published a "housewife's letter from Palestine" by Vera Rosenbaum-London:

> *Dear Esther, yesterday I met your husband, who showed me your last letter and asked what every husband asks who has arrived before his wife: "My wife wants to know what she should pack." Now, I don't want to be responsible for you leaving your mattresses behind but bringing your giant pull-out table, so I want to share my experiences with you, even though in Palestine more than anywhere, the saying is true: What do all experiences have in common? Everybody makes their own.*[1]

The majority of German immigrants arrived in Palestine between 1933 and 1938. Hence—unlike those who fled in haste in early 1933, and also unlike those who came following the outbreak of open terror at the end of 1938—they had the time and, because they were mostly middle class, the means as well to make the necessary arrangements for an orderly migration. This included exploring the conditions of the country; timing their emigration; making administrative preparations to gain the required documents; obtaining a visa; negotiating with various German government bodies, the British consulate, and shipping agencies; and planning the actual physical journey. Those who could afford it even made exploratory trips to evaluate potential places to settle and sources of livelihood. They also attended language classes and vocational retraining, organized by the Palestine Office of the Zionist Organization. This organization, under the auspices of the Jewish Agency, was solely responsible for German-Jewish emigration to Palestine. It was in contact with most of the later immigrants because it had to allocate certificates to them and deal with the formalities of their emigration from Germany, but it also provided them with information, consultation, and counseling. This chapter, following the process of the immigrants' pre-migration, physical journey, arrival, and first absorption in various different spaces and scenes, highlights the interaction between the perspective of the immigrants, on the one hand, and of the absorbing authorities, on the other.

AN INVASION OF *LIFTS*

Packing was one of many crucial activities in the pre-migration stage. The immigrants-to-be were keen to seek advice on what items to bring to their new homeland: husbands who had immigrated before their wives asked their acquaintances and then reported back home, while those still in Germany sought advice from friends already living in Palestine. Others followed the coverage in the newspaper *Jüdische Rundschau*, studied the extensive publications of Zionist organizations such as the *Aliyah-Informationen* (Aliyah News) and the *Informations-Rundschreiben des Palästina-Amtes Berlin* (Newsletter of the Berlin Palestine Office), and eyed the catalogs of businesses specializing in relocation to Palestine, the most prominent of which was N. Israel, a huge Berlin department store that had its own Palestine Department. Equipment advertised to the immigrant-to-be ranged from mosquito nets, through clothing and stoves, to ready-made houses.[2] As Marion Kaplan shows, most of the logistical work of preparing for migration was female work. Women were considered responsible for breaking down the household and packing, and were hence targeted by these materials. Men, on the other hand, were seen as the decision-makers regarding where to settle and invest.[3]

Shipping an entire household was a new phenomenon in the history of immigration to Palestine. Unlike the immigrants of earlier waves, many German Jews not only brought luggage with them on the ships but also sent furniture and household goods in large wooden containers, so-called *Lifts* or *Liftvans*. These *Lifts* had to be declared in advance and packed in Germany under the eyes of German officials; they would then arrive several weeks after the immigrants. In addition to transporting households from Germany to Palestine, these containers also quickly became a distinguishing mark of this immigration wave in the eyes of the absorbing society: soon after the beginning of the "German Aliyah," *Lifts* were to be seen everywhere, in courtyards, on street corners, and in fields. As temporary storage rooms, they can be explored in three different ways: in terms of what was supposed to be in them, what was actually shipped, and how this practice of shipping *Lifts* was received.

The Palestine Office and the immigrant organization Hitahdut Oley Germania (HOG; Association of Immigrants from Germany) published helpful lists for middle-class immigrants of what to bring and what to leave

FIGURE 3. A customs official observing the packing of the *Lift* of the Meyer family, Rheda, 1937. Photographer: Andreas Meyer. Reprinted with permission.

behind. These lists called for change: the new clothes, furniture, and personal belongings needed to match Palestinian conditions. Clothes needed to be of a functional and robust material, suitable for the hot climate and manual work. Recommended wear included straw hats and tropical helmets for protection from the sun; stout shoes, polo shirts, and khaki trousers galore for men; and simple, airy dresses and work clothes for women. Clothing, it was stressed, should be of simple design.[4] For example, immigrants were explicitly urged not to bring elegant beachwear or dresses of delicate fabrics. Thoughtfully chosen garments would spare housewives intensive laundry procedures as well as allowing the immigrants to fit in with the sartorial culture of the Yishuv and the values and norms expressed in it. In other words, their attire should enable them to blend into the new society rather than stand out as German bourgeois fresh off the boat. In commenting on a draft of the *Aliyah-Informationen*, for example, the HOG asked the editors to change a paragraph on recommended clothing so that the German Jews, "who already had a tendency to dress up too much, would not bring elegant beachwear with them."[5]

The furniture also needed to suit the Palestinian conditions. The advice given was generally to pack as few and as practical items as possible. In packing, immigrants needed to bear in mind the new conditions they were moving to: climatic (heat, humidity, dust, and vermin), social (high rents and a lower standard of living), and dwelling conditions (small apartments, often shared). A piece published in *Jung Wizo: Monatsschrift*, the monthly magazine for young members of the WIZO (Women's International Zionist Organization), declared: "It is hardest for those who bring their European customs to Palestine and stick with them. One is used to a large apartment with heavy furniture and luxury items, but all this would be a terrible burden for the women once in Palestine."[6]

The absorbing bodies in Palestine assumed that bringing an entire German middle-class household would complicate integration. Once they had arrived with all their furniture, it would be much harder for such immigrants to lower their standard of living, because they would then feel obliged to search for a larger and more expensive flat. And because the immigrant women were going to be expected to manage homemaking under more difficult conditions, without the help they had previously had, and most probably in addition to a job, the goal of this advice was to help them minimize housework through careful consideration of what to pack. Women were therefore encouraged to pack mattresses and metal folding beds instead of upholstery or large wooden pieces of furniture, wool blankets instead of comforters, and neither big carpets nor large curtains. Light, small pieces would fit better into the smaller flats with lower ceilings in Palestine; sturdy material would be better able to resist humidity and dust and easier to clean and disinfect. Books, typewriters, radios, and gramophones are also found on the lists. Because they were considered to be standard items in a middle-class household, immigrants were expected to bring these as well. The immigrants-to-be were urged to sell any items not suitable for Palestine before they left Germany, in order to avoid the high prices for storing *Lifts* and paying moving companies to transport them from the harbor to one's apartment and to conserve resources for necessary purchases and other emigration costs.[7]

The Palestine Office advised bringing a variety of kitchenware and domestic appliances, such as Primus stoves, sewing machines, and clothes irons. It was explicitly recommended not to bring luxury items, such as champagne glasses, chandeliers, or very large tablecloths for huge tables. In Palestine, it was explained, the immigrants would have neither the room nor the opportunity to host large social events as they had done in Germany. However, women should bring a few tableware items and cooking utensils in the luggage that traveled with them, which would enable them to cook meals for their families right after arrival instead of spending their precious cash in restaurants. Just as important, doing their own cooking for their loved ones would facilitate a swifter integration, as it would help create "domesticity in the difficult early period of acclimation."[8] This kind of advice on what to pack is but one example of the attempt of the absorbing bodies to prepare both male and female immigrants for a change of profession, class, and living standard. Despite all these anticipated changes in Palestine, the responsibility for breaking down their old household and creating a new one in Palestine was consistently assigned to women and not to men.

This material distributed by the Palestine Office provided valuable information for the new immigrants, compiled as it was with extensive knowledge of the situation in Palestine and with the goal of swiftly integrating the new immigrants, rather than being shaped by financial interests, as were the catalogs of private suppliers. However, the material also clearly reflected the Zionist agenda of founding a new society. It was important to leave behind *galut* (a derogatory Hebrew term for "diaspora") attitudes, habits, and belongings even within the home and in the private areas of personal dress, personal belongings, and furniture. It should be noted that the German Jews who had to move into more cramped conditions even within Nazi Germany itself also had to engage in these discussions about what objects to take and what to get rid of. There were a variety of positions on the subject, ranging from getting rid of as much "unnecessary ballast" as possible to keeping precious items for the next generation.[9] The Jewish community asked those who were moving to get rid of any objects that were no longer needed, such as crystal glasses, chandeliers, and fine dishes. Both groups, then—those who stayed in Germany and made internal household moves there, and those who left the country—were asked to adapt their standard of living and give up the bourgeois habitus associated with having such items in their homes.

Many German-Jewish immigrants to Palestine, however, failed to heed these guidelines. Some may simply never have read them and "expected nothing but blue skies"; others read them but rejected or ignored the underlying agenda and hoped for the best.[10] Many, however, feared the immigration to an "uncivilized" country and wanted to be forearmed. Emotional considerations far outweighed the practical and ideological aspects of packing for Palestine. For all of these reasons, furniture was eventually brought even though it was large and heavy, even though houses were small, and even though bringing it would cause extra (female) work. The same was true for elegant clothing, fur coats, and even dirndl-style dresses that did not match the climatic conditions, workplace requirements, or normative dress codes that the immigrants would encounter in their new country. Miriam R.'s mother insisted on bringing all of the furniture from their four-room apartment; Yohanan B.'s parents brought "1 meter [of shelf space of] Schiller, 80 centimeters of Goethe, and the Brockhaus [encyclopedia]" instead of Primus stoves or khaki shorts; and Fritz Wolf's parents-in-law brought a supply of candied cherries from Germany to open on special occasions.[11] All of these items were brought in *Lifts*, soon to be seen in courtyards, on street corners, and in fields from Tel Aviv to Nahariya.

Because immigrants shipping an entire household was a new practice in

FIGURE 4. The unloading of the *Lift* of the Meyer family in Nahariya, 1938. Photographer: Andreas Meyer. Reprinted with permission.

Palestine, it gave rise to a new nickname for the German-Jewish immigrants: *Liftmenschen* or *Lift* people. As Albert Baer wrote in the *Jüdische Rundschau*:

> Palestine has not seen an immigration like this one from Germany. It is not only people that arrive but also furniture, furniture, furniture, all shipped with the well-known *Lifts*, whose debris can be found on the construction sites of Hadar HaKarmel, labeled with the names of the German cities and the shipping agents who shipped them; a Palestinian kid walking through the streets can learn German geography.... Lately, people have realized here that these *Lifts* have an important meaning for a colonial country, but it is a different and more important one than the one that was intended in Europe. The pieces of furniture are mostly unnecessary but the *Lifts* have been used recently as kiosks, garages, shacks, construction site huts, and the like.... In colloquial speech, the German immigrant and his *Lift* are referred to as *Liftmenschen*, a variation on the term *Luftmenschen* [air people] that was used by German Jews, before that, for the "poor Eastern brothers in faith." As unsuitable as this European furniture is for the country,... the country is just as unprepared for this invasion of *Lifts*.[12]

The fact that the new immigrants are described through the *Lift*—both by way of the object itself and through the immigrants' practice of arriving with it—indicates how the German Jews, whose presence immediately changed the face of the Yishuv, were perceived by the established inhabitants in their new homeland. The pejorative term *Liftmensch* was a new creation that expressed the sometimes amused, sometimes malicious reception of German Jews in Palestine. It articulated how the position of those who had once looked down on the *Luftmenschen* had now been completely reversed: in the Yishuv, the former "poor brothers from the East" were the dominant political and cultural group, while the German-Jewish immigrants were perceived as clueless, embarrassing, poorly prepared newcomers, stuck in their past lives and literally importing their alien habits and belongings in their *Liftvans*. But the fact that they were categorized according to the old conflict of Western versus Eastern Jews also shows that the old-timers themselves were not free from a past they still used as a point of reference. Schadenfreude at the reversed conditions was expressed through insulting ethnic humor from the side of the absorbing society, targeting the newcomers' alleged rigidity, alienation, and exaggerated deference to their own former status. While these jokes can be understood as a corrective for the newcomers' seemingly unfitting behavior, they also clearly follow the genre of Eastern European Jewish jokes about stupid Gentiles who are always outwitted by the Jews—here, the German Jews take the place of the Gentiles.[13] *Yekke*, the infamous and most common nickname for the immigrants, was also an import from Europe, where Eastern European Jews had already used the derogatory term to describe their German-Jewish brethren. The epithet targeted the German Jews' assimilation to their non-Jewish surroundings, expressed, among other things, by wearing a jacket instead of a caftan. In Palestine, the term received a new connotation, describing the German Jews' lack of assimilation to the informality of Yishuv society.[14] At times, the especially insulting suffix *-potz* (Yiddish: penis) was added. Unlike Yekke, however, a formerly negative concept which underwent a shift in meaning and is broadly familiar in present-day Israeli society, the term *Liftmensch* is now forgotten.

For all of its negative connotations, the term *Liftmensch* also underlines the fact that their personal belongings were thought of by these immigrants as "a piece of home." Despite both the costs and the counter-instructions by the absorption apparatus, they brought dressers, clocks, armchairs, and dishware with them from Germany. In fact, many of these objects can be found to this day in the apartments of the German immigrants' descendants. Looking on these *Lifts* as cabinets containing meaningful items opens a window into the process of building a new home in this specific immigration process. They highlight the differing perceptions of what was needed to create such a new home, by the immigrants, on the one hand, and by the absorbing authorities, on the other.

TO NEW BEGINNINGS: THE PASSAGE TO PALESTINE

For most German Jews, migration to Palestine began with a journey by train from Germany to one of the port cities of southern Europe, which took a day or two. There, usually in Trieste or Marseille, the immigrants embarked on a ship to Palestine, where they disembarked five days later in Tel Aviv or Haifa.[15]

At the beginning of the journey, friends and families would accompany the emigrants to the train station to bid them farewell. Hans Jonas remembers his last moments with his parents:

> Everything was ready: I had my train ticket and papers, my suitcases were packed and the arrangements had been made for my furniture to be shipped to Palestine. . . . As we walked in the garden—our last time together—suddenly, as if on signal, we all broke out in the most heartrending sobs. Up to then not a tear had been shed . . . but now that the moment had come and the last half hour, the last ten minutes, were upon us, we cried our eyes out.[16]

These last moments together have been described as a devastating experience. While at this point, the emigrants could not know what would eventually happen to those staying behind, parting from their loved ones was inevitably painful. Even spouses were often separated from each other: while the German Aliyah was considered a family immigration, families often did not immigrate all at the same time but rather in a chain migration, as will be discussed in depth in chapter 5. Especially in the first years of the immigration wave, from 1933 to 1936, this meant that husbands often immigrated before their wives, who followed several months later. The relief of leaving

Nazi Germany was thus tied up and tempered with anger, frustration, and anxiety for dear ones left behind as well as about the unknown future ahead. Yissakhar Ben-Yaacov, who left Hamburg's Dammtor train station with his parents in September of 1933, describes how, in the final minutes before the train left, his father tried desperately to convince his relatives to follow them as soon as possible.[17]

The train ride from Germany to the port cities of southern Europe, therefore, took place in a tense atmosphere. As the emigrants watched the familiar landscapes and towns drifting by, they had to grapple with the unbelievable fact that the very land that they had felt a part of was now forcing them to leave. In addition, the immigrants were anxious that something could still go wrong, and along the way, many endured bullying by police officers, border control officials, and ordinary German fellow passengers.[18] Georg Herlitz, for example, who left Germany in 1933, describes a humiliating body search by male German customs officials, carried out on himself and his wife and daughters, which left them all deeply upset.[19]

The second part of the physical immigration, the sea voyage, was very different. In Trieste or Marseille, the immigrants embarked on their five-day voyage to Palestine. As they left the ports of Italy or France, aboard ships with such telling names as *Gerusalemme*, *Palästina*, or *Tel Aviv*, the pressure of the first part of the journey decreased.[20] Now, as Justus Klimann wrote in a letter from aboard the ship *Tel Aviv*, which carried him and his wife from Trieste to Haifa, the ship "was our world for a few days."[21] The cultural historian Joachim Schlör has stressed the importance of the journey as part of the emigration process for the German Jews. The passage was a liminal space: now, the migrants had time, a forced break between the old and new homelands, and this time was filled with reflections as well as anticipations, rest as well as activity. Even though the physical journey from Germany to Palestine was usually the shortest part of the immigration process, it was decisive in the overall experience because of its emotional intensity; contemporary sources (such as letters and newspaper articles) as well as autobiographies and oral history bear witness to this. People had time to collect themselves, released from the pressure of escaping Nazi Germany and not yet under the pressure of their immediate absorption into Palestine.[22]

The majority of the German Jews arrived before the outbreak of terror in 1938 and still had the means to afford a ticket on sophisticated ships. These ships were different both from those that had brought the previous waves of immigrants to Palestine and from the rusty wrecks that would later bring the illegal immigrants of the "Aliyah Bet" over the Mediterranean Sea. The ships that brought the immigrants from Germany provided comfortable, sometimes even luxurious, facilities, entertainment programs, and dining options. The conditions of the passage were enjoyable for most immigrants, almost like a pleasure trip, and letters from the ships were often written in a light, humorous tone. To be sure, not all passengers could afford tickets in first or even second class; many had to spend the passage in the crowded, windowless third- and fourth-class compartments. However, because it was a successful economic undertaking to transport immigrants, especially on the Trieste-Haifa line, the shipping companies strove to make it a pleasant trip even for those in third class. Yissakhar Ben-Yaacov, for example, cited above regarding his father's comments as they left Hamburg in September of 1933, then continued the voyage with his parents aboard the Lloyd Triestino line's ship *Italia* and mentions that a festive menu for Rosh Hashanah was offered even for those in third class.[23] The newly established Jewish Palestine Shipping Company, meanwhile, broke with the usual system and had only one class for all its passengers.[24] The ships provided entertainment including music, dancing, games, movie screenings, and even beauty contests. The passengers also enjoyed tourist activities like sitting on the deck, sunbathing, watching the landscape drifting by (including attractions such as the canal of Corinth), and even leaving the ship for short excursions.[25] For many of the German-Jewish passengers, this voyage was the first time in a long time that they could relax and feel like human beings again, after having been subjected to increasing humiliation and persecution in Germany. As Heinemann Stern wrote: "Sun, warmth, and light delight body and soul.... We move our deck chair into the blazing sun, stretching out in the pleasant warmth, dreaming into a dolce far niente lacking time and space.... That there is still a place like that for us."[26] The passage was not, of course, a restful experience for everyone. Especially for those with health issues, older passengers, women with children who were following their husbands and had to take care of the children alone during the journey, and pregnant women, the experience of the passage on the ship could be taxing. The social worker Frieda Weinrich reports about several women who gave birth onboard ship and had to endure labor, birth, and caring for newborn babies under improvised conditions.[27]

The voyage also gave the immigrants the opportunity to prepare for their new life. The long hours between meals could be put to use studying publications such as *Hebräisch für Jedermann* (German: Hebrew for everyone) or material prepared by the Palestine Office and the HOG for distribution among the passengers, such as the comprehensive *Bordmerkblatt* (German: ship bulletin).[28] The latter, compiled by the HOG, provided information on the landing process, suggestions for cheap hotels and restaurants, and referrals to immigration hostels and the HOG support centers.[29] Zionist organizations hosted talks and lectures in which topics relevant to life in Palestine were discussed. The food served in the dining halls included previously unknown Oriental food staples, providing a foretaste of what was to come. The first taste of olives during the voyage, in particular, made a lasting impression on many immigrants.[30]

Participating in social life on board the ship was more than just a way for the passengers to entertain themselves. It enabled the immigrants-to-be to consult with others on possible places to settle, schools for their children, workplaces, and investment options. Passengers were especially keen to find out as much as possible from those who had already gotten established or from native Palestinians returning home. Jenny Aloni wrote about the ubiquity of these discussions: "conversations, everywhere conversations, . . . as if the whole ship were nothing but a net of conversations."[31] Contacts made during the passage often proved important in the later absorption process. Ben-Yaacov's parents changed their mind about settling in Haifa after talking with other travelers aboard who praised the benefits of Tel Aviv. Miriam S., immigrating without her parents, made friends with a girl her age whose parents later "adopted" her. Sometimes travelers who met on the ship even formed a community and lived together after arrival.[32]

One activity that was especially enjoyed from deck chairs to dining hall was observing and categorizing the other travelers. The majority of the passengers on the ships were other German immigrants. They ran the gamut of

FIGURE 5. Female emigrants dancing on the ship to Palestine, ca. 1934; Photographer: Herbert Sonnenfeld. Source: Jewish Museum Berlin, FOT 88/500/11/018 purchased with funds provided by the Stiftung Deutsche Klassenlotterie Berlin. Reprinted with permission.

the immigration from Germany: middle-class families with kith and kin, fathers on advance scouting trips, mothers with children following their husbands, elderly parents, and pioneering youth traveling in groups. There were also immigrants from other countries, Palestinian Jews returning home, tourists visiting the Holy Land, Christian pilgrims, priests, and nuns, as well as soldiers of the British Empire from countless countries. In his diary, Martin Hauser, a young German immigrant en route from Trieste to Jaffa, described the scene on May 24, 1933:

> A deck chair at the end of steerage, above me the light blue sky, under me the dark blue sea, ... around me a "human mass." Who knows all the people who were assembled here, who can say their names? *Haluzim* [pioneers] with backpacks, short trousers, open shirts; Hassidim in black suits with yarmulke and sidelocks; middle-class immigrants with families, real tourists from West European countries. . . . Old and young, Sephardim and Ashkenazim.[33]

As this description suggests, the voyage also provided a first glimpse of Yishuv society, with its cultural, religious, ethnic, and class frictions. Within this potpourri of people, the most notable fellow passengers were the *Haluzim* (Hebrew: pioneers) heading to Palestine, differentiated by their looks and behavior from the middle-class immigrants. Their presence became a topos in stories of the journey. Only a few meters away from the gentlemen's lounges and bridge tournaments for the middle-class passengers, there they were: dancing the hora and singing the "Hatikva," the male and female pioneers dressed in the iconic short trousers and open shirts. As this was the first time the middle-class immigrants had encountered actual pioneers, they regarded them with curiosity. While some observers perceived them as far too loud and tumultuous, most were favorably impressed with their proud, life-affirming attitude.[34] Cheery, young, and healthy, these pioneers came to embody the iconic "revitalized Jews" about whom the German Jews had read day in and day out in the *Jüdische Rundschau* and other Zionist publications. These pioneers were mostly German Jews themselves, who had undergone preparatory agricultural training known as *Hahshara* (Hebrew: preparation) and were to join a kibbutz. In the eyes of the other passengers, they had already transformed themselves according to the Zionist impetus.

The pioneers evoked somewhat different reactions depending on whether they were male or female, though. The male pioneers received universal acclaim. The distinctiveness of their physical appearance, apparel, and behavior suggested a transformed masculinity: tough, strong, and muscular, their bodies largely visible due to their shorts and open shirts, coming to build the country and conquer its soil. They were identified as the iconic role models of Zionist masculinity.[35] These features seemed to defy the vicious anti-Semitic stereotypes of Jewish men as physically flawed and pathological. Hans Bernkopf, a young physician who traveled to Palestine in the summer of 1934 aboard the *Italia*, was so impressed with the *Haluzim* that he spent all of his days with them in steerage, even though he had paid for the much more comfortable second class. To his parents, he wrote full of excitement about his new acquaintances, who made his fellow middle-class passengers look boring. The pioneers on the ships provided a peek into the hegemonic masculinity of the new society that all were heading for. In a first attempt to adapt to this model, many men changed their apparel immediately after their arrival, literally exchanging cravat for khaki.

This ideal masculinity was not accessible to all German men, however. In fact, the middle-aged, middle-class men on the ship appeared the complete opposite of the pioneers, as the journalist and author Gabriele Tergit pointed out: "They stand at the railing, in their urban suits, in long trousers. The wind comes, the sun, but the only thing that makes them look sporty is their caps; they look like men to whom their doctor has said: 'your sedentary occupation demands that you take a cruise, calm your nerves.'"[36] The elusiveness of this masculine ideal, we can suspect, probably increased the anxiety of the male immigrants over what would happen to them after their arrival. They must have worried about their lack of importance in their communities and networks, and the loss of their careers and professions left behind in Germany—which had previously provided them with self-esteem and a positive image of their masculinity. What was in store for them?

And while the male pioneers received almost universal acclaim, the female pioneers were met with more mixed reactions. Their iconic image portrayed them as independent and tough, replacing bourgeois femininity with often androgynous physical features and unisex clothes, aiming to work side by side with their male comrades at building the country. The ideal of the *haluza* (Hebrew: female pioneer), disseminated through Zionist publications, served as a role model for many young female immigrants from Germany, too, who aimed to transform the status they had had in Germany. For Lotte Pinkus, for example, the journey offered the chance to define a new Jewish identity in a gendered form. Pinkus, who already lived in Palestine, was now on her way back from Germany, where she had gone to help her mother with breaking up the household. During the trip, a fellow traveler, a Christian pilgrim, approached her and asked her to change into a skirt because an archbishop was about to embark. Lotte answered him confidently: "I am really sorry, but I am a Jewish woman and I wear trousers!"[37] For her, being a Jewish woman from Palestine was already linked to being a *haluza*, a female worker of the Jewish community, who wore trousers as a principled statement of her changed class affiliation and concept of gender and nationality. She defended this decision proudly against the demands of the Christian man. It was just this kind of self-assertive attitude that attracted

Hans Bernkopf to the female pioneers, whom he preferred to the middle-class passengers.[38]

For others, changing to a new kind of femininity was simply seen as necessary, but not necessarily positive. Irna (Shlomit) Mueller, a young girl who immigrated in 1933 with her sister and her mother, recalls: "During the voyage, our mother gave us a lecture on "Zionism": from this day on, no more makeup, no corset, no silk stockings, and a few more *no*'s that I have forgotten. In short, we were thoroughly brainwashed."[39] Even though Irna's mother had not been not involved in Zionism before leaving Germany, she "briefed" her daughters during the passage on how they would have to change. Strikingly, Irna's mother understood the Zionist urge for transformation mainly as a negation of her own former decidedly bourgeois femininity, expressed in the form of clothing and makeup. To enable her daughters to integrate themselves into the new homeland, she prompted them to renounce this femininity while they were still on the ship.

And finally, while for some immigrants, changing femininities seemed either positive or, at least, necessary, there was also an opposite attitude: the rejection of female pioneers as masculinized women. Gabriele Tergit identifies the distinctive femininities of different types of women on board: "The mother is an old, elegant Berliner.... She lies in the deck chair, thin, pale, and beautiful, with posh high-heeled black shoes. Her daughter wears boots and a windbreaker, under that an open sports blouse, her straight hair cut short in a manly style. She is short and plump, a nice, efficient worker; she will go to the countryside, milk cows, and feed chickens."[40] In the course of her descriptions, Tergit implies that the days on the ship are to be the last days of the mother's previous life as a middle-class woman. Soon, she will have to cast off her best-selling novel, blanket, and immaculate skin and declare her former life to have been a mistake. Instead of a life consisting of nice clothes, marriage, children, and caring for her household, she will now have to see "caring for cows and the planting of orange cuttings in the dry earth under the blazing sun as the goal for future generations, for whose sake she must sacrifice herself."[41] After her arrival, she will literally have to stand up from the deck chair and start working on Palestinian soil. The topos of "working the land" used here is more a reflection of the contemporary Zionist discourse than it is an actual prospect—it is in fact more likely that this elegant woman will become a household helper or a waitress than that she will plant orange trees. Nevertheless, the anticipation of change was realistic: Tergit correctly assumes that for a middle-class woman from Germany, immigration will entail a loss of class, status, and standard of living.

The pioneer daughter, on the other hand, Tergit indicates, has already undergone the necessary transformation through *Hahshara* and is now equipped with the necessary qualities for "building up the land." For Tergit, she represents both the generation and the femininity of the future, while the young woman's mother belongs to the past. The two women's respective femininities are not only expressed in their different apparel (high heels versus boots) but also embodied: the mother is thin and of delicate build, while her daughter is strongly built and of tomboyish appearance, as Tergit observes. The *haluza*, in some ways like the "New Woman" of the Weimar Republic, rejected not only the Jewish diaspora identity but also bourgeois norms of femininity, and was, hence, going too far. Denying female pioneers any hint of traditional femininity created an anxiety that the New Hebrew Woman would be stripped entirely of her beauty and femininity.

This attitude is also expressed in the account of the immigrant Fritz Wolf, who vividly describes a scene in which a group of male and female pioneers were dancing on deck: "The lads, stocky and muscular, wore short trousers and heavy boots, and the girls, in the same blue shirts and scarves, threw their huge weight around the floor without any grace. . . . Despite their pendulous breasts, plump hips, and huge bottoms, they were girls without sex: working animals and conquerors of the land."[42] Wolf's take on this scene is an explicitly negative male gaze on women. While the male *haluz* is acceptable, maybe even attractive, the female is clearly not, and Wolf felt nauseated by her. This was his first direct encounter with female pioneers, and he was strongly repulsed by their physical appearance and behavior. There are two particularly telling elements in his depiction of these women. For one thing, he ridicules their bodily features: plump, broad-bottomed, and clumsy, they clearly take up too much space. To him, this is a deviation from the middle-class gender norm that he deems appropriate. For another thing, he desexualizes them. Despite their female physical attributes, "they have no sex," as he writes: they are assimilated to their male comrades in clothing and behavior, and they also intend to pursue physical work and till the land like men. In Wolf's view, their

Zionist commitment to "conquering the land" masculinizes these women. During the ship voyage, he felt the change in the wind for gender identities, which fanned his fears of what to expect in Eretz Israel.[43]

The liminal space of the voyage created room for discussion of the place of gender and its transformation in Palestine. The sight of the pioneers, in particular, triggered discussions about gender identities among the passengers. The way they observed others from their deck chairs in this space between the old and new homelands, between Trieste and Tel Aviv, was not only a way to pass the time. The contemporary Zionist discourse of transformation was translated into gendered terms, and a transformation of gender identity was expected by many German Jews. The observations made during the passage expressed their anticipation—sometimes anxious, sometimes gleeful—that, among the changes they were about to undergo, questions of the body, beauty, and gender would also be at stake.

PALÄSTINA WIE ES WIRKLICH IST . . .
LANDING AND DISEMBARKATION

After a week on board, the journey ended. Palestine suddenly became real in an overwhelming culmination of lights, smells, heat, and noise. The new immigrant Herbert Wolff summed up this impression of arrival with the words: "This is the Orient; Europe is behind us."[44] The moment a ship anchored in the harbors of Tel Aviv/Jaffa and Haifa, it was approached by Arab porters in small boats. These porters entered the ship and flocked on deck to unload the luggage from the vessel. Gad Granach, who immigrated in 1936, recalls the shock felt by the German immigrants arriving in the tumultuous, chaotic setting of a Middle Eastern port: "At first I thought we had arrived at the wrong wedding—the harbor was full of Haurani [Syrian] laborers running around in their brightly colored clothes and blue-painted eyes. All of them looked like Genghis Khan to me. I overheard a distinguished-looking German Jew say to his son, 'Herbert, I think we've arrived ten years too early.'"[45] The majority of the German immigrants brought with them an Orientalist attitude, through which they viewed the Arabs, most likely never having met any Arabs before. The strangeness of these Arab men, their physical appearance, language, and rough manners evoked feelings of apprehension and fear among the new immigrants. And not only was this their first contact with Arabs, it was a very physical one. Due to the local conditions in Haifa, the passengers had to leave the ship using a bridge, while their luggage was transported in rowboats. Ben-Yaacov writes, "Those who were afraid of crossing the gangway, which was not very stable, were given a piggyback ride by an Arab, as if they were a sack of flour, with no regard for their sensitivities."[46] In Jaffa's port, meanwhile, which was too small for the ships to dock in, Arab stevedores took the passengers ashore in rowboats, as they fretted about losing their luggage or, worse, going overboard themselves.[47] The immigrants felt overwhelmed, intimidated, and utterly confused by this reception. Ulli T. describes the shock of arrival: "We had a book called *Palestine As It Really Is*, but . . . when we arrived here in Jaffa . . . and we were forced to leave the ship in little boats, and *oy ve avoi*, that was catastrophic, and the Arabs! . . . And I cried: I want to go back!"[48] The shock of this interaction dominated the experience of arrival. It has been described in countless accounts, many of which are almost literally identical, both in contemporary documents and in interviews conducted decades after the events.[49] Even children and youngsters, who on the whole coped better with the whole immigration process, were as shocked as their parents at this first sight. This experience of the arrival as a shock was not unique to the German Jews: immigrants from Poland in those same years, as well as immigrants from earlier years, describe the scene in the same way.[50]

The encounter with the Arabs was, however, only one part of the disembarkation procedure. Upon a ship's arrival in the harbor, the Harbor Police and Immigration Commission boarded the ship. All passengers had to receive vaccinations and undergo a compulsory physical examination conducted by a medical officer of the British government, either on board or before leaving the harbor.[51] While for most this was only a formality, the physical examination was the last hurdle to clear, and in fact not all could clear it.

According to British Mandate law, immigrants to Palestine were supposed to be both physically and mentally healthy. All potential immigrants and their dependents were hence required to obtain a health certificate before their immigration. Those suffering from infectious diseases or severe psychological illnesses, prostitutes, and persons without any means were forbidden entrance to Palestine. Disqualifying illnesses included epilepsy, leprosy, syphilis, open tuberculosis, and all illnesses considered by the medical officer of the government to be a threat to public health. Also barred from entry were persons suffering from an infectious or contagious disease; persons not immunized and unwilling to be immunized; and persons unwilling to comply with a possible disinfection, physical examination, or quarantine as prescribed by the medical officer of the government upon landing in Palestine.[52] Immigrants arriving with capitalist and dependent certificates needed to comply only with these general regulations, while those who arrived with a labor certificate, regulated by the Jewish Agency, were required to obtain an additional health certificate by a fiduciary doctor of the Palestine Office. These immigrants were not supposed to suffer from illnesses of the kidneys, endocarditis, arthritis deformans, pernicious anemia, leukemia, or malignant tumors. The physical examination was intended to determine their suitability for physical labor and quick adaptation to the climate. A 1926 manual for the physical examination of immigrants by the Health Council of the Palestine Zionist Executive, which was still in use in the 1930s, divided the potential immigrants into three groups: group A, healthy men aged eighteen to forty-five; group B, specialized workers, not as healthy as those in group A but without serious illnesses, as well as women and children who were not in group C; and group C, persons who were weak or suffering from illnesses, mental or venereal diseases, or physical deformities. Members of group C were not to be allowed to enter Palestine.[53]

The Palestine Office warned potential immigrants from Germany who had chronic illnesses not to immigrate to Palestine because of the climate, the harsh working conditions, and the nonexistent welfare system. Both the British Mandate and the Jewish Agency had regulations in place to prevent immigrants with chronic physical or mental illnesses from entering Palestine, but they did not completely succeed in this attempt—many tried to enter Palestine anyway because they did not want to be separated from their families or because they had nowhere else to go. In some cases, the German physicians failed to diagnose the illness in the first place; in other cases, the immigrants fell ill after the initial examination and then tried to conceal their diseases in order not to threaten their immigration. If medical officials detected such conditions during the physical examination upon arrival, the potential immigrant faced serious problems. Mentally ill immigrants, for example, were regularly sent back to Germany.[54] There were also cases of immigrants who arrived with a labor certificate but were physically unable to work because they suffered from epilepsy or other illnesses. The absorption apparatus argued that social problems were caused by such mistakes in the selection of the immigrants by the Palestine Office and, because they could not support these immigrants forever, urged for them to be deported.[55] Unsuitable immigrants, called *Olim bilti matimim* in Hebrew, were a constant bother for the immigration apparatus, and the German Department repeatedly complained to the Palestine Office in Germany about having sent them.[56] Miriam L.'s brother, who had Down syndrome, was one such unsuitable immigrant. Even though he had relatives in Palestine who vouched for him, he was not allowed to leave the ship in Palestine, Miriam recalls. Miriam herself was suffering from mumps at the time of their arrival. However, she managed to conceal this fact. Miriam's mother tried to commit suicide on board because of the threat that the family would either be torn apart or all have to sail back to Germany. Luckily, however, they found a solution: family members interceded on their behalf and they were able to continue on the ship to Egypt, and from there they made it back to Palestine by rail. Others were not so lucky and were indeed sent back.

After the ship's passengers were cleared by the physician, a commission consisting of British and Jewish officials started with passport and visa control. Representatives of the Jewish Agency then allocated each passenger a porter for the transport of his or her luggage to the harbor. These porters were mostly the abovementioned Arabs. Once ashore, the immigrants received vaccinations against typhoid fever and smallpox, passed through customs and claimed their luggage, and then were finally allowed to leave the harbor.[57] The physical part of the migration was now over, and with their first steps outside of the harbor, the immigrants' absorption into Palestine began.

DISAPPOINTED AND DEEPLY HURT: RECEPTION AT THE HARBOR

Most immigrants, men and women alike, and both grown-ups and children, perceived the landing procedure as chaotic, unprofessional, and intimidating, with corrupt officials asking for gifts of money, or *baksheesh*. Unlike most of the earlier immigrants, many of the German immigrants brought more luggage with them than they could carry on their own, complicating its transport. Ben-Yaacov's family of three, for example, brought eleven pieces of luggage. As a result, so-called harbor hyenas immediately besieged the immigrants, taking advantage of their confusion and lack of Hebrew and offering overpriced services.[58]

The immigration apparatus, which regarded the arrival and first impressions as crucial for the new immigrants and the process of their further integration, was aware of this initial shock. Therefore, the apparatus devised a multitude of systems to support the newcomers. One important measure was the *Hafendienst* (German: harbor service) set up to receive the immigrants arriving at the ports.[59] A novelty in the Yishuv, this HOG reception mechanism offered advice to the new immigrants on all relevant matters, including dealing with customs, receiving their luggage, finding a driver to transport it, and, most importantly, where to stay on the first night.

Two groups of newcomers figured prominently in these debates by the absorbing authorities: male veteran Zionists and young women. As the HOG soon realized, arrival in Palestine was experienced as a shock not only by immigrants who were complete greenhorns and had chosen Palestine for prosaic reasons, without any particular expectations, but also, more often than not, by veteran Zionists. Hundreds of these veteran Zionists decided to immigrate to Palestine after 1933, and many of them were dissatisfied with what they found. Max Kober, a veteran Zionist himself who had immigrated in 1933, noted in a letter to Georg Landauer of the German Department in February of 1934:

> *There are so many people who are deeply hurt by the lack of any kind of reception or support upon their arrival. . . . I would argue . . . that these few pounds per month . . . would be an excellent investment. In general, so-called "first impressions" are crucial. Many veteran Zionists are arriving now, loyal members of the organization and the funds [i.e., the Keren HaYesod, the fundraising arm of the Jewish Agency; and the Keren Kayemet, the land-purchasing fund], and they feel forsaken beyond measure, . . . with no welcoming word. Get a list once a month from the Hitahdut, from the KH [Keren HaYesod] folks, etc., with the names of all of those arriving, and you will be able to capitalize on these few dozen letters for the KH. You need to understand the mentality of these people—they want to feel caressed.*[60]

Kober, who worked for the Keren HaYesod in Haifa, argued that the immigration apparatus needed to act on behalf of these men because of their strong commitment to the Zionist cause prior to migration. In his mind, they deserved a special reception because of their history of Zionist activism in Germany. Many veteran Zionists felt the same way. To that end, Kober requested that the German Department take special measures, such as preparing individual welcome letters to several dozen such immigrants per month. In his opinion, the special status of these immigrants justified the allocation of funds to this cause; not only that, but the more content the new immigrants were, the more likely they would later be to support Zionist institutions and the immigration apparatus through donations. What makes Kober's request remarkable is the fact that veteran Zionists already belonged to a network that was extremely beneficial to them. Objectively speaking, they already had better starting conditions than did other immigrants. Fraternity brothers who were already established in the new country advised fraternity brothers prior to their immigration and then welcomed them at the harbor, offered them a first place to stay, helped them to find apartments and jobs, and finally, introduced them to the cultural life of the Yishuv.[61] However, these immigrants expected something more: an official welcome.

Hugo Schachtel, who like Kober was both a veteran Zionist and a new immigrant, articulated this position in a letter to the German Department:

> *Right now, a number of people are arriving from Germany who used to hold a certain position in the Jewish communities [there] and who will only gradually be able to establish and integrate themselves here. These individuals, often no longer young, have a hard time finding their bearings here, and suffer from this "loneliness." Within the German Olim [immigrant] community, these people have often held a certain role and have influence. We know these types from our practical KH [Keren HaYesod] work, and therefore we want to suggest the following procedure: the executive, or the "German Central Bureau," should welcome these people with a letter signed by Dr. A. Ruppin.... We believe that this would be extremely beneficial, both from a Zionist point of view and ... for the practical work of the KH, because people suffer most from feeling unappreciated.*[62]

Schachtel, like Kober, advocated special treatment and an appropriate welcome for these immigrants. He also referred to the common perception that it was harder for veteran Zionists to become integrated in the society of

Palestine than it was for complete greenhorns, because the Zionists arrived with illusions about both the character of the Yishuv and their own role in its society. They were sorely disappointed that they did not receive adequate credit for their longtime involvement in the Zionist case but were treated, instead, as ordinary immigrants. The lack of any appropriate welcome at the harbor, Schachtel suggests, may have been the catalyst for the crisis of integration experienced by these Zionists. Hence, the apparatus should take action to prevent such disenchantment. By paying the Zionists the desired respect, negative influence and agitation within the German-Jewish community could be averted. It is remarkable to note that many documents referring to the difficulties of the veteran Zionists explicitly mention their emotional state, which is referred to as being disappointed and hurt. In other words, these immigrants were being focused on not because of their material need or lack of practical support—as was the case for immigrants without means—but because of their psychological need. This was a rare case of the immigration apparatus taking the immigrants' emotions into account.[63]

The German Department and the HOG expected that veteran Zionists would voice their anger and disappointment and thereby influence others within the immigrant community, be it within the Keren HaYesod, the HOG, or in private circles. As a result, these two institutions went to great lengths to provide an appropriate welcome for the Zionists. The opinions of the veteran Zionists mattered, they had agency, and their fate remained a concern of the apparatus. While there were also female veteran Zionists, who were surely also disappointed by the reality of Palestine, they are hardly ever mentioned in this discussion. Not only were men discussed here because they were men, but because they were the fraternity brothers of those in charge of their absorption. The men in charge of the immigration apparatus were committed to them and very well able to relate to the deep fear of becoming a nobody in the new homeland, where former achievements no longer counted for anything. The discussion about making sure they were welcomed can therefore also be read as an attempt by their male peers to massage their shattered self-esteem and bruised masculinity.

A second group that figured prominently in the discussions about the reception immigrants met with at the harbor was the group of lone female immigrants. Unmarried women over the age of seventeen made up about 10 percent of the immigration from 1933 through 1938, or about 4,000 people. About 3,400 of these arrived as holders of labor and capitalist certificates and not as dependents.[64] Women who immigrated without being part of a family or a group and who were not joining a kibbutz were a particular focus for the social workers of the absorption apparatus. The beginning of their life in the country was especially scrutinized, as an article published in March 1934 in the *Jüdische Rundschau* shows: "The first weeks in the new homeland are the hardest for the young haluza, and even more so when money and housing are lacking—the malady of Haifa and Tel Aviv. Girls in such a situation are thankful for every kind word and especially responsive to advice and promises."[65] While women who were going to join a kibbutz were seen by the immigration apparatus as already belonging to a secure, stable network, women who were alone in the cities were not. These new immigrants from Germany, commentators noted, were different from the lone female immigrants of earlier immigration waves, who allegedly "knew what they wanted: to go to the countryside!" and who, as Zionist pioneers, were secure in their personality and in their path in the new country. These newly arrived women from Germany, by contrast, stayed in the cities, without any social framework or any connection to the building up of the country.[66] This, such was the fear, would put an unknown number of young single women in a vulnerable position, prone to being lured into prostitution. There was thus a real fear that these women might fall into prostitution, combined with a general disapproval within the Jewish Agency, and within its subsidiary German Department, of the concentration of this immigration wave in the cities.

In published material, the dangers that were named were social isolation and distress caused by the difficult housing and job markets, while the danger of prostitution was only hinted at. In internal discussions between the respective bodies, however, this concern was expressed explicitly from the beginning of the mass immigration. The issue of lone female immigrants in the cities was addressed both in internal discussions—within the HOG, among social workers, and in the respective bodies within the Yishuv—and in newspaper and magazine articles.[67] At the center of this discussion were the port cities of Tel Aviv/Jaffa and Haifa. As both of these contained a mixed population of Jews and Arabs, they were seen as a dangerous potential meeting ground between young, inexperienced women and Arab men or British soldiers on leave. The Jewish national community and the British authorities had somewhat different perspectives on prostitution, though they both disapproved. The Mandate authorities were more concerned with questions of "social hygiene," while the Yishuv's take centered on the project of nation building: Jewish women were to serve as "mothers of the nation," as the moral gatekeepers for the state-in-the-making.[68] The German immigrant apparatus adopted the general approach of the Yishuv. Their differing approaches to the subject prompted conflicts between British government social workers and the social workers of the immigrant apparatus.[69]

The prostitution of Jewish women in the port cities had been a matter of discussion within the relevant bodies for years, but became especially prominent after the mass immigration from Germany began, as Henrietta Szold observes. In the summer of 1933, the director of the Jewish Agency in the Haifa Bat Galim neighborhood adjacent to the port suspected that procurers were boarding immigrant vessels and beguiling immigrant girls. Due to a lack of funding, this suspicion could not be investigated at the time. In 1934, the year in which almost ten thousand immigrants from Germany arrived— the highest yearly amount of the whole immigration wave—the discussion intensified. A few incidents launched a new discussion of the involvement of newly arrived female immigrants from Germany. In February, the existence of a brothel run by German-Jewish immigrants in Jaffa, the Bar Royal, was discovered—a shocking, shameful incident for the HOG and the German Department, especially because the operators had been supported by social workers of the HOG. At least one of the prostitutes was of German-Jewish background as well and was detained and apparently deported.[70]

Also in February of 1934, a Haifa resident, Willy Goldschmidt, ombudsman for the Zionist committee for Austria, complained about the prostitution of newly arrived German girls in Haifa. Goldschmidt lambasted the female immigrants' love of luxury as the reason for their prostitution. In addition, he insinuated that there were cases of German-Jewish women being involved in sexual relations with Arab men to whom they would tell political secrets. Goldschmidt's letter, although much of it was hearsay and exaggerated, touched a nerve, precisely because it touched upon the fear within the Yishuv of prostitution as a mixing ground between Jews and Arabs. It expressed the general Yishuv attitude of frowning upon any romantic or sexual relations between Jews and Arabs.[71] The letter was passed from institution to institution and sparked a discussion between the HOG, the German Department, and even the London Executive. After listening to several complaints and reports, Georg Landauer embraced the idea of a female social worker as necessary.[72] Henrietta Szold, in charge of social work within the Va'ad Leumi, addressed the accusations herself. She rejected most of Goldschmidt's allegations as unverified rumors and tried to bring the discussion back to a pragmatic approach, concentrating on German women who were lured into prostitution upon their arrival and on ways to deal with this problem through investigation and social work.[73]

Following Goldschmidt's claims and, apparently, other complaints of the same kind, funds were appropriated both to investigate the situation and to provide a female social worker specifically to engage with these young women on the ships—funds that had not been previously allocated. In the following months, Szold placed Frieda Weinreich, a senior German social worker from the HOG, as a *Schiffsfürsorgerin*, a ship social worker, on ships that arrived carrying immigrants from Germany. While she had been appointed to investigate the plight of young women and the danger of prostitution, she also advised women in general about their early days in the country. In published material, her position was defined as complementing the work of the Jewish Agency "regarding protection, advice, information, and support for women and girls traveling alone, as well as families with children." For women who arrived alone with their children, it turned out, Weinreich was a particularly valuable asset during disembarkation: "Here she holds the small children while the mother sorts the luggage, there she organizes a baggage porter and helps the flustered woman with an infant in her arms to clear customs quickly."[74]

After visiting nine ships as a harbor social worker, Weinreich reported back to Szold and the Immigration Department that, while her work had proved to be of great benefit to women of all ages traveling alone, she could not find any evidence that procurers were beguiling young women. Subsequently, in May of 1934, Szold's request of 20 Palestine pounds per month for the continued support of women traveling alone was denied, on the grounds that there was no apparent danger to the women. While the support of a harbor social worker for women and girls was seen to be helpful, David Beharel, treasurer of the finance department of the Jewish Agency, informed Landauer and Szold that there were no longer funds for this work in the budget.[75] Beharel further argued, in a letter to Yitzhak Greenboim, that prostitution, though he acknowledged it was a problem, was an international issue and hence not the responsibility of the Jewish Agency. He added that there were only very few cases of women in danger, as most of them came either in groups as pioneers, or else as dependents who had been invited to come.[76] Reluctantly, Szold had to dismiss Weinreich, because she had no funds to pay her with.[77]

Although the work was discontinued for lack of funding, the social workers criticized the Jewish Agency's policy, pointing out that the problem had not gone away and calling for change. Gusta Strumpf, for example, founder of a *Bet Haluzot* (home for pioneer women) in Haifa, repeatedly weighed in on the discussion of prostitution and pointed out the problem to the German immigration apparatus. In December of 1934 she turned to Arthur Ruppin, pointing out that the problem of single women in the cities was anything but solved. She rejected as wishful thinking the Jewish Agency's argument that pioneer women all came in groups and were hence in no danger. Instead, she argued, young women would stay in the cities whether this was politically desirable or not, and the apparatus needed to come to terms with this situation. She pointed out the importance of taking care of these young women while they still had a positive attitude toward the Yishuv, so that they could be shown the "right way" and be integrated into both the labor market and society.[78] In her opinion, the young women from Germany were less prepared than earlier immigrants and suffered from the difficult housing conditions, and were therefore especially in need of support. Because the *Bet Haluzot* contributed significantly to this attempt to keep the new immigrants away from prostitution, she requested financial support from the immigration apparatus.[79]

Ina Britschgi-Schimmer of the German Department also asked for help for those single women who lived not in *Batey Haluzot* but rather on their own in the cities. Because they spoke no Hebrew and had problems finding jobs, they tended to feel very lonely and could become "morally unstable."[80] Indeed, female immigrants without means, a family, or a network, and who lacked sufficient language and professional skills, were by definition in a very difficult situation. While there is no way to assess the actual scope of prostitution among German-Jewish women, it is obvious that the social workers of the immigration apparatus cared for the well-being of this potentially vulnerable group of immigrants. However, there was also a strong undertone, in this discussion, of a questioning finger pointed at the moral stamina of young women. It was only single women who immigrated without their husbands or parents—and not single men in the same situation—who were defined by the authorities as being "alone." In the new society as in the old, women were defined by men, and lone female immigrants suffered from being doubly patronized, as single women and as new immigrants. Given the prevailing ideology, which perceived women as the moral gatekeepers of their community and linked female sexuality to this endeavor, it is not surprising that single male immigrants, 16.5 percent of the German-Jewish immigration, were not seen as being in danger of becoming morally unstable. Nor was the sexual health of these men apparently seen as a concern—they were either not considered to be potential clients of prostitutes, or else mixing in that form was not perceived as dangerous to themselves or to the Jewish community. In the light of the surplus of young single men in the Yishuv, as well as of those men who immigrated months before their wives, it is remarkable that men are absent from these reports and concerned letters. In their case, being single was not perceived as a factor that impaired them in any way.

Another significant absence from this discussion is the taboo subject of sexual harassment within Jewish society. Gretel M. recalls multiple occasions on which she was sexually harassed by male colleagues, both on the kibbutz where she lived and in the cities where she worked at a restaurant. Complaining to the police was futile, she added, and might have meant losing her job. She had to defend herself on her own, as she had no family in Palestine: "I was completely alone here, I had no one."[81] In her autobiographical novel, Jenny Aloni, another young woman who immigrated alone, described many incidents of sexual harassment and attempted rape, all by Jewish men. The owner of the restaurant where she found a job as a dishwasher touched her against her will; the head waiter groped her, kissed her, and, when she resisted, openly bullied her every day at work; and a fellow student almost raped her.[82] Sexual harassment affected the lives of female immigrants in general, but especially those without a network or the support of their family. This plight, however, was not discussed by social workers or the apparatus.

NOT ANOTHER COUNTRY, BUT ANOTHER
WORLD: FIRST STEPS IN PALESTINE

Finding temporary housing was the primary task of each immigrant on his or her first day. The luckiest ones were those who were able to stay for a time with family and friends and receive advice and support, and who did not have to deal all alone with the hardships of this "other world" right from the beginning. Immigrants enrolled in a *haluz* program were usually brought to their respective kibbutzim, which took care of their elementary needs, like housing, work, and insurance. For those who could afford it, hotels, hostels, and pensions existed en masse in the port cities. Places run by other immigrants from Germany were especially popular, as they were German-speaking and provided German food and hospitality.[83] Female pioneers without means could stay in *Batey Haluzot* for the first weeks. Founded by the Women's Workers' Council in the 1930s, these provided homes for pioneer women in Haifa and Tel Aviv (later also Jerusalem). Hundreds of women stayed in these hostels, which later also offered vocational training for the women. Beginning in 1933, the HOG absorbed the cost of board and lodging for young German women staying in the hostels.[84]

Immigrants who arrived on a labor certificate and had registered before their immigration could stay inexpensively at *Batey Olim* (immigration hostels) run by the Jewish Agency when they first arrived. They could use their time while staying at the *Batey Olim* to look for work and an apartment. However, many of the newly arrived immigrants considered the conditions at the *Batey Olim* to be far from ideal. They were crowded, noisy, dirty, disorganized, and lacking in privacy. Many new immigrants also fell ill during their first days in the country, both as a result of the immunizations and because of the completely different climate.[85] In particular, the WIZO complained, the *Batey Olim*'s utter lack of family-friendliness was taxing for women and children.[86] Meta Frank, who arrived in 1934, chronicled her first night at the *Bet Olim* in Bat Galim, Haifa:

It was unbelievably hot.... In our European clothes, we were dressed utterly wrong. Also, dinner was anything but appealing.... I was completely intimidated and just did not know what to do.... During the night, I suddenly woke up: I had been bitten all over!... Turning on my flashlight, I realized to my horror that the bed was full of bedbugs.... I didn't dare go back to bed but left the room.... I looked up at the beautiful starlit sky and thought of home. How would I bear all this?[87]

Many new immigrants, both men and women, went to bed on their first night in Palestine disturbed by their new reality, intimidated by the landing procedure, and worried about their prospects for the future. Whether or not they had read publications such as the abovementioned *Palästina wie es wirklich ist* (Palestine As It Really Is), they were generally almost completely unprepared for the reality of their new homeland. In the words of Curt Wormann, "This Aliyah from Germany did not come merely to another country, but to another world."[88] Even worse was the situation of immigrants with no means whatsoever. If they had not registered for Jewish Agency hostels before their immigration, and if they had no acquaintances to rely on, they could find themselves temporarily homeless. Along with the *Va'ad haKehilla* (the community council), the HOG supported destitute cases by giving them vouchers for groceries and paying school tuition for their children as well as their rent. They also built tent camps for them. However, because space there was limited, in the summers of 1938 and 1939 some immigrants had to sleep on the beach under the open sky.[89] And finally, some immigrants, especially the refugees coming after 1938—many of whom had been imprisoned in concentration camps and were "broken in body and spirit"—not only needed the HOG to provide them with everything from clothes and kitchenware through furniture and loans for their rent, but also required social work and sometimes even medical stays in convalescent homes.[90] Private initiatives by and for immigrants were established, too, such as a collection of groceries for immigrants in need, a *Kleiderkammer* (free clothing store) collecting clothes, and a *Mittelstandsküche* (middle-class soup kitchen), almost entirely organized by women.[91]

Because the immigration apparatus considered the immigration hostels run by the Jewish Agency to be unfitting, they founded new hostels catering to the needs of the new immigrants. Unlike the *Batey Olim*, these were also available for immigrants who did not have labor certificates. The HOG hostels in Haifa and Tel Aviv featured more spacious and modern facilities and were particularly well suited for families, unlike the Jewish Agency–run hostels. Hebrew classes were taught on site, and a German social worker was at the immigrants' disposal to help organize their new lives and advise them about workplaces, vocational training, schools, and medical treatment. With these hostels, the apparatus aimed to ease the stress of the first days in the country and help Palestine become home for the immigrants as quickly as possible. With this end in mind, the focus of the social workers was on women. Men were not specifically addressed and did not appear as the object of social work at this point. It was the unequivocal opinion of the immigration apparatus that women were the sine qua non for the integration of their families. As the social worker Sara Berlowitz put it, "As mothers and wives they are responsible for certain tasks from the first day on and hence lack the option of a slow, healthy acclimatization and assimilation. Their double task is to adjust both themselves and their relatives to living here."[92]

Women—and only women—were offered "Palestine cooking" classes at the hostels so that they would have fewer problems adapting once they moved out. The immigration apparatus assigned them the role of creator of a new home for their families from day one, a role that included both homemaking and emotional support. And even in those first days, women were also already seen as potential providers for their families, given that it was easier for women to find temporary jobs than for men. Hence, further services were provided to ease the women's workload. While they had the option to cook for their families at the hostels, they could also choose to receive full board instead, inexpensively.[93] Another service was the presence of a childcare worker who could take care of the immigrants' children, enabling both parents to look for an apartment and workplaces. For the same reason, the HOG also supported some parents who sent their children to children's homes, *kibbutzim*, or Palestinian families in the countryside for the first weeks and months.[94] While women were expected to be the main caregivers, a separation from their children was accepted for the sake of a quick integration for the entire family.

While they stayed in the hotels, hostels, or with family, the new immigrants then also had to search for an apartment. In the cities, where three-quarters of the immigrants preferred to live (a ratio matching the preference of the Yishuv population in general), this task was extremely challenging. Different cities attracted different segments of the German-Jewish population. Tel Aviv, the cultural center of the Yishuv, where a third of the immigrants settled, attracted mostly those in commerce and the liberal professions. Haifa, where close to a quarter of them stayed, was attractive to those in the liberal professions, industry, and the technical professions, while Jerusalem, where only about 15 percent found a home, attracted small shop owners, academics who sought work at the Hebrew University, and religious immigrants.[95]

Home building lagged behind the actual need, which led to a lack of housing and exorbitant rents. This situation continued throughout the 1930s, especially in Tel Aviv, the city that attracted the majority of the immigrants. To help the immigrants swiftly find places, the offices of the HOG provided a registry of available rooms and flats. A private market of housing agencies also came into existence, with German immigrants establishing themselves as realtors for more recently arrived German Jews. Others asked friends or simply walked through the streets, checking posters or advertisement pillars. This proved to be difficult and time-consuming, because most immigrants did not read Hebrew well, if at all.

Beate D. remembered standing with her parents in front of advertisement pillars for hours, tediously trying to make out the Hebrew handwriting for advertised rooms. Those very same pillars also held death notices for those killed in attacks during the Arab unrest, immediately confronting the new immigrants with the dangerous reality of their new homeland.[96]

Many of the immigrants, not yet familiar with the reality of the housing market, initially wanted to find apartments that met their standards from Germany, and this as quickly as possible. The waiting period, living in hostels without their belongings, was taxing, and they yearned to "finally have again what they so dearly missed: their own home, the familiar surroundings of the Europe they had left behind, their own books and pictures, their clothes and appliances."[97] As a result, they often misjudged the situation and began by renting apartments that were too expensive for them. Ilse B.'s father, for example, initially rented a five-room apartment, until he realized that he could no longer afford that standard of living. Like many others of their compatriots, the family was forced to move into smaller and smaller apartments. Eventually, the whole family found itself in one single sublet room.[98]

German Jews living in Germany under Nazi rule had already undergone a process of being forced to leave their homes and move into more restricted apartments, as well as spaces shared with others. Guy Miron has discussed how for German Jews their whole world was shrinking around them and how this dramatically changed the experience of being at home in Nazi Germany. This was due at first to declining incomes and the resulting impoverishment, and later to the Nazi laws that required Jews to leave their homes. This process began during the early years of Nazi rule and intensified over time.[99] Many of the German Jews who immigrated to Palestine, however, made the move early in the Nazi years, which explains the feeling of a dramatic loss of standard of living in many contemporary documents as well as in the discussion of the absorbing authorities, despite the situation in Nazi Germany at the same time.

THEY WERE ALL YEKKES: GERMAN-JEWISH SUBCULTURE

The immigrants faced countless hardships, difficulties, and disappointments as they tried to set up the basics of their daily life in their first weeks and months in Palestine. In consultation hours and letters, the apparatus was confronted with complaints about the arrival process, the general lack of organization, and the many shortcomings of their new homeland, such as in this complaint by a new resident of Haifa: "For weeks now there has been a huge hole in the middle of Hadar HaKarmel, and the bus schedule is crossed out with a pencil and unreadable."[100] Additional complaints addressed the lack of housing and the exorbitant prices for renting an apartment as well as the lack of solidarity and the harsh welcome given to them by longtime residents.[101] As the weeks and months went on, this list grew to include futile attempts to find a job, health issues, conflicts with established residents of Eastern European origin, and, later, the effect of the immigration on marriages and family relations. In addition to the objective hardships of their migration, an important reason for these frustrations can be found in the fact that German Jews arrived in Palestine with manifold illusions. Veteran

Zionists, in particular, had expected to find a New Hebrew culture and were more often than not disappointed to find it only on the kibbutzim, while the feeling in the cities was one of "coming to an Eastern European shtetl."[102] Others felt they had been misled by the coverage of the *Jüdische Rundschau*, which had allegedly drawn a picture of life in the Yishuv as an "eternal Hora dance" and made the Yishuv appear to be a European country.[103] Now, they had to come to terms with the fact that "at the borders of the European enclaves, Asia begins, as one comes to realize on a daily basis."[104] The perception of the German Jews that they had come to the Orient, to Asia, to the Levant, was crucial to their overall immigration experience and self-perception in the new homeland, and they often phrased their criticism in terms of West versus East, order versus chaos, as I will discuss at greater length in chapter 2. Margulies-Auerbach, like countless other contemporary commentators, ridiculed this critique from the immigrants:

> They apparently find it inappropriate that this poor Yishuv did not prepare more and better working opportunities for them, that the rents are suddenly as high here as in all other countries, that the streets are not as clean, the children not educated to European standards, that the synagogues follow Polish rites ... that the markets are not clean, the restaurants not to their taste, that the waiters in the restaurants do not compare to the standards of the big German hotels.[105]

One of the results of this feeling of disappointment was the establishment of a German-Jewish subculture (even beyond what one might expect as a general tendency of immigrants). Immigrants who came as children and adolescents managed in most cases to integrate quickly into Yishuv society through school, youth movements, and their peers. They learned fluent Hebrew within a short time and intuitively adapted to the new culture, behavior, and appearances. Those German Jews who came as adults, on the other hand, tended to adhere to their own language and habits and, most importantly, continued to stay within their landsmanshaft even after the initial period of absorption. Whether within the framework of the official landsmanshaft—in other words, the HOG, with its organized leisure activities and continuing education—or in privately established circles of families and friends, the immigrants continued to bond and stay connected with their compatriots. Joining a landsmanshaft, "a local association of those arrived from the same country, city, or region," was a conscious and deliberate act of identification with a cultural group, as Anat Helman notes. In the 1930s, more than twenty such landsmanshaftn existed in Tel Aviv alone. However, the German landsmanshaft was by far the strongest, best organized, and most efficient.[106] Curt Wormann, himself a participant in the establishment of the cultural work of the HOG, called this activity an *Aufbau im Übergang* (building up during transition), playing on Ernst Simons's phrase *Aufbau im Untergang* (building up during decline), which described the organized work of the Jewish communities and organizations in Germany after 1933.

The HOG avoided the term *landsmanshaft* because it evoked negative implications in the Yishuv, like adhering to a *galut* (diaspora) attitude and using foreign languages instead of fulfilling the national obligation to learn Hebrew. Instead, the immigrant organization emphasized its mission to foster the cultural adaptation and integration of the new immigrants into their new homeland while also helping to minimize their feelings of isolation and uprootedness. Through Hebrew language classes and lectures on a wide variety of issues, ranging from history and political institutions to the climate, geography, and food of Palestine, they aimed to make the newcomers familiar with their new surroundings. In the process, the absorption apparatus used the German language with the immigrants during the transitional period, as a tool to help facilitate their integration into the Yishuv. Although the Yishuv criticized the de facto landsmanshaft, the HOG defended its work as a mediator between the immigrants and the society, envisioning a process of integration "from the individual immigrant via the HOG into the Yishuv."[107] As Lavsky has noted, this practice was unique to this group of migrants.[108]

The practice of staying close to one's own compatriots was also visible in the process of residential differentiation in neighborhoods. The newcomers tended to move to places where compatriots already lived: "You went to see an apartment on the second floor, and underneath it there lived a doctor from Berlin, and opposite was a librarian and former owner of a bookshop in Munich, so they were all Yekkes."[109] German-Jewish ethnic neighborhood formation occurred most famously in Rehavia in Jerusalem, Ahusa in Haifa, and the area around Ben Yehuda Street in Tel Aviv. Here, the immigrants soon established myriad small businesses, restaurants, shops, hostels, and cafés, followed later by an infrastructure of religious congregations, libraries, and schools for German children. These businesses served the double role of satisfying the specific desires of this group and attracting more new immigrants. For those immigrants who settled in the middle-class agricultural settlements established by the Rural and Suburban Settlement Company (RASSCO), such as Nahariya, Ramot HaShavim, Kfar Bialik, and Gan HaShomron, this tendency was even stronger. Because these places were often relatively isolated, and populated solely or mostly by fellow German Jews, the immigrants were able to adhere to German customs and the German language and separate themselves more from the rest of the Yishuv than immigrants who settled in the cities were able to do, at least initially.[110] And yet, as I will discuss in chapter 2, although the immigrants may have preferred to mingle mainly with their compatriots, they were nevertheless also in constant contact with their host society. Their often negative experiences, however, as well as the sheer size of their immigration wave, further enforced their tendency to prefer to mingle with their own compatriots.

Coffeehouses were of particular importance in this context. From the perspective of the immigrants, they offered a place to escape crowded housing and provided meals for those who had no kitchen at their disposal or for the single men—and women—who were not used to cooking for themselves. The massive influx of German immigrants led to the founding of scores of new coffeehouses throughout the country, and especially in Tel Aviv. Anat Helman mentions that in the 1930s, the number of cafés per capita in Tel Aviv was on par with that of European capitals.[111] Many of these newly founded coffee shops were replicas of famous cafés in Germany, where they served German cheesecake with whipped cream, German was spoken by both waitstaff and guests, and one could read German newspapers and drink what the Germans considered good coffee.[112] Cafés also served an important social function. The Yishuv was still a small community, and in the cafés, new immigrants could find and reunite with friends from Germany with whom they had lost contact after immigration.[113] For those living in the countryside, coffeehouses were also of crucial importance: a village would often only have one café, which became the central meeting place for the village. Some cafés even advertised themselves with this promise, as in this slogan for a coffee shop in Haifa: "Where do you meet your friends in Haifa? At Café Curtoni!"[114] Coffeehouses also provided an excellent opportunity for networking with fellow compatriots, as Hugo M. recalls: "You met a lot of people all at once. You went to eat where the others ate. There were certain restaurants that provided a 'visa' to enter Tel Aviv's Yekkish society."[115] Becoming a regular at a particular café could also serve as a form of escapism, especially for those who felt that they had not managed to integrate themselves. Ilse B.'s father, who was unemployed and embittered by his fall from being a wealthy merchant to a "nothing," went to the Schach Café in Haifa every day. This coffeehouse, where he could be with his kind—German men in similar situations—provided him with a space in which things were still the way they were before he migrated. The coffeehouses provided a shelter for many immigrants who had not yet found a job and who felt lonely in their new country. As Eva W. remembers it, these cafés were "always full, packed, but the patrons usually drank only one cup of coffee and then continued to sit there all day."[116]

However, visiting a café was not always a peaceful experience: reading German newspapers in public became frowned upon, especially from the end of the 1930s and increasingly so in later years, with the association of the German language with the Shoah.[117] While coffeehouses were an important space for the new immigrants, the absorbing society was ambivalent. Many residents enjoyed the new establishments and what they had to offer, but, as Liora Halperin shows, the official Yishuv received such German-speaking places of leisure as a sphere in which the use of Hebrew—which was supposed to be promoted, according to the collectivist ideology of the nationalist labor movement—was under threat.[118] The prevailing attitude was that instead of founding their own separate landsmanshaft, new immigrants ought to integrate themselves into their new society. And this was to be achieved, first and foremost, by learning and speaking Hebrew, rather than one's mother tongue, not only in official but also in leisure contexts, even though in actuality there was great language diversity among the residents of the Yishuv.[119]

The German Jews' practice of forming ethnic enclaves was certainly not unique, neither for the context of migration to Mandatory Palestine nor in comparison with contemporary and earlier migration movements. Sociospatial differentiation, the "tendency for people with distinctive characteristics and cultures to reside close to each other in cities thereby forming distinctive neighborhoods," is characteristic for minorities and migrants in general.[120] Research has pointed out that living together in enclaves can serve members of minorities in many ways: it can facilitate mutual support as well as help to preserve their group identity and lifestyle. It can also be a choice that is made out of fear of being exposed to the mainstream society.[121]

For the immigrants, the subculture they formed often made it easier for them to accept the reality of their new homeland. However, this isolationist tendency may also have strengthened conservative desires among parts of the immigrating group. In times of tremendous change, and given the fact that immigration entailed multiple challenges to traditional male prestige, male immigrants in particular searched for places where everything was seemingly the way it used to be. This has been shown for other countries of German-Jewish refuge, where these places—whether immigrant clubs or cafés—became "enclaves in which things were as they should be," as Steven Lowenstein has put it.[122] Lowenstein argues that this must be seen in relation to the naturally conservative character of immigrant organizations, as a place where immigrants could associate with their fellow immigrants and continue to preserve old customs and belief patterns. It tended to be the more tradition-minded immigrants who joined these groups.

The HOG did not fulfill this desire in the same way as did immigrant organizations in other countries, because it was committed to integrating its members into the host society. However, one place where this did happen for the German-Jewish immigrants was in their intellectual gatherings. Many German Jews joined intellectual circles, where they regularly listened to and discussed lectures with their peers. The prominent Zionist Georg Herlitz and his wife initiated a *jour fixe*: every Friday, they invited other German Jews to their Jerusalem apartment.[123] Other famous circles included that of Max Brod and Walter Grab.[124] While (as in the case of Herlitz's wife) women were sometimes involved in the hosting of these events, they were a minority among the participants; the only one established by a woman was the Kraal Circle in Jerusalem, founded by Else Lasker-Schüler. There were no exclusively female circles, which is not surprising, given the double burden the immigrant women had to shoulder. There is evidence of informal networks of women, but these had a very different character. Female immigrants established shopping cooperatives with neighbors, and in the tradition of German female charity organizations, as mentioned above, volunteers collected groceries for families in need and founded initiatives including a middle-class soup kitchen and a charity clothing collection.[125] Among the intellectual circles, some were explicitly male spaces. Hans Jonas, for instance, was in extensive contact with his fraternity brothers and other veteran Zionists when he first arrived in Palestine. With some of them, he founded an all-male intellectual circle that met on a regular basis to discuss philosophical issues in German. This so-called Pil Circle was later joined by other famous Zionists, such as Gershom Sholem. In his memoir, Jonas describes the circle:

> An important trait these friends shared was that they were all unmarried.... The fact that we were unattached was useful because the men in our group had plenty of free time. We had no wives waiting at home to demand that we devote Sabbath afternoon to them instead of engaging in endless talk with other men. Over the years, as one man after another married or remarried, it turned out to have a detrimental effect on the group.[126]

In his memoirs, Jonas highlights the explicitly men-only character of his network even across the distance of years. Strikingly, the presence of women just as spouses—not even as participants—was interpreted as disruptive to this network. The question of whether female participants could have added intellectually to these meetings does not seem to have arisen for Jonas and his peers. Jonas does mention that, after several years, women were allowed to participate, but none ever came. In the tradition of the men-only KJV fraternity (*Kartell Jüdischer Verbindungen* / Cartel of Jewish Fraternities), many such circles continued to exist in Palestine. In addition to the obvious element of mutual aid, they also served to reassure their membership of their role as men in a time of gender turmoil. The mainly male members of the various intellectual circles, whether scientists, authors, or Zionist activists, were searching for a way to preserve their legacy, not only politically or philosophically but also as a way to cope with their double loss of significance. As men who had once felt important both to their families and to their communities, they now had to adjust to a reality in which they were not relevant to the intellectual or political discourse of their host society, and in addition, they had to learn to accept the fact that in the initial period in Palestine, many women became the providers for their families, as we will discuss in chapter 3. While in Palestine everything was supposed to be different, male-centrism and all-male networks continued to exist within the immigrant community.

CONCLUSION

The pre-migration phase, the physical movement from the old to the new homeland, the arrival, and the initial absorption were critical phases in this migration—both from the perspective of the immigrants themselves and in the perception of the absorbing authorities entrusted with the organization of this process. This chapter, following the sequence of these events, has shed light on the level of experience, the level of policy, and the interaction between the two in various spaces. In the newcomers' first encounter with Palestine, gender came into play in various ways. The discussions during the voyage highlight the fact that gender identities were expected to change in the new homeland. For some, this anticipation was welcomed, while for others it was a cause of anxiety. The shock of arrival, then, was experienced by men and women alike. However, while both were confused and overwhelmed at the magnitude of their tasks, their methods of coping were different, as were the roles prescribed to men and women by the absorption apparatus in this initial phase. A look at the internal discussions of German-Jewish officials within the immigration apparatus and related organizations in the framework of the immigrants' reception at the harbor reveals normative doctrines and convictions that shaped the policies of the immigration apparatus. These discussions not only distinguished between men and women but among different kinds of women (in terms of age, form of immigration, and marital status) and different kinds of men (in terms of age and membership, or not, in the network). Another central question, from the perspective of the absorption apparatus, was who was considered to have agency and who was not. For the apparatus, mothers and wives were crucial to their families' adjustment and responsible, as gatekeepers in a time of transition, for forestalling crisis. However, they were not seen as politically relevant, nor was the apparatus worried that they might feel disappointed, hurt, or angry, or that they would voice their grievances within the immigrant community.

TWO

We Are the West in the East

GENDERED ENCOUNTERS IN
MANDATORY PALESTINE

IT WAS A HOT AUGUST day in 1934, and from a buzzing Jerusalem café, the young immigrant Hans Bernkopf was writing to his parents back in Germany:

> There is hardly anything more interesting than sitting in a sidewalk café and watching the different types of people who constantly pass by; firstly, all of the Jewish types you could think of, starting with the worker in the blue blouse, through Yemenites, to the caftan-wearing Jew—nobody is absent; then all of the different Arabs, Bedouins with scarves on their heads..., then fellaheen with their tarbooshes, and Arabs and Jews in European dress, some very elegant, the ladies made up, and in between all the little brown children, among whom it is already hard to distinguish between Arabs and Jews; heavy traffic, in the middle a group of Arabs riding on mules with lots of screaming, sometimes even a camel, buses, an unbelievable lot of traffic. It is notable that every second woman is pregnant. Girls, just like you see them on the Kurfürstendamm, English soldiers, local police—you cannot imagine this scenery colorfully enough.[1]

The practice of sitting in cafés was common among the newcomers from Germany. Here, one could not only meet old acquaintances and network with compatriots but also soak in the mixture of people passing by. Bernkopf's letter draws a comprehensive picture of the highly heterogeneous scenery that immigrants to Palestine found in the 1930s. The figures he observes run the gamut of Mandatory Palestine's society: "Oriental" and Ashkenazi Jews, Arabs, and British Mandate soldiers; men and women, old and young, religious and secular, modern and traditional; camels and cars. As the Israeli historian Anat Helman writes, "In a society where people are strangers to each other, they judge each other by what they see."[2] Like Bernkopf, the new immigrants literally looked around to orient themselves in the face of an overwhelming wave of impressions. And as they did so, they categorized their fellow citizens by visual features and tried to make sense of what they saw in order to understand connections and closeness as well as borders and boundaries.

Although the immigrants formed a unique subculture in the Yishuv, as discussed in the previous chapter, they were in contact with all the groups making up Mandatory Palestine society. The intensity of each interaction depended on a variety of factors. The most crucial distinction to be made is between interactions occurring within the organized Jewish community, the Yishuv, and those that took place outside of it. Encounters with the British and with Arabs were generally more limited than those with fellow Jews, due to Palestine's political realities. The Arab majority and the Jewish minority formed different entities, living in a de facto dual society. Nevertheless, despite the increasing enmity between them in the 1930s, they still interacted, due to their spatial proximity—mostly in the cities, but also to some degree in other places.[3] As for the British, although they were ever-present as the colonial power, personal interactions with them in daily life were generally scarce. Because neither the Arabs nor the British were part of the Jewish community, contact with them fell under close scrutiny in the contemporary discourse of the Yishuv. German-Jewish newcomers arriving in Palestine found themselves in the middle of an ongoing struggle over the boundaries of the state-in-the-making. Any crossing of the boundary between Jews and non-Jewish groups was perceived as "contested contact," as Deborah Bernstein demonstrates. Such boundary-crossing was seen as a potential threat to the national project and therefore objected to. As Bernstein further argues, it was mainly women who were observed to cross boundaries, and Yishuv public opinion strongly objected to Jewish women socializing with "men on the other side," barely differentiating among shared leisure time, romantic relations, and prostitution; these were all perceived as equally illegitimate.[4]

Within the Yishuv itself, there was ethnic friction between European and non-European Jews. The latter group consisted of Sephardim (who had lived in Palestine for generations) as well as various Jewish communities of Middle Eastern and North African descent. Despite their different origins and heritages, these groups have been subsumed under the term *Oriental Jews* or, in modern terminology, *Mizrahim* (Hebrew: Easterners).[5] The political, administrative, and cultural world of the Yishuv was dominated by Jews of Eastern European background, and the newcomers from Germany therefore met them constantly in their everyday lives. Contacts with Mizrahi Jews were less frequent, and the quality of these encounters was different, occurring mostly in the framework of employers and employees or providers and recipients of social work. Except with the Eastern Europeans, such contact occurred in the public sphere rather than in interpersonal settings. Individual factors, such as the sex, age, living situation, and livelihood of the given immigrants, were also relevant to the conditions of encounters. Jerusalem was more heavily shaped by the Mizrahi communities than was the rest of the country; most of the settlements were dominated by Ashkenazim. And finally, older immigrants tended to stay within their own landsmanshaft, while the young went to school with other Jewish children from different backgrounds.

This chapter explores encounters with the various groups from the perspective of the new immigrants. As discussed earlier, the shock of being in Palestine was often expressed in terms of Europe versus the Orient or West versus East. By and large, German Jews perceived themselves as Westerners in possession of superior education, culture, and the "secondary virtues" needed in modern societies, such as reliability, punctuality, cleanliness, etc. They expressed their apprehension toward the East, including Arabs, Mizrahim, and Eastern European Jews, using the derogatory term *Levantinism*, which expressed a perception of the new homeland and its residents as unreliable, unprofessional, and ultimately inferior. Scholars describe such "othering" of non-Western Jews in Israel as "internal orientalism."[6] The immigrants' own self-perceived Western-ness played a crucial role in how they perceived themselves vis-à-vis their new homeland and host society.

THE REENCOUNTER OF OSTJUDEN AND YEKKES

The German Jews, who, like the Eastern European Jews, belonged to the Ashkenazi group, strengthened Ashkenazi dominance in the Yishuv. However, neither the new immigrants nor the established residents of Eastern European background perceived this as a unifying element between them. In fact, this inner-Ashkenazi conflict was the most crucial one for the German Jews. This was due, firstly, to the overwhelming presence of Jews of Eastern European and Russian background in Palestine: they formed the demographic majority in the Yishuv by the time the German Jews arrived. The new immigrants encountered them daily as neighbors, shop owners, landlords, teachers, employers, and colleagues. Secondly, the two groups had a conflictual entangled past in Europe, exemplified in the conceptual pairing of *Ostjude* and *Westjude*. These terms, which arose at the turn of the twentieth century in Europe, described the highly ambivalent relation between Western and Eastern European Jews, revolving around assimilation to Christian culture by Western Jews, on the one hand, and adherence to the Yiddish language and traditionalist Judaism by Eastern European Jewry, on the other (what Steven Aschheim calls the clash between caftan and cravat). The massive immigration of Polish Jews to Germany, especially after World War I, made this issue more concrete for German Jews.[7] They often approached their Eastern brethren—constant reminders of the ghetto existence they aimed to leave behind—with feelings of superiority and rejection. *Ostjuden*, a highly derogatory term, expressed stereotypes of backward, aesthetically unpleasing, inferior outsiders.[8] As Kalmar and Penslar write, Ostjuden were considered "half-asiatic" and perceived in Orientalist terms by both Western Jews and Gentiles.[9]

While most German Jews, pre-migration, had clearly perceived their Eastern European brethren as inferior, now, in Palestine, they encountered the reverse situation. Now they were Yekkes, outsiders, unable to adapt properly to the new conditions, while Eastern European Jews were politically, culturally, and demographically dominant. For both newcomers and old-timers, this old conflict remained a key reference point. Both continued to think in terms of Eastern and Western Jews and the negative attributes connected to each. Irith Cherniavsky, writing from the perspective of Polish immigrants, has claimed that there was also a sense of empathy, even admiration, among the Polish immigrants for the German-Jewish immigrants.[10] This was, however, apparently not felt by most of the German Jews. They also brought from Germany the pejorative terms Yekke and *Ostjude*. A genre of insulting "ethnic humor" arose, which, along with the epithet Yekke, expressed schadenfreude at the reversed conditions.[11] Because Eastern Europeans and Russians were the Yishuv's political and cultural elite, they were the one group that had the power to harshly criticize the new immigrants.

The basic critique of the newcomers, offered in both personal encounters and public debates, was that they were unwilling to change their lifestyle and refused to assimilate to Yishuv society.[12] But the new immigrants barely read the Yishuv's Hebrew publications in their first years in the country; they continued to rely primarily on German-language newspapers. The *Jüdische Rundschau* and the *Mitteilungsblatt*—both outspokenly committed to the Zionist project—therefore translated the criticism and delivered it directly to the new immigrants. Here, German-speaking veteran residents of the Yishuv delivered their critiques of their German brethren, such as in this 1934 article in the *Mitteilungsblatt*: "They form colonies of emigrants in the three cities of the country and continue with the life that they led in Berlin or other German cities. They want their businesses, convenience, entertainment, want to read their German newspapers."[13] The three-part criticism consisted of an ethnic element, a class element, and a settling of old scores. But the ethnic part formed the core of the critique, alleging ethnic separation through the landsmanshaft, ethnic neighborhood formation, and continued use of the German language. German Jews made up the biggest immigration wave to Palestine so far. By the end of 1936, German Jews already numbered 35,000, making them the third largest ethnic group in the Yishuv, after Jews from Poland and those from Russia. They eventually made up one-fifth of the Yishuv population. This fact alone drew extra scrutiny to this group of immigrants from veteran residents. More importantly, though, the prevalence of the German language in both private and public aroused anger, hostility, even occasional violence.[14] As Liora Halperin shows, continuing to use one's mother tongue instead of learning Hebrew was perceived as laziness, contradicting the Zionist concept of labor and sacrifice.[15] And while suspicion of the German language first arose from its speakers' alleged refusal to speak Hebrew, it soon became enmeshed with the political situation in Germany: German was now the language of Hitler.[16] The class part of the critique concerned the immigrants' alleged adherence to bourgeois culture. German Jews, it was bemoaned, would import alien practices and ideas that might threaten Yishuv culture.[17] Adam Rubin has used the term *cultural anxiety* to describe the prevalent feelings of the political and cultural Yishuv toward the absorption of German immigrants; it was feared they would interfere with the creation of a homogenous New Hebrew culture and society. It was a common trope in the hothouse atmosphere of those years to denounce German Jews for destroying the Yishuv's pioneering spirit, Zionist ideals, and socialist ethic with their urbanism, hedonism, and alleged materialistic affinity for luxury shops, a bourgeois lifestyle, and sophisticated clothes.[18] Consumerism and luxury became derogatory terms in the Yishuv of the 1930s, as Helman has pointed out.[19] And finally, the score-settling part of the critique, in connection with a generally dismissive approach toward new immigrants by more established ones, faulted German Jews for their arrogant attitude toward the achievements of the Yishuv based on their bias against Eastern European Jewry.[20]

The immigrants were well aware of the criticisms directed at them. In November 1933, Else Bodenheimer-Biram, of Haifa, wrote a letter to her friend Georg Landauer, of the German Department of the Jewish Agency for Palestine, in which she summed up the prevailing attitude toward the new immigrants:

This is how the argument goes: The Germans ruin the prices. They are to blame for everything getting more expensive. They live too luxuriously. Why can't they live in tents, as we did? Why do they need to boost the prices for apartments? Why can't they walk instead of paying 20 piaster for a car that should only cost half that? Spinney cannot keep up with the bacon supply because the Germans eat it all, and more of the like. In fact, all of the animosity that the Jews voiced in Germany against the Ostjude is now being paid back with 100% interest.[21]

Like most German immigrants, Bodenheimer-Biram, understanding the criticism as a direct response to German Jewry's previous treatment of Eastern European Jews, therefore saw it as biased and unhinged. Bodenheimer-Biram pointed out that even though German Jews suffered from the housing crisis like everyone else, they were singled out for attack as having caused it.[22] The argument about German Jews eating bacon, targeting their alleged lack of religious observance, recalls the critique of Western Jewish assimilation to Christian society back in Europe. However, the new immigrants' lack of religious observance—consuming nonkosher food, desecrating the Sabbath, etc.—was a side issue in this critique.[23] The main issue was the national interest, which required rejecting foreign products in favor of those created in the Yishuv by Jewish agriculture and industry (*tozeret ha'aretz*). And while the whole group was attacked for its allegedly harmful behavior, female immigrants were particularly targeted, as the consumers who should have been strengthening the Yishuv economy instead of buying foreign goods, as I will discuss more thoroughly in chapter 4.

The profound and comprehensive criticism aimed at the new immigrants included all aspects of their lives. In addition to their consumption patterns, it explicitly addressed their leisure and private lives. Indulging in allegedly alien habits was considered harmful to the emerging national culture. Jazz music, for instance, was popular among the newcomers, and advertisements in the *Mitteilungsblatt* and the *Jüdische Rundschau* frequently promoted events featuring German musicians, such as: "Visit in Tel-Aviv: Layla. Jazz on two pianos. Composer Hans Schlesinger on the piano." These "foreign" musical preferences of the German immigrants were repeatedly criticized as going against the desired Hebrew culture. The social worker Helene Hanna Thon, for example, complained in the *Jüdische Rundschau*:

> A young couple that had difficulties abroad, but was lucky enough here to do well right away, goes to a café to listen to jazz every day after work. A longtime resident tries to speak to them about this. "You are both new here; you still don't know the country and its institutions, you still have a lot of work to do to learn the language of the country. Is there nothing better to do with your evenings than listening to jazz?" They look like scolded children: "But we've had such a hard time, and we want to enjoy our freedom here. In the whole world, they dance to jazz—why not here?" . . . "No, it

doesn't work like that. . . . It starts with jazz in the evenings—and where does it stop?"[24]

The immigrants quoted here explicitly refer to the lack of personal freedom they experienced in Nazi Germany and their desire to live their lives according to their own wishes now. Many new immigrants experienced such criticism—targeting even the music they enjoyed—as an imposition. As Halperin shows, though, such policing aligned with the official position of the Yishuv, where social control was especially palpable in the leisure sphere.[25]

Apprehension, even hostility, toward newcomers was expressed not only in newspaper articles but also in the daily interactions that took place mostly in hierarchical relationships. Conflicts with Eastern European landlords, for example, were a common experience for German Jews. The newcomers constantly bemoaned the fact that their naïveté, and their unfamiliarity with the specifics of life in Eretz Israel, were taken advantage of. Many German immigrants initially had to live in a single sublet room, sharing a kitchen and bathroom. Landlords who would not let them cook in the kitchen or wash their laundry, and even limited their use of the toilet, were more often than not interpreted as settling old scores. The immigrants encountered mockery and hostility that they interpreted as directly related to the shared history back in Europe. Eva W., who came to Palestine as a girl, recalled: "The landlord of our house . . . was from Lodz, and he hated the Yekkes—he loved to take money from them, though. The Ostjuden were so full of hate. This man couldn't pass me in the staircase . . . without pulling my pigtail and saying: Yekkete!"[26] Eva described being constantly bullied and harassed, as a young immigrant girl, by this older man, the landlord. Her powerlessness incensed her: "Every time he did this I wanted to kill this man; this is how deeply I was hurt by this impudence!"[27] Several categories intersected to create an unbearable situation for her: gender, age, old-timers versus newcomers, and the landlord-tenant hierarchy. But the main category for her interpretation of the unpleasant daily encounters with her landlord was the conflict between Ostjuden and Yekkes. Other immigrants also recalled their landlords making them pay outrageous rents, charging them for the entire house's water supply when they only lived in one small part of it, or even stealing from them. Ilse B. remembers, about her family's landlady: "I had a few things from Germany that I clung to. That was a piece of home, and she stole it, and that was terrible for me.... We did not say anything; my parents did not say anything, they were so anxious. We were so intimidated here."[28] Here, the landlady virtually stole a part of Germany, a "piece of home," from the immigrants. Because of the multiple power relations at play, the immigrants found themselves powerless and frustrated in their host society. We should note that while the difference in ethnic backgrounds was not necessarily the reason for the landlady's alleged theft, the newcomers themselves saw it that way, and it was crucial to their interpretation. This powerlessness that the immigrants experienced, not only in interactions with their landlords, also affected power structures within family units: Ilse, like many other children, began to perceive her parents, especially her father, as impotent vis-à-vis the receiving society.

Children also experienced hostility at school, where they were bullied for being "Yekkish" by both classmates and teachers. Abraham M. recalls being called out in school for dancing the tango instead of the hora: "How can you? Ballroom dancing—what is that? That's terrible!" he recalls his classmates reacting, adding "that meant we were odd, we didn't belong, we were *borganim* [bourgeois]."[29] Like the grown-ups, the children were mocked for their German accents, different clothes, and distinctive habits. However, children usually adapted more easily, quickly learning Hebrew and changing their appearance so they would not automatically be recognized as Yekkes.

CAPITALIST MOMMY'S BOYS AND KURFÜRSTENDAMM LADIES

For adults, the situation was more difficult. In their interactions with the authorities, which were highly hierarchical anyway, discrimination was felt particularly strongly. The infamous request by the city of Tel Aviv that letters be written only in Hebrew, not in German—an almost impossible requirement for new immigrants—was seen as an act of revenge. Georg Goldstein, a resident of Haifa, complained about a clerk at the *Va'ad HaKehilla* (community council) who told him that she couldn't help him and then added: "You should have stayed in Germany." Goldstein found this extremely insulting; it was obvious to him that she would not have said this to "her own people."[30] Some

FIGURE 6. A German Jew purchases orange juice at an outdoor stall in Palestine, 1936. Copyright: United States Holocaust Memorial Museum. Photograph Number: 66408. Provenance: Ralph Blumenthal. Reprinted with permission.

discrimination was even more explicit. The job description for a clerk position in the Haifa municipality included the desired qualification of "immigration before 1933," code for non-Germans.[31] Discriminatory remarks about their ethnicity were part of the experience of many immigrants in the labor market, whether as kibbutz workers, domestic workers in the city, or construction workers. The immigrants suffered from their lack of *protektzia*, a derogatory term used by German Jews for what they saw as Eastern European nepotism.[32] In addition, German-Jewish men were sometimes demeaned as insufficiently masculine, stereotyped as overtly intellectual and physically weak. Both contemporary Zionist discourse and anti-Semitic ideology attributed these negatively marked characteristics to Western Jewish men. Such negative features of the diaspora were to be overcome in Eretz Israel over the course of the "normalization" of the Jewish people (see chapter 3 for more detail).

Among other things, such stereotypes meant worse chances at scarce positions. In conflicts in the workplace, ethnicity, class, and masculinity could intersect, as the following example demonstrates. In 1937, bus drivers in Haifa were in a conflict over whether to stay independent or form a cooperative, a conflict that was about to culminate in a lawsuit. Erich Badrian, a recent immigrant from Germany involved in this quarrel, reported to his fraternity brothers in the KJV (cartel of Jewish fraternities) that the lawsuit was supposed to stop the influence of the German Jews and stabilize the power of the established residents. Badrian described meetings of the drivers' cooperative where German Jews were told to "go back to Hitler" and that "Hitler was still a man of honor for not killing them before they got here." The criticism was framed in terms of gender and class. Badrian said his opponents claimed German Jews had "ruined the socialist character of the cooperative so that poor drivers couldn't enter anymore, were against the Histadrut [the General Organization of Workers in Eretz Israel], endangered the unity of the movement, and, in general, were capitalist 'Mommy's boys.'"[33] Thus, German bus drivers were both blamed for endangering socialist character and unity and mocked as spoiled, effeminate boys.

And yet, although "Yekkish" men were ridiculed and criticized, they were not as heavily attacked, as potential threats to the emerging Hebrew culture and its unity, as "Yekkish" women were. The stereotype of female immigrants from Germany as vain, fancy, bourgeois, egotistical "Kurfürstendamm Ladies" (after the famous Berlin boulevard) was an extreme version of the critique of the already "othered" German immigrants. These women allegedly only cared about the latest fashion and elegant houses, rather than building up the country, thereby ignoring the sacrifices of earlier immigrants who had drained swamps, constructed colonies, and risked their lives.[34] This classification aligns with the general discourse in the Yishuv contrasting middle-class and proletarian femininity.[35] However, it explicitly constructs these women as German. The Jerusalem-based author Moshe Yaakov Ben-Gavriel made this explicit in a 1933 article in the *Jüdische Rundschau*:[36]

> We don't like to see people trying to import inappropriate customs and practices. For example, the housemaid who . . . is banished to the kitchen table. No, dear [female] friend, here the custom is that the housemaid is part of the family, that she eats with the family, and that she, too, does not work on the Shabbat—just like you, madam, who work much less during the week than the comrade housemaid. And while I am at it, madam, I want to humbly call your attention to the fact that now you have the opportunity to overcome the unwelcome stereotype of the Kurfürstendamm Lady. You surely know what I mean, as you are shamefully if not completely aware of it when putting your lipstick into your purse that so fantastically matches your tea dress.[37]

Ben-Gavriel constructed the Kurfürstendamm Lady as a clearly recognizable type, distinguished from veteran female residents by her behavior and apparel. She is the carrier of a bundle of negatively connoted features—unproductive, bourgeois, decadent, snobbish—embodied in her appearance, lipstick, elegant clothing, and accessories: the opposite of the productive proletarian "comrade housewife." Remarkably, Ben-Gavriel, himself of Austrian origin and only in Palestine since 1927, presented himself in his letter as a "veteran Palestinian." The harsh critiques of their German brethren by Ben-Gavriel and others were surely partly motivated by the desire to establish themselves as old-timers. Indeed, as Irith Cherniavsky has shown for the Polish-Jewish press reporting on the German immigrants, the intense criticism directed at them argued that German women would cause Polish and Russian women to emulate this negative lifestyle.[38]

Ben-Gavriel's article started a controversy, fought out in readers' letters to both the *Jüdische Rundschau* and the *Mitteilungsblatt*, regarding German-

Jewish women's behavior and appearance. Most of the letters disputed Ben-Gavriel's assertions. They did not seem to take exception to his point about the treatment of domestic workers; relations with servants in Germany were indeed very hierarchical, and many immigrants struggled to accept the Yishuv approach to domestic help. But most of the letters addressed his description of the appearance of female immigrants. Albert Baer of Haifa addressed Ben-Gavriel directly in the *Jüdische Rundschau*:

> You as a resident of Jerusalem should be aware that lipstick is used to a great extent by the local population, especially by women from Poland and Russia. There were already beauty salons for the "daughters of Jerusalem" before the German immigrants arrived, and if you took a closer look you would realize that only a very small number of the female German immigrants hold on to these European customs in Palestine. I am sure that they will not even adapt to this custom now that they have the model of the local population.[39]

While Baer acknowledged the negatively charged phenomenon and its imported character, he inverted its origin: not German women, but established immigrants from Poland and Russia, were to blame for this "lipstick femininity." The same was true, he continued, for the alleged luxury pursuits of German-Jewish women in beauty salons. Addressing the accusation of endangering Hebrew culture, he wrote that if there was a danger of "infection" from this decadent behavior, it would be Eastern European women who spoiled German women, not the other way around. Baer closed by remarking that he trusted German women's ability to resist this temptation. A few months later, as the discussion spread to the *Mitteilungsblatt*, a Mr. Katz took a similar line:

> There is almost nothing that the German Aliyah is not attacked for once in a while.... An article published last year in the *Jüdische Rundschau* ... even went so far as to say that the women of the German Aliyah move in an especially showy way and that they attract attention for their exaggerated use of makeup and powder. It wouldn't have been too difficult for the author of that article to figure out that the women whose looks he was criticizing are obviously and almost completely women whose birthplace wasn't Germany.[40]

Katz recalls Ben-Gavriel's accusations as more extreme than they actually were. This indicates that such complaints were not an isolated incident but an ongoing discourse; Ben-Gavriel was advancing arguments that the immigrants had already heard many times. Katz's outrage is not over the use of lipstick and powder themselves but about their exaggerated use, attributed to Eastern European women. Ben-Gavriel's attack on the modesty of "their" women spurred writers like Katz to push back against the phantom of the Kurfürstendamm Lady. The subtext here is that, if such a phenomenon exists, it must be attributed not to *real* German Jews but to those who were born in Eastern Europe.

The focus on the alleged looks of female immigrants was essentially a critique of an adherence to a German culture and lifestyle that was understood as separatism. In the discussion that Ben-Gavriel initiated, the question of desirable and undesirable femininities in Palestine intersected with the categories of appearance, class, and ethnic background against the context of the emerging Hebrew culture. Immigrants were indeed highly visible. German immigrants were, at least during the first period in Palestine, easily identified not only through language but also through a distinct look.[41] It is therefore no coincidence that the critique addressed sartorial culture. Clothing was an important element in expressing belonging to one or another of the different groups in the emerging culture. The values of the pioneers building the country, leaving the diaspora behind, were expressed in khaki trousers and simple, unadorned dress, while elegant clothing, lipstick, makeup, and nail polish were seen as markers of middle-class diaspora identity.[42] However, it was not the case that other city-dwellers did not dress well, nor in fact that the majority of the immigrants dressed as described. Earlier, female immigrants from Poland had suffered similar gendered criticism. In the 1920s, Polish women were condemned as licentious whores and women of cultural vacuity by their Russian predecessors. However, unlike the Yekkes, these women still dressed traditionally, in a recognizably Jewish way. But in the 1930s and 1940s, the Yekkes became the perfect "other" for such accusations, identified with hedonism, a "craving for luxury and snobbishness," and a "foreign spirit."[43] They were perceived as so different from the rest, Helman writes, that the Easterners felt a sort of solidarity against them.[44]

Attacks on the looks of female immigrants aimed to pressure them to conform in appearance and behavior, abandoning their middle-class German standard for a proletarian Yishuv standard. Ben-Gavriel's accusations are in line with the general ideas and conflicting images of the *Ivria Hadasha*, the New Hebrew Woman.[45] Appearance featured heavily in these debates. The ubiquitous derogatory nickname Yekke derived from male clothing, but women's apparel was at the center of the discussion. Male immigrants' looks were frequently ridiculed (knee socks with sandals; gloves and parasols; knickerbockers and tropical helmets), but not perceived as threatening the emerging national culture. Both in Ben-Gavriel's critique and in his readers' reactions, women are seen to serve as gatekeepers.

This debate—both the critique and the responses—consisted of men speaking about women. Ben-Gavriel explicitly inspected and evaluated the appearance of a woman who was blushing under his gaze—a prototypical example of male objectification of women.[46] For his respondents, however, these accusations stood out from other critiques: while immigrants faced all sorts of criticism, accusing "their" women took it too far. These respondents also objectified women: both those of their own community, on whose behalf they allegedly spoke, and the "other" women (unanimously perceived as Eastern Europeans), who were attacked in return. The male German discussants were not willing to allow the interpretational sovereignty of the Eastern European–dominated Yishuv to extend to othering "their" women's physical appearance.

THE OTHER SIDE:
THE GERMAN-JEWISH GAZE ON THE OSTJUDEN

As now established, the German-Jewish minority experienced mistreatment and criticism by veteran residents of the Yishuv, both in public debate and from men and women on the street. The German Jews felt regularly excluded, discriminated against, and othered by Eastern European Jews. These encounters involved the shared experience of being part of a powerless minority, mistreated by a powerful majority. Any criticism of the situation in Palestine, they felt, was quashed by veteran residents with remarks like "We didn't ask you to come; go back to Hitler."[47] However, the newcomers also delivered harsh criticisms: the aversion was mutual. While the attitude of veteran residents in relationships of power over German immigrants (as employers, landlords, municipal workers, etc.) had serious practical relevance for the new immigrants' everyday lives, the newcomers' gaze on veteran residents had no such ramifications—but it *was* relevant to their own self-understanding. The newcomers' conception of the veterans was shaped by an Orientalist gaze. Jews from various Eastern European states, as well as Russia, were perceived as one hegemonic bloc by the new immigrants, many of whom felt a strong aversion toward them. This perception, one immigrant recalled, was imported from Germany: "At home, I always heard how people talked about the Ostjuden. That they had so many children, etc. . . . And I always thought that they must have horns. . . . And here, everything was full of Ostjuden, and I realized that they are people, too, just like me."[48]

The reversed power conditions in the Yishuv profoundly challenged this feeling of superiority: German Jews were now the new immigrants who had to start from zero, resulting in what has been called a simultaneous complex of superiority and inferiority.[49] This was true not only for middle-class urban immigrants, but also for kibbutz pioneers, as Gad Granach recalls. He describes this reciprocal relation as "a constant tension between the Jews from Eastern Europe and us German Jews. The cultural gap was huge. Our living habits differed, we dressed differently, ate differently, and furnished our rooms differently. The East European Jews looked down upon us while we made fun of them. Naturally, we thought of ourselves as more intelligent than them and culturally superior."[50] Among the German Jews, feelings of superiority were expressed in terms of culture, status, and education as well as appearance, the body, and hygiene. Sometimes the sense of superiority was expressed in outrageous terms, such as in this 1934 letter from a Mr. Sachs to friends in Germany: "Palestine is a beautiful country, full of natural beauty, oranges, wine, etc. The only downside is the Yids, mainly the Polacks, whom you would need to kill. . . . Life here is very interesting, the filth unspeakable, but you can keep your own home as neat as you wish. Come here, and you will become an anti-Semite. I will shortly open an SA here."[51] Sachs's letter was intercepted by the authorities and, though it was clearly sarcastic, was perceived as so offensive that the German Department within the Jewish Agency considered deporting him. While this example is extreme, condescension toward Ostjuden was common among the German-Jewish immigrants. Offensive statements were rarely found in newspapers, where such expressions were deemed inappropriate. In autobiographies, such criticisms could be found, though presented in a milder form, as Miron has shown. This probably reflects an attempt by their authors, writing with many years' hindsight, to adapt to the Israeli narrative and the Zionist impetus.[52] In interviews, however, notions of superiority were expressed quite frankly. Ruth M. described her schoolteacher as "such a Polish type," wearing "a filthy white dinner jacket to teach the Yekkish children. That did not fit. He chewed gum, we weren't used to that, . . . and then he stuck it on the table. . . . He couldn't stand us, and we couldn't stand him."[53] Themes of apparel and hygiene were common in statements of disdain toward Eastern Europeans. In this description, the filthy and uncultivated teacher, who appears intellectually inferior, is directly opposed to the German Jews. Apparel and appearance were also at the center of Eva W.'s gaze on Eastern European women:

> They [the Germans] were much neater in their appearance . . . because the Western Europeans differed in that from the Eastern Europeans. For example, a grandmother! Among us, a grandmother looked like her daughter, just a little older. . . . But among the Ostjuden she was a Babushka! She wore old rags, she was disheveled, and she was run-down. . . . She had given up on herself, so to speak.[54]

Eva W. used the appearance of elderly women as an example for her claim that German Jews were neater—a classic stereotype about Ostjuden in Germany and a topos of Orientalism. This lack of neatness, she asserted, not only made Eastern European grandmothers look much older and less attractive than their German-Jewish contemporaries, but also dramatically affected their self-esteem. The gaze on Eastern European women—in this case by a woman—is also relevant in light of the above discussion of the Kurfürstendamm Lady. In addition to their alleged lack of personal hygiene, Eastern European women were also criticized for overt showiness in their use of makeup and jewelry—recalling nouveau riche stereotypes—while German-Jewish women were allegedly much more modest.[55] The author Gabriele Tergit, for example, claimed that Eastern European girls in the Yishuv were "made up to their eyeballs."[56] Old stereotypes against the Ostjuden brought over from Europe became enmeshed with bias against the Yishuv's female pioneers: working on the kibbutzim, they were considered masculinized, having rejected not only the Jewish diaspora identity but also bourgeois norms of femininity.[57] German men and women shared this sentiment: Beate D., for example, described her experience of a kibbutz where she lived briefly. Most of the kibbutz residents were Eastern European Jews who, Beate believed, abhorred the few German immigrants, making it very hard for them to integrate. Beate noted:

> The women of the kibbutz wore trousers, but the trousers were really ugly, ... and they had all worked really hard in the past and were real pioneers, and we weren't. That was also a reason why they hated us. And their legs were so varicose, awful. And they were in general terrible figures.... When they had babies, they all sat together on a bench to breastfeed the babies and ... that was so repulsive, terribly repulsive.[58]

The inversion of the Zionist ideal of the *haluza* (pioneer) is striking: the body of the hardworking woman is rejected exactly because of its obvious signs of hard physical work, making her disheveled and unattractive. The description of breastfeeding makes Beate's focus clear: women that she perceives as aesthetically displeasing are performing a—in her mind—very private act collectively, in public, showing themselves as uncivilized and primitive. Here again, the construction of Ostjuden as physically inferior, aesthetically displeasing, and repulsive reflects Orientalistic terms and themes imported from Germany. But this construction of Eastern European women also reflects the negotiations of different femininities in Palestine.

Ironically, many German-Jewish immigrants had family roots in Eastern Europe themselves. One in five German Jews was descended from Eastern Europeans—which could explain the emphasis they placed on distancing themselves from their Eastern European brethren. These ancestors were often kept a secret out of shame. Ilse B., for instance, went into utter shock when, once in Palestine, she learned that her parents were Ostjuden themselves. Her family was so assimilated to German ideas and behavior that she found this unimaginable.[59] However, in Palestine, German Jews who had been born in Eastern Europe often tended to identify with the German landsmanshaft rather than the Eastern European majority.[60] There was naturally some ambiguity. The immigrant Adolf B., for example, born in Germany to Eastern European parents, felt the need to distance himself from that part of his heritage. He deeply admired German culture but because of his family background had never truly felt part of the German immigrant community.[61]

While many Jews who had immigrated to Germany from Eastern Europe, especially in the years following World War I, perceived themselves, along with their descendants, as Germans, this identity was rejected by parts of the German-Jewish community even after their immigration to Palestine. Yehiel Ilsar, the son of parents from Galicia but who had lived all his life in Germany until immigrating to Palestine, described this attitude. In 1937, he proposed to Miriam, herself a new immigrant from Germany. Her parents were outraged:

> My social status was not high enough. "Who is he, where does he come from, who are his parents, apparently they are *Ostjuden* . . . ? The *Dichter* [this is a pun; see below] is out of the question for our only daughter Miriam. Western Jewish academics of worthy status court her. If Miriam is not willing to give up the *Dichter* we will send her to an aunt in the United States."[62]

Here the word *Dichter*, literally "poet," is a play on words, as Ilsar had a job sealing pipes, *dichten* in German. Along with his being considered an Ostjude, this clearly points to the element of class: as a simple worker, not an academic, he is considered an unworthy match. Ilsar describes how Miriam's parents' behavior continued at their wedding and beyond:

> When Miriam and I stood under the huppah, everybody stared, and the guests asked "who is that, is that the groom?" The rabbi who married us spoke in detail about the status and history of Miriam's family, which all the guests knew anyway. My parents and my name were not even mentioned. . . . Later, I learned that Miriam's parents had told her: "We will not give you a dowry, this marriage will last only a few weeks." Shortly after the wedding, Miriam fell ill with jaundice. . . . After her recovery, Miriam told me that her mother was initially convinced it was not jaundice but an early pregnancy, and took her straight to a gynecologist, indirectly asking for an abortion.[63]

The category of Ostjuden was remarkably strong in the consciousness of these German Jews. As Ilsar's example demonstrates, this mistrust was sometimes directed even at Jews who had been raised in Germany but were of Eastern European origin. As one immigrant said, "Someone just needed to tell me his name, and I already knew, he is from Galicia."[64] The fact that German Jews in Palestine continued to identify veteran residents of Eastern European descent, along with some of their compatriots from Germany, as Ostjuden can be read as an unwillingness to accept the political and cultural superiority of Ostjuden in the Yishuv—an act of defiance in the face of the circumstances that, of all people, those very Ostjuden now had the power to criticize the German Jews. This Orientalist perception of the veteran residents then became conflated with the nationalist demands of the New Hebrew culture. German-Jewish immigrants, it seems, were often unwilling to appreciate the achievements of the Yishuv because they identified those in power as Ostjuden. There was an omnipresent notion that German-Jewish immigrants were the victims of Ostjuden trying to settle an old score. They saw the treatment they received as stemming not just from their immigrant status but from their German-ness: that they were discriminated against "because we were Yekkes" or "because they were Ostjuden."

Whether the conflict between Yekkes and Ostjuden ever came to an end is an open question. Some observers perceived a change in the relationship toward the end of the 1930s. At that point, Helena Hanna Thon, for example, notes that the "embittered opposition" between the two groups has diminished and is now found only in "those circles which cannot release themselves from the grip of the old ideology," particularly men.[65] Others opine that the hostility ended with the founding of the state of Israel and the war of independence (and German Jews' participation in that). As the interviews show, however, stereotypes against Eastern European Jews continued to exist. An extreme example is a reader's letter published in the *Yakinton*, the monthly magazine of the organization of German Jews and their descendants, *Irgun Yozey Merkas Europa*. In the summer of 2012, an outraged female senior citizen expressed her apprehension over a joint event of the *Irgun Yozey Merkas Europa* and an organization committed to the heritage of Eastern European Jewry: "I think this kneeling before the Ostjuden is inappropriate. Did they ever apologize to us or voice their regret for what they did to us, the Yekke immigrants, in the 1930s?... Just as the German people asked the Jews for forgiveness, so should the Ostjuden."[66] More than eighty years after immigration, then, some immigrants still use and think with the categories of Yekkes versus Ostjuden.

"INTERNAL OTHERS": ENCOUNTERS WITH MIZRAHIM

Unlike their history with Eastern European Jews, most German Jews had never encountered "Oriental" Jews before immigrating to Palestine. By the time the new immigrants arrived, Sephardim and "Oriental" Jews had become a minority within the Yishuv. In 1938, Sephardim and members of communities of Persian, Yemenite, Kurdish, Turkish, Bukhari, Syrian, and other similar (Mizrahi) origins made up 23 percent of the Jewish population.[67] While some Sephardim of the old Yishuv were well established and educated, most Mizrahim lived at the margins of Jewish society, resided in neighborhoods with less access to health services and other resources, and worked in low-income jobs.[68] In Yishuv society, as Kalmar and Penslar write, Mizrahi Jews were therefore located in a "liminal zone between the European Jew and the Arab" and subjected to a Zionist form of Orientalism: while there was a romantic fascination with the "authentic, pure" Mizrahim, they were also largely viewed, with a patronizing mixture of pity and scorn, as primitive, feminized, irrational, and weak. Contemporary Zionist discourse, aimed at Westernizing the Yishuv, regarded "Oriental" Jews as a malleable group in need of reform and modernization.[69]

This general approach of Ashkenazi Jews toward "Oriental" Jews in the Yishuv was shared by the German-Jewish newcomers. Many felt a striking sense of superiority toward non-Western Jews, in both discourse and encounters. The "internal Orientalism" typical of Zionist discourse was also expressed in the *Jüdische Rundschau*'s Palestine coverage, where German Jews could read about the culture and heritage, the culinary and religious customs, of the Yishuv's "Oriental communities." Mizrahi culture was presented as interesting from a folkloristic standpoint and "Oriental" Jews described as beautiful, devout, with a rich and colorful tradition.[70] They were mostly presented as stereotypes, however, not individuals, and as inferior to Western Jews in every possible way. The most common topic in the journal's coverage of Mizrahim was social welfare. Scholars researching social workers in the Yishuv, many of whom had migrated from Germany or been trained there, have discussed them as trailblazing professional women entering the public sphere and praised their collective contribution to the Yishuv.[71] But this positive assessment has recently been challenged, most decisively in Dafna Hirsch's work on hygiene discourse and its inherent construction of "Orientals" as the "mirror image of the human ideal associated with hygienic conduct."[72] Itamar Radai notes that Helene Hanna Thon, one of the most famous activist social workers in this field, saw social work as an attempt to prevent Mizrahi Jews from lowering the economic and cultural niveau of Yishuv society.[73] Such critical assessments of Mizrahim were also crucial for the self-perception of German-Jewish immigrants in social work or related fields.

The Palestine correspondent Gerda Luft, for example, up in arms against the living conditions of Mizrahim in Tel Aviv, wrote an article for the *Jüdische Rundschau* entitled "Tel Aviv: Two Cities." She juxtaposed and contrasted the city's vibrant, modern, comfortable, beautiful part ("a victory of the West") with the living quarters of Yemenite, Kurdish, and Circassian Jews (the "other world" of Tel Aviv).[74] Luft bemoaned the grave conditions in these quarters: neglected buildings, unpaved roads, and lack of sufficient garbage disposal. She criticized the city council for not addressing these problems, but also described the residents with pejorative stereotypes, clearly distancing herself from them: "A colorful mess of dark faces, of men with beards, of girls and women wearing headscarves, with frizzy hair and thin legs, of children tumbling over each other with flies on their noses."[75]

The description of the residents' skin color and the condition of their hair and beards, along with the emphasizing of the chaotic mass, do not serve the criticism but, rather, evoke ideas of Mizrahim as essentially different, non-Western—implying that they are at least partially responsible for their situation.[76] In juxtaposing the "two different worlds," Luft perceives "a coexistence of progress and stagnation, of Europe and Asia, of convenience and utter distress." It was clear to herself and her readers which side of this comparison she and the other German immigrants were on. Her article concludes with a request that the government and the city council be more committed to ensuring that the "slums of Tel Aviv" be "paved, cleaned, ventilated, renovated."[77] Luft's request that the neighborhoods of the Mizrahim be cleansed is not accidentally phrased.

As Hirsch has shown, debates about the Mizrahim by Yishuv social workers were conducted using the terminology of hygiene. Mizrahi Jews were conceived as having poor personal hygiene and being lazy and neglectful, hence in need of instruction. Social workers therefore served as mediators of Western culture to the Mizrahi population. German social workers who joined the Yishuv's developing field of social welfare crucially influenced it.[78] They, too, saw their mission as teaching "modern hygiene instead of superstition and Oriental neglect" (as the social worker Nadja Stein phrased it) to members of the Oriental communities.[79] In general, the focus of social work was on women and children. The alleged inferiority of Mizrahi women came into play especially in their role as inadequate mothers, making home visits in the Yemenite quarters necessary. Because the German social workers were also female, this was essentially a discussion by women about women. The encounter between German-Jewish and Mizrahi women as, respectively, providers and objects of social work, staged different femininities: while the German social workers attempted to call attention to the plight of underprivileged residents of the Yishuv, they also presented Mizrahi women as dull, primitive, passive, and hence opposed to themselves, the white, civilized, modern, Western, clean, superior German women.[80] The superiority the German women felt toward their Mizrahi counterparts was also expressed visually, in pictures of social workers in European dress in front of little ramshackle houses in Tel Aviv's Yemenite quarter or together with Mizrahi women.[81]

The female German new immigrants were supported in this perception by Emma Esther Smoira, chairwoman of the Women's International Zionist Organization (WIZO). In a programmatic article published in the *Jüdische Rundschau*, she enumerated the alleged differences between "Oriental" women and women from Germany. Mizrahi women "stand at a lower level of civilization; there is still the need for a big educational measure to be undertaken. For the time being, they are more objects than carriers of our work." German-Jewish women, by contrast, already "possess many skills that could be of great use for the women's organization and the community," such as a "high level of culture, emancipation, and sense of community."[82]

While they, too, needed to be trained in Zionist thought, they were regarded favorably for the Zionist project precisely because they were from the West.

Outside the framework of social work, interactions also occurred in the realm of the labor market. Encounters between employers and employees are hierarchical by definition. Descriptions by German Jews express how much such encounters were also shaped by the new immigrants' self-conception and their profound Orientalism. The notion of an essential difference between Easterners and Westerners in looks, dress, behavior, culture, and morals was ubiquitous and intersected with notions of gender, marking the differences in both masculinities and femininities between "Oriental" and German Jews. "I have to say, my eyes nearly popped out of my head: These are also Jews, these are also humans. They were so primitive!"[83] This is how Ruth, whose family ran a laundry business that employed Syrian Jewish women, described her first impressions of those women, adding that her parents made the workers shower before allowing them to start work. Mizrahi women were also hired as domestic workers, especially in the first years of the German Aliyah, when German families still had more financial resources. They were clearly hired because they would work for lower wages than other domestic workers. In a *Jüdische Rundschau* article entitled "How Much Does the Household Cost in Palestine?" Gerda Luft explicitly promoted hiring Mizrahi instead of European domestic help in order to save expenses. She recommended hiring Mizrahi women or even children. Neither Luft nor the editors of the *Jüdische Rundschau* apparently found any ethical problem with this.[84] Others, however, criticized this practice by well-to-do European women as outrageous.[85] An echo of such discussions about not treating Mizrahi women as equals can be heard in the fact that in oral history interviews, many pointed out that their domestic help was treated *respectfully* and *equally*.

Because of language problems (the German immigrants did not yet speak Hebrew, let alone Arabic), interaction with domestic workers was relatively minimal and mainly involved instruction. In descriptions of such encounters, the general perception of Mizrahi women as inferior is enmeshed with the new immigrants' self-conceptions as modern and emancipated in their gender relations. The journalist C. Z. Kloetzel, for example, who immigrated in 1933, wrote about his Persian domestic help in the *Jüdische Rundschau*.[86]

The relationship between this woman and his wife was good, he observed. They spoke in "Oserith" (*oseret* is Hebrew for domestic help), with hands and feet, and in a mixture of German, Persian, and Hebrew, which was apparently enough to enable them to exchange recipes. Regarding his relationship with the domestic worker, he wrote:

> For me, our *oseret* cherished an unchangeable admiration that was however mixed with a quiet resentment. First of all, I am the "Baal habajith"—for every Oriental woman . . . the dear representative of God on earth. Secondly, I am a "Sofer" [scribe] . . . Thirdly, I threatened to do terrible things to her should she ever dare . . . to touch anything on my desk. Fourthly, I sometimes offer her cigarettes. Therefore the admiration. The quiet resentment stems from two sources. Firstly, she sometimes catches me throwing out the kitchen garbage for my wife. . . . That is unworthy of a man, a landlord, and an author in her eyes. And then, on hot summer days, I often sit at my desk dressed only in bathing shorts. That is obviously perceived as obscene where she comes from.[87]

Kloetzel described a very hierarchically structured situation: a wealthy, educated white man employing a seemingly uneducated and unemancipated "Oriental" woman. The fact that this woman, though from a highly conservative society, worked to provide her family with income might actually have challenged his notion of her as passive, submissive, and backward. This woman, very likely either born in Palestine or having already lived in the country a long time, clearly occupied the lower position in this encounter, not only through the employer-employee hierarchy but also because of the discourse and practices within the Yishuv and those that the immigrants brought from Germany. Kloetzel's idea of the servant adoring him for being a *baal ha bayt* (Hebrew: head of the house), while obviously flattering to him, marked her as unliberated and simultaneously marked the German Jews' gender relations as modern and emancipated. In the same piece, Kloetzel also wrote about the perceived cultural differences between him and Persian Jewish men, mentioning that his Persian barber tried to treat him with powder and perfume after his haircut, as he was used to doing for his Persian customers. Kloetzel fought against this, much to his barber's dismay. In Kloetzel's eyes, such body care with herbs and perfumes was emasculating and inappropriate.[88]

The same attitude is palpable in Martin Feuchtwanger's account of the Yemenite domestic workers he employed. He describes them as primitive women, completely controlled by their husbands and fathers, who decided when and whom they married and where they could work: "The Oriental man lets his wife work hard," which is why "Oriental" women always looked tired and worn-out and aged quickly. Such statements are notable in light of the labor market conditions and the fact that many German women had to provide for their unemployed husbands, as the next chapter will discuss. Observations about "Oriental" Jews served as a foil for how newcomers perceived themselves in terms of relations between men and women. Feuchtwanger portrayed Yemenite domestic workers as active and determined in negotiating their working conditions and aware of their rights. Though illiterate, Feuchtwanger mentioned, they were all well aware of the minimum wage, and no one would work for less. But the general Orientalist attitude was so strong that such behavior was not recognized as contradicting the stereotype of passive and submissive women. Feuchtwanger mentioned that he and his wife chose their domestic workers from an "Oserot market" in Tel Aviv, at the entrance to the Shuk (the large outdoor market). He was pleased with the opportunity they could provide to a "Negro girl," "a little savage, not yet at home in this country," who knew about neither indoor plumbing nor how to eat with a knife and fork before working for him and being provided with such opportunities. Feuchtwanger, himself a new immigrant, was confident: "We have the duty to lift their level of culture, to make education accessible to them, to raise their standard of living, to let them participate in our life." Although they "would not know our notions of agreements and duties," they "needed to be treated as equals."[89]

In line with this general attitude, socializing is rarely mentioned—for example, invitations of former employees to weddings or a bar mitzvah. There was also hesitation about entering into romantic relationships with Mizrahi Jews: Miriam S., for instance, found it out of the question to marry the Yemenite man who proposed to her.[90] This continued to be true for the second generation of immigrants, confronting the mass post-1948 immigration from Arab countries. Gitta B. noted that her parents and their friends were strictly opposed to their children marrying Mizrahi Jews in later years: "Most of the Yekkish families were not happy if their children dated . . . Moroccans or Syrians or Iraqis, who counted almost like a mixed marriage."[91] And Alisa E. remembered the many prejudices she encountered when she married a Bukharan Jew, something previously unheard of in her community: "That was very strange here; I was the first to intermingle."[92] German Jews had very particular ideas about whom to socialize with and, at least for the first generation of immigrants, this usually excluded Mizrahi Jews. Even while calling for improvement and equal participation, the sense of superiority in some of their statements is striking. It also indicates that the only encounters they could imagine with Mizrahim were hierarchical, not eye-to-eye. This strong feeling of superiority also made it humiliating to compete with Mizrahi Jews for resources. In 1937, the Jerusalem branch of the Hitahdut Oley Germania (Association of Immigrants from Germany) claimed: "In a city like Jerusalem, which is overwhelmingly inhabited by an Oriental population, a European Jew, if he is still dressed reasonably well, seems much less in need of help than an Oriental Jew, who shows up with a dozen children. However, the subjective level of distress need not be lower." For German immigrants, it was added, it was an imposition to sit in the same waiting rooms with "people of very different origins and a very different standard of living."[93]

Feelings of superiority toward Jews from Arab countries were not unique to the German Jews, but part of the overall attitude of the Yishuv. The same attitudes have been described as coming from Polish immigrants in those same years, for example.[94] However, the new immigrants from Germany profited from this ethnic hierarchy: just arrived in the country themselves, often facing severe hardships, at least they weren't starting at the bottom of society.

THE ARAB QUESTION: ENCOUNTERS WITH ARABS

The mainstream attitude toward Arabs in the Yishuv of the 1930s was negative and generalizing. In earlier decades, romantic Orientalist perceptions of Arabs as Hebrews or as noble savages, even as a model for the New Jew, albeit minority positions, had existed in the Yishuv. In the 1920s and 1930s, however, there were violent clashes between Arabs and Jews, and encounters became increasingly tense. Interest in Arab culture disappeared, and the dominant image of Arabs become that of not only a primitive and inferior culture but a cruel enemy.[95] So where did German Jews stand? Most German Zionists belonged to the left and liberal-left. In the conflict with the Arabs, they advocated a position of *Verständigung*, or coming to terms, aiming at peaceful coexistence and, to varying degrees, a binational state.[96] Some of the most prominent German-speaking proponents of a binational solution, including Kurt Blumenthal, Robert Weltsch, Arnold Zweig, Martin Buber, and Georg Landauer, immigrated to Palestine and continued to be active in this cause in pre-state Palestine. They helped to form binationalist organizations such as *Brith Shalom* (Covenant of Peace) and, later, the *Ihud* (Unity), both of which were dominated by German-speaking intellectuals.[97] However, while some of their members, like Arthur Ruppin, figured prominently in the political elite of the Yishuv, these organizations were small in membership and, because they were politically opposed to the Yishuv majority position, eventually failed.[98] It is also important to note that these were the positions of relatively small intellectual circles that were not necessarily shared by the rank-and-file of immigrants. For one thing, most German Jews arrived during the Arab Revolt of 1936–1939, when frequent terror attacks caused them to fear for their lives once again—unlike in most other countries of emigration. For another, German Jews, including the *Verständigungs*-Zionists, arrived in Palestine with a firmly Orientalist approach toward the Arabs. This attitude was often vividly confirmed in their first encounters upon arrival at the ports of Haifa and Jaffa. Dark-haired, dark-skinned, shouting Arab porters became synonymous with the Orient for these newcomers. Martin Hauser described the arrival scene in his diary:

> Porters in dusty, sweaty shirts and trousers that hang from their legs like sacks climb up on ropes, their feet in dirty old shoes of all colors. Black eyes look from under the clothes and rags that are wrapped in all possible and impossible ways around their heads; before you realize it, your suitcase is gone, and you are carried on the arms of one of these fellows to the rocking boat.[99]

The pejorative tone of such descriptions in contemporary sources is ubiquitous. Even though most German Jews were seeing Arabs for the first time, what they observed was informed by what they had heard and seen in newspapers, movies, and fiction. The books of Karl May and the like had shaped their idea of the Orient; in the Berlin Palestine Office's information material for new immigrants, T. E. Lawrence's *Revolt in the Desert* was even recommended as preparatory reading.[100] Such literature could also lead to sexualized perceptions of Arab women: Fritz Wolf, for example, has described his fantasies of harem life, belly dancers, and hookahs upon arrival.[101]

Most German Jews perceived Arabs as strange, at best, and as uncivilized, inferior, and potentially dangerous at worst. However, there were some everyday encounters between German Jews and Arabs. In the mixed towns of Jerusalem and Haifa, they were sometimes neighbors, or landlords and tenants: Avraham M. remembered playing with the children of the Arab landlord in Jerusalem. Even though they were strongly encouraged not to buy Arab produce but only *tozeret ha'aretz* (products of the country), homemakers bought groceries from Arab shop owners and marketers because they were said to have better meat and cheaper produce. German-Jewish physicians treated Arab patients, and many German families employed Arab laundrywomen. These women regularly worked in the homes of German Jews, but due to the lack of language skills on both sides, little to no communication took place. The laundrywomen were described as primitive and hardworking but able to eloquently express their needs (amount of money, breakfast, etc.).[102] Encounters also took place in the agricultural villages established by German Jews: Arab salespeople delivered food to Nahariya and, as residents proudly recall, were even taught to speak some German. A picture of a Mrs. Klimann, one of the founders of Kfar Shmaryahu, hugging two Arabs from surrounding villages bears witness to the good neighborly relations that business contacts could establish.[103] And yet, while there were many accounts of friendly neighborly relations, Arabs were nonetheless generally feared and abhorred, such that Jews avoided contact with them. Ilse B., for example, was afraid of returning home alone late after work (there was not sufficient public transportation) to an area in Haifa where many Arabs from the Hauran in Syria lived.[104] As Miron has shown, there is only scant grappling with the Arabs in the autobiographies by German Jews that cover that time. If interactions are recalled, they are mostly not personal interactions, and they are used only as a backdrop for the main narrative. Miron understands this as reflecting a perspective that the writers adopted over time: the standpoint of the national Zionist narrative.[105]

These contacts, or attempts to avoid them, occurred in the context of tense political relations. The Yishuv frowned on buying food from Arabs instead of purchasing *tozeret ha'aretz*, literally a "product of the country," or employing Arab cleaners instead of *avoda ivrit*, literally "Hebrew work," both elements of the attempt to strengthen the Jewish sector of the Yishuv economy by employing Jewish instead of Arab workers and purchasing only products produced by Jews—these boundaries were clear to the German Jews. To most immigrants, the Arabs belonged to the primitive Levant and stood for chaos, dirt, and unreliability. This perception—like the gaze on "Oriental" Jews—was often described in terms of hygiene: a physician complained about the mess Arab patients left behind in waiting rooms, which would deter preferred German patients; a female immigrant declared: "An Arab passed me—and I already had a flea."[106] The immigrants embraced the attitude of the Yishuv (and the British) and felt culturally superior toward the Arabs. From this viewpoint, Arabs formed one monolithic bloc of strangers, which included no modern, educated individuals.

In the othering of Arabs by German Jews, the gender dimension figured prominently. Martin Feuchtwanger wrote:

> We, the newcomers, saw the Arabs but had nothing to do with them. We saw the men in their abayas, the white head scarves, the strange trousers, the women, some of them veiled, mostly dressed in black. We saw the children, who were mostly neglected. The women, with tattooed faces and arms, carried baskets on their heads and held their infants at their bare breasts.... At first, we were astonished by these exotics, by this oriental ado, but after a few days, we got used to it. We had hardly any contact with the Arabs; our neighbors, friends, and partners were Jews.[107]

Like Feuchtwanger, many German Jews perceived Arab society and its norms as primitive, lacking common decency or responsibility. A commonplace was to juxtapose Arab and Jewish women. In this example, the perception of Arab women as negligent mothers was connected to their toiling in physical labor, expressing the middle-class immigrant's gendered class consciousness. Public breastfeeding, exposing women's bare breasts—perceived as a primitive practice of the lower classes—takes this image to its extreme. The journalist Gabriele Tergit for example, who traveled across the country writing about her observations, stereotypically portrayed Jewish women as emancipated, tilling the land like men, smoking, in short trousers, as opposed to the veiled Arab women, working under primitive conditions, dressed in traditional clothes, and completely subordinated to their husbands.[108] German immigrants identified with this attempt by the Yishuv to present itself, through its women, as modern, enlightened, and progressive: the very opposite of the backward, primitive, chauvinistic Arabs.

The *Jüdische Rundschau*, according to the political agenda of its publisher, the outspoken *Verständigungs*-Zionist Robert Weltsch, was committed to the enlightenment of its readers both in Germany and in Palestine. In its supplement, the *Palästinablatt*, the *Jüdische Rundschau* covered not only the political situation but also recent developments in Arab culture, religion, and daily life, such as the opening of schools, founding of new newspapers, and inner-Arab reforms. Lectures and classes organized by the Hitahdut Oley Germania presented more liberal thoughts about the Arabs in Palestine. These lectures touched not only on theoretical questions but also on practical suggestions. In early 1936, the *Jüdische Rundschau* published a series of articles on "The Arabs in Palestine" following requests from readers, who were eager to know more about their neighbors. A "Palestinian specialist," Menahem Kopeljuk, wrote comprehensive, informative articles about Palestinian history, demography, religion, society, and culture. Kopeljuk, a Russian-born scholar and translator from Arabic, was part of a group of writers and intellectuals who, according to Jacobson and Naor, "believed they had a role to play as possible mediators between Jews and Arabs."[109] For his German-Jewish immigrant readers, above all, he provided concrete advice on how to behave properly when meeting Arabs in everyday life. Such knowledge was needed, Kopeljuk made clear, because most Arabs would not know anything about European concepts and behavior. Remarkably, especially for 1936, these articles were written with the clear intention of facilitating contacts between (German) Jews and Arabs. Next to advice on how and in what terms to greet Arabs (not *Salaam Aleikum* but *Merhaba*, and no Arab curses) and how to behave when hiking in Arab villages (no spontaneous whoops of joy) or when visiting mosques (no shoes), relations between the sexes also figured prominently in the essays. The part on "Habits and Morals," advertised by the *Jüdische Rundschau* as a must-read for all German immigrants and tourists, highlighted the status of women in Arab society: "The special position of the woman in Muslim society is responsible for all those relations, opinions, and ideas that seem strange to Europeans used to free relationships between men and women."[110]

Even though the Arabs' attitude seems primitive, Kopeljuk insisted, careful behavior respecting their customs should prevent the Jews from offending the Arabs' norms of decency. In the long term, such thoughtful behavior could prevent conflicts between the two groups. Female immigrants should dress properly when in contact with Arab men (no short trousers) and not engage in "liberated" behavior with men in front of Arabs to prevent hurting their feelings. Men, on the other hand, should try to avoid contact with the other sex altogether "to prevent misunderstandings or wrong situations." When visiting Arab houses, they should use the door knocker to give the women of the house the possibility of retreating to another room. While aiming to enable friendly contacts, Kopeljuk made it clear that careless interactions could be dangerous, even life-threatening, for new immigrants. When hiking through the countryside in Arab areas, women should always be as covered as possible, exchanging their iconic short trousers for a skirt. In general, women were warned against hiking alone in Arab areas, where they were in danger of being robbed and even greater danger of being raped. They should only hike in the company of several men, as one man alone was not enough to "defend their honor." In the Yishuv, rape was seen primarily as a crime not against the individual woman but against the national collective.[111] New female immigrants in particular, not yet familiar with the customs of the country, were seen as potential targets of rape by Arab men.

The fear that Jewish women might be raped by Arab men was immense. The *Jüdische Rundschau* published many stories of almost-raped girls and women.[112] Helene Hanna Thon, for example, reported on a young German woman who fell into conversation with an Arab man as they walked along a rural road. Following European norms, she shook his hand when making her farewell—and in doing so, according to Thon, unintentionally signaled that she was a prostitute. The man then tried to rape her, but passers-by saved her at the last moment.[113] In these reports, newly immigrant women were in particular danger, because of their naïveté and unfamiliarity with the different culture, of being raped by Arab men. Another context where women needed to be extremely careful when interacting with Arabs was at the beach. An article in the *Jüdische Rundschau* described the following scene at a Tel Aviv beach, where new immigrants, both male and female, were photographing one another, observed by Arab passers-by:

> One of the girls approaches them [the Arab passers-by] and tries to explain something to them, speaking in German (which they obviously don't understand) as well as through gestures. When they don't seem to understand her, she suddenly tears the headscarf . . . off the head of one of the young Arabs and puts it on herself in order to be photographed in this silly disguise. The Arab lets all of this happen with a good-natured smile, even though this must seem very inappropriate to him. In any case, the informal gathering of men and girls is strange to him and is surely a cause for distrust regarding the morals of the girls—and that misunderstanding is one we cannot struggle against, because we cannot make our opinions on such personal issues conditional on the Arabs' opinions. However, in Arab tradition, taking away the head covering is a disgrace, something you do to an enemy to humiliate him. Here, the fact that it was a woman who took it away must have been even more unpleasant for him. . . . Even if he understands that it was not intended as an insult, he must perceive it as a lack of respect.[114]

While the main message of this article was that Arab locals should be treated with respect even though they seem backward, it also hinted at other questions, such as the behavior of Jews at the beach and the generally "liberated relationships" of Jewish men and women. While these could not depend on the Arabs and their perceptions, Thon wrote, new immigrants—especially women—needed to be aware of the possible consequences of their thoughtless behavior. The allegedly shameless behavior of Jews on the beaches of Tel Aviv was discussed repeatedly in the contemporary press of the Yishuv, complaining that men and women who dressed in revealing beachwear, mixed and mingled, and undressed in public were observed by Arab men walking the beaches of Tel Aviv to view the bathing Jewish women.[115]

In both these cases—hiking in the countryside and sunbathing at the beach—women were perceived as the most vulnerable part of the Yishuv, needing to be extra careful to avoid too-close contact. While this addressed the actual fear of being raped, it also enforced boundaries between Arab men and Jewish women, in this case German immigrants. The concern was not just rape by Arab men, but immodest behavior by Jewish women. The fear of boundary-crossing by Jewish women in the cities was repeatedly discussed by the absorption apparatus and its social workers in the 1930s. Rumors spread of young women lured into sexual relationships with Arabs, or even prostitution, in the harbor cities of Haifa and Tel Aviv, as discussed in the previous chapter. Accusations were made about the immorality of female German immigrants, including that some were unfaithful to their husbands and had Arab paramours to whom they passed political secrets. Cafés were generally perceived as areas of potential contact between Jewish women and non-Jewish men.[116] A confidential report on the "state of morals" of the new immigrants in Haifa investigated the café scene, but came to the conclusion that serious transgressions were rare. The real danger was seen in young immigrants' inability to differentiate between Jews and Arabs:

> Many girls who are not familiar with the special situation of the country make the acquaintance of men at cafés, for a dance, whom they do not at first recognize as Arabs, or they are not aware that such relationships can be dangerous for their reputation within the Jewish community; they get involved with these men in a close relationship and it cannot be foreseen how such things end. These are typical events, especially in a café in Hadar. . . . Sometimes, European women who have already been in the country a long time—women of all social classes, from the salesgirl to the "high society lady"—also have temporary relations with different Arabs, but these are rare cases, and these women are not interested in money.[117]

Thus, the new immigrants crossed boundaries unintentionally: because they did not notice them, could not recognize Arabs, or were unaware that such relationships could harm their position in Jewish society. For the absorption officials, it was more important to teach young women to avoid such contacts than to try to reach those women who deliberately chose such relationships and already seemed to be lost causes. Neither male immigrants nor Jewish men in general were discussed in this context, whether as potential customers of prostitutes or as romantic lovers unaware of boundaries. Men, even those constantly called naïve Yekkes, were not seen as being in that kind of danger, nor did they pose a threat to their community or the Yishuv. It was women who had to serve as gatekeepers for society's morality by avoiding intermingling. The *Jüdische Rundschau* conveyed the idea that it was the responsibility of the female immigrant to avoid any contact—whether hiking, at the beach, or in cafés—that could cause negative effects for herself or for Jewish society as a whole. Although these articles could in fact be useful preparation for real encounters between German Jews and Arabs, the contested character of contacts between the sexes became obvious. Idith Erez notes that because Arab women in the 1930s mostly stayed home, out of the public sphere, such meetings were primarily between Arab men and Jewish women.[118]

German Jews, by and large, perceived Arabs through an Orientalist lens, involving feelings of superiority, othering, fear, and rejection. This served their own self-perception in Palestine, assuring themselves of their Western identity, while the Arabs were the complete other. Gender played into this othering in various ways: as a way to show one's own superiority; in marking the dangerous otherness of Arab culture; and as a barrier against intermingling. Research on Orientalism and German Jews in Palestine has discussed how the academic study of Orientalism was transferred to the emerging state. But Orientalism was not simply a scholarly discipline for a few professional Orientalists and teachers of Arabic; the firmly Orientalist gaze was a crucial way for the majority of immigrants to observe the absorbing society, interact with various groups, and understand their own place within that society. In the case of interactions with Arabs, the boundaries between the two groups were much clearer to the immigrants than in the case of the second non-Jewish group in Palestine: the British.

LEHITANGLES, THEY SAID . . . MEMORIES OF THE BRITISH[119]

When the German Jews arrived in Palestine, the relationship between the Yishuv and the British was politically cooperative. Because the Yishuv leadership assumed that the British Mandate was temporary, and would eventually enable the foundation of a Jewish state, the British were accepted, even if ambivalently, as both allies and occupiers.[120] While political relations deteriorated after the 1939 White Paper, which limited the immigration of

Jewish refugees from Europe, and even more so with military operations by the Yishuv against the British and with the anti-British terror, cooperation continued in various spheres. Many Jews worked in the government sector of the economy (e.g., in administration, municipalities, police), putting them in daily contact with British personnel; socially, however, there was little interaction between the British and members of the Yishuv.[121] While the initial conditions at least theoretically enabled encounters, the Jews of Palestine and the British were generally not perceived as being part of the same society and, as research shows, preferred not to intermingle, so that contacts were mostly limited to professional relations. It is not surprising, then, that in the collective Israeli memory, the prevalent narrative about the Mandate era is the aversion of Jews in Palestine to "perfidious Albion," as well as the anti-British struggle. Research on the subject has only recently begun to question this dominant motif and to explore the British influence on Israeli historiography.[122]

British men and women based in Palestine—not only soldiers but also civil servants, police officers, teachers, missionaries, medical officers, and their spouses and children—stayed and socialized within the British expatriate community. They evidently preferred the company of their fellow Englishmen for various reasons: because they knew their time in Palestine was limited; because there was a language barrier; but also because of their attitudes toward the natives, who, through the prevailing Orientalist lens, were not regarded as equal. While a few British were interested in Jews and Zionism, most found it impossible to socialize with the Jews, seeing them as overly self-confident, unmannered, tactless Eastern Europeans who barely spoke English and could be suspected of Bolshevism. A. J. Sherman suggests that most of the British were not fond of the Jewish inhabitants of Palestine and more likely to be pro-Arab.[123]

In the Yishuv, meanwhile, intermingling was seen as undesirable because of the desire to create a Jewish state with a unique Hebrew culture. Yizhak Abbady, head of the Mandate government's central translation bureau, who penned one of the very few publications dedicated to this matter, went so far as to claim that there was simply no mutual interest between the two groups because of cultural and emotional distance.[124] While such declarations express the social reality of the colonial society, they must also, crucially, be understood in the light of the taboo-like nature of the attitude toward socializing, particularly between British men and Jewish women. And yet, the Yishuv's official attitude regarding socializing was not unequivocal: the Yishuv establishment did organize social encounters between Jews and the British, including hosting British soldiers in Jewish homes and arranging hospital visits, lectures, cultural events, and dances. In spite of the potentially transgressive nature of such encounters, the perception that women were better suited for hosting and catering activities put them at the forefront of this endeavor.[125]

German Jews met and interacted with the British in various settings. Because the majority of the British stationed in Palestine were men, these were encounters of German immigrants of both sexes with male British personnel. Any British women were usually wives of high-ranking personnel. Given the contemporary discourse, this is crucial, because women were the focus of potential boundary crossings. Hitahdut Oley Germania (HOG), the Association of Immigrants from Germany, was cooperative and loyal to the Mandate. This attitude was also expressed in practical questions. For example, unlike the Histadrut, the HOG employment services tried to find jobs for immigrants in the non-Jewish sector as well, placing immigrants in positions with the British Mandate (e.g., as policemen, in the British administration and British-owned companies, and as household help in British families in Palestine and surrounding countries). Other encounters in the labor market included German physicians who treated British personnel and German immigrants who worked as waiters in cafés frequented by British officers.[126] From 1939 onward, German Jews also enlisted in the British Army.[127]

In further exploring encounters between the new immigrants and the British, we face a methodological problem. Contemporary newspapers tended not to discuss such socializing, because it was contested. While some contemporary ego-documents do mention interactions, by far the most fruitful source is oral history interviews. Interviewees spoke more often about encounters with the British during leisure activities—for example, in sports clubs, at cafés, and at dance events—than they did about those that occurred in the professional or political sphere. This is especially remarkable in light of the fact that it was leisure-time connections, rather than ones in the professional sphere, that tended to be censured as potential boundary crossings.

One kind of place that brought certain German immigrants and British officials together was sports venues. The Haifa rowing club, founded by German Jews who had brought both their rowing boats and rowing itself to the country, was allocated the necessary area for rowing practice by British officials, who rowed as well.[128] At a Jerusalem horseback-riding club, established by a former lawyer from Hanover, German Jews and British personnel trained together. The Haifa tennis club was used by both the British and well-to-do German families. Ruth B. and her family spent all of their leisure time at this club with British and other well-off European families. Encounters at such sports venues were not random but arose from shared cultural practices. Sports that were enjoyed in both Great Britain and Germany provided a space where British and German interests intersected in Mandatory Palestine.[129] Unlike spontaneous meetings in the public sphere, repeated encounters at such venues made it at least theoretically possible to get to know the other more intimately. It is crucial to point out that joining such clubs required a certain socioeconomic standing. Hence, the German Jews who could afford this were immigrants of means who had not (yet) lost their capital. Likewise, those British who frequented such establishments would have been not simple soldiers but higher-ranking officials.

Coffee shops and restaurants were places of encounter in the public sphere—between waitstaff and customers, or between patrons of the same establishment. In general, British soldiers on leave were desired patrons in cafés, and owners tried to recruit them as customers, sometimes requiring waitresses to socialize with them to boost consumption.[130] Some upscale venues in the cities also held afternoon dances, attended by well-to-do Jews, British officers, and wealthy Arabs. For some German Jews, the presence of British soldiers at cafés signaled a more sophisticated cultural life. For Ruth M., then a teenager, these men were more attractive than those locals she met in Haifa, "where everything was red, communist, or socialist."[131] To her, British soldiers in cafés served as a mark of class and quality due to their background, education, and lifestyle. British soldiers also frequented cafés and restaurants in more remote settlements established by German immigrants. For example, in Gan HaShomron, German-Jewish entrepreneurs opened a café catering especially to British soldiers, and in Shavey Zion, a little hotel, Lotte Eisenberg's Dolphin House, mostly hosted British soldiers. In Kfar

Shmaryahu's small café, British soldiers were welcome visitors, and Nahariya, which became a tourist resort with a distinctively European character, attracted many British soldiers, too.[132]

In Nahariya, which under its first mayor, Oskar Mayer-Wolf, was decidedly pro-British and had excellent relations with the British administration, the local youth allegedly began to emulate the looks and the lifestyle of the British soldiers.[133] The relative geographical isolation of Nahariya and of other secluded agricultural villages founded by German Jews may have strengthened this tendency. However, a similar phenomenon was also described in Haifa, where German bus drivers emulated British apparel: "All the drivers imitated the English way, wearing nicely pressed khaki shirts and khaki shorts with wool stockings and a pipe stuck down the side."[134] In Jerusalem in the late 1930s, the writer Gabriele Tergit observed that German Jews went outside "dressed in tuxedos, at 40 degrees Celsius, because the British, too, wear tuxedos."[135] The Yishuv's dress culture was famously informal, and this alleged adherence of German Jews to formal attire made them the butt of jokes.[136] The British were similarly ridiculed, as these examples demonstrate: they, too, allegedly wore suits and even gloves in the Levant's heat. But those British whom German Jews observed in the public sphere made a good impression. Their dress stood out in Palestine. This appreciation for British attire also needs to be understood against the background of the commonly expressed sense of the inferior apparel and hygiene of the Yishuv's Ostjuden, as discussed above. In fact, German immigrants' praise of the British may be seen as a reaction to the criticism that they themselves faced in the 1930s and 1940s from veteran residents.

The common perception of the British as gentlemen went beyond attire and polite manners and was often connected with masculinity. The constant reference to the British as "absolute gentlemen," both in contemporary documents and in hindsight, expresses respect for the polite way they treated girls and women, in contrast with the local Jewish population's allegedly ruder behavior. However, this reference also had another dimension: the socializing of British men with Jewish women. Some immigrants found this wish for companionship of some form understandable: "Of course, these Englishmen, they had no girls, they came and looked around, and when they liked a girl they asked her for a dance," Ruth M. remembered. She and her friends were among those dancing with British soldiers, "gentlemen per se," as she, too, emphasized.[137] In descriptions of socializing with British soldiers, remarks that everything was harmless constituted a topos. Hedwig Lehmann, for instance, who stayed in the famous Haus Cohen during a vacation in Nahariya and went to a "soldier dance" there, a reception with charming British soldiers, wrote: "Everything joyful and harmless and the young guys were thankful and happy. Here one really makes efforts to be on good terms with the soldiers, often organizes music and dance events for them and there always is a thankful audience."[138] Rafael T. described the British who visited the café in Gan HaShomron as "extraordinary men," adding, "they never touched a woman."[139] Alisa E. reflected the same sentiment about the British soldiers she met in Kfar Shmaryahu: "great guys and extraordinarily polite."[140]

These recurring references to the socializing between British men and German women as harmless indicate that the new immigrants were aware of the discourse on boundary construction within the Yishuv and the attempt to prohibit Jewish women's transgressive behavior. While the new immigrants were much more sympathetic toward these boundaries as they applied to interactions with Arabs, the interviewees regarded socializing with the British as harmless. Arab men aroused much more fear and apprehension than did the British.[141] However, not everyone thought everything was harmless, and not all British soldiers were perfect gentlemen. Miriam R. recalled a drunken British soldier sexually harassing her and a friend in a lonely Haifa neighborhood one night. The girls, trained in combat sport by the (Zionist paramilitary) Haganah, defended themselves and overcame him.[142] It seems likely that there were other attempted assaults by British soldiers, especially because the British were famous for having imported their heavy drinking habit.[143] However, in other interviews, they were not remembered as drunk or violent, nor would such men have fit the notion of kindred spirits. Overall, both in memory and in contemporary discourse, any mention of sexual harassment by the British remains taboo.

The affinity of some of the new immigrants for the British did not go unnoticed. Avraham M., who as a boy attended horseback-riding classes in Jerusalem, recalls how this was received at his school: "Horseback riding was *lehitangles*, meaning cozying up to the British. . . . That was painful to hear, but on the other hand, I really enjoyed the horseback riding. . . . The riding school was used by the English, but that did not bother me at that time."[144] *Lehitangles*, "to become/make yourself English," refers to a bourgeois lifestyle associated with the British: engaging in sports like rowing, tennis, horseback riding, or ballroom dancing; specific fashions; but also the purchase of (nonkosher) British food at Spinneys, the British import supermarket.[145] *Lehitangles* designated not only closeness to the British but also a set of allegedly alien dispositions brought into the Yishuv—elements that were not in line with the desired national culture of the state-in-the-making. Criticizing the new immigrants for imitating the British was part of the broader criticism of the German Jews' alleged adherence to bourgeois norms in general. But while appreciating and emulating the British was one thing, romantic or sexual encounters were another. Despite the general sympathy, as one immigrant put it, everyone was well aware that "the audience was not fond of such relationships."[146] Even those with an outspoken affinity for the British rarely established romantic relationships with them. In general, A. J. Sherman notes that only a very small number of relationships between British men and Jewish women resulted in marriages. According to him, the British most likely to mingle with Jews were those of lesser rank who sought opportunities for intimate relations with Jewish women. Golani and Reich estimate that about two hundred marriages and hundreds of relationships were established.[147] The German-Jewish immigrants were aware of the contested character of such liaisons, the disapproval of the public, the gloating cautionary tales published about the eventual failures of such relationships, and the occasional violent responses to actual or presumed interactions between British men and Jewish women.[148] Even in the small number of actual relationships, however, contemporary discourse focused on women as the potential transgressors.

In the case of the new immigrants from Germany, this suspicion of women was also expressed in anxiety on the part of the absorbing society that single female immigrants might engage in commercial sex—especially in the port cities, which were seen as a dangerous ground for mixing between inexperienced young women and British soldiers on leave, as well as Arab men.[149] In Haifa, for example, one complaint lambasted prostitution among new female immigrants from Germany. The female immigrants' alleged "love of luxury" and unwillingness to give up a certain standard of living—as already noted in the discussion of the "Kurfürstendamm Ladies"—were cited as possible reasons for their sexual relationships with British men. While German men were mocked for emulating the British, German women were at the center of the debate over contested intermingling. A focus on women as transgressors has also been perpetuated in Israeli literature, theater, and film since the foundation of the state of Israel.[150] The research literature and Israeli cultural production continue this perception of women as those who primarily cross boundaries. However, encounters between German Jews of both genders and the British in general were characterized by at least partial (and maybe overriding) ignorance of the attempts at boundary construction. And while these encounters may have included romantic interest, that was neither the sole nor the most crucial aspect of this affinity.

For some, appreciating the British was a political question. As Rafael T. put it, the British Mandate was the best era for Jews: "We never lived as well as under the British."[151] Hilde S., who worked professionally with many Englishmen, shared that sentiment, adding that unlike most Yishuv residents, "I did not dance in the streets when the Mandate ended."[152] For these interviewees, the British had guaranteed peace and stability. Such remarks must also be understood in the context of the security issues that these interviewees have witnessed their entire lives. Eitan Bar-Yosef, who analyzes "colonial nostalgia" in post-1967 Israeli culture, argues that fictional friendships and romances between the British and the Jews in Israeli literature express a longing for the Mandate as a cosmopolitan haven and must be seen in the context of the Israeli occupation and the failing peace process, hence reflecting less actual encounters in Mandatory Palestine than they do the Israeli present.[153] In the case of German Jews, this praise for the British as guarantors of stability can be understood in the framework of their dramatic migration to Palestine: their forced emigration from Germany, the dramatic downward social mobility and anti-Jewish violence they experienced in Palestine, and their sense that the local elite handled the situation badly, made the British appear to be a force of reason and civility. Mostly, however, appreciating the British was a cultural rather than political question.

For certain immigrants, British cultural influence was even more important than that of the Yishuv. When she turned fifteen, Ruth B. refused to continue going to the Hugim School in Haifa, like most German immigrant kids. Instead, she insisted on going to the Haifa English High School for Girls, where she hoped to receive a better education and the opportunity to study in Great Britain after graduation.[154] Her decision to leave the Hebrew school system angered her Zionist father, who told her: "I did not come to Palestine so that my daughter could be educated at an English girls' school." For Ruth's father, working and socializing with British clients was acceptable—the latter in clear opposition to public opinion at the time. But he considered Ruth's decision to opt out of the Hebrew school system out of the question. Nevertheless, she eventually prevailed. In her eighties at the time of our interview, she fondly, almost defiantly, stated: "In a way, I am a product of the Mandate—and I say this deliberately. . . . The whole English way of living had a formative influence on my life."[155] Unlike Ruth B., most German immigrants of the 1930s and 1940s interviewed here did not personally interact with the British, though they recalled an affinity and perceived cultural similarity with the British. The perceived cultural similarities between Germany and Britain led to an appreciation for the "civilized manners" of the latter and a perception that they were kindred spirits in the Levant. This praise for the British—especially seventy years after they had left the country—can also be understood as self-praise for the German immigrants themselves. The British and the German Jews both saw themselves as Westerners in a country shaped by "Orientals" and Eastern Europeans.

As mentioned earlier, the reflections of the interviewees do not represent German-Jewish immigrants as a whole. Most of them belonged to the Association of Israelis of Central European Origin and identified strongly with a distinctive German-Jewish heritage that had made a meaningful contribution to the state of Israel and was deemed worthy of preservation. While such interviews, thus, cannot measure the actual scope of interactions in the 1930s and 1940s, they do express an affinity of the interviewees for the British that resulted from their struggle to establish their place in the new society—as seen in both the contemporaneous discourse of the Yishuv and that of present-day Israel. Appreciation for the British can be read as an orientation tool for the immigrants, a means of cultural self-identification with the "West," not just in the 1930s but also to this day. The interviewees' affinity for the British serves as a foil for their suspicion of the Ostjuden and rejection of the dominant Eastern European model in their new homeland.

For new immigrants who were dismayed at veteran Yishuv society, the British provided an alternate model of people in power: well-dressed, educated, and polite.

Whether or not the British saw the German Jews any differently from how they saw the rest of the Yishuv has not yet been researched; studies have hitherto generalized British interaction with the Jews. The cultural similarities between the two countries of origin may have facilitated a different approach by the British, who appreciated the politeness, "civilized manners," and cultural contributions of the German Jews, as opposed to the rest of the Yishuv. Likewise, it is unclear whether German Jews were the only group in the Yishuv who felt an affinity for the British. While it has been claimed that other than the Sephardim of the Old Yishuv, German Jews were the only members of the Yishuv who socialized with the British, this assessment seems to be a stereotypical othering of the German newcomers as not fitting into Yishuv society due to their allegedly bourgeois norms.[156] Clearly, given the political and social situation, public opinion frowned on encounters between Jews and the British. On the other hand, given the size of the British presence (numbered in the tens of thousands from 1939 onward), it is likely that more interactions took place than are remembered today.[157] After all, despite its generalizing and collectivist ethos, the Yishuv was not a monolithic society.

CONCLUSION

While German-Jewish immigrants established a unique subculture, they did not live in a bubble. From the moment they set foot on the shores of Palestine, they became a part of their new society. Many German Jews had no meaningful interactions nor personal relationships with members of all the various other groups. However, through simple observation, they had to grapple with the nature of the new society and their place within it. In the eyes of the new immigrants, all of these groups, apart from the British, belonged, to varying degrees, to the "East." They hence observed them with an Orientalist gaze, which explicitly included the veteran Eastern European residents of the Yishuv. The most decisive conflict for German Jews was not between Ashkenazim and Mizrahim, or Jews and Arabs, but rather this inner-Ashkenazi conflict. This was the only encounter where the German Jews experienced discrimination themselves. In interactions with the other groups, German Jews did not notice or were not necessarily interested in how they were perceived. In the encounter with Eastern European Jews, however, they not only realized the perception of the veteran residents but also reacted to it.

The public debates to which the German-Jewish immigrants were subjected through newspaper articles, the absorption apparatus, and the opinion of men and women on the street, as well as the ideas of the immigrants themselves, expressed different expectations, for men and for women, of how to behave and what their responsibilities were in such encounters. In interactions with non-Jewish groups, it was mainly the task of female immigrants to avoid the risks of such contacts for themselves and their community. In the immigrants' perception of the absorbing society, their Orientalist gaze intersected with class and gender: observed gender relations, especially in the realm of labor, were compared with those in their own group. The common comparisons drawn by German Jews of the different women and their femininities shed more light on the self-perceptions of the German Jews than on their actual counterparts. In their gaze, gender added to perceptions of inferiority and superiority. Female bodies are central in these discussions, both in the attempts at boundary construction and in the perceptions of the immigrants. The sense of working women as ugly, masculinized, primitive, or exposed in the case of Ostjuden, Arabs, and Mizrahim is deeply connected to the close and intricate relation of gender, class, and the body as markers of difference. The myth that, as a marker of their gendered class identity, middle-class women did not need to work was soon to be shattered for the German Jews, however, as we will see in the next chapter.

While the Westernization of the Yishuv has been described as a main objective of Zionism, the German Jews, who embodied this Western ideal in many ways, were criticized and found offensive because of two main factors: the settling of an old score from an imported conflict and the demands of building a new society and culture in which separatism, a bourgeois lifestyle, urbanism, and consumerism were associated with German Jews and perceived as potentially threatening. On the other hand, the ways in which German Jews constructed other residents of Mandatory Palestine enabled them to perceive themselves as culturally superior Westerners vis-à-vis the absorbing society. This self-conception of German Jews as *the* Westerners of the Yishuv continued into statehood. In the wake of the post-1948 mass immigration of Jews from Arab countries to the new state of Israel, Georg Landauer phrased this attitude paradigmatically in a *Mitteilungsblatt* article in May 1952: "German Jewry could be a crucial factor in the dynamic of a cultural process in the country. It must not be overwhelmed; it must not abandon itself. We are the West in the East. It may be the fate of our own German-Jewish dynamic to accelerate the orientation towards the West."[158]

THREE

Capable Women and Men in Crisis?

GERMAN JEWS IN THE YISHUV LABOR MARKET

IN JUNE OF 1936, AFTER having carried out thousands of consultations per month, the Tel Aviv branch of the HOG declared: "It seems that we need to categorize three quarters of the male job seekers as difficult to integrate."[1] In every city, the HOG offices had to deal with such job seekers, some of whom had already been in the country for several years. These men could not be placed through the normal services but depended on social welfare or loans, and hence posed a problem for the integration process in the authorities' eyes.[2] The Yishuv in general and the absorption apparatus in particular had closely watched developments in Nazi Germany, looking for ways to facilitate German Jews' immigration to Palestine. But—and this contradicts today's common perception of German Jews as well-to-do migrants—the absorbing authorities in the Yishuv also had grave doubts, due to German Jewry's social, demographic, and occupational profile, about the prospects of integrating these immigrants into the labor market. In their search for a solution, they considered female employment to be of paramount importance.

Given the initial condition of the Yishuv economy—underdeveloped, shifting between prosperity and depression, with construction and agriculture at its center—integrating this population posed immense problems. During the prosperous years of 1933 to 1935, it was relatively easy for immigrants to enter the labor market. But after 1935, when the Yishuv economy was in recession again, it became much harder. The so-called Arab Revolt (1936–1939), the Mandate's restrictive immigration policies, and the outbreak of World War II in 1939 contributed to the crisis. The majority of the German immigrants arrived precisely during these years and, therefore, in the midst of economic crisis. If, the Jewish Agency and the apparatus worried, these immigrants failed to integrate, it could be fatal both for them and for the absorbing society. Thus, measures were taken to avoid that scenario. One was an organized effort by the apparatus to monitor the immigrants, assess their respective level of economic integration, and provide help accordingly. As economic crisis and unemployment were especially damaging to new immigrants, the apparatus was keen to find out which of them were particularly vulnerable to the crisis for occupational, psychological, or physical reasons. Thus, throughout the 1930s, the German Department and the HOG conducted a variety of surveys on the integration of the German Jews into the labor market. This group of immigrants was much more closely examined than any earlier immigration waves had been, both because of its sheer size and unfavorable pre-migration profile and because the absorption apparatus consisted of their own brethren, including many social scientists trained for this kind of research. This chapter investigates how gender mattered to the apparatus's evaluation of the situation as well as to the conclusions it drew and the policies it chose to implement. It then turns to the perspective of the immigrants themselves, exploring the experiences of male and female immigrants in the labor market and how they coped with occupational change, unemployment, and the loss of their former status.

MONITORING THE IMMIGRANTS

Immigration statistics documenting the occupational and demographic structure at the time of arrival in Palestine reflect a difference between the profile of the newly arriving immigrants and that of German Jewry before emigration.[3] Before 1933, more than 60 percent of the Jews in Germany worked in commerce, 23 percent in industry and handicrafts, and 12.5 percent in public services and professions. Close to 48 percent of German Jews were forty years old or older in 1933.[4] After migration, while the proportion of liberal professions among the immigrants remained high, their average age was younger, the number of those working in commerce dropped, and the number of those working in agriculture rose. Most significantly, only 28 percent of the immigrants worked in commerce. While they still constituted the biggest overall occupational group among the immigrants, this was a remarkable decrease compared to the numbers for pre-Nazi German Jewry. Another significant difference between the immigrants and Jewry in pre-Nazi Germany was the proportion of those working in agriculture. Among the immigrants, more than 17 percent worked in agriculture while in Germany; this number had been less than 2 percent. This unique composition of the German Jews who immigrated to Palestine derived from the fact that many had changed their profession in preparation for immigration. The proportion of liberal professions among the immigrants (20 percent), on the other hand, originated in the persecution that was directed against members of this group in Germany, causing them to leave Nazi Germany early in greater relative numbers. Half of this group were physicians. In addition, the average age of the immigrants was younger than that of German Jewry on the whole: only 12 percent of immigrants were over fifty.[5]

These numbers were regarded favorably by the authorities, but their significance was seen as limited, as they only indicated the status quo at the moment of arrival. They did not predict successful integration, as the apparatus soon realized. For instance, those immigrants who entered with a labor certificate were expected to easily find work in the Yishuv, for they had proved to the Palestine Office in Germany that they were physically and occupationally prepared. But in fact, they had not all been sufficiently trained in their new occupations.[6] Nor were all of the immigrants who entered with a capitalist certificate actually wealthy. In 1934, the majority brought no more than the required 1,000 pounds, the HOG realized.[7] Such a sum, though, was only a reserve; it was not a large fortune. It also became clear to the authorities that some had only borrowed the money in order to have the required amount to get out of Germany as quickly as possible; others lived on their savings instead of finding a job right away or invested in unprofitable businesses. Instead of securing the economic future in Palestine, then, capital could hinder integration, because it slowed the process of coming to grips with a new reality.[8]

The absorption apparatus quickly began to collect its own information, assembling data on immigrants through the HOG and the recipients of its services as well as through surveys and reports. Its findings revealed a large-scale occupational change taking place primarily as a concession to the economic situation and the limited possibility of finding work in former professions. Most evident were a decrease in commerce and the liberal professions and an increase in industry, trade, and agriculture, as well as a sudden, decisive increase in female participation in the labor market. In the cities, the main new occupations were construction for men and domestic work and the catering industry for women; in the countryside, for both sexes, it was agriculture. This occupational segregation by gender, and the "way stations" of construction and domestic work, were analogous to the general situation in the Yishuv. Also analogous was the fact that the absolute majority of women were concentrated in the lowest segment of salaries, at 0 to 5 Palestine pounds (LP) per month, while most men were concentrated in the segment of 7 to 10 LP.[9]

The immigrants' occupational changes also brought social changes: changes in class affiliation through the shift from white-collar to blue-collar work and from self-employed to dependent employment. This development was accompanied by downward social mobility, through lower salaries, temporary jobs as unskilled workers, repeated changes of occupation, and unemployment. Even for those who underwent occupational training, the poor salaries and the high rents in the cities made it almost impossible to subsist on such salaries alone.[10]

The authorities wanted to know how the German Jews were dealing with these changes and tried to identify any developing problems within the mass immigration so as to provide suitable solutions. Thus, they classified the immigration into weaker and stronger parts. In general, the immigrants in the cities were the focus. This is where most of the immigrants lived, and their situation worsened each year of the mass immigration. This was especially palpable in the male immigrants' high unemployment rate. As the mass immigration wave continued and the situation in Germany deteriorated, more and more immigrants needed social help. Surveys of hardship cases in the German

Aliyah were compiled to estimate their severity. Mostly, these were unskilled workers who had to support big families with unstable jobs and were, therefore, most affected by changing conditions in the job market. Additional attributes of this group were its high average age and the fact that these men had to do physical labor but were not prepared for it, and their health therefore quickly failed. Most of them held professions that were regarded unfavorably in the Yishuv, but tried to stay in them nevertheless, while those who had undergone occupational change were often insufficiently trained.[11]

Pioneers joining kibbutzim, as well as those settling in agricultural villages, on the other hand, were widely perceived as integrating easily.[12] And in the cities, skilled workers in construction and related fields had little problem finding jobs. Those who underwent occupational change to "productive" professions, such as physicians who became drivers or lawyers who became plumbers, were lauded in surveys. They were regarded favorably not only for their occupational transformation but also for their adaptation to the proletarian living standard of their new occupation, including how they dressed and furnished their houses, as well as the fact that their wives did not employ domestic help. Such cases were not in the majority, though. The apparatus focused its investigations, therefore, on those who tried to remain in their original occupations, such as those in the liberal professions, agents, merchants, and academics, all of whom who had trouble finding stable jobs. The two main in-depth surveys of the 1930s, carried out by the social scientist Ina Britschgi-Schimmer and the economist Hilde Oppenheimer on behalf of the German Department, investigated the occupational distribution of adult immigrants in the cities, their integration into the labor market, and their overall socioeconomic conditions.[13] Both reports paid special attention to the employment of female immigrants.

Married women mostly immigrated as dependents, rather than as holders of their own certificates and were therefore, according to the immigration regulations, not supposed to join the labor force. However, given the families' severe economic situation, many of them entered the workforce shortly after arrival anyway. Most worked (intermittently and poorly paid) as unskilled domestic workers or in the informal sector, providing services such as tailoring, mending, or baking in their homes. Often, these married women were not additional earners but supported the family alone while their husbands were either unemployed or underwent retraining. Married women worked out of economic need: because of their husbands' low salaries, intermittent employment, and unpaid vocational training, and/or because they needed to support additional family members, such as elderly parents. Sixty percent of working married women contributed up to 4 LP per month to the family income; 30 percent contributed 4 to 8 LP per month.[14]

Both in Germany and in the Yishuv, women had traditionally stopped working outside of the household when they married. In Germany, after World War I, more women became gainfully employed due to the worsening economic situation. However, female employment in the Jewish sector was still lower than that of the general population. After marrying, most wives left their employment to become homemakers. (In 1933, about 27 percent of all Jewish women in Germany aged fifteen to sixty-five were gainfully occupied, most of them in commerce.) This changed involuntarily with Nazi rule, when married women were increasingly forced to step in for their newly unemployed husbands.

In the Yishuv in the 1930s, the proportion of women in the labor force was also about 27 percent. But among female immigrants from Germany, this number rose decisively. Britschgi-Schimmer discovered that in 42 percent of the marriages she sampled, women were part of the labor force, a number that "proves the willingness of these women to be an active part of founding an existence."[15] In the countryside, where 25 percent of the immigration wave settled, full female participation in the labor market was seen as a necessity. Therefore, the total number of employed women was most likely even higher.[16] The limited availability of data and the absence of any unifying statistics regarding married and unmarried women as well as urban and rural workers mean that these figures only allow for a tentative appraisal. However, they do indicate a sudden and dramatic increase in female employment and hence a major change for the immigrating group. There was little doubt that the breadwinner-homemaker model that had been valid for middle-class families in pre-Nazi Germany would have to change in Palestine.

In these surveys of immigrants in the cities, men and women were assessed differently. Women in the labor force were described as "women of valor," who took great sacrifices upon themselves, as Britschgi-Schimmer put it: "It was of crucial importance what moral strength the woman could mobilize for building a new life, to what extent she could positively contribute, whether by securing existence or by creating an atmosphere that eased her husband's struggle and contributed to making their home a refuge."[17] Among the men, though, Britschgi-Schimmer identified a variety of problems that affected their integration into the labor market. For example, almost 50 percent of the male immigrants did not start working right away. She sensed an absence of willpower among many men—mostly the academics and merchants—who did not immediately accept the change to unskilled labor, and whom she described as indecisive and hesitant, as opposed to the women. Oppenheimer, too, detected a potential crisis especially among men, particularly those who were older and unemployed, and who had to subsist on their capital, pensions, and other benefits. Despite their lack of income, Oppenheimer noted, they tried to keep up their former bourgeois lifestyle; meanwhile, they suffered from severe psychological and physical problems: illnesses, lack of money and support, language problems, but also disappointed expectations, anxiety over lost social status, and distress about the future. Oppenheimer characterized these men as "indecisive, unstable, depressed, and inclined to grumble,"[18] estimating that one quarter of those she surveyed would need social help soon, while three quarters could manage with the help of their capital income and could hence be seen as integrated.

It is notable that the two main surveys of the absorption process were conducted by professional women who were new immigrants themselves. Oppenheimer and Britschgi-Schimmer presented their findings, including their concerns about gender issues, to the policy-makers of the apparatus.[19] They drew attention to the potential crisis for men as well as the crucial importance of female participation in the labor market. The importance given to these studies by the authorities shows that their assessment resonated with the apparatus.

DISCUSSING THE IMMIGRANTS

The surveys of and statistics compiled on the German Jews were not only discussed within a circle of experts but also widely circulated in the immigrant media. The *Jüdische Rundschau* and the *Mitteilungsblatt* frequently published results of surveys and reports as well as articles on the labor market.

Due to the unique context, the authors and contributors were immigrants themselves. But while rank-and-file immigrants also wrote about their labor market experiences, by and large this debate took place among the functionaries of the absorption apparatus and was, hence, a debate *about* the immigrants. The coverage of the integration of German Jews into the labor market served potential immigrants, informing them about desired and suitable occupations as well as overcrowded and "unproductive" ones, deploying the well-known Zionist aspiration to "normalization" and a "return" to productive occupation.[20] But the media outlets, serving as mouthpieces for the apparatus, also directly addressed the immigrants already in Palestine, pushing the agenda of the apparatus by condemning adherence to *galut* (diaspora) and middle-class attitudes while celebrating successful transformations. The juxtaposition of men and women was central to these debates.

In 1938, an article in the *Jüdische Welt Rundschau* entitled "The fate of the Jews from Germany" compiled a typology of male immigrants from Germany, proposing three unsuccessful types. The first man does not want "to start a new life but to continue with his old life in the new country. He wants to continue working in his old profession, to retain his social situation." The second man studied law in Germany but was blocked by the political situation. He then learned to be a locksmith and came to Palestine with almost no capital. Because of his insufficient training, he couldn't find work as a locksmith but became an unskilled worker, with recurring periods of unemployment. Because his situation is so hard, he often thinks: "You have no future here! Leave if you can!" The third man, aged forty, immigrated as a capitalist. He wants to use his money to establish a factory or a workshop, but although he is highly motivated, he fails. What all three types have in common is their apparent failure to integrate successfully into the labor market. Various reasons are provided for this failure—wrong mindset, wrong occupation and training, and insufficient skills for dealing with the new reality. These types serve as a foil for the types who *have* succeeded: all of the successful immigrants settled in the countryside—in an agricultural village, a *moshavah* (privately owned agricultural settlement), and a *kvuzah* (small communal rural settlement)—and who are happy "because they had trust in the country."[21] Given the contemporary Zionist ideology, this assessment is not surprising.

The immigrant media, reflecting the survey findings and statistics, categorized male immigrants according to their potential success or failure. Certain men were regarded favorably, mostly young, healthy men with agricultural or industrial training. Those in the cities, who had unfitting occupations or insufficient training, were seen as problematic. The most difficult element in this latter, already problematic group was soon identified as fathers over thirty-five. These men, the data showed, often failed to support their families in Palestine—whether because of being in the wrong profession, being insufficiently trained, making bad investments, lacking Hebrew skills, or due to psychological and physical problems. The very ones who in Germany had been the main breadwinners, one of the largest immigrant groups, became the epitome of problematic immigrants in the eyes of the authorities in Palestine. As the HOG reported in 1933, "A great many of these fathers are trained not at all or insufficiently, so they have to work mostly in unskilled labor. For older men, unused to physical labor, this is very difficult."[22] Changing occupations was especially difficult for men who had already worked successfully for ten or twenty years in a totally different career.

The apparatus saw age thirty-five as the upper boundary for transition to physical work; this age therefore became a synonym for hard-to-place men.[23] Because unskilled physical work was initially the way station for immigrants with unfitting occupations, these men posed a dilemma for the absorbing bodies. Connected to their age was their general physical condition, which made them unfit for physical work. The *Jüdische Rundschau* repeatedly emphasized the need for physical fitness in all immigrants, including women. Everybody would find a job in Palestine if they were willing to accept "sore hands and a sore back," as Gerda Luft wrote in 1933.[24] Such nonchalant declarations, ultimately expressing an expectation that immigrants should risk their health, were backed up by stories of transformation eagerly published in the *Jüdische Rundschau*: physicians who became construction workers, academics working as farmers, and former students on the docks, often illustrated with a picture.[25] Similarly, the following letter by a middle-class settler in Pardess Hana, published in the *Jüdische Rundschau* in 1936, dismissed health concerns as a mere excuse: "The easiest thing . . . is getting used to physical work. In fact, almost no settler has failed in this regard, and most of them are older than me, and I'm 40. Willingness to work is crucial, and this is important to say to all those sitting around in the cities because they are 'not capable of physical work' or because 'their wife is too weak.'"[26] Not only age and physical health but also psychological state were seen as possible reasons for failure to integrate. The surveys and articles noted that men over thirty-five found it especially hard to give up their bourgeois lifestyle and come to terms with the lower living standard demanded by their new jobs or, in the worst case, unemployment. Even though the immigrants were told that there were no class distinctions in Palestine and therefore it was an illusion that their change of occupation meant a fall in social status, this was of little comfort to those who had been proud of their professional achievements and middle-class status in Germany. As the apparatus noted, many men proved psychologically unequal to all the changes involved in the task of building a new life. Their resulting exhaustion hindered their "inner integration."[27] Such men could be found at all socioeconomic levels. The Haifa HOG's inquiry perceived them as hardship cases, the obvious losers of immigration.[28] But this psychological crisis also affected those who were seemingly integrated into the workforce. As Oppenheimer pointed out, physicians and dentists faced no immediate existential crises, but potential psychological crisis loomed despite the fact that all of these men had brought assets: "Even for those who have years' worth of reserves, the fact that their doctor's office is not getting started begins a process of attrition, with the daily fruitless waiting for patients." Whether living off their reserves was seen as a disaster per se, or whether they hadn't brought much capital or were already older and saw no perspective for occupational change, "at this point, the internal crisis [was] more common than the external one."[29]

An article in the *Jüdische Rundschau* entitled "Integration Difficulties" describes the phenomenon:

> It is precisely in wealthy circles, which have no immediate worries about food, that many stand on the outside and complain, no matter what. These are mainly middle-aged people and, most often, men. It is easy to see what they are missing: a sphere of influence. This group includes physicians who once had large offices and are now more or less idle, as well as former entrepreneurs who once had a full working day and now don't know what to do with their free time.[30]

The author points out that these formerly busy men now "live[d] in a void." This group also included many "veteran Zionists." For years, these men had been active in Zionist organizations in Germany, but the reality of Palestine shocked them. Most of all, they were utterly disappointed by the lack of gratitude for their former activities. All these men who could not adapt were described as bitter, frustrated, complaining, and unthankful.[31]

In this discussion, living in the countryside was presented as an alternative for older men. Men who decided to join agricultural villages instead of living the allegedly unhealthy, hectic urban life were described as changing both physically and mentally, becoming happy and content, healthy and masculine, confident and free—men who fulfilled their role instead of living in a void.[32] A piece in the *Jüdische Rundschau* quotes a settler in Herzliya, doing the physically demanding work of pouring concrete:

> At first, I could not stand in the same line with the young ones because I could not keep up with them, but now I am agile and strong enough to keep up with them, and I take great delight in that. . . . I have hardly lost any weight, but I am now tan, made almost entirely of iron-hard muscles, have no health issues whatsoever, and feel great in general.[33]

While the fathers in the villages might not have experienced the frustration of unemployment that their peers in the cities had to cope with, they did have to endure hard physical labor and a dramatic change in their way of living—problems due to the sudden change to physical work are hardly discussed, and this coverage paints the fate of these men very optimistically. Nor did everyone have the necessary capital for settling. A 1939 article entitled "Jewish Academics in Agriculture" discussed former physicians, journalists, and lawyers now working as agricultural day laborers in Magdiel, a *moshavah*. The author, J. Bar Tikva, praised these German academics as men who occupied their rightful place, who were healthy, strong, and fulfilled by their new work, and who now hid their old diplomas and never wanted to return to the cities. He spoke glowingly of these men—gray-haired physicians, narrow-chested teachers, slender classical philologists, now doing taxing physical work that only seemed to do them good—ending with the exclamation: "These are the men Palestine needs."[34]

As opposed to such men, older, frustrated, failing men are a trope in the contemporary discourse. They lacked power—the power to work, to decide what to do and where to live, to provide and support—and thus, they lacked the central attributes of masculinity in the contemporary conception. They seemed to be the diametric opposite of the young, healthy, virile pioneers building the country, as well as of those older men who were willing to work in agriculture despite their age.

Women were discussed differently. From the beginning of the mass immigration, immigrants could read in the *Jüdische Rundschau* and the *Mitteilungsblatt* that the middle-class model of the husband as provider was over and that all women—not only young, single women but also married, middle-aged housewives—would need to become part of the labor force in some form. In 1937, for example, the *Jüdische Rundschau* published a typology of female immigrants in the labor market, entitled "Job-Seeking Women":

> 33 years old, high school diploma, five years of office work (to save for the long-desired medical studies), political change, must stop studying, 1.5 years *Hahsharah* [training] in agriculture and domestic science, marriage, immigration to Palestine where her husband finds a good position as an architect. With the Arab Unrest, he becomes unemployed and since then, she needs to work in various positions, under harsh conditions, as an *oseret* [maid] or caretaker. Another one is 44 years old; in Germany she lived the bourgeois life of a lawyer's wife and caring mother of three. Immigrated in 1933. The 1000 pounds they brought with them were invested without any luck and are lost. The husband cannot be integrated into the labor market. The woman and her 14-year-old daughter have registered at the employment service.... There is also the mother who was "sent for," aged 68, who hoped that she could just live in her married daughter's household. But now her son-in-law is unemployed, and she doesn't want to be a burden on them and hence aims to earn some money, too.[35]

These short case descriptions are examples from the HOG employment service's files. They include homemakers and schoolgirls as well as older women who had been sent for as part of the "parent immigration." The range of immigrants included here makes it clear that the authorities saw women as a promising and not-yet-exhausted pool of workers. The enthusiastic tone of these discussions of women in the labor market—both in the surveys and in the press—is striking. Women are described as brave, tough, determined, and devoted, and their initiative and strength are constantly praised. The social worker Frieda Weinreich, for example, lauds the female immigrants, writing: "'I am willing to accept every job,' this is their motto, and one admires the strong will, the bravery, and the readiness to adjust of one who takes up the heavy burden of providing for her family."[36] The fact that many of these women were married and had been homemakers before immigration was particularly emphasized. In addition to homemaking and caring for the needs of their husbands and children, they now also had to secure their families' economic survival. Some authors even declared that women were able to adapt better per se, because of their superior practical and manual skills.[37]

While it was often noted that women carried the heaviest burden in immigration, they were not expected to experience this situation as a crisis, whether physical or psychological, like the men. Instead, they were expected to prove themselves in the light of this challenge, to "keep [their] cool and accept the unavoidable with a smile," as one author put it.[38] These assumptions can be found in countless articles in the *Jüdische Rundschau*, which declare that, despite the difficulties, women were responsible for their families' and their own successful integration.[39] This discussion of women contrasts strongly with that of men. Women's age and physical fitness (which were after all comparable to those of the men of the immigrating group) are hardly ever mentioned as hindering elements for their integration into the labor market. Despite their triple burden (work, homemaking, and caring for their families), women's illnesses or breakdowns were barely discussed. Furthermore, women's changes in class affiliation and occupation are simply not addressed as grounds for psychological or physical difficulties. But nor were the possible positive effects of the work on their bodies much discussed. While men working in "productive" occupations were presented with the prospect of "steeling" their bodies, no such promises were made for women working as domestics, cleaners, and cooks. Stories of metamorphosis applied only to young women, former city dwellers who were now interested in nothing but greenhouses and manure ("from a real Berlin girl to a real Palestinian girl") or "daring" young women working on construction sites.[40]

There was very little negative attention paid to women in the labor market. If voiced, it was aimed mostly at job-seeking women who were only looking for "leadership positions."[41] The social worker Helene Hanna Thon, for example, provides the negative example of a counseling interview with a young woman from Germany: instead of a suitable profession for Palestine, she studied philosophy. Now (like so many immigrants) she wants to find a job as a secretary, but her knowledge of Hebrew, English, and French is too poor. As a last resort, she would be willing to work as a domestic aide, but she does not know how to cook or clean, as Thon snidely notes.[42] The woman described here as a poorly prepared, naïve, selfish, and un-Zionist female immigrant served as the antithesis of the desired woman. This undesirable woman was not willing to leave behind her old class affiliation and status and lacked all those attitudes of the women of valor, who self-sacrificingly took on any work. While men and their failures were often discussed in tones of compassion and pity, women who were unwilling to meet expectations were harshly criticized. Such cases, however, were the exception rather than the rule in the German Zionist media and were apparently intended to serve as a deterrent.

The discourse of the 1930s described the social reality of female immigrants in the labor market as disclosed in surveys. At the same time, it articulated the demands that the apparatus expected them to meet. They were charged with the ideological task of securing the success of their families and their community by excelling at classical female skills of self-sacrifice and bravely pulling themselves together to get through the difficult period. This juxtaposition of problematic, bitter, and sometimes failing men, on the one side, and hardworking, self-sacrificing women, on the other, was disseminated almost unanimously, both in newspaper coverage and in surveys. Thus, men and women were discussed in relation to one another: the male problems of integration made female work necessary. While male immigrants were seen as prone to failure, female immigrants were seen as capable of overcoming this crisis. This notion was also prevalent in the implementation of policies to support the immigrants' integration into the labor market.

SUPPORTING THE IMMIGRANTS

There was no adequate support system for the absorption of the immigrants of the German Aliyah, so the HOG and the German Department established one on their own. They provided a variety of services for immigrants in the cities who were having trouble entering the labor market. While at first they concentrated only on the most difficult cases, more immigrants turned to them for help as the economic crisis deepened.[43] The most important support tool was job placement services. The HOG founded its own employment services throughout the country. They provided general advice about the labor market, mediated between employers and immigrants, and looked for jobs in fields that were not covered by the Histadrut. Because the HOG wanted to complement the existing job placement system, it did not place immigrants in companies that already had agreements with the Histadrut. However, many immigrants preferred the HOG's job placement services, because they had more trust in their landsmanshaft and a certain apprehension toward the Histadrut.[44]

Every year, thousands made use of the overburdened HOG's employment services. And while at the beginning of the immigration wave, most of the job seekers were male, women soon flocked to the employment services as well.[45] As the HOG did not work with businesses that had agreements with the Histadrut, young, skilled workers most likely turned directly to the Histadrut. However, the rising number of female immigrants seeking jobs was understood as an expression of the economic crisis and the need to provide for their families when their husbands became unemployed. The HOG embraced this attempt and was eager to help job-seeking women. The HOG's statistics show that the number of women using their employment services rose constantly. While in October of 1933, only one-third of the employment services' clients were women, six months later that proportion had risen to 40 percent.[46] In 1937, 50 percent of the employment services' clients were women, 35 percent were men, and 15 percent were youth under eighteen.[47] It quickly became clear that not only were women the majority of the employment services' clients, they had also started to outnumber men in successful placements, for it was "very obvious that it is much easier to find a stable occupation for a woman than for a man."[48] The number one placement for women was in domestic work, comparable to the Yishuv labor market in general. Both former homemakers and academically or commercially trained women were placed here. To a lesser degree, they were also placed in office work and in craftwork.[49] Domestic work was especially feasible for new immigrants. Unlike the much more desired office work, it did not require much Hebrew or English. From 1934 on, the majority of all vacant positions were in domestic work and therefore considered only for women.[50] Men were placed in a variety of fields, mainly as artisans and unskilled workers, in the trades, as business agents and salesmen, and, in singular instances, as skilled specialists in industry. With the economic crisis, unemployment also became palpable in the female professions, and the employment services were overrun with women searching for jobs. But while there was very little demand for male workers, women could still be placed in this field, partly because Jewish homes that had previously hired Arab domestic help now wanted Jewish workers.[51]

Initially, the apparatus was skeptical about whether the German women, who had employed domestics themselves in Germany, would be able to work in this occupation. A HOG report by Grete Turnowsky-Pinner noted that this redeployment to domestic work caused the women physical and psychological difficulties but, because this work was intended to be temporary, that was not seen as a problem.[52] As the economic situation worsened, however, the authorities took the female immigrants' willingness to work as domestic help for granted, and the women's problems were increasingly trivialized. Women who only wanted to work in wealthy homes or leadership positions were criticized, such as "Ms. J. B. from Karlsruhe, age 48, immigrated a year ago with minimal financial means, still unemployed, seeks a self-employed, 'leading' position as a housekeeper in business."[53] In response to such women, the WIZO declared that there was already an oversupply of well-trained veteran resident women who cooked perfectly and spoke Hebrew. Thus, these allegedly spoiled German women were warned that Palestinian homemakers would hire someone else if they didn't agree to accept any position offered to them.

Crucially, female workers were paid much lower salaries than men, despite the narrative of heroic women disseminated in the immigrant media. The HOG was well aware that female immigrants were seen as cheap labor, working mostly as unskilled help in temporary and poorly paid positions. Female writers complained several times in the German Zionist press about this attitude toward female immigrants, especially the low salaries, sometimes 50 to 70 percent less than men were paid, which was seen as an upsetting imbalance in the new society. However, there was no attempt by the immigration apparatus to address this issue.[54] The employment of married women during the depression was also controversial in Yishuv society for another reason: cases of high-dual-income couples.[55] At the end of 1939, for example, a reader of the *Mitteilungsblatt* suggested that in cases of dual-income couples, the women should be forced to stop working so that there would be more positions for unemployed families. He went on to say that his proposal did not apply to cases where both spouses were working to survive, but only to high-earning academics and employees of national institutions.[56] For the immigrants from Germany, this discussion was finally not particularly relevant, because there were so few cases of such high-income couples. Female immigrants primarily held domestic household jobs, which were not attractive to men. But in their internal communications, the HOG and the German Department did suggest hiring men for the office jobs usually held by women within the apparatus. This suggestion was made for very divergent reasons, as one informal meeting between representatives of the HOG and the KJV (the men-only Cartel of Jewish Fraternities) shows. The social worker Frieda Weinreich, representing the HOG, supported the policy for the sake of the women who needed to leave their children at home to do these jobs (because their husbands, though unemployed, were apparently not taking care of them). The KJV representative, on the other hand, along with some of the other HOG and German Department representatives, was interested in providing more paid positions for veteran Zionists, arguing that they should be preferred over women for positions within the apparatus.[57] Members of the apparatus were constantly looking for positions for their fraternity brothers and other veteran Zionists, sometimes also for the sake of their mental health. One former lawyer, for instance, had failed to make a living on his own and, after suffering a nervous breakdown as a result of his failure, was now supported entirely by his wife. Because he was in danger of experiencing another collapse, his fraternity brothers within the apparatus sought to get him "some small office position as occupational therapy."[58] Another new immigrant, Martin Scheftelowitz, who knew the social worker Frieda Weinreich personally, received tremendous help in the placement process: "I explained to her that I had been told that here one needs to forget all one's education, and do manual labor. But I was too weak to carry orange boxes in Tel Aviv harbor. Ms. Weinreich explained that that wouldn't be necessary and placed me in a position as an accountant right away."[59]

Vocational training was another pillar of the HOG's support of immigrants. The problem of occupational adjustment was twofold: younger immigrants needed to be trained, and older immigrants needed to be retrained. The apparatus noted that the reason for male unemployment was not only a lack of vacancies but also a lack of trained workers. Employers in the Yishuv repeatedly criticized the level of occupational training or retraining that male immigrants had undergone in Germany. As a result, the German Department and the HOG collected funds to organize courses for redeployment and further education and to create or support proper training facilities in the cities. Training for men focused mainly on construction, metalworking, and related fields. For family fathers without financial means, the HOG also established *kvuzot*, groups to teach them easy-to-learn professions. There were relatively short courses, such as a four-month course in construction; longer ones, such as an eight-month brickmaking class, and classes of up to twelve months for carpentry.[60]

Women were trained by the WIZO or the *Moezet Hapoalot* (Women's Workers Council, part of the Histadrut), for example in the domestic sciences school in Tel Aviv. The WIZO had complained for a long time about the lack of education and skilled training in urban professions for girls and women. The result, they argued, was that women mainly had poorly paid, unskilled jobs. In collaboration with the immigration apparatus, they therefore established special training for female German immigrants, mostly in domestic work, such as cooking, laundry and ironing, and infant care, but also in stenography, tile-laying and -making, floor-laying, varnishing, painting, and upholstery. This training was intended to enable them to find steady, well-paid employment.[61] As the economic crisis worsened, WIZO functionaries warned that men would be given preferred placement even in jobs usually held by women. Therefore, they argued, it was especially important to provide adequate training to women. But they found it increasingly difficult to defend this position to the absorbing bodies, and as a result the WIZO received less funding and was therefore less able to provide help.[62]

Because immigrants were not usually able to earn money during their training, they received loans through the apparatus. The amounts of these loans show that the apparatus invested more in men's vocational training than in women's. Britschgi-Schimmer observed that in 1933 and 1934, women received an average of 9.7 LP for their training, while men received an average of 15 LP.[63] This differential allocation of money reflected the assumption that female employment was temporary, while male training needed to be more thorough because the man was expected to eventually be able to provide for the whole family again. It also reflected the fact that, in spite of the changed social reality, the apparatus still saw women largely as dependents of their husbands and, therefore, secondary to them and to their education, which translated into less financial support for women's training.

To support German immigrants without means, a credit institution, the *Kupath milveh shel Oley Germania*, was founded. This institution cooperated with several banks and other institutions to enable the founding of small business enterprises. It gave loans designed for those who, because of age or physical or psychological problems, could not be placed through the regular employment services and who could therefore only make a living if they were self-employed. Recipients were especially families with children, as well as those who had no security with which to secure regular loans. Single immigrants capable of working were not supposed to receive these loans, nor were those who aimed to work in already overcrowded occupations.[64] The loans, approved for the purchase of equipment, appliances, tools, small machines, vehicles, furnishings for cafés, etc., were modest: generally between 20 and 50 LP, for up to four years, at 5 percent interest. The kinds of businesses the recipients aimed to establish included "lunch tables," laundry services, sewing services, newsstands, and small bakeries. The loan applications document all the various problems of the German Aliyah, especially its lowest strata, as in this example:

> G., a 50-year-old man, and his wife were sent for by their son, who has been unemployed since his parents arrived. Subsequently, his father . . . has been trying to make a living doing unskilled physical labor to support himself and his wife. He has already collapsed three times in the process. His wife is a seamstress, but is often ill. The sewing machine they brought with them was damaged on their journey.[65]

The family received the loan for a sewing machine and was thus potentially enabled to provide for themselves, through the woman's work, and thus overcome difficulties caused by age, illness, and lack of suitable occupation.

In this case, as in many others, family members who had been sent for as dependents by residents of Palestine could not be supported because their adult children subsequently lost their job.

The social crisis is palpable in the requests for loans for men who were either unemployed or unsuited, because of their age, fitness level, and/or health, for placement in physical work, and who therefore needed to either run a small business together with their wives or be supported by them. The applications usually included letters of recommendation and information about the applicants' marital status, number and age of children, Zionist activity before immigration, and the situation of both the husband and the wife.[66] The WIZO also supported women, through loans for work in home industries. These loans were explicitly intended to enable women to continue caring for their families while working from home. Mrs. L. from Breslau, who immigrated in 1935 with husband and child, was supported by such a loan from the WIZO. Her husband had initially worked as a pediatrician, but then fell ill and had to give up his practice, and Mrs. L. now had to support her family: "The WIZO recommended a home business to her so that she could stay at home and look after her sick husband and her small daughter. WIZO gave her a loan and the opportunity to make experimental designs for painting glass. She now earns a good deal of her housekeeping money, besides fulfilling her duties as a wife and mother."[67]

In most cases, the men were named as the applicant for the loan, even though they were not able to work themselves. But widowed or deserted women also appear in the documents, needing to support their families alone. Charlotte Meyerstein, aged twenty-eight, a chauffeur, was the sole breadwinner for herself and her parents and was granted a loan of 65 LP to purchase a car; a deserted woman was enabled to establish a beauty salon. It was always taken for granted that married women would be gainfully employed, and if a married woman was not working in addition to homemaking, this was explicitly mentioned, along with the reason (for example illness, disability, pregnancy, or caring for children). Immigrants who wanted to receive a loan were first expected to show that both husband and wife were working or at least willing to work.[68] Pfefferman and De Vries have shown that gender bias prevailed on the loan-granting committees in the Yishuv in general. Women wanting to be entrepreneurs were perceived as transgressing gender norms by going beyond the accepted sphere of the home. Therefore, Pfefferman and De Vries point out, women applying for loans explicitly noted the absence or incapacitation of their husbands to show that they were forced to choose this path.[69] However, in the case of the German-Jewish immigrants, male applicants also mentioned their wives' status in their loan requests, as well as in other correspondences with the authorities. They knew that they had to provide this information, because meeting these expectations of the apparatus was essential for getting a loan.[70]

Despite the various attempts to support the immigrants in entering the labor market, the German Department mentioned as early as 1934 that "grave social problems ha[d] arisen" among the new immigrants, especially in the large cities, problems that could not, given the limited budget, always be solved.[71] These cases were handled by social workers, who focused in particular on refugees, immigrants without means, and families with many children, as well as young single women (as discussed in chapter 2). They were given, variously, temporary housing, rent loans, furniture, clothes, childcare, and medical care. With the economic depression, the HOG reported more cases of crisis. Now veteran immigrants were also becoming unemployed, unable to pay their rent, and even going into debt to buy groceries. This last was considered especially significant, as that would only happen when a family's savings were entirely depleted.[72] Many "capitalists" needed support now as well—some who had come on the capitalist certificate had received the required 1,000 LP from friends, while others waited years for their *Ha'avara* transfer money from Germany.[73]

Most German-Jewish immigrants had belonged to the middle class and never been in contact with social welfare before immigrating, especially since they left Nazi Germany early and thereby escaped much of the impoverishment that the Jewish community in Germany was increasingly subjected to. When they experienced downward social mobility in Palestine, they first had to overcome their inhibitions about asking for help. Many were afraid of becoming social work "cases." Frieda Weinreich described the case of Ludwig Eckstein, who arrived in 1933 on a tourist visa and had been a lawyer in Germany. In Palestine, he did manual road construction work. But the work was too physically demanding for him, so he changed careers again, to work in an office. When he was fired from that position he could not find work in that field again and tried to survive by selling insurance, but did not succeed there either. As a result, Weinreich wrote, Eckstein had sunk into poverty, lived in an unhealthy cellar, and ate poorly, but out of pride refused to accept help.[74]

Women who asked for support but were unwilling to take up employment were regarded negatively. The HOG reported on the case of a family with three children in which the father, a locksmith, could not find a steady income, but the mother rejected temporary work as a maid.[75] In another case, a family was in distress because the husband, who had been interned in a concentration camp, was unable to work because of what he had suffered there. Despite his condition, his wife was unwilling to accept a position working as an infant nurse. The social worker noted snidely that the work would allegedly remind her of the concentration camp.[76] Instead, the woman tried to make a living at various menial jobs but lacked the necessary stamina; in addition, her sick, bitter, and egotistical husband made her suffer. Thus, the family existed solely on social welfare.

As already noted, the immigrants were aware of the apparatus's expectations and made a point of mentioning the situation of husband and wife both. Julius Reisapfel, for example, immigrated in 1934 as a worker. He was sent to work in agricultural labor, but as the wages were too low and there was not enough work, he could not provide for his family adequately. His wife, he explicitly noted, could not join the labor market because she needed to take care of their baby. Reisapfel therefore asked for help because they owed money for their groceries and needed furniture and such small things as laundry detergent.[77] The social worker Bella Preuss provided support for another family that had become destitute because the wife began to suffer from a heart condition from the change in climate. Her husband needed to care for his wife and therefore could not work.[78]

The absorbing authorities' policies were based on different tasks, responsibilities, and allowances for men and for women. The absorbing bodies expected men to fail, calculated for it, and adjusted their agenda accordingly. Women, on the other hand, were put under tremendous psychological and ideological pressure to succeed. While it was considered rather normal for men not to be able to provide for their families, women's ability to stand in for their husbands was taken for granted. At the same time, however, the fact that the apparatus provided so many fewer funds for female education and that there was such an overwhelming lack of protest against their low wages kept women in the lowest strata of the labor market. These policies and their implementation shaped the experiences of the immigrants in the labor market.

EXPERIENCING THE LABOR MARKET

The experience of entering the labor market and the accompanying obstacles were explored in studies conducted by the absorbing bodies as well as through their ongoing support system. But of course these documents expressed the perspective of the absorbing bodies. Likewise, while the *Jüdische Rundschau* was eager to publish letters by immigrants voicing their observations, these letters largely focused on experiences of positive transformation through occupational change. In the ego-documents that depict the experience of the labor market from the perspective of the immigrants themselves, the impressions are much less positive. These documents bear witness to how the immigrants coped with the demands of occupational change, what the ramifications were for both their physical and psychological well-being, and how male and female immigrants reacted to the apparatus's requirements. In the following, I will concentrate on the experiences of occupational change in the cities that were shared by large segments of the immigrating group.

For male immigrants, working in construction was a common and taxing experience. Most thought of it as a transitional job to make enough money to start a business, or until they could return to their old profession. However, the experience was profound, as Martin Hauser describes below. Hauser, a dental technician, immigrated in the summer of 1933, at age twenty. On June 2, 1933, four days after arriving, he wrote in his diary: "Searching for a job in Tel Aviv. No prospect of work as a dental technician at all. Solution: Doing as opportunity offers. The kitchen porter in the restaurant is a medical doctor, the window cleaner a junior lawyer. I will try construction."

As the weeks went on, he continued his entries:

> June 12, 1933: Back from *Lishkat Avoda* (the labor exchange). "Occupation?–Dental technician. (Questioning look.)–Born when?–1913–Where

from?–Germany (oh, another Yekke. I shall hear that many more times). Construction. You think you will be able to do that?–I will try (doubting shrug of the shoulders). So, off to construction I go.

June 22, 1933: Since the day before yesterday, work in bridge construction, chopping with the *turiah* [an agricultural tool, comparable to a hoe] and bringing out the earth. Hands are full of blisters. What's going to happen?

June 26, 1933: Again tried in vain to get work. Yesterday I worked in a restaurant in Yaffo as a dishwasher (broke two plates). Today I went to Haifa to consult with fraternity brothers. Good prospects of work as an office boy.

July 4, 1933: Since Sunday, I've been working on the construction of a chocolate plant in Ramat Gan. Needed to heft heavy iron poles. Yesterday so wrecked that I was too tired to eat dinner. Today I am completely exhausted; I will take a break tomorrow. Sometimes I feel desperate … am I ruining myself, because I do not have enough strength? What is going to become of me?[79]

Hauser's experience was very typical for an urban worker at the time.[80] Because there was no demand for his original profession, he started working at intermittent positions allocated to him at the labor exchange, mostly in construction. These temporary jobs barely enabled him to make a living, and also exhausted him to an extreme degree. Hauser was afraid not of getting "a sore back," as the *Jüdische Rundschau* had euphemistically phrased it, but of permanently ruining his health, even though he was still young and able-bodied. For older immigrants, it was worse. The critical ramifications of such jobs for their health, both mental and physical, were mentioned by Britschgi-Schimmer, who found that 40 percent of the immigrants suffered from various illnesses, mostly related to the new climate and the demanding physical work.[81] For older men, the experience of heavy physical work was much more taxing, and they tried to avoid it. Those who did not continue in their former professions were most interested in working in offices or as bus drivers. However, for an office position, connections were needed to get the job in the first place, and language skills were required to do the work. Working as a bus driver, meanwhile—a popular occupation because it was comfortable, permanent, and provided a safe income—was only possible for those who could afford to become a member of the cooperative (with a deposit of 500 to 700 LP).[82] Older men often tried to establish small businesses with their wives, both in formal settings (cafés, shops, guesthouses) and informal ones (boardinghouses, home food production). In chapter 5, in the context of family dynamics, I document in more detail the practice of couples setting up small businesses called *Mittagstische*, or lunch tables.

As economic conditions in the Yishuv deteriorated, it became more and more common to see immigrants peddling soap, combs, or washcloths, or walking from door to door as salesmen. Not only the physical exhaustion of jobs like construction work, but also the humiliation of some of these jobs, drove some male immigrants to despair and, apparently, even to suicide. Martin Feuchtwanger, a journalist and publisher whose own experience running a *Mittagstisch* with his wife was actually very positive (see chapter 5), wrote:

> A former notary told me that he had offered articles to the editors of newspapers and magazines, he had attempted to work as a translator, he had tried to find a modest position or menial work in dozens of shops and factories, he had even tried to make a few pounds with picking oranges, and that now he was at the end of his tether. The next day, he hanged himself from a tree.[83]

While some immigrants managed to stay optimistic and see this as a transitional phase in their lives, others could simply not endure it.

How was the labor market experienced by women? For German-Jewish women in Palestine, whether academics or homemakers, students or retirees, it was a universal experience to do domestic work. "Suffered a lot, interrupted her medical studies, here an *oseret* [maid], did not know how to work, treated badly, washing the socks of strangers."[84] This passage from an interview by the journalist Gerda Luft contains some of the main features of this work in condensed form: the deep social fall and change of class associated with working as a domestic servant, the maltreatment by employers. It also points to the important fact that many women were not adequately prepared for the occupational change to being a domestic worker. The skills required for domestic work did not come "naturally" to these female immigrants; quite the opposite. They needed to learn the work in the same way that men needed to learn construction work. The fact that Luft uses the Hebrew term *oseret* instead of the German word for "maid" was common, as with the use of *poel* for "worker." This may be because of the Zionist take on domestic work: Palestine was supposed to be a society without classes, and *Dienstmädchen* was too reminiscent of the conditions in Europe. Furthermore, the use of the Hebrew word indicates that this work was new to the German immigrants and the German expression did not seem to fit, maybe also because it was too humiliating in its associations.

While some women tried to better their skills through classes at the WIZO, others just saw this as a transitional stage to something better (whether another job or returning to being a stay-at-home housewife) and sought no additional training. Even those who were familiar with domestic work in Germany found the working conditions here very different: in a new climate, and with new machinery and materials for cleaning and cooking. Meta Frank, who worked as a household help, described the difficulties:

FIGURE 7. Instructor Henriette Albach (left) demonstrating the use of the Primus kerosene stove to students who want to immigrate to Palestine, Berlin, 1936; Photographer: Herbert Sonnenfeld. Source: Jewish Museum Berlin, FOT 88/500/43/002, purchased with funds provided by the Stiftung Deutsche Klassenlotterie Berlin. Reprinted with permission.

standing for hours in the heat, cooking without gas but using a Primus cooking stove, preparing previously unknown food, and having to fight vermin on an unprecedented scale.[85] Jenny Aloni, who worked as a cleaner at one point, was not even given proper equipment, but had to throw the waste out with her bare hands.[86] Many women working as domestic help complained about maltreatment. Household workers were in a vulnerable position because they worked in their employers' private homes. Everything had to be negotiated with the employer—number of rooms to be cleaned, meals, breaks, etc.—for those not hired through the Histadrut. Most domestic workers (like the immigrants in the cities in general) were unorganized, as theirs was mostly temporary work.

The employers included established residents of Eastern European origin, British families, and, especially at the beginning of the immigration, other German immigrants. Initially, German families could still afford to hire household help. They often wanted to hire German domestic help so that communication would be easy and cooking and housekeeping would follow the norms they knew. This did not always translate into positive relations. Gretel M., who worked for a year in the household of a wealthy German family, remembers: "In any case, they weren't nice, . . . they treated me as a servant, of course, . . . one level down. . . . It was not common to talk with the lady of the house in private."[87] In the German Zionist press, female employers, especially, were repeatedly called on to change such attitudes toward their employees in Palestine. The kind of employer-servant dynamic that was imported from Germany was not supposed to have any place in the new society (see also the "Kurfürstendamm Ladies" debate, chapter 2). While maltreatment by German employers was openly discussed in the German Zionist press, conflicts with Eastern European veteran residents were not. Ego-documents provide ample evidence of these complicated interactions, though. Ilse S., who immigrated in 1938 at age twenty, worked three times a week as a maid, three afternoons as a nanny, and once a week as a laundress. She worked only for German families "who were also immigrants, and knew where they came from."[88] Because she was trained in domestic work, she earned relatively good money. She belonged to a minority of immigrants who were prepared for the Palestine labor market. Only once, she states, did she work for a Russian family—but left after a short time, "because they treated me like an *oseret*."

Ilse B. recalls her shock on her first day of work for residents of Eastern European origin, her first-ever contact with veteran residents:

> These were people who had lived here for a long time already, and you wouldn't treat a dog how they treated me. ... First of all, I had to mop the floor. Then, at lunch, I had to serve them while they ate, then take the cold food back to the kitchen. And they said: now you can eat the cold leftovers. Of course, I was indignant and very unhappy. I came home and had a crying fit. I swore to myself that I would never work in a household again. I would beat stones on the streets, I would accept any work, but never again in a household.[89]

The deep humiliation that Ilse B. describes must be understood in the context of both her occupation and her employers' background. Many German-Jewish families had hired domestic help themselves back in Germany and looked down on this occupation. The sudden experience of being on the other side of this relation was traumatizing. Another complicating factor was the historical conflict between German Jewry and the Ostjuden. Not only did these women have to work in an occupation not befitting their former social status, they had to do this work for a group they themselves had looked down on before their immigration.

Working as a maid may have felt humiliating, but alternatives were hard for women to find. The fact that Ilse B. mentions stone-beating shows an awareness of the existence of this occupation for women, but it was hardly a viable alternative; extremely few women did such work. Ilse B. had no choice but eventually to work in domestic employment again. For younger women, next to domestic work, jobs in catering were common, too: working as waitresses, dishwashers, and kitchen assistants in restaurants, cafés, and guesthouses. As with male immigrants, women frequently alternated between temporary jobs and periods of unemployment. This was especially hard for single immigrants, who had no one else to rely on. Jenny Aloni describes the difficulty of finding a job, often only for one day a week, and not even always getting paid. She worked as a cleaner, in ironing, as a server for a *Mittagstisch* for German immigrants, then as a dishwasher in a Jerusalem restaurant. This last job was physically taxing, as she describes in her autobiographical novel:

> The tiny kitchen was hot and airless. . . . The soapy water burned the skin of her hands. They became saggy and wrinkled and were soon covered with wounds, which burned and did not heal. Sometimes a glass broke, and the shards cut into her fingers. The joint of her right hand became inflamed from polishing the glasses. Fine wire pieces from the steel wool used for cleaning the aluminum pots penetrated her skin and festered. Her back hurt from bending over the sink for hours.[90]

Domestic work and catering, the most common female jobs, were physically taxing and perceived as humiliating, but there was almost no alternative. In the more desired occupations of saleswoman, typist, and correspondent, where many women would have loved to work, they faced great difficulties if they didn't speak Hebrew or English. Very few German women worked in factories or workshops, partly because of the low wages but mainly due to the negative associations of being a "worker." As noted earlier, married women, in particular, turned to work in the informal sector, mending and tailoring clothes or providing board and lodging. Professional women also had trouble finding anything other than menial jobs. Their career options were even more limited than men's were, especially for mothers who also needed childcare. Beate D., a gynecologist, for example, needed to leave her infant in order to finish her practical studies. In general, female physicians had more trouble finding positions than men did: an article in the *Jüdische Rundschau* points out that women were not placed in responsible positions in the countryside, first because it would be too dangerous for them, and second because they would not be accepted by the patients.[91]

Former professional women suffered from this interruption of their careers just as men did; as the journalist Gabriele Tergit wrote in 1934: "Painfully I realized that I am of no use to anyone, except for my husband and my son. Sometimes, very rarely, I write a few little things. A few German-Jewish newspapers print them."[92]

While rank-and-file male immigrants suffered from unemployment and were hard to place, as we have seen, professional men who were veteran members of Zionist organizations had a decisive advantage. There were veteran Zionist women, too, but the apparatus did not treat them equally. The HOG, the German Department, and related organizations such as the *Ha'avara* were sought-after work places, including for professional women. But when it came to the allocation of high-ranking positions, women were more often than not disregarded. Male veteran Zionists were at an advantage when looking for a position within the apparatus.[93] Both the HOG and the German Department were male-dominated, and while women served on committees there, they seldom held important positions. Those women who did get to be part of the networks, including Gerda Luft, Margarete Turnowsky-Pinner, Bella Preuss, and Ina Britschgi-Schimmer, were often outspoken advocates for women-oriented policies and brought gender issues to the fore. But these women did not reach the organizations' highest ranks and were sometimes openly discriminated against.

Another woman who worked for the apparatus was Hana Majofis, a social worker who had worked in the Berlin Palestine Office as an emigration advisor for more than a decade. After her own immigration, she was promised a leading position at a transitional camp in Haifa for immigrants without means, but then the German Department informed her that they would not hire her after all. The reason provided was that, in spite of her extensive work experience, as a woman she was not fit for the position. Majofis resisted angrily, pressing for the position she had been promised. She argued that she was second to no man and simply the best-qualified person for it.[94] After Georg Landauer intervened on her behalf, she then got the position. However, after only two months, she was suddenly fired, replaced by a man backed by several male members of the HOG who were not supportive of a woman in a leading position and claimed she lacked the necessary assertiveness.[95] Majofis wrote to Landauer again, humiliated and furious over her treatment:

> *I dreamt that I could prove to these people that a woman can do it not only as well as, but better than a man.... All of a sudden, Tanne summons me and lets me know that in Jerusalem it has been decided that I should go to the Va'ad HaKehilla [community council] instead because the camp should be led by a man. When I asked if I had failed,... Tanne told me... that I had done very*

well, but that he had the feeling that I was not equal to the job. I don't know if you can understand how terrible this is for me, to fail like this, after working independently for two months in a job that I loved.[96]

Majofis was especially hurt by the form of her dismissal. Behind her back, the HOG Haifa had found a male replacement to whom she had to hand over her job the moment she was told that she had been fired. For Majofis, it was clear that her replacement had better connections within the apparatus, which apparently justified the way she had been treated.

Majofis was not the only highly qualified female professional to be discriminated against within the apparatus. Britschgi-Schimmer, the author of the influential survey discussed above, received no permanent position after conducting her study and felt that the German Department consistently dismissed her as "just a WIZO lady" and that her excellent qualifications went unrecognized.[97] Gerda Luft supported Britschgi-Schimmer's claim, noting how inconceivable it was that a woman with her skills should not be given a position while many less-skilled men received positions in the apparatus.[98] The solution offered to Britschgi-Schimmer by Werner Senator of the German Department speaks for itself: for her to receive a permanent position, one of the other women working for the HOG would have to give up her position or minimize it to 50 percent.[99] In another case, when a leading position for social work organizing in the Tel Aviv HOG was vacant and the hiring commission was still undecided, Alfred Landsberg (the former head of the Zionist Federation in Germany) praised the candidate Max Pomeranz to Georg Landauer while dismissing Frieda Weinreich as unfit for a leading position, and asked Landauer to influence other members of the commission to support Pomeranz as well. Weinreich was a seasoned social worker and fluent in Hebrew, while Pomeranz, as Landsberg admitted, had no prior knowledge of social work and did not speak Hebrew. His advantages were being a man, and therefore deemed more suitable for a leading position, as well as being a veteran Zionist and a father who needed employment. Moreover, Landsberg explicitly notes that his hiring would make prominent German Zionists very happy.[100] And while the participation of married women in the labor market was taken for granted, Hilde Oppenheimer felt the need to assure her then-boss Arthur Ruppin that he could continue to count on her after her wedding: "Please excuse that I cannot wait for you today. The reason is of a personal nature and a little unusual. Two hours ago, I married Dr. Killian Blum.... I can assure you, I believe, that the efficiency of my work will not suffer."[101]

Despite all the praise for the bravery and willpower of German women, the prevailing gender bias within the absorption apparatus did not change. These women were veteran Zionists and a part of the apparatus, but they were discriminated against nonetheless. A few years after Hana Majofis was fired from the camp, she summed up her bitter experience to Landauer: "You know, Georg, ... when it comes to important decisions and changes, etc., a woman, no matter how competent she is, really feels that she is 'only' a woman."[102]

LETTERS OF COMPLAINT

Some immigrants may have kept their anger, pain, and frustration to themselves, but others discussed it within their families or circles of friends. Many also chose to address the apparatus directly, in letters of complaint written to the German Department and the HOG. Immigrants are not usually familiar with the style, formalities, and cultural codes that letters to authorities require. The German Jews in Palestine, however, could turn to two organizations founded especially for their needs, staffed with other immigrants from Germany who shared a similar background, and, maybe most importantly, whom they could approach in German (unlike other authorities of the Yishuv, such as city councils). In many cases, the writers also knew people in these organizations and tried to make use of this personal connection in their requests, resulting in a lesser degree of "social distance." Mostly, the authors of these letters were the very same older men who, as we have seen, had problems integrating into the labor market. One of them was Kurt Beer, who wrote to Georg Landauer in November of 1937, asking him to find him a position:

> *I am 40 years old; I was a lawyer and notary in Berlin. In July, 1933, I entered with my wife as a tourist and stayed in the country. As a veteran Zionist, and according to the advice of the Palestine Office, I tried to undergo occupational*

change. All my attempts (learning to become a carpenter and a shoemaker) failed due to the negative attitude of my employers. Although I am physically disabled (I have a scar on my leg) I did hard physical work as a poel [worker] at Assis for a long period. All my attempts to find a more suitable job failed, and so I was forced to trade in chocolate among my acquaintances in Tel Aviv. Our financial situation worsened more and more because my wife could no longer work after she gave birth to our son in 1935. Our physical exhaustion, the illegality, and the bad economic situation forced us in July 1937 to stay with relatives in Prague who were able to host us temporarily.[103]

Beer attends to the specific requirements of communication with the authorities, introducing himself with his age, former profession, and membership in a network ("veteran Zionist"), a pattern that most letters follow. The elements he incorporates in his letter are in fact representative of most of the letter writers, including themes that were common to the experiences of many (male) immigrants: unsuccessful occupational change, conflicts in the workplace, the effects of age and the body, downward social mobility, and the importance of female work. Beer proclaims that while he met the requirements of the authorities, he failed to succeed in Palestine. This caused an economic, legal, and physical crisis for him and his family. And this is outrageous in his eyes exactly because he "did everything right": he is part of the network; he acted according to the advice of the Palestine office and underwent occupational change to physical and blue-collar work against all the odds. He deploys the elements of age, former profession, and physical fitness—which were constantly discussed in the newspapers as problematic features—to pinpoint his level of willingness to act according to the request of the apparatus. In his mind, the reason he failed in spite of this was the negative attitude of his employers. He seems to assume that he does not need to elaborate on the hostility he was met with, given that the mistreatment of German Jews by the "old-timers" of Eastern European origin was a buzzword in those days.

Beer describes the dramatic downward social mobility of a one-time lawyer, a highly respectable profession by German-Jewish middle-class standards. Eventually, he became a small trader in the informal sector. Becoming a worker was already a social decline, but at least it was compensated through the ideological framework of Zionism; trading in chocolate, however, was humiliating and not acceptable in either conceptual framework, neither German-Jewish middle-class nor Zionism. To explain his family's extreme relocation to Prague, he adds that his wife could no longer work after giving birth and his income was not enough to support his family alone. Beer's letter also addresses legal status. Being illegal, he was in a most vulnerable position, constantly faced with the danger of deportation. The combination of not being part of the in-group (subjected to hostility) and illegality was a particularly difficult one for the new immigrant.

This was not Beer's first communication with the authorities. One year earlier, he had written a letter to the Keren HaYesod (United Israel Appeal, a fundraising organization) to protest the use of a picture of him with the caption, "From a Lawyer to a Carpenter." He wrote that he had ultimately failed in undergoing occupational change because of his lack of *protektzia* (a derogatory term for what they saw as Eastern European nepotism) and the unfair system, and was therefore now forced to trade in chocolate. "The correct caption should now read: From a lawyer to a chocolate trader. I want to ask you to stop using this picture immediately, as it is de facto wrong."[104] This is an interesting example of the refusal of an individual immigrant to be monopolized by ideology. He did not want to be used to illustrate success stories of occupational change. Even though the difficulties of occupational change seemed in many cases to be only temporary, this is not what the immigrants experienced: for Beer, his failure seemed to be permanent.

The hostility the immigrants met with is an important point in many of the letters. A letter from Shlomo Juengster provides yet another angle on this phenomenon. Juengster, who immigrated in October 1933 as a pioneer, was a lathe operator but earned so little money that friends had to support him with food. Due to the economic crisis, he had been fired and been unable to find a new job since then. He wrote to Moshe Brachmann of the HOG Tel Aviv:

> *Of course, I am a member of the Histadrut, and since I became unemployed, I've attended their labor exchange for metalworkers three times a week. But so far, I haven't gotten even one day of work. There is no question that workers were needed during this period, whether in my profession or some kind of "Avoda shrora" [literally "black labor," referring to unskilled physical work]. But although I always asked politely, I was put off from day to day. Meanwhile,*

others, even single men, got work; those who stood out for their rowdy behavior or those who have what they call "protektzia" from the highest ranks. But it is not my character to gain attention in such a way, and I still believed in justice. I want to mention, by the way, that I am not in arrears with my payments for the Histadrut, even though it was extraordinarily difficult for me to pay them. Naïvely, I believed that I was more likely to be considered because of that, but here too I was wrong.[105]

Juengster sees two reasons for his lack of success in getting a job through the Histadrut. It seems to him that first, one has to act out a certain kind of masculinity, and second, one needs to be part of a network and have *protektzia*. While Juengster behaves calmly, politely, and according to the norms he is used to from Germany, he sees around him the opposite behavior—and those who make noise and trouble and act aggressively get the jobs, even though they are not married. Access to the major resource of work is dependent on a certain performance of masculinity, one that is rough and aggressive. Juengster cannot bring himself to behave in such a way because of his "nature" and because it does not meet his standards of justice. Even though this would boost his chances, he claims, he is not able to change. In addition, and he identifies this as the second crucial point for success, he is not part of the right network. Even though he does everything "right" from a Zionist point of view, including belonging to the Histadrut, paying membership fees, learning a productive profession, and attending their consultation hours, he has no *protektzia* and as a result he finds the *Vatikim* (veterans) / Histadrut clique to be completely closed off to him, as well as corrupt and untrustworthy. Nevertheless, what he does have—a crucial resource for immigrants—is a private network of acquaintances who provide him with food and other things and advise him (more or less successfully) on which occupation to learn. Eventually, it is through his marriage that he is able to live, as his wife supports him financially. Juengster is so convinced of the importance of his wife's job and her role as a major breadwinner in the family that he resists taking an unstable job as an agricultural worker, because that would endanger his wife's job.

Belonging or not belonging to networks and the society as a whole was a huge issue in the letters, as Hans Falkenstein's letter also shows. Falkenstein, thirty-five, wrote to Landauer in 1938. He had been a judge in Germany and an active member of the Zionist movement. Due to a conflict with the leader of the Haifa branch of the HOG, he could not pursue his career and was unemployed. His goal was to find a job within the framework of the German Department or the HOG. The major problem that Falkenstein saw was his lack of integration into Yishuv society. He felt like an outsider—and that seemed outrageous to him.

> *A Zionist, an active member of the movement, well prepared, . . . who speaks Hebrew and English, is, after two and a half years in the country, left with nothing. It is not that I did something wrong or was not adequate to a task—nobody gave me a chance. I do not know if you, Dr. Landauer, can understand what it means to be on the outside like this, and I do not want to talk about it too much. Also, I will soon have to take care of my parents. My wife's medical practice supports us at the moment, with great difficulty, but it can't support four people, and we have no savings. It is of utmost importance that I get help now. I appeal to you, do not just put this letter away; and do not forward it to Haifa. Because whom else can I turn to?*[106]

It is common for an immigrant to feel isolated and uprooted, but Falkenstein cannot accept this, and complains about it to the German Department. In his eyes, he deserves to be treated better for two reasons. First, he had been an active member of the Zionist movement in Germany, and second, although he doesn't say so explicitly, he indicates that the position he held in Germany should win him better treatment now. In terms of his membership in the Zionist movement: even though he did everything right—worked in the movement, learned Hebrew—this has brought him no success. The fact of being on the outside poses a tremendous crisis for him, but he sees his crisis as being caused solely by the outside world, no fault of his own. His age, thirty-five, also poses a challenge: "It is almost impossible to integrate somebody my age into the workforce." In terms of his professional credentials and his former position, he begins the letter by introducing himself with his exact professional position, the kind of examinations he took, and the specialization he had gained while in Germany. This is all irrelevant to the absorbing authorities because he cannot continue to work as a lawyer anyhow, but it is highly relevant for him as an individual: his past has shaped his identity, and his achievements are a source of pride that he is not willing to leave behind. This kind of biographical factor was mainly relevant for men.

Falkenstein lives on his wife's medical practice, but because they will have to take care of his parents shortly and he has no income himself, the family is in distress. He cannot stand the chasm between this new life and his former life and is unwilling to accept the immigrant's fate: starting from zero, being an outsider, being unemployed, and doing subaltern work.

As discussed above, their failure to integrate had a strong physical dimension for these men: it got under their skin. They experienced themselves, especially in the light of the Zionist cult of youth and virile masculinity, as unequal to the transition to physical, subaltern work and therefore powerless and dispensable. Most of the letters touch upon this subject; some make it the centerpiece of their complaints, like this letter from Gustav Kahn, who wrote to Werner Senator at the beginning of 1938:

> *I have been in the country now for two years. For the first six months, I worked for a store selling dairy products. Since then I have worked as a deliveryman for the Aviv bus company. I am already 38 years old, and I need to change occupations for health reasons, because I have already suffered two nervous breakdowns. If I were younger, then certainly I wouldn't suffer from this harm to my health.*[107]

Kahn does not explain in detail what exactly caused his nervous breakdown, but he seems to assume it will be clear to Senator. The work of a deliveryman is a hurried, other-directed activity that requires being outside a lot. Kahn directly links the harm this job is doing to his health to his "old" age of thirty-eight years. He interprets this age and its correlation with his physical health as a disadvantage in the labor market: he can no longer do just any job, like younger men can. The dynamic he describes is one of downward social mobility, from the work of a statistician in Germany, through sales work, to making deliveries. Even though Kahn outlines his situation in just a few sentences, the changes he describes to Senator are dramatic. One needs to remember that disclosing these most intimate problems to an authority was often an act of despair. Being fit and able-bodied was a requirement for most of the jobs the German Department and the HOG suggested to the immigrants. Those who did not meet this standard, like Kahn, had to pay a high price, both psychologically and healthwise.[108] In Germany, they had been considered men in their prime; in Palestine, they were "too old." These men could not transform "from a Zero to a Hero," as younger ones, at least theoretically, could. They were no longer judged according to their former professions or education; instead, they were judged by their bodies and age against the omnipresent Zionist cult of youth.[109]

The available letters provide descriptions of the hardships these men had to face: a lack of integration into the labor market, a lack of integration into society, and a lack of networks. On the other hand, the letters also unintentionally show how immigrants coped with this situation: through shifting work patterns within family units, relying on private and family networks, and trying to (re-)build and strengthen networks from their country of origin, discernible behind the declarations of being veteran Zionists.[110] However, many men apparently exaggerated their membership in and importance to the Zionist movement. The sources show that prominent figures within the movement usually did receive better treatment, even when they did not meet all the standards. Prominent veteran Zionists from Germany even received help when they were completely physically unfit for life in Palestine; in such cases, it is usually mentioned that while the men are unable to work for physical or psychological reasons, their wives will be able to work.[111] Given the character of this correspondence, then, it is likely that some of the writers exaggerated certain elements of their experience to increase their chances of receiving the desired support. The constant mentioning of their wives' work is not a mere description of social reality but also an expression of the immigrants' understanding of the authorities' conceptual framework, in which married women were also expected to work. The hardships these men experienced were clearly gendered: their image of their own masculinity as strong, able providers underwent a change. They lost their power, both financially and socially, and as former breadwinners who were now dependent on their wives' income, felt forced to call on the authorities for help.

WOMEN OF VALOR

Who has toiled from morning to night?—The woman
Who has cleaned and who has sewed?—The woman
And when we were short of Piaster [Ottoman monetary unit],
Who went to do the outside work?—The woman, the woman, the woman

*Who dragged stones to build the Quisch [street]?—The woman
Who showed how hard one can work?—The woman
And for every finished house,
Who was called to do the outside work?—The woman, the woman, the woman.*[112]

It was not only in newspaper articles and in surveys that the women of the German Aliyah were commended. In ego-documents, the same enthusiastic rhetoric is used, describing the female immigrants as brave, tough, and determined. Women were lauded for taking up any job while also being homemakers and bearing children. This concluding section examines this praise and sheds light on its meaning. The employment of married women was decisive for the success of this immigration wave because of its character as a family immigration. In order to prevent a crisis, the void that was left by the many "failing" men had to be filled somehow. Consequently, female work, both paid employment and unpaid homemaking, became visible and was discussed in public debates and within the immigrant communities. First and foremost, this was an acknowledgment of the changing social reality and changing gender roles within the immigrating community. But beyond acknowledgment, it was also appreciation. The way in which men showed respect for the work of women expressed a sincere thankfulness. While this thankfulness was not remembered by every man in hindsight, in contemporary sources it was ubiquitous. Women were literally lauded in song, as the opening quotation just above, from immigrants in the agricultural village of Bet Yitzhak, shows. Especially in the countryside, where female work was an unconditional premise, women were lauded:

> I only wrote of myself and did not mention the most important thing—and that is my brave little wife. I am strengthened by my exercise regime, but my wife surprises me more every day. I knew that she was dedicated body and soul to building our existence here, that no sacrifice was too great for her. But the way she works in our vegetable garden, in addition to all that, is admirable. Today she surprised me by building a kitchen table on her own . . . while she used to be afraid to stand on a ladder and wash the windows.[113]

This letter is a typical example of how women were often admired for the transformation they had undergone, which indicates by contrast how they had been perceived in Germany—whether the change was indeed in the women themselves or whether men had simply not previously perceived the work their wives did. Men paid tribute to women and their work in the cities as well, as in this passage by Martin Scheftelowitz memorializing the female immigrants: "On this occasion, the bravery and hard work of the women of the Aliyah from central Europe should be remembered. . . . Women who belonged to the upper middle class in Central Europe did not hesitate to work in strangers' households or in hotel kitchens or to create pastry for strangers in their own homes."[114] Strikingly, there are hardly any sources that describe the changing gender roles and responsibilities as a threat to or humiliation for men. Instead, the emphasis is on an appreciation of working women. But this does not mean that there weren't men who felt this way. Men who had lost social and economic power might very well have felt humiliated and ultimately ungrateful to their wives whose entrance into the labor market ensured their survival.

The humiliation that *was* expressed was the result not of dependence on wives' incomes but of treatment by society at large. And the accolades for female immigrants by their male counterparts have a different character than the debate in the immigrant media and the apparatus, which, while also expressing appreciation, was aimed at integrating the immigrants. However, the songs of praise sung by the male immigrants were also not free of ambivalence. I want to focus here on the commonly encountered statement that the process of absorption was easier for women, as in the following passage by Martin Feuchtwanger:

> These women and girls who were new in the country had had a big house and been used to giving orders to maids, nannies, and laundresses. Now they were grateful to be able to clean the floors in strangers' houses, to cook, do the laundry, and iron. Women, it seems, can integrate more easily than can men. Skillfully and without complaining, ladies transformed themselves into servants, and in many cases provided for their husbands and children.[115]

This conception of women as more easily able to adapt—to the country of immigration in general and to its labor market in particular—has also been held by historians of the German immigration to Palestine as well as by historians of the German-Jewish emigrants in general.[116] To challenge this notion, I want to look at two main points made in the above quotation that are mentioned in many other sources as well: first, that it was easier for women, and second, that they did not complain.

Was integration into the labor market indeed easier for women? The features of women's and men's absorption discussed throughout this chapter should raise doubts about this claim. The labor market had more use for women than for men at this point. But given that women worked in poorly paid, temporary positions; that overwhelmingly male networks continued to exist and privilege men; that women were given fewer training opportunities and ultimately seen as a stopgap support, with men expected to take over again eventually; and that gender bias continued to operate within the apparatus and beyond—given all of this, such a claim should be regarded with skepticism.

Men failing to integrate are topoi in contemporary documents, while failing women are indeed harder to find. However, from social welfare documents and oral history, we do know that there were ailing immigrant women who needed support, which should not be surprising, given the triple burden they had to shoulder. Ruth L.'s mother, for example, fell ill every year for several months; according to her daughter, it was a psychosomatic illness caused by the unbearable impositions of life in Palestine.[117] Yohanan B., too, directly opposed the conviction that absorption was easier for women. His mother worked twelve-hour shifts as a private nurse, then came home, cleaned the apartment, and cooked. His father, meanwhile, worked as a sales representative by day and managed a café in the evenings:

> For my father, despite it all, it was much easier. My mother always wondered, why didn't we go to America, which would have been much easier for me? I guess she was right. For her it was harder, she had to work much more. When my father went to work in restaurants, etc., there was always a little chitchat, but for my mother, it was a mad rush to manage everything in the day. There she had people working for her, and here she did everything alone. She came to terms with it eventually, she hardly ever complained ... at least not in front of us children.[118]

The claim that women did not complain is conspicuous: it lauds an allegedly essential character trait of women. Sacrificing themselves in silence and without complaint was part of a normative idea of femininity, both in the cultural-religious framework of the *Eshet Chayil* (the tribute to the "woman of valor") and in the context of 1930s German Jewry. Within the Jewish community in Germany, Marion Kaplan has shown, women were increasingly charged with protecting their families, their communities, and their faith against the Nazi state.[119] Given the persecution and distress, they were expected to take any job offered while continuing with homemaking and easing emotional distress in their families—competing demands that were almost impossible to satisfy, as Stefanie Schüler-Springorum has noted.[120] In other words, female immigrants had already faced such demands before their immigration. Zionist functionaries and social workers from Germany brought this discourse to Palestine. The praise for female immigrants should thus be understood as a continuation of the German discourse, imported to Palestine as well as other countries of exile. While shattered men were an accepted phenomenon, overworked women are described as having no alternative. They likely complained less about their illnesses and challenges than men did, because they were well aware of the expectations of the apparatus and their community and family: to be strong. But did women not complain at all? And if not, why not?

First of all, we do have examples of female complaint. Most letters of complaint were indeed written by men, probably because they felt entitled to complain publicly. But this behavior is not based on essential traits of men or women. The public discourse provided information that immigrants may well have used both to understand their reality and shape how they asked for help. Women who complained to functionaries about their own health issues were often not met with compassion. Hilde Nesselroth was married to a former lawyer who could not find any work, so she had to support the family alone for years. When she became severely ill with angina and could no longer work, she wrote to Werner Senator in 1938: "Dear Doctor Senator, is there no way at all to find work for my husband, who is really extraordinarily smart and skilled . . . ? I will add to our income again once I am healthy again, but it can't continue like this, that I ruin myself and my husband is without occupation!"[121] Nesselroth notes that her husband was a paying member of the Zionist Association for Germany, even though he had no income in his final years in Berlin. Senator replied that he was shocked by her letter, but that he was unable to help. In another desperate letter, a female immigrant wrote that because her husband could not find work, she had to start working as an *oseret* a mere month after delivery, even though she had severe health problems. Due to the lack of childcare, she needed to take care of her baby in addition to working. Thus, she earned less money because she constantly had to leave work to nurse.[122] A copy of the letter, which was intended to be private, was passed to the German Department. Landauer commented: "Some of the complaints might be right.... Nonetheless, there is no justification for this exaggerated reaction."[123] Women immigrants, just like men, strategized in their communication with the apparatus. Complaining, it seems, was not perceived as particularly promising.

A final argument for women's alleged greater ease of adaptation is that women are less status-conscious than men. It has been argued that women may not have experienced the social descent from employing a servant to becoming one as intensely as men, since women's status had always been determined by that of their father or husband anyway.[124] But it is doubtful that women suffered less from the loss of status. Middle-class women, who had to work double days—both as workers and as homemakers—in Palestine, may very well have suffered a tremendous loss of self-perceived status. Viewing their employment as temporary may not have helped. The lack of documentation of failing and complaining women does not prove that they were all heroines in the spirit of *Eshet Chayil*, that it was easier for them than for their male compatriots, or that they were "better" immigrants. The authorities' expectations left little space: women had to succeed at migration. There was no space for them either to complain or to fail.

CONCLUSION

It is so easy to say it, and it sounds so good: first it was bad, then acceptable, and finally pretty good. But only someone who also lived in Palestine at that time can understand how difficult were those thirteen years from 1939 to 1953, those grueling daily struggles.... Only [that immigrant himself] can know how often he wanted to throw in the towel, to give up, how many times he lay awake at night, staring into the darkness and saying to himself desperately: "I can't take it anymore, I can't go on like this." Still, he did.[125]

This is how Martin Feuchtwanger summarizes the immigrant's struggle for economic absorption. Most German Jews were unprepared for the labor market when they immigrated to Palestine in the 1930s and therefore experienced occupational change, menial and temporary jobs, downward social mobility, and a change of class affiliation. Nazi rule had radically transformed the social and economic life of German Jews, depriving them of their income, careers, homes, and possessions. However, as mentioned, most of the immigrants to Palestine had left Germany before the complete erosion of their socioeconomic position there. The serious economic struggle this group faced, at least in their first decade in the country (and sometimes longer, as noted just above), contrasts with the popular image of the German Jews as well-to-do immigrants who may have suffered cultural trauma, but not severe economic hardship. The focus by much of the research literature on the professional contributions of certain groups and individuals, as well as the emphasis on the immigrants' eventual successful integration, rather than the economic struggles most of them underwent during their first years, have reinforced this impression.

German-Jewish professionals were indeed crucially involved in industry and production, commerce and consumer culture, banking and finance, architecture, the tourist industry, medicine and medical services, science and academia, the judicial system, technology, and high culture. But while those who managed to stay in their original professions and eventually enable the modernization and professionalization of the Yishuv and the later state of Israel in these fields dominate popular memory, they were a minority within the immigrating group. Most physicians, to look at just one example, could not live on the income of their original profession for at least their first decade in the country. To survive, many physicians worked two jobs at once, with their main income coming from the second job: physician and mirror manufacturer, physician and timber dealer, physician and insurance agent, physician and bus monitor.[126] Some professional women, too, managed to integrate into the labor market in the Mandate period, for example in the fields of medicine, social work, and architecture; however, they remained a small minority.[127] Most female workers were concentrated in lower-ranked female occupations and held temporary, unskilled jobs, which resulted in low wages.[128]

The success of the immigrants' integration is a question of perspective. For the absorbing society of the Yishuv, the immigration was doubtless a blessing, as it brought with it the German immigrants' private capital, knowledge, and professional skills, which created Jewish jobs, strengthened the Jewish demographic factor within Palestine, and helped to shift political dominance from the diaspora to the Yishuv leadership.[129] From the immigrants' perspective, however, things look different. Most immigrants suffered severe downward social mobility and distress for many years, and even those who brought large sums of capital with them could not as a rule continue to maintain the same living standard they had enjoyed in Germany.

The one thing that did eventually change the socioeconomic fate of the immigrating group as a whole had less to do with the eventual success of those professionals than with international politics. The individual reparations that were paid as a result of the 1952 Luxemburg agreement between Israel and West Germany were an attempt to restore the social and financial status of individuals and to compensate for financial loss due to National Socialist persecution. These *shilumim* (Hebrew: payments), as they are referred to in Israel, included restitution of property and collective, in addition to individual, reparations. Only a small part of Israeli society received individual reparations, almost all of them immigrants from Europe. The group receiving the highest payments by far were Israelis of German origin. In the 1950s, struggling to absorb a massive immigration wave of Jews from Arab countries, as well as Holocaust survivors from Europe, Israel was under an austerity regime, with shortages of food and other essential supplies. While the reparation agreement had a generally positive effect on the Israeli economy, the payments especially helped the recipients of German origin to significantly raise their living standard and that of their children.

Integration into the labor market posed a formidable challenge for the immigrants as well as for the apparatus entrusted with their absorption. Gender, intersecting with other factors such as class, age, and the body, played an important role in the monitoring of the immigrants, in the debates about them, and in the policies governing redeployment training and loans, as well as in the immigrants' own experiences. While many of the difficulties in this process were borne by the immigrating group as a whole, women and men underwent them, and were perceived as undergoing them differently, as this chapter demonstrates.

FOUR

How to Cook in Palestine?

HOMEMAKING IN TIMES OF TRANSITION

IN AN ARTICLE PUBLISHED IN the *Jüdische Rundschau* in December 1934, the journalist Gerda Luft pointed out the manifold challenges facing the homemaker in Palestine:

> She needs to learn a new form of housekeeping, and that often without help, or without sufficient help, which is something she is not used to. Housework and caring for the children fatigue her; she suffers from the climate; she does not sleep enough. And it is mostly she who feels the social decline in all the little things that make life comfortable. The information and preparation that had been directed at her abroad did not help. She had been told that it would be hot in the summer, but few have the imagination to really picture how hot it will be. It is only once you have had to clean the floor while dripping with sweat, when you yearn for a cold bath three times a day, that you begin to understand what heat means. A great deal of humor and serenity are required in order not to give up in the face of never-ending daily difficulties, from the smoking Primus [kerosene stove] to sour milk, from crowded schools to ants in the pantry.[1]

As Luft vividly illustrates, homemaking was radically changed by the migration to Palestine.

Close to 30 percent of all immigrants were married women.[2] Prior to immigration, most had been responsible for the housework in their families and were not gainfully occupied. After the Nazis' rise to power, the unemployment of former male providers had increasingly made female employment necessary. But because, as I have already noted, most German Jews who immigrated to Palestine came during the early years of Nazi rule, this provider-homemaker model had still largely been the norm for them until they immigrated. In Palestine, this changed; here many married women had to provide for their families through gainful employment, as I discussed in the previous chapter. But notwithstanding this major change, women also continued to perform the household duties in their families, working what feminist scholars have called a "double day."[3] Housework included a variety of tasks: cleaning, laundry, maintaining clothes and other household items, as well as shopping and preparing meals. Care work, such as caring for children and taking care of sick or infirm family members, as well as emotional support for the family, was performed within the household, often simultaneously with other domestic tasks. The contemporary documents continued to use the terms *homemakers* and *housewives* even though these women in many cases had ceased to be solely homemakers, holding gainful occupations in addition. Accordingly, I will use the word *homemakers* in the following to refer to those individuals who performed the unpaid task of homemaking (whether or not they also had paid employment). This chapter discusses the changed practice of homemaking and its ideological implications, both from the perspective of the immigrants and from the vantage point of the absorbing authorities.

CHALLENGES OF HOMEMAKING IN PALESTINE

During the late nineteenth century, ideals of home and domesticity had become a crucial part of the bourgeois German identity, as Nancy Reagin has shown. This "domestic identity" was also internalized by German Jews.[4] Climatically, geographically, technically, and socially, however, Palestine was very different from Germany, and all of a homemaker's duties needed to be adjusted to the new conditions: the weather conditions of a subtropical region, the processing of unknown food, the handling of unfamiliar household appliances. Homemaking in Palestine therefore posed a tremendous challenge for married women, who were automatically regarded as responsible for it. As Luft indicates in the above quotation, even the vast array of information for potential immigrants that specifically targeted homemakers could not entirely prepare them for the reality of homemaking in Palestine.[5] Some women, who in Germany had been mainly occupied with representative tasks, literally did not know how to perform such household tasks, as Eva W. remembers:

> My mother had to give up learning Hebrew pretty fast because she had such a heavy struggle for existence. Look, my mother had never cooked, she could not cook at all, she could not iron, let alone mop the floor.... My father came to the country bringing his linen suits; well, have you ever tried to iron linen? That is the hardest thing of all. Soaked in sweat, she ironed these linen suits, and obviously, you only wear them once, then they are rumpled again.[6]

It was not until they had been in Palestine for several years that her father was willing to exchange his linen suits for simpler materials that meant less work for her mother. For several years, in other words, this family held on to customs that had been brought from Germany and were embedded in their class consciousness, but did not match the changed conditions in their new homeland. The resulting additional work was performed by women who attempted to maintain these customs despite the completely changed situation. In addition, given the socioeconomic conditions of the immigrants, homemakers generally needed to perform these various tasks in the household with less help than they were used to. Running the household with so much less help, or even all alone, and in worse technological and climatic conditions than they had known in Germany, meant an enormous change for these middle-class homemakers. Ruth L., who immigrated with her family as a ten-year-old girl, in 1936, recalls that while in Germany her mother had had a nanny, a laundrywoman, and an ironing woman; "now she was alone and had to do everything on her own, and it was hot, and there was little room."[7] Employing domestic help had been the norm in German-

Jewish middle-class families prior to Nazi rule. While many immigrant families initially continued to employ full-time household help in Palestine, most of them gradually reduced the hours of their domestic help, or ended up doing without it entirely, as a way to reduce living expenses.[8]

Miriam R. remembers that when her family first moved to Palestine, they hired a full-time domestic helper to assist her sick mother; only later did they realize they could not afford this and reduced the helper's time to just a few hours daily. The relation to these domestic aides was different in the Yishuv than it had been in Germany. The *Jüdische Rundschau* felt the need to instruct the immigrants on how to treat their employees, informing them about the differences between the housemaids they had employed in Germany (usually young Christian women who lived with the family) and the domestic workers in the Yishuv, mostly veteran residents of Eastern European origin who were organized in the Histadrut, the General Federation of Jewish Laborers in Palestine. It was common among the new immigrants to complain about how demanding the domestic workers were: they had many requests, and adhered strictly to the contracted hours, and this was hard to accept for the German Jews, who had been used to a more servile attitude from their cooks, cleaners, and nannies.[9] Miriam R. recalls that she and her family were outraged when the cleaning lady insisted on eating with them and not in the kitchen, as they had told her to do. Reluctantly, they agreed, even though "she had no table manners." This anecdote illustrates the antipathy of the new immigrants toward the Eastern European Jews, which became intertwined with their aversion to the Histadrut. Miriam R.'s father even composed a song about the various domestic workers who had been sent to them by the Histadrut, mocking their work ethic:

> *Osarot, Osarot, may God protect me from your work*
> *Before you find the dustcloth*
> *The eight hours are over*
> *And you need to go back to the Histadrut*
> *Osarot Osarot.*[10]

The fact that Miriam still remembered this song some eighty years later, word for word, including the incorrect pronunciation of *osrot*, Hebrew for "domestic aide" (her father probably did not know how to correctly pronounce the plural form when he wrote the song), indicates how often this song must have been sung in her family.

For washing sheets and other large linens, a very physically demanding and time-intensive chore done by hand, most of the German women still received help. The laundrywomen, who would come to each apartment several times a month, were not organized in the Histadrut but were almost entirely Arab women or women of "Oriental" Jewish origin. The employment of Arab women was frequently criticized in the Yishuv because, not being "Hebrew work," it was seen as undermining the goal of supporting the Jewish economy. The immigrants, however, defended themselves with the argument that veteran residents also employed mostly Arab women for this task.[11]

One main challenge facing the German homemakers was the local food and its preparation. Common Palestinian vegetables like eggplants, zucchini, and citrus fruits, which were inexpensive and abundant, as well as food staples like bulgur, olives and olive oil, hummus, and tahini, were unfamiliar to the German immigrants, who had trouble getting used to their preparation and taste. Other common ingredients, like garlic, were known but often rejected because of their associations with Eastern European cuisine. Some immigrants had tried to prepare for cooking in Palestine with special classes while still in Germany, but the majority was completely unprepared; I will discuss their challenges in more detail in the following section. Many immigrants were repelled by the markets and shops in Palestine, which they saw as primitive, inferior, and unhygienic.[12] These conceptions were strongly influenced by the Orientalist gaze the German Jews brought to Palestine, which was often framed, as discussed earlier, in terms of hygiene. Gerda Luft wrote about one female immigrant who was so disgusted by the hygienic conditions in Palestine that she wore gloves throughout her first year in Palestine so as not to have to touch anything.[13] Even household measurement units differed in Palestine, where the Ottoman system of ounces and rottels was used. And to make things worse, even these units differed between the cities of Palestine: one ounce was 240 grams in Tel Aviv and Jerusalem, but in Haifa, only 213 grams; one rottel was 3 kilograms in Tel Aviv and Jerusalem, but only 2.5 kilograms in Haifa.[14]

The ideological implications of shopping were new for homemakers, too. The Association of Immigrants from Germany / Hitahdut Oley Germania (HOG), as well as articles in the immigrant media *Jüdische Rundschau* and *Mitteilungsblatt*, constantly called on the immigrants to purchase *tozeret ha'aretz* (Hebrew: product of the land) products only. *Tozeret ha'aretz* designated goods were produced in the Yishuv by Jewish agriculture and industry, as opposed to goods produced by Arabs in Palestine or products imported from other countries. Because women were seen as primarily responsible for shopping, they were especially targeted by these calls, and commentators repeatedly blamed the immigrants for pressuring shop owners to provide them with imported German products (for example the laundry detergent Persil) instead of accepting the domestic products of the Yishuv.[15] Such behavior, it was lamented, would end up ousting *tozeret ha'aretz* goods.[16] This criticism was in line with the Yishuv's general critique of the German immigrants as being too luxury-oriented, as I discussed in chapter 2.

The technical equipment for cooking, washing, and baking used in Palestine also created difficulties in homemaking. Nothing symbolizes this better than the infamous Primus, a kerosene stove that was used for cooking in most Palestinian households in the 1930s. It was initially imported from abroad, but beginning in 1936, the Tuval Company produced an Eretz Israeli Primus.[17] The German immigrant Martin Scheftelowitz described the centrality of the Primus in these words: "I learned quickly that for life in Palestine, three capital Ps were needed, namely 1., the Pound, or Piaster, ... 2., Protection, called *Protekzie*, which was even more important than money, and 3. Primus: a moody kerosene stove."[18] Many immigrants brought their own furniture and household items with them in the large wooden *Liftvan* containers (see chapter 1), but the homemakers still needed to adapt to the challenge of the Primus, because cooking with gas or coal was very expensive in Palestine. While electric stoves were already being advertised and sold in the Yishuv in the 1930s, especially to German immigrants, they were too expensive for the majority to afford.[19] The Primus, meanwhile, often referred to as the "horror of the housewives," was loud, hard to operate, heat-generating, and dangerous: it caused many injuries.[20] In comparison with the stoves that were common in Germany, which used coal, electricity or gas, the Primus was clearly a step backward for the homemakers. Recipes had to be adjusted to the new cooking conditions. In order to reduce the heat and noise produced by the Primus and to save fuel, housewives avoided meals that had to be cooked for a long time. For baking, an aluminum pot called the *Wundertopf* (German: wonder pot), which could bake a cake without an oven, was used as an extension. However, immigrants frequently complained about the characteristic hole in the middle of the cake created with the *Wundertopf*. The Primus was also used for heating, as described in this 1937 *Jüdische Rundschau* article entitled "The Worries of the Housewife":

> How can one keep the apartment warm with a kerosene cooker? The housewife needs to carry it with her: From the kitchen to the children's room, from the children's room to the living room, from the living room to the bath. As long as she is alone, that is doable. But once husband and children come home, the worries about moving the stove around do not stop. Everyone sits in one room, and the housewife needs to keep order and peace so that the husband can read, the children can do their homework, and she herself can cook on the stove.[21]

This article, like so many others, held women responsible, in their roles as wives and mothers, not only for making do as they ran the domestic sphere with the limited resources in their possession, but also for keeping the peace in the family. Homemaking as a practice was thus embedded in the task of creating a new home for their families in the new homeland—an issue that will be discussed at greater length in the next chapter.

There were other practical obstacles for the homemakers in their daily activities. Storing food was problematic due to the hot climate and the absence of refrigerators. Instead, blocks of ice were used to cool the food. These ice blocks, as well as petroleum, were delivered daily by salesmen walking through the streets. There were hardly any electric refrigerators used in private households in Palestine in the 1930s; those German Jews who had brought their own refrigerators soon realized that these could not withstand the heat and frequently broke down. A popular joke of the time took this issue on: "A Yekke family wins a refrigerator in the lottery. When the delivery service rings the doorbell at 2 o clock in the afternoon, the lady of the house opens the door dressed in a robe and refuses to accept the delivery because it has arrived during the Schlafstunde [nap hour], when no disturbance is permitted."[22] While this joke is clearly part of the genre mocking the immigrants for their lack of flexibility and their deference to rules, even when that was to their disadvantage, the punchline relies on the tremendous importance of refrigerators in Palestine, on the one hand because they were in short supply, and on the other because of what they represented for the immigrants.

Another aggravating factor for homemakers was the apartment situation. Subletting was the most common way of dealing with the shortage of flats and the high rents. A 1936 survey of the immigrant organization HOG found that more than half of the immigrants in the three big cities, as well as in the large agricultural settlements, were subtenants.[23] This also included couples and families, who could often not even afford the tiniest flat, but only a single sublet room. It was, however, especially difficult to find a property owner willing to let a whole family live in one room. Another 20 percent of immigrants lived in one-room or one-and-a-half-room apartments, so that altogether, about three-quarters of the respondents had to live either as subtenants or in one-room apartments. A 1935 HOG survey covering the most socially disadvantaged sector of the German immigrants in Haifa found out that in almost 70 percent of cases, one room was occupied by three or even more persons.[24]

Many of the interviewees, who had been children and adolescents in the 1930s, recalled the crowded conditions. Eva W. remembers how economic need forced her family to sublet rooms. She had to share her room with a girl who paid for board and lodging; another room was rented out to two students, her mother slept on the couch in the living room, and her father, a physician, slept on a folding bed in his office.[25] Jacob M. had to share the bedroom with other tenants of the flat, an elderly couple.[26] Yissakhar Ben-Yaacov actually had to sleep in the bathtub for the first ten months, because there was simply no other place in the apartment.[27] Immigrants who had families in Palestine could stay with them for a while, but because of the crowded conditions, this, too, was a taxing experience. After leaving the Bet Olim in Haifa, Meta Frank and her husband moved in with an uncle who had fallen ill. Because their relatives had to sublet the other rooms, Meta and her husband had to sleep and eat with the sick uncle, his wife, and child, all of them together in one room.[28] Sometimes people not only lived but also worked in these shared apartments: Martin Feuchtwanger and his wife Trude Loevy, for instance, had subtenants, a hat salon, and a *Mittagstisch* (a small cafeteria; see chapter 5), all in one apartment.[29]

When families had to live in sublet rooms because they could not afford an apartment of their own, this created a variety of problems. Shared bathrooms and kitchens meant that time slots needed to be painstakingly organized with the other tenants, and conflicts were unavoidable. This situation also forced many immigrants to eat out despite their dwindling financial resources. Yair C., who lived with his wife and two other families in one flat, remembers: "The landlord was an unlikable man with an unlikable wife, ... they had a little girl ... and she cried all night. And we were three families, but only had one bathroom, one toilet."[30] This landlord, like many others, did not let the subletters use the kitchen. Yair C. recalled that instead, they had to cook on a tiny, dark, closed balcony a few floors up from their room, where they could use a Primus stove but had no possibility for storage.[31] Ilse B., too, described the humiliating experience of her mother, who was not allowed by the landlady to use the kitchen: "When we arrived in the country, we had no clue about how things were. My parents rented a place, only temporarily.... And there, we only had one room, and therefore my mother had to cook with a Primus stove on the floor."[32] In this scene, the way they had to cook exemplifies the immigrants' overall experience of downward social mobility. Ilse B.'s mother, who had employed several domestic servants in Germany, was now forced to do the cooking herself, with a Primus stove, on the bare floor of the room that served also as the whole family's bedroom—a telling example of the severe erosion of the ideal of domesticity to which bourgeois Jews had been accustomed.

The newcomers felt misunderstood, noting a lack of empathy for their plight among their host society. For many new immigrants, the interactions with landlords who were veteran residents of Eastern European or Russian origin were especially tense. Countless complaints bear witness to defraudation as a constant problem, ranging from exorbitant rents, through deceptions (e.g., making a new immigrant pay for the whole house's water bill), to the theft of belongings by landlords or neighbors. The fact that such acts took place in the immigrant' own homes made them especially hard to endure.

Eventually, their lack of space and dwindling financial resources would force the immigrants to sell their furniture and belongings—the very belongings their families had cherished for generations and that they had brought with them all the way from Germany in their *lift*. Their whole lives shrank, sometimes to a single room for a whole family. The immigrants were not used to such a limited living situation, and many had to change their perceptions of how a family had to live. In Germany, before Nazi rule, the separation of spheres had been a defining aspect of the bourgeois home. The majority of German Jews had internalized this idea. Nazi policies, though, made it increasingly impossible for those Jews remaining in Germany to maintain a bourgeois habitus in domestic life, as Guy Miron has recently shown.[33] In migration, too, the concept of home and domesticity needed to be entirely changed. Most of the immigrants who now dwelled in crowded conditions had lived in bourgeois homes before their migration, typified by a division of rooms into public and private, with no intermixing of living and working. In addition, men and women, children and parents, had spent most of their days in separate spheres. For many immigrants, privacy was now almost nonexistent and male privileges, like the *Herrenzimmer* (a separate dedicated men's study room), vanished. One new immigrant complained bitterly about this lack of privacy. In a letter to an acquaintance in Germany, he described visiting a friend who had to share one room with his whole family. At one point he was asked to turn away because the wife needed to breastfeed her newborn baby. This was outrageous to him, both because he had never seen nursing before and because this made the total lack of privacy so evident.[34]

Cleaning, too, had to be done differently in the new homeland. The hot, humid Middle Eastern climate; the characteristic sandstorms that filled the flats with sand in the spring and fall; the lack of refrigerators; the dirt and grease caused by the Primus; the fact that the apartments usually had floors made of stone rather than wood; and the extensive presence of vermin: all these demanded different cleaning methods. Household customs, such as the common use of petroleum in Palestine to clean and to prevent infestation, seemed odd to the new immigrants. In addition, cleaning and hygiene were crucial issues because of the prevalent illnesses. New immigrants were especially prone to falling ill because of the new climate, the unaccustomed makeup of the food and drinking water, as well as the conditions in immigrant hostels and other crowded housing.[35] Outbreaks of dangerous illnesses, including typhoid, dysentery, diphtheria, malaria, bubonic plague, tuberculosis, and pappataci fever, as well as common eye infections and skin diseases such as boils and rashes, deeply frightened the new immigrants. Many of these illnesses were transmitted through contaminated food or contact with human waste, which created a lot of pressure to maintain strict cleanliness and hygiene. Homemakers were seen as having the primary responsibility for shielding the health of their families, as constantly discussed in the *Jüdische Rundschau, Mitteilungsblatt*, and publications of the HOG. In 1935, for example, the *Mitteilungsblatt* issued a brochure for new immigrants, in cooperation with the Kupat Holim (the public health fund), that became standard reading material. Entitled "Illnesses and Hygiene in Palestine," it gave information on health and illnesses, hygiene, the climate, and appropriate clothing. The article "What and How Should the Immigrant Eat?" explicitly asked immigrants to avoid drinking or having ice cream on the streets and beaches, as these were seen as a risk. And fruit and vegetables were supposed to be soaked in a chemical solution of potassium permanganate for twenty minutes before eating.[36] Many immigrants, anxious to stay healthy, complied with these instructions.[37] Questions of hygiene and homemaking under conditions that were considered extreme were an important topic for German Jews in other parts of the world as well, most notably in Shanghai and in South America. So-called European practices of hygiene were considered to be under threat in these places, and the immigrants were warned of tropical illnesses that could be caused by the slightest slip in household routines.[38]

Homemaking in Palestine then, often conducted in addition to gainful employment, was a heavy burden for female immigrants. While individual conditions differed according to the respective immigrants' socioeconomic and family backgrounds (some could afford domestic help, while others could not, for instance), for many homemakers the scope of all their household tasks barely left time for recreation or social activities. Else Bodenheimer-Biram, for example—who was a prominent Zionist, held a PhD in sociology, and had been active in many charitable organizations in Germany—complained about this in a letter (mentioned in another context in chapter 2) to Georg Landauer, the secretary of the German Department of the Jewish Agency for Palestine. Noting the need for educational work among the immigrants, she pointed out: "I cannot do this work myself now because I have no maid and need to do all the housework myself, and because this work is physically very demanding for me, I cannot afford to be involved in volunteer work."[39]

The absorbing bodies were well aware what an imposition this all was for the immigrants, who had been used to so much better living conditions in Germany. The authorities understood that it was women who worked to bridge the gap between the old life and the new. Ina Britschgi-Schimmer, for example, noted: "The crowding in the apartments is especially hard to bear for many immigrants from Germany, who were used to good and comfortable living conditions.... It is striking that in spite of all these difficulties, most of the flats visited were clean and in good shape. One could sense that the women try, with all their might and against all odds, to maintain order in their apartments."[40] Like other contemporary surveys and newspaper articles, this one is full of praise for the female immigrants. However, the fact that these articles remained remarkably silent about men's homemaking responsibilities meant that the praise also implied a demand that women be responsible for providing and maintaining domesticity, even under these dreadful conditions.

While both men and women suffered from the housing conditions, only women were asked to compensate for them. This ideology also prevailed in the new society of the Yishuv. While homemaking became a highly visible part of the migration process in this debate, and there was a great deal of awareness of the burden on the homemakers, the absorbing bodies, for the time being, allowed men to continue with their pre-migration routines, without expecting them to take on new tasks in the home.

However, it was not just the immigrant media and the absorbing authorities that extensively discussed homemaking; it was also, frequently, individual immigrants. Fritz Wolf, for example, who settled in Nahariya and initially lived with his sister and brother-in-law, made these observations:

> I already knew: there are no maids here. Gretel did all the housework herself. It was only fair for me to make my own bed. Back in Germany, Anna, our maid, had done that. Another reality: no maids. That meant a lot of extra work for Gretel. Well, I would manage to make the bed alone. Of course, this was a small thing to do, but it was very real. This takes a certain amount of time every day.... But who does the dishes and cleans the floor if

there is no maid? And there was no cook, either, so Gretel had to cook. The chickens needed to be taken care of: Gretel took care of them.... When I returned from the bathroom, the table was already set for breakfast. Gretel did it. All these things were trivialities ... but somebody needed to do them. Why does Hans not set the table? He should set the table. Gretel took care of the chickens; she got dressed; she set the table.[41]

Wolf provides a very detailed description of Gretel's double burden of homemaking and farm labor. The absence of household help (which had been a feature of middle-class homes in Germany) suddenly makes homemaking visible to him. As a result, he is indignant with his brother-in-law: in Wolf's opinion, the family's changed social conditions should have been reflected in a sharing of the household duties.[42] Old traditions imported from Germany, such as the special, opulent Sunday breakfast that Gretel still clung to in Nahariya, seem out of place here and cause her even more stress, Wolf notes.[43]

After he moved out of his sister's house into his own home, Wolf needed to deal with food preparations, under difficult conditions, on his own. The fact that he was single and had to perform homemaking tasks alone certainly added to his sudden awareness of the burden of female work, not only in Gretel's case but also for other female immigrants. Wolf, who was an avid writer and wrote songs for local musicals, praised the valor of working women in many songs, as in the following scene from his 1939 *Die grosse Parnosse*:

> *Who does the laundry? Cuts the roses?*
> *Takes care of the ill? Stitches the trousers?*
> *Who washes the children? Empties the potty?*
> *And gives Anise drops against coughing?*
> *Who scours the floor? ...*
> *Who bakes a cake on Friday*
> *And only has one piece of it?*
> *Who comforts the kids when they cry*
> *And kisses the husband to calm his fury*
> *And breastfeeds the kid*
> *And in between looks after the chickens,*
> *Who knows who these creatures are?*
> *The women—honor them.*[44]

In his praise for the women of Nahariya, Wolf acknowledges the fact that these working women were responsible for homemaking and childcare in addition to their work in the fields and the chicken coop. He asks his male audience to respect the work of their wives and to start helping them. Like Wolf, many male immigrants became acutely aware of the scope and importance of homemaking though their migration to Palestine, whether because they could not afford domestic help, because they were unemployed and mostly stayed at home, or because the newcomers' crowded living conditions simply made it impossible to ignore this work.

"AT THE SERVICE OF THE HOUSEWIFE": ASSISTANCE, INSTRUCTION, AND CONTROL

Because of the new and challenging conditions presented by homemaking in Palestine, there was a strong need for orientation and advice among the immigrants. The absorption apparatus, well aware of the importance of homemaking and the workload of the women performing it, responded to their needs in various ways: through information, advice, and intervention. One practical measure was a placement service for domestic workers, in particular for helping overworked homemakers, which the HOG promoted in these words:

> Who does not know the worries and complaints of the overworked, worn-out housewife who has to suffer nerve-wracking daily battles with all the plagues of daily life! Children lie in bed with a cold and need to be taken care of; it rains into the tiny bedroom/living room; the kitchen is covered in soot from the Primus; and in the middle, the dirty laundry, the piles of socks that need darning, linen that needs mending. How she longs for a little relief, a pair of hands to help her out; how she yearns for ... a nice concert, a good lecture, a get-together with friends.... The placement service of the HOG is at the service of the homemaker.[45]

While the absorption apparatus recognized the homemakers' workload and acknowledged their need for relief from this burden, potential help from their husbands was not seen as a potential mode of relief; instead, the remedy was seen in paying other women for their assistance. The HOG established a "homemakers' advice service" that provided guidance on questions of homemaking and cookery, and the WIZO (Women's International Zionist Organization) offered services such as classes in housekeeping, infant care, and cooking.[46] "Palestine cooking" was also taught, in German, in immigrant hostels. The social worker Sara Berlowitz, one of the organizers, describes the cooking class and its social component for the immigrant women:

> We had received a big kitchen for our class, and because the correct preparation of Palestinian vegetables was equally important to all the women, it was much nicer and more practical to stand together with the neighbors around the Primus and be taught how to prepare tasty and healthy dishes from the unknown Palestinian vegetables. Even when our conversation changed to topics unrelated to cooking, these were important questions for these women.[47]

Social workers from the HOG and WIZO also paid home visits to the newly immigrated homemakers to assist them in these questions as well as to help take care of the sick and advise on baby care. Nadja Stein described the need for such home visits in light of the mental state of the desperate, confused, worried women who "cry because of the Primus; because of the flies, mice, and ants in their bad accommodations; they do not know what they should buy, where they should shop, or how they can feed their families, and for many of them this is the first time they have had to do the laundry and clean."[48] In 1936, Sara Berlowitz told the WIZO news service about the advice she provided to German immigrants she visited in their homes. She described, for example, the case of "a brave little woman," almost destitute, who had come with her husband to Palestine via Holland and had no friends or family whom she could ask for help. Berlowitz discussed with her the many different daily duties, how to organize the day, and the necessity of not doing the most difficult tasks in the midday heat. She also advised her on what pieces of furniture were and were not useful in Palestine because of the danger of vermin, and lastly, showed her how to clean the beds thoroughly once a week with petroleum and insecticides. To other homemakers, Berlowitz explained or demonstrated, for example, how to whipstitch a suit for a little boy out of a dress, how to make an eggplant casserole tastier, and how to cook with various other vegetables.[49] WIZO home economics instructors also visited the German immigrants who settled in agricultural villages. For several weeks in 1938, for example, a WIZO itinerant teacher instructed the women of the newly established village Shavey Zion in homemaking and cooking.[50]

The goal of the home visits and the other services provided to homemakers was to facilitate their tasks, and these visits did, on the one hand, provide valuable advice and practical help for homemakers, especially those who were socially isolated. On the other hand, however, they also contained a crucial element of social control. This is conveyed in many publications in the immigrant media. In 1934, the social worker Helene Hannah Thon published an assessment in the *Jüdische Rundschau* under the telling title of "Freedom and 'Freedom': Experiences with New Immigrants":

> Visiting a family that had a beautiful home in Europe, we find an untidy living room; leftovers on the table wrapped only in paper; and children wearing nothing but their oldest clothes over their underwear. "Why don't you make it a little cozier here for yourself and your children?" "Because here we want to be freer than before and not do trivial work all day long." "And what do you want to do with this freedom that you gain from abandoning a clean home?" The answer I receive from her is vague and insufficient and does not support the idea that there are higher duties for this woman than keeping her house and her children as clean as possible, both from the inside and the outside, for the sake of the country.[51]

Both in personal encounters and in the immigrant newspapers, social workers discussed this duty to keep the house clean: not only for the sake of preventing illness, but also to guard against moral disintegration, associated with the alleged negligence that members of the apparatus identified with the new immigrants. It is difficult to assess whether this allegation of a tendency to let go of hygienic standards was grounded in reality or whether such stories were, instead, intended to act as a deterrent. As Nancy Reagin has persuasively argued, the demand for pristine cleanliness had been a norm deeply internalized by German bourgeois housewives, including German Jews.[52] And as I have noted, the fear of illnesses caused by a lack of hygienic standards was also a primary concern for the immigrants themselves.

This fear of slips in the household routine must be understood in relation to the general discourse in the Yishuv of that time. In the Zionist discourse on homemaking, as Ofra Tene demonstrates, it was the homemaker's main task to create a proper Eretz Israeli home: Zionist, modern, clean, and effective.[53] As Liora Halperin has shown for the sphere of language, the self-conception of the official Yishuv centered on support for the national project through pioneering and sacrifice, and relaxing this commitment was perceived as lazy and feared as a retreat into chaos.[54] In the case of German homemakers, this was phrased in the terminology of "letting go," especially with regard to hygiene. A special issue of the *Mitteilungsblatt*, dedicated to immigrants' health, shared this suspicion that immigrants might "let themselves go." The author Siegfried Kanowitz wrote that "the tendency of immigrants of a higher living standard to let themselves go under worsening conditions is terrifying." If this "tendency to filthiness" became a habit, it could cause a plethora of health dangers. And while the alleged negligence of the immigrants, as detected by social workers and others, was a general critique, directed at all newcomers, it was only women who were actually reprimanded here. Kanowitz urged mothers to clean their homes rigorously in order to keep their children healthy: "The first commandment is absolute cleanliness in the house, even under the most primitive conditions and even given the severe workload of keeping a house clean in a hot and dusty climate, in a tiny apartment, and without domestic help." The author recognized the difficult conditions of homemaking for the new immigrants, but still demanded strict obedience to the rules he presented as normative. His detailed instructions included: "The floor needs to be mopped daily; the apartment always needs to be kept neat; never keep leftovers around; the toilet needs to be cleaned every day; and rooms need to be aired thoroughly."[55] He admitted that striving to fulfill these principles would mean a great deal of trouble, work, and effort for a mother, but on the other hand, she would prevent a lot of grief and harm. This article, like many similar ones, fanned fears that letting the household routine slip could harm families, putting them at grave risk of health problems.

While this discourse was mainly led by the absorbing bodies and social workers, there were other voices, too. Questions of hygiene and illness in relation to nutrition were also a recurring element in advertisements targeting the new immigrants throughout the 1930s and 1940s. They, too, targeted this same weak spot, intimidating homemakers with all kinds of illnesses that they could cause their families and themselves by thoughtless behavior. Whether they were promoting domestic goods, or imported ones, advertisements exploited this fear that the new immigrants had. A German entrepreneur from Tel Aviv emphasized that the imported butter he sold was absolutely pure and without harmful additional ingredients. "Buying butter is a question of trust," he added, in a bid to draw fearful immigrants to his shop.[56] Meged advertised its *tozeret ha'aretz* olive oil with the claim that they only produced oil according to modern scientific standards, warning homemakers that buying a cheaper alternative could endanger their family: "To protect your health, buy only Shemen Oil."[57] Assis claimed in a promotion that responsible mothers would only use that company's products to prepare food for their children.[58] An advertisement for Matok sugar cubes declared: "The sugar cubes sold in loose form throughout the country are subject to dust, fleas, ants, and other squalor. Every careful homemaker who wants to secure her health should from today on request and purchase ONLY the hygienically wrapped CRYSTAL SUGAR CUBES in *tozeret ha'aretz* packages."[59] An especially remarkable tailor-made advertisement, which appeared in the *Mitteilungsblatt* in 1935, showed a professor lecturing in a university auditorium on the health benefits of Shemen Oil.[60]

This discussion of health and hygiene also took place in the Hebrew-speaking press of the Yishuv during those years, where it targeted not only female immigrants but women in general.[61] As Sachlav Stoler-Liss demonstrates, the emphasis on strict hygiene was used to define the proper mother as opposed to the improper mother. The latter was overtly envisioned as being Mizrahi or belonging to the Old Yishuv. As Stoler-Liss further points out, embracing this role of the proper mother was by no means a natural choice but rather the consequence of an "unremitting program of indoctrination, education, and regulation that formed the subtext of the apparently innocuous medical advice provided to them."[62] On the one hand, the absorbing bodies saw German-Jewish women as capable of carrying out the task of being proper mothers and homemakers. As discussed in the framework of the interaction between German-Jewish social workers and Mizrahi families, female immigrants from Germany were regarded favorably for the Zionist project because of their allegedly higher cultural level. In addition, the majority of the social workers handling instruction for German homemakers were either immigrants from Germany themselves or had been trained in Germany. However, the discourse presented here demonstrates that the female immigrants from Germany, too, were constantly reminded and reprimanded that they must never let their household regimen slip, even in the slightest way.

FIGURE 8. Cover illustration of *Wie kocht man in Erez Israel?* by Erna Meyer, Tel Aviv, 1936.

VON DER SEELE BIS ZUR KEHLE: COOKING, COOKBOOKS, AND ZIONISM IN THE KITCHEN

The instructions regarding proper hygiene were part of the broader work that concerned itself with the newly immigrated homemakers from Germany. During the 1930s, this debate was pursued by journalists, nutrition and health experts, social workers, and other members of the absorbing authorities (many of whom were female professionals), as well as by entrepreneurs and advertising companies. Both the advice and the advertisements targeting the German Jews constantly referred to an eager, hardworking homemaker who had to keep her house clean, her family healthy and content, and her food fresh and beneficial. One topic of special concern in this debate was cooking—of all the different aspects of homemaking in Palestine, cooking stood out. On the one hand, it was the realm in which the most confusion existed and where the need for orientation was therefore the greatest. What to eat and how to feed one's family multiple times a day was more crucial for homemakers than how to clean the floor or wash the laundry. On the other hand, it was also the most emotional aspect of homemaking: food choices and taste preferences were directly linked to the immigrants' pasts, to the memories of their loved ones in Germany—and hence to a part of their identity. The question of how the relocated German-Jewish homemakers were supposed to cook in their new homeland was addressed in cookbooks as well as in a plethora of articles, newspaper columns, and brochures published in the 1930s. From the perspective of the absorption apparatus, the transformation of one's diet was connected to other required transformations, as an article called "Cook Palestinian!" made clear: "Time and time again, the Palestinian immigrant is called to undergo economic, occupational, sometimes also psychological transformation, but never is he asked to make a culinary shift, even though the dull continuation of European cuisine in Palestine must cause constant indigestion."[63] This was supposed to change.

One of the most active and famous participants in this debate on cooking in Palestine was Erna Meyer.[64] Meyer herself emigrated from Germany to Palestine in 1933. She had been a well-known expert on home economics and the rationalization of housework, repeatedly publishing on these issues in Germany before she migrated.[65] Once in Palestine, she contributed to the writings of nutritionists and home economics experts who dealt with questions of health and eating patterns from a Zionist perspective. In addition to two cookbooks, Meyer also had a column in the *Mitteilungsblatt,* wrote articles for the *Jüdische Rundschau*, delivered lectures on "Palestinian dishes" with demonstrations and tastings, held cooking classes and counseling hours for German homemakers, and presented homemaking instructions during the 1934 Tel Aviv fair.[66] Meyer's first cookbook after migration, *How to Cook in Palestine*, was published in 1936 in Tel Aviv on behalf of the WIZO.[67] It appeared in German, Hebrew, and English, but notwithstanding the three languages, its main target group was newly immigrated women from Germany. The book was a smashing success with the new immigrants, as Nadja Stein reported in a positive review soon after publication: "The book, long anticipated by the public, created a furor, and soon it could be seen under almost everyone's arm."[68] Erna Meyer became a household name with homemakers, who even requested autographs from her.[69]

How to Cook in Palestine was obtainable at WIZO offices, in bookstores, and in grocery stores for the price of 10 piaster. It included extensive recipes for both warm and cold dishes, instructions on the use of cooking equipment, and articles on health issues. A chapter on the WIZO's activities called upon homemakers to join this women's organization. A German-Hebrew kitchen dictionary was intended to enable women to talk about their housework and communicate with salespeople, in stores and markets, who were not of German origin. Meyer also provided tips on cleaning, laundry, and household maintenance in the book, but cooking instructions were at the center of her advice. Reviewers such as the prominent Zionists Nanny Margulies-Auerbach and Theodor Zlocisti praised the book. Margulies-Auerbach described it as a "beautiful and joyful read," providing healthy and tasty recipes even for inexperienced homemakers. And beyond that, Margulies-Auerbach pointed out the deeper meaning that she saw for the immigrants of homemaking and cooking, in the "preservation of family and community through healthy, inspiring meals, adjusted to climate and income; the preservation of a good mood in bad times through friendly and beautiful things."[70] Zlocisti praised the book in the *Mitteilungsblatt* as part of the "revolution of Jewish cuisine" in Palestine that would, through cooking, include the whole person, "von der Seele bis zur Kehle"—from the soul to the throat.[71]

Meyer's standpoint on cooking in the new homeland was based on the conviction that Zionism needed to be realized in the kitchen, too. The title of her book already expressed this: "how to cook in Palestine" suggests the existence of a normative Palestinian cuisine with a distinct character that homemakers need to adjust to—even though such a national cuisine did not exist at the time. In the first paragraph of her introduction to *How to Cook in Palestine*, Meyer declares: "We housewives must make an attempt to free our kitchen from its Galut traditions.... We should wholeheartedly stand in favor of healthy Palestine cooking. We should foster these ideas not merely because we are compelled to do so, but because we realize that this will help us more than anything else in becoming acclimated to our old-new homeland."[72] Instead of cooking as they did prior to immigration, homemakers are supposed to "free" both themselves and their kitchens from obsolete customs. They are supposed to overcome the diaspora identity through a new way of cooking, thereby entrenching themselves in their new homeland, Palestine. Meyer prompts her readers to acquaint themselves with "healthy Palestine cooking": a cuisine based on the local vegetables and fruits. Immigrant women are expected to overcome their reluctance toward typical Palestinian food staples like eggplants, zucchini, olives, and okra. This produce, Meyer argues, is healthy, inexpensive, and always available in Palestine, and hence provides for countless variations of nutrient-rich dishes. Her book contains an abundance of recipes using these products. Such cooking, she writes, will keep the families of the homemakers healthy and avoid illnesses caused by adherence to European cooking traditions in Palestine. (These illnesses were also discussed by other authors, such as the nutritionist Heti Horwitz-Schiller, who warned of kidney stones, acidosis, and gastrointestinal illnesses if the immigrants did not change their diet.[73]) Typical German dishes, rich in fat and meat, are to be avoided altogether, and the classical ingredients of German cuisine, such as potatoes, which were often expensive in Palestine, should be replaced by cheaper and easily accessible alternatives like bulgur or rice. Butter, finally, should be replaced by olive oil: the brands Shemen and Meged are often specifically recommended in her recipes.[74]

Because Meyer was an active proponent of the rationalization of homemaking, all the dishes she suggested were selected according to their nutritional value, taste, cost efficiency, and how filling they were. Both in texts and illustrations, the housewife is urged to work as professionally and efficiently as possible, saving her time, strength, and health. (Before Erna Meyer, Greta Turnowsky and Gerda Luft had already called for Zionism to be combined with the rationalization of homemaking in the Yishuv; they organized an exhibition by the WIZO on this subject as early as 1930.[75]) Illustrations in Meyer's book demonstrate, among other things, how to sit or stand correctly while performing certain cooking activities in order to prevent fatigue, exhaustion, and back pain. Erna Meyer was convinced that in Palestine, the rationalization of housework was even more necessary than it had been in Germany, because in Palestine the homemakers were forced to work under worse technical and climatic conditions. For the sake of rationalization and efficiency, she recommended electric stoves despite their price.[76] But because cooking was in fact done mainly on Primus stoves, recipes had to be adjusted accordingly—avoiding complicated and time-consuming dishes—in order to reduce heat and noise and protect the homemaker's health. In her column, Meyer also constantly reminded her readers of the principle of rationalization. She suggested, for example, keeping a book about supplies, or using a chart she had prepared to keep track of weekly consumption of each product, in order to minimize waste of groceries that would not keep due to the climate, in order to deal with the lack of storage possibilities, and in order to decrease vermin.[77]

Meyer made it very clear that in Palestine, homemakers were now responsible not only for their own family but also for the Yishuv as a whole. The homemaker's contribution to the support of the state-in-the-making should be through consumption: "We buy *tozeret ha'aretz*. Of course we do!" she prompted her readers.[78] In the struggle to support the developing national economy of the Yishuv, it was the homemaker's responsibility to "vigorously strive to buy local products" and convince her family to do the same.[79] Because the companies Shemen and Assis had underwritten the publication of Meyer's book, their products are often mentioned by name. In her newspaper column as well, she aimed to educate her readers to demand *tozeret ha'aretz* products while shopping and to decline attempts by shop owners to persuade them to buy foreign products. While *tozeret ha'aretz* consumption was an economic necessity, Meyer also associated these products with health benefits. An example of a meal plan for the summer months according to her guidelines consisted of the following courses. First, for appetizers:

a cold soup made from zucchini or red beets, a fruit soup, a chilled milk soup, or tomatoes and white cheese. For the main course: a vegetarian meal with a filling side dish of rice or pasta and shredded cheese or, alternatively, a filling eggplant dish such as eggplant dumplings. For a meaty main course: beefsteak, because it could be prepared quickly and with little heat. And for dessert: chilled fruit desserts.[80] And finally, for special holiday meals, Meyer suggested inexpensive alternatives to traditional dishes. For Hanukkah, for example, she recommended a "Kmo-Honigkuchen" (as-if-honeycake), based on *tozeret ha'aretz* dates instead of expensive honey.[81]

Meyer acknowledged that homemakers in Palestine were burdened with so many responsibilities that they were often not able to keep up the custom of preparing three-course meals as they had done in Germany. She hence recommended simple, filling meals, such as stews, especially for women living in agricultural villages. Such meals would "leave them time to work in their gardens while still enabling them to feed their families adequately."[82] But Meyer reminded homemakers that beautifully setting the table and serving meals in an appetizing way were also important parts of the meal and should not be neglected.

The cover design of the book reflects its conceptual framework. It shows a woman cooking with a Primus stove while intently reading her copy of *How to Cook in Palestine*. Next to her can be seen fresh Palestinian vegetables and fruits, beautifully arranged on a plate. On a balcony against a Palestinian landscape, her family, a husband and two children, waits for her to serve the food. This illustration reflects the conditions of the time of the book's publication, 1936: woman, man, and children have immigrated as an intact family—no one is missing, as they will be in later years due to the National Socialist terror and the increasing difficulties of receiving certificates from the British authorities. Nor has this family been forced to live and eat in a single room, as was the case for those immigrants who had already experienced downward social mobility. And this woman, despite the changes in her cooking, is preparing and serving the food all on her own: neither her children nor her husband assist her. This detail, too, is in line with the contents of *How to Cook in Palestine*. While calling for a radical transformation of cooking and consumption, Meyer continued to perceive homemaking, in a conservative way, as a female task. And although she addressed the many hardships of homemakers, men were not addressed as active partners in the housework. Meyer preserved a traditional vision of labor that kept women in the kitchen, but at the same time, she politicized the seemingly "private" practices of consuming and cooking. Thus, the newly immigrated homemakers were assigned an important role in the nation-building project. In her second German cookbook, *Menu in Times of Crisis*, Meyer further emphasized this approach, suggesting that homemakers should create a national Palestinian dish made completely from local products. Her proposal was bulgur with tomato sauce and white cheese—satisfying the need to support the developing Jewish economy as well as the guidelines of a healthy, filling meal according to nutritional science and the rationalization concept, because this dish was easy and quick to prepare.[83]

Erna Meyer's "healthy Palestine cooking" was a new creation. While she made use of produce that grew in Palestine, she provided no recipes of Mizrahi or Sephardi, let alone Arab, origin, and neither did other authors who were published in the *Jüdische Rundschau* or the *Mitteilungsblatt*. Nadja Stein, who was also active in the cooking debate, went even further than simple omission, stating that Oriental food was "in stark contrast to our Western- and continental-oriented eating culture and in many aspects also contrary to the insights of our modern nutritional science."[84] As with questions of hygiene, here as well arguments that were presumably scientific served as a way to define the kitchen as a place of boundary construction, with the goal of Westernizing the Yishuv. Eastern European cuisine, too, was criticized as unhealthy, because, as Meyer and others argued, it used too much fat and too few vegetables. Meyer proposed a completely new Palestinian cuisine, using *tozeret ha'aretz* ingredients and based on modern nutritional science, the concept of the rationalization of the household, and Western hygiene. She dissociated it from Jewish diaspora cooking (whether Western or Eastern European) as well as from the culinary influences of the Old Yishuv, non-European Jews, and the Arabs of Palestine. This was in line with the general Zionist discourse on cooking of those years, which aimed to create a Zionist cuisine identified as Western, healthy, and scientific while simultaneously delegitimizing both local and Eastern European influences.[85]

The absorption apparatus, with its publications on "healthy Palestine cooking," was not the only force attempting to influence and instruct homemaking in Palestine. Companies and entrepreneurs also addressed German homemakers in their household instructions and advertisements, in an effort to promote their goods and services. They, too, intervened in the debate over how homemakers should cook and consume in Palestine. And these private initiatives also argued that they wanted to relieve the burden carried by female immigrants, providing them assistance in the form of guidebooks and cooking instructions, though not necessarily from a Zionist perspective. The most prominent example of such attempts was *The Household Encyclopedia for Erez Israel*. As its subtitle revealed, it aimed to be a "guide for housekeeping, health, and education." The *Encyclopedia* was published in German and Hebrew by the advertising company Pirsum Sahavy.[86] This company was founded by the German entrepreneur Ludwig Goldschmidt, who immigrated to Palestine in 1935 and subsequently changed his name to Sahavy. The four-volume *Encyclopedia* was handed out free of charge between 1939 and 1940 to grocery store customers in Tel Aviv.

The *Encyclopedia* differed in many respects from *How to Cook in Palestine*. Firstly, while many recipes were presented throughout the book, it also included other fields of domesticity. Hundreds of entries, listed alphabetically from A to Z, dealt with such subjects as cooking, cleaning, and household maintenance, but also beauty, health, parenting, marriage, and etiquette. Advertisements appeared next to the relevant topics (for example, a painkiller would be advertised next to the entry on headaches). What constituted the housewife's crucial tasks was understood differently here than in Meyer's book; the *Encyclopedia* also included the traditional outward-facing tasks of a middle-class German homemaker. For example, readers were asked to take care of their appearance through gymnastics, cosmetics, clothes, and the right accessories, as well as being advised on how to properly host and entertain guests. In the introduction, the publisher described the job of the homemaker like this:

> It is the housewife who is responsible for the happiness of the family. Today, her work is harder than ever before—but there is also no task that is more fulfilling for a woman today than to be the lady of the house. The *Household Encyclopedia* aims to be her loyal assistant in this endeavor.... All the advice and information that the lady of the house might need, she can find here.[87]

FIGURE 9. Cover illustration of *Das Haushalts-lexikon für Erez-Israel*, published by Sahavy Advertising, Tel Aviv, 1939/1940.

The *Encyclopedia* put the relation of the homemaker to her husband and children in the center. The responsibility of the "lady of the house" was caring for her family, not caring for the nation or the land. Stating that housework was "harder than ever before" hinted at the double burden of housework and additional employment that was common among German immigrant women. However, the publisher constructed homemaking as the most desirable task for women, even in times of crisis. This responsibility of the homemaker was expressed throughout the book. Thus, cooking was described as "one of the most responsible tasks and the main basis for the well-being of the family."[88] Aversion and reluctance to cooking, the *Encyclopedia* indicated, occurred mostly among women who felt insecure about their cooking skills. It therefore suggested that they take a cooking class in order to overcome this aversion.

One remarkable feature of the *Encyclopedia* is the fact that, despite its name, large parts of it are completely lacking any indication that this knowledge was to be used in Palestine. This is also reflected in the cover of the book, which shows pictures evoking a German middle-class household, such as a beautiful living room and a roast on a well-laid table. Nothing in these images links the publication to Palestine: no palm trees, no Primus, no eggplants. This tendency also manifests itself in the recipes: eggplants and zucchini are not even mentioned; and while it is explained what olives are, they are not used in any of the recipes. Instead, there are recipes for classic German and Central European dishes, such as spätzle (a Southern German pasta dish), roast with gravy, or real Vienna schnitzel. Dessert suggestions include apple pie, pancakes, Sachertorte, and of course whipped cream (*Schlagsahne*). There are hardly any references to adjusting dishes because of the climate, the wish to avoid imported products, the aim of saving homemakers time and energy, or the increasingly difficult economic situation of the immigrants. On occasion, some remarks do take a reduced budget into consideration, for example when olive oil is mentioned as a cheaper alternative to butter, in recipes for cheap spreads and recipes using substitute ingredients, or in suggestions about how to repair household devices instead of throwing them away. A few entries deal with the use of kerosene and give instructions on how to cool food without a refrigerator (namely, by storing it in a vessel with cold salt water). There are also some references to the double workday of many homemakers, for example in an advertisement for a Tel Aviv sausage stand: "Vacation from the household: every housewife should take time off once a week—without cooking or doing the dishes. The best way for her to get some rest is a meal at the sausage stand at 8 Ben Yehuda Street, where you can eat as well and as cheaply as at home!"[89] The concept of the rationalization of homemaking is apparent here, in passing, as well; women are asked, for example, to keep track of the family budget by noting all expenses and to work more efficiently, for example, by sitting when ironing.[90]

While the book contains few hints that it is intended for use in Palestine, there is advice throughout the book about evening dresses, cocktails, food, and etiquette that are probably more an expression of the memories of the bourgeois life lived back in Germany than any reflection of the actual conditions in Palestine, which for many immigrants were restricted by their proletarianization.

Unlike Meyer's book, the *Encyclopedia* was the commercial initiative of a company, rather than the publication of a political group of the Yishuv. Goldschmidt-Sahavy did not feel particularly obligated to Zionist values, and hence the book advertises not only domestic but also imported goods; the meaning of *tozeret ha'aretz* products is not specifically explained. Given the eclectic character of the *Encyclopedia*, some entries and advertisements even contradict each other. For example, one entry deals with olive oil and its advantages over butter, while an entry on the next page praises butter as one of the healthiest products available.[91]

Like Sahavy's *Encyclopedia*, which specifically advertised products to German homemakers and took the form of homemaking instructions, the advertisements in the *Mitteilungsblatt* also often used the language and style of cooking instructions in their promotions. Assis, for example, published a series of advertisements in 1935 and 1936 that were designed to look like a homemaking advice column:

> Being a housewife in Palestine is not easy, especially when you have just come to the country. The climate, attitude toward work, and way of life are all different and unfamiliar. This is why we believe that the practical suggestions and recipes that we will publish here regularly will be welcomed by homemakers. These are recipes . . . from the most experienced and successful nutrition specialists in the country![92]

All the recipes and hints published in the column recommended Assis products, of course.

The homemaking discourse of the 1930s, consisting of cookbooks, guidebooks, and other forms of instruction, did not finally provide any definitive answer for how to cook in Palestine. Both in *How to Cook in Palestine* and the *Encyclopedia*, however, homemaking is charged with meaning above and beyond the mere execution of household tasks. Depending on whether Zionist ideology and its demands are embraced or treated with indifference, contrary directives are given to the homemakers. Erna Meyer's position clearly reflects the Zionist ideology and the demands of the absorbing Yishuv society for the transformation of the new immigrants. Healthy Palestine cuisine, the Zionist version of homemaking, would enable cheaper, healthier, and more efficient cooking. At the same time, it would allow the homemakers to become fully integrated and valuable members of Yishuv society and part of the nation-building project. In Meyer's publications, the kitchen is constructed as a place of change and of a new identity. *The Household Encyclopedia*, meanwhile, did not demand any ideological contribution to the nation-building project, as it was indifferent to Zionism. It addressed homemakers mainly as consumers who could choose whatever pleased them from its offers. In contrast to Meyer's monolithic style, the *Encyclopedia* was a conglomerate of authors, styles, and ideological positions. Through its conception of homemaking and cooking, it encouraged its readers to preserve the German-Jewish cuisine in Palestine. The attitude expressed in the *Encyclopedia* indicated a perception of the kitchen as a place of memory and tradition. This attitude can also be read as a refusal, on the part of some of the immigrants, to accept the demands of the receiving society for radical transformation and all-encompassing change.

HAZILIM BURGER OR WIENER SCHNITZEL? THE IMMIGRANTS' CUISINE

Guidebooks provide insights into the norms that women were supposed to follow in their homemaking. As normative literature, they lay down rules for the allegedly private realm of housework and nutrition within a family. The characteristic element of this directive literature is the fact that it simultaneously both constructs and reflects societal norms. These guidebooks for newly immigrated homemakers in Palestine reflect the different positions—not only on homemaking but also on absorption in general—that existed in different sectors of 1930s Yishuv society. These guidebooks indicate that women, because they were perceived both by the absorption apparatus and by their own families as responsible for homemaking, found themselves pressured by conflicting demands: to preserve, on the one hand, but also to change, on the other. However, these publications cannot shed light on the actual implementation of these norms. After all, the immigrants cooked in their own kitchens, with their own pots and pans, and ate off their own dishes, out of the public eye.

So what did homemakers actually cook in Palestine? In an article in the *Jüdische Rundschau*, Heti Horwitz-Schiller described the food preferences of German immigrants in Palestine in these words: "They want Brussels sprouts and potatoes, ... and instead of eggplants and zucchini they demand sausages, poultry, and meat."[93] Indeed, at least in their first years in the country, the food served in immigrant families remained definitely German. Regarding the meals prepared in Shavey Zion, a German-Jewish enclave close to Nahariya that had been established almost entirely by German immigrants from the village of Rexingen, one member noted in his diary that the cooking remained "Rexingen-style: Pretty often and pretty much meat. There are Rexingers who are picky, who do not want to change their habits; they do not eat rice, no tomatoes, let alone olives."[94]

This example also hints at the fact that the question of what was cooked depended not only on the intentions of the homemakers but also on how accepting their families were, or how much they complained. Ruth L. remembers that while her mother's cooking was adapted due to the heat, at least on Friday evenings for Sabbath dinner, the dishes stayed German: "Every Friday evening we had our family evening, as we called it. My uncle came with his wife, and my grandfather and friends of the family, and we ate herring with potato salad."[95] Lieselotte R. recalls that she tried to prepare lighter meals for her family after they moved to Sde Warburg, "but my husband needed his fried potatoes every day, it just did not work without fried potatoes."[96]

The menus of restaurants, cafés, and lunch diners, which were established by and for German immigrants, also of course catered to German tastes. That was why the immigrants visited them in the first place. Advertisements for German-style lunch (*Mittagstisch*) venues explicitly mentioned that "German cuisine" or "German home cooking" was offered.[97] This included lots of potatoes and meat and side dishes of vegetables and salads (but hardly any eggplants, okra, or zucchini), as well as typical desserts such as compote and cake. Due to the prices of ingredients, different cooking methods, and the climate, the recipes were usually altered from their original forms, but they were still recognizable as German cuisine.[98] In spite of the heavy promotion of the Shemen brand of olive oil, butter did not disappear—not from the immigrants' kitchens and not from the newly established bakeries that prepared German cakes and pastries, either.[99] Advertisements for bakeries and cafes explicitly promoted their products as using butter instead of oil. This was a question of taste, but also of price: many homemakers did not buy the *tozeret ha'aretz* butter from Tnuva, preferring instead the cheaper, imported butter from Poland, Holland, or Australia.[100]

It is not only the produce that was cooked but also what did not get used that is relevant. In addition to Levantine food staples such as the unpopular eggplants, hummus, and tahini, this also included garlic, which some German Jews abhorred because of its association with Eastern European Jews.[101] Eva W. recalls how her mother gathered recipes from her domestic helpers to learn cooking, because when she arrived she had only known how to prepare one dish—pot roast. One new recipe that she tried to master in vain for a long time was pickled cucumbers. "One day, the *oseret* [servant] told her that she needed to use garlic for the pickled cucumbers. We had never had garlic in our kitchen. And then, she brought this piece of garlic home, and my father came into the kitchen and saw it and threw it right out of the window."[102] This example is very telling: the mother, responsible for food preparation, and inspired by her domestic worker, wanted to try out a new dish. The father, who was not involved in the cooking at all, was not willing to accept this change and threw the abhorred ingredient out of the kitchen. In his eyes, this use of garlic was a reprehensible act of assimilation to the Ostjuden. Others also referred to the culinary conflict between the German immigrants and Eastern European veteran residents. An article in the *Jüdische Rundschau* stated jokingly that the potato fritters served in German immigrant cafés were so tasty that even Ostjuden came to eat them and were willing to make peace with the disliked Yekkes because they enjoyed their fritters so much.[103] A Meged advertisement, using the headline "Strudel oder Apfelkuchen?" took the same line, joking about the conflict between new immigrants and veteran residents in terms of culinary preferences.[104]

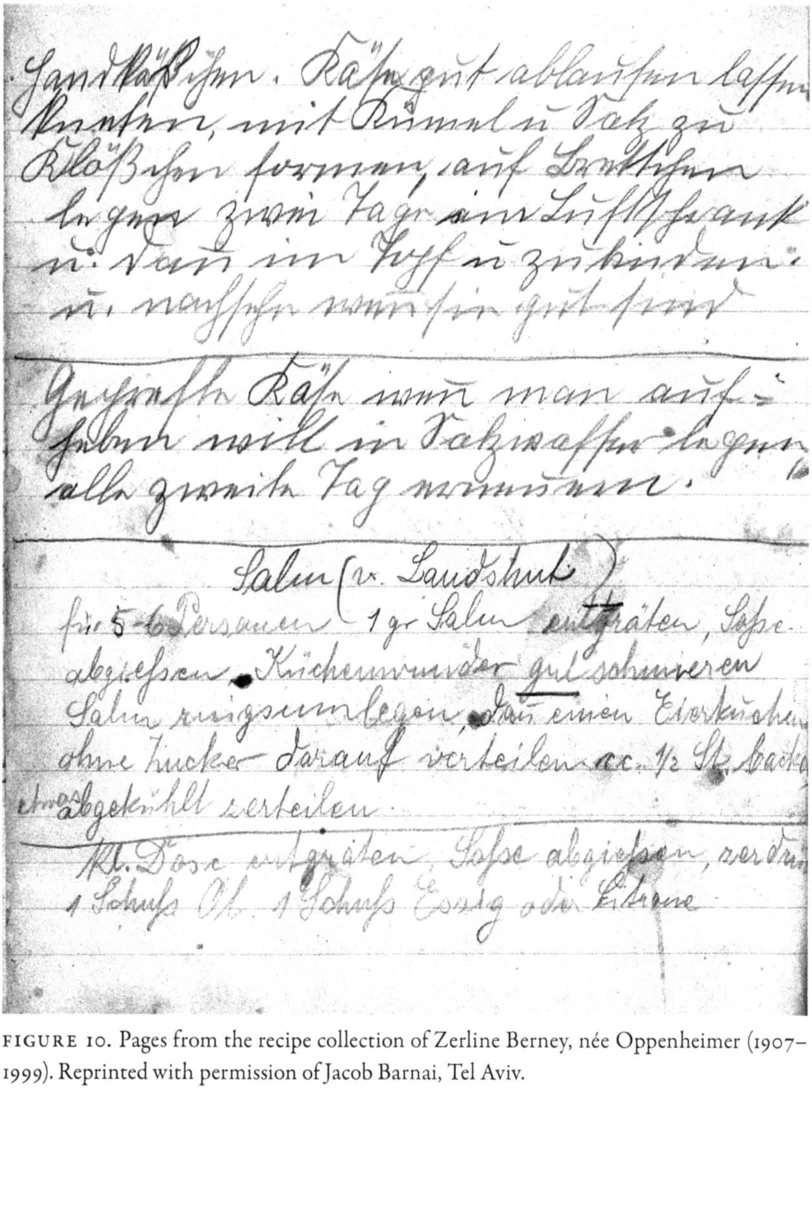
Sandkäßchen. Käse gut ablaufen lassen kneten, mit Kümmel u. Salz zu Klößchen formen, auf Brettchen legen zum Tage im Luftschrank u. dann im Topf u. zudecken u. nachsehen wenn sie gut sind

Gequellte Käse wenn man aufheben will in Salzwasser legen alle zweite Tag wechseln.

Salm (v. Landshut)
für 5-6 Personen 1 gr Salm entgräten, Safte abgießen. Küchenwunder gut schmieren Salm ringsum legen, dann einen Eierkuchen ohne Zucker darauf verteilen ca. 1/2 St. backen
etwas abgekühlt verteilen
Kl. Dose entgräten Safte abgießen, verdünnen
1 Schuß Öl 1 Schuß Essig oder Zitrone

FIGURE 10. Pages from the recipe collection of Zerline Berney, née Oppenheimer (1907–1999). Reprinted with permission of Jacob Barnai, Tel Aviv.

Orangenrecept (v. Nußbaum)

cc 8 große Orangen (nicht geschält) werden 2-3 Stunden in Salzwasser gelegt, dann dünn geschnitten, die Kerne entfernt, dann die Früchte mit der Schale 24 Std. in kaltem Wasser stehen lassen. Dann kocht man die Früchte mit dem Wasser cc 1 St. in löslich wieder 24 Std. stehen, mischt sie mit Zucker, Kilo auf Kilo. Kocht die Menge noch 1x1 Std. füllt sie in Gläser. 2 Zitronen dazu.

Ein gutes Rezept. 4 Orangen 2 Zitronen
(Sanitätsrath)
2 Grapefruit ½ Kaffel Zucker Äpfel geschält, Läuschen daran lassen klein geschnitten. [...]

Sandwich Aschhaumschalen. Die Schalen 3 x 24 Stunden in Wasser legen, nach je 24 Std. frisches Wasser, dann mit frischem Wasser 20 Minuten kochen lassen. Wasser ab[...]en Schnitze schneiden. Soviel Schalen so viel Zucker. Zu 1 Pfd Schalen etwa ½ Weinglas Wasser kochen bis Zucker eingekocht 2½ bis 3 Std.

An important group of sources for shedding light on immigrant cuisine are private recipe collections. It was common among German-Jewish homemakers to compile such private collections for personal use. Such recipe collections seldom survive—they were usually heavily used and were splashed, stained, and the like. But Zerline Berney's recipe collection was one that did make it through intact. Berney, née Oppenheimer (1907–1999), came from a religious Zionist family from southern Germany. At the end of 1932, before immigrating to Palestine, she married Friedrich Berney. In Palestine, Berney lived first in Ramataim, but in 1935, she and her husband moved to Sde Ya'akov, a religious agricultural village where many members of her family eventually settled.[105]

While still in Würzburg, Zerline Berney started to write recipes down in a notebook in preparation for her immigration to Palestine; throughout the 1930s and into the 1940s, she continued to gather recipes in her notebook. Her collection is composed of a variety of materials. While still in Germany, she wrote typical German and German-Jewish recipes and fine baking recipes in the first part of the book. These were apparently gathered from family members so that she would be able to prepare these meals in Palestine after immigration. They are written in beautiful handwriting. She also glued in many recipes clipped from German newspapers; in some cases, she later noted possible adjustments next to the recipe so that it could be made using the produce of Palestine and the simpler cooking equipment she now possessed. Her collection also includes notes on home remedies (for example, for burned skin or warts) as well as ideas for homemade cleaning solutions. In Palestine, while the majority of Berney's recipes remained committed to German cuisine (with lots of cauliflower, potatoes, peas, and specific dishes like *Jägertorte* ["hunter's cake"], herring salad with sour cream, and mustard pickles), small changes almost immediately become visible. She started to use the measurements used in Palestine (rottel and ounce), and she altered traditional recipes with substitutions for ingredients that were apparently not available in Palestine: making "Pischinger Törtchen" with arrack instead of rum, chocolate cake with dates instead of honey, cheesecake with white cheese instead of the German *Quark* (curd cheese), and the like. She also noted alterations that were made necessary because of cooking with a Primus stove.

A few pages from Berney's time in Sde Ya'akov are dedicated to recipes that make use of eggplants and zucchini, using their Hebrew names, *hazilim* and *kishuim*, as well as olives. First, Berney wrote down how to prepare these previously unknown vegetables: "peel, cut into slices, salt, then let them rest outside in the sun." Then she wrote down ways to use the produce in her cooking. A lot of her recipes were clearly inspired by Erna Meyer. Berney apparently wrote them down in order to document the recipes she had mastered and that came out well, in order to be able to repeat them. Her recipes clearly document the abundant supply of eggplants, tomatoes, grapes, and oranges in Sde Ya'akov, inspiring many recipes such as *hazilim* [eggplant] cutlets, *hazilim* salad, and *hazilim* with hard-boiled eggs or with mayonnaise. Countless orange recipes document their use in fruit salads, cake, jam, syrup, and fruit soup. Many recipes are vegetarian, reflecting the high price of meat, while vegetables were much cheaper and always available toward the end of the 1930s. Next to some recipes, Berney noted the year when she first cooked them ("1938 cooked for the first time") or made comments ("very good jam!"). Quick, everyday recipes for steamed zucchini are listed next to complicated, time-consuming cakes. The number of cakes, tarts, cookies, and pastry in the collection is stunning, especially given the cooking conditions. For baking, the Berneys had built an outside stone oven, which saw heavy use.

Berney also added recipes to her collection that she apparently wrote down while visiting friends—there are recipes that had been written on the backs of envelopes, on restaurant bills, and the like. She also included recipes that relatives, friends, and neighbors had provided, sometimes within letters that she then inserted into the book as they were sent to her (for example, an "especially delicious yeast cake" or "Sara's fish recipe"), or in other cases that she then copied into her book with a note about who had given it to her: fish soup from the Landskron family, the Berneys' neighbors; an orange dessert recipe from the Nussbaums, in-laws from Haifa; various recipes from her sisters-in-law; many jam recipes from Sara; Celine's tomato paste; and Fanny's cake. All of these recipes were discovered by Berney during her first years in Palestine, apparently during family gatherings, and she wrote down the recipes for the ones she liked in order to be able to prepare them herself.

Because Berney only wrote these recipes for her own use, the instructions are informal and the measurements often vague ("plenty" or "as desired"), with visual cues ("stir until the dough drips from the spoon in thick drops"). It is worth noting that once she was in Palestine, the handwriting and arrangements of Berney's recipes also changed: from beautiful handwriting and carefully arranged entries back in Würzburg to hastily scrawled entries in Sde Ya'akov. Given the workload of homemakers in agricultural villages, discussed earlier, this is not surprising. Zerline Berney's cookbook reflects an eclectic cuisine, a symbiosis of both cherished family recipes from Germany and newly acquired recipes using food staples of the Levant. Her cuisine in Palestine, which has been preserved for posterity through her private cookbook, combines memory and change. For instance, "Apfelstrudel mit Schlagsahne" coexists with a newly created date and honey cake; *hazilim* steaks appear next to German potato soup. Changes are made as needed; a new product is tried and added to the stock of the familiar recipes from Germany in an ongoing process.

CONCLUSION

"Wie kann dieser Haushalt flutschen / Ohne Mutschen, ohne Mutschen?"[106] ("How can this household run smoothly, without Mutschen [a nickname], without Mutschen?") asked the immigrant Fritz Levinson, in a song praising the housework of his aunt, Minna Baer, who lived in Haifa with her husband, the physician Ludwig Baer. In the song, Levinson included Minna's many different tasks within the household: cooking, cleaning, caring for her children, paying bills and welcoming visitors, as well as her additional work in her husband's medical office. This poem and many others like it, as I discussed in chapter 3 in the framework of the discourse of "women of valor," praised the female immigrants. In the Yishuv of the 1930s, there was no lack either of praise for the practice of homemaking or of attention to it, as I have discussed in this chapter. Housework was not an invisible and private practice but highly visible and publicly discussed, from a variety of different positions. Immigrant cuisine was exposed to many demands, requests, and warnings, from social workers, cooking instructors, shop owners, and advertising companies, as well as from family members. This cuisine was, however, also enriched by unknown produce, and new and old recipes from cookbooks or relatives. Cooking was also a social process: recipes were exchanged between friends and relatives, in letters and in private conversation; people learned from each other. Cooking was hence at once a place of memory (remembering a former life in Germany and surely, also, the family members left behind) and change. However, there is no evidence that men started to share the burden of the housework. Apparently, despite all the changes that homemaking underwent in Palestine, the notion that women were solely responsible for it was not challenged. The question of *who* should cook in Palestine was not raised.

From the side of the absorbing apparatus, the home, along with the homemaking practices it entailed, was considered to constitute an important site of nation-building and national responsibility. As such, it was subjected to scrutiny and control. From the immigrants' side, however, the kitchen was also seen as a place to be protected—as a place to preserve heritage, identity, and community.

FIVE

Qualities That the Present Age Demands

GENDER AND THE IMMIGRANT FAMILY

DURING THEIR LAST MOMENTS ON board, just before landing, the passengers immigrating to Palestine streamed onto the deck to try and spot their loved ones in the waiting crowd at the harbor. Those families that had not immigrated all together experienced the arrival of the later immigrants as an emotional reunion, a final closing of the circle of chain immigration. For Shlomit Mueller, who along with her mother had followed her father to Palestine after months of painful separation, the long-awaited reunion remained etched in her mind:

> On September 15, 1933, we left the "Roma" in the harbor of Haifa as a refugee family. I still recall the yellow-and-white-checkered linen dress I wore. My father wore short khaki trousers and a khaki-colored hat on his head. When he saw us,... he started crying and almost fainted because we looked so gaunt, pale, and frightened. And with this, a new chapter of our life began.[1]

This account of their reunion records the minutest details, including the clothes they were wearing: Shlomit was in a dress from Germany, while her father was already sporting khaki trousers, the "uniform" of Palestinian men. For Shlomit, this moment signified the beginning of a new phase of her life. The physical part of the immigration was now over, and the process of absorption began. For families, this entailed unique dynamics. The absorbing bodies considered the German immigration to Palestine family immigration: about two-thirds of the immigrants came as families. However, not all of these entered Palestine together. As depicted above, chain immigration had physical and psychological ramifications for the women and children staying behind, as well as for the men who preceded them. After arrival, facing the process of absorption together, as a family, yielded many benefits to immigrants, such as not being alone in an unknown country, having familiar faces around, being able to continue speaking in one's mother tongue, sharing memories from the earlier life, and, generally, providing a support system. But migration as a family unit also fundamentally influenced relations and dynamics, both between spouses and between children and their parents.[2]

Families were also a central concern for the absorbing bodies in Palestine and for the Mandate power—family cohesion was considered crucial to the immigrants' successful integration, and signs of potential disintegration were therefore scrutinized. This chapter discusses the significance of families in the migration process from both macro and micro perspectives. First, it analyzes the effects of immigration law on families. Second, it demonstrates how immigration regulations and expected gender roles in Palestine both led to changed marrying strategies among the immigrants. And finally, this chapter addresses post-immigration family dynamics, both between spouses and between parents and children.

CHAIN MIGRATION AND FAMILY REUNIFICATIONS

While most German Aliyah immigrants came within family units, the family members did not necessarily all immigrate at the same time; they often arrived successively, in a chain migration, as in the case of Shlomit Mueller.[3] Especially in the first years of the immigration wave, from 1933 to 1936, husbands often immigrated before their wives and children, who followed several months later.[4] Permission for other family members, such as parents or siblings, to come as well could later be requested using category D certificates, for dependents reuniting with their family. These policies were based on the British Mandate authorities' understanding of gender and family status as well as, to a lesser degree, the gendered perception of the Jewish Agency, which allocated the labor permits. The British intended the need for natural growth within the community to be achieved by allowing men and women to enter in equal numbers. However, most women immigrated as dependents, while most men immigrated as permit holders. In each year of the German Aliyah, men were the majority of the immigrants to Palestine. The difference was especially pronounced from 1933 to 1935, when 54 percent of the immigrants were men and only 46 percent were women. This was due to the Jewish Agency's allocation of labor certificates mostly to men.[5]

Many married men emigrated first, without their spouses, in order to establish themselves abroad before their families joined them. This practice was widespread among immigrants arriving on capitalist certificates. The men came to Palestine first, searching for job opportunities, housing, settlement, investment options, schooling, etc., to facilitate their relatives' subsequent ar-

FIGURE 11. Emigrants on a ship to Palestine, 1935; Source: Jewish Museum Berlin, 2008/5/57, Donation of Orna Leshem. Reprinted with permission.

rival and integration. While this process aimed to make integration easier, it was driven by and could reinforce a power imbalance between the sexes. It followed a logic that assigned tasks in the new homeland, including the decision about where and how to live, to men, while women were left to deal with issues in the old homeland. During this period, men who went ahead were free from the pressure of persecution; meanwhile, the women dealt with the authorities in Germany as well as the breaking up of the household and sometimes also of businesses, while simultaneously performing domestic care work. After the 1938 pogrom, wives of imprisoned men arranged for their release and enabled them to flee while the women themselves stayed in Germany to break up the household and negotiate the terms of emigration with authorities, consulates, and shipping agencies. As Marion Kaplan argues, this behavior was based on the conviction that men were in greater danger and that even the Nazis would retain traditional respect toward women.[6]

Due to British immigration law, the women remaining behind were completely dependent on their husbands. The German-Jewish immigration apparatus never explicitly suggested separate immigration; the immigrants came up with this process themselves. Individuals within the German Department did sometimes recommend that fathers arrive six months before their families in order to settle in and search for a job.[7] But the Palestine office in Berlin, as well as the HOG, also warned of the risks of separate immigration. If the immigrants did not negotiate with the British consul before leaving Germany, it could have grave consequences for the dependents. If, when a husband departed, he did not specify that he intended for his family to join him, his dependents would not be allowed to enter Palestine. In 1934, after a year of immigration from Germany, a solution was reached: the certificate owner had to make sure that upon his departure, visas were issued for all his family members remaining behind; his dependents then received a copy of the capitalist (category A) certificate.[8] In addition, upon his arrival in Palestine, the family father had to inform the authorities when and at what port his family would subsequently immigrate. While the legal situation for families immigrating separately could be solved in this way, other problems caused by the practice continued: the spouse remaining behind had to face a period alone, in increasingly hostile Germany, as a single parent, in addition to enduring the effects of a months-long separation.

An especially difficult legal situation arose when men entered Palestine on tourist visas but with the intention of staying, becoming legal residents, and then requesting permission for their family members to join them. Palestine residents could request dependent certificates for other family members, including wives, parents and grandparents, children and grandchildren, siblings, nephews, and nieces. But tourists had no such secure legal status: their own position was vulnerable, and if caught with an expired visa, they faced deportation. At the same time, their families in Germany literally depended on them, as married women could only enter Palestine as dependents. More than twenty thousand tourists entered Palestine from Germany between 1933 and 1938; several thousand of them stayed on illegally after their visas expired. Authorization to settle in Palestine, with the accompanying right to request dependent certificates for their wives, was eventually granted to 3,228 tourists from Germany. When tourists applied for residency, a family reunion was seen as the most important reason for granting them legal status.[9]

In the German Aliyah, the largest group of immigrants considered illegal by the British were these "tourists" who overstayed their permits. One of these was Miriam R.'s father. In the summer of 1933, he was in imminent danger of being arrested in Germany and therefore went to Palestine on a tourist certificate. Back home, his wife and their daughters (Miriam and her sister) broke up the household in a hurry and then fled via Czechoslovakia to Geneva. From there, they were supposed to follow him as soon as possible. But as a tourist, not yet a legal resident, he was not able to sponsor them as his dependents. They ended up stranded in Switzerland for seven months, with no legal way to follow him and no possibility of returning to Germany. With almost no money left and nothing but summer clothing, Miriam, her mother, and sister had to endure the winter in Switzerland before her father could obtain the necessary documents for them to finally reunite in Palestine.[10] Her father in Palestine, meanwhile, could only worry, powerless to help his dependents. The ramifications of these separations for the fathers in Palestine can also be seen in Erwin Mansbach's story. Mansbach, too, had entered Palestine on a tourist certificate in 1933, while his wife and children stayed in Germany. Not yet a legal resident himself, he could not sponsor their immigration. In a letter to Georg Landauer of the German Department, a personal acquaintance of his, Mansbach described his ordeal:

> You see, I have already been separated from my family for seven months, and one might think that one day more or less no longer makes any difference. But the truth is that both my wife and I are desperate. My wife's letters are terrible. She isn't really a complainer, but her nerves are truly frayed. I, on the other hand, suffer from nervous diarrhea, alternating with a total inability to eat. On the outside, I try to keep up—and so does my wife—attempting to appear calm. I write you this because I need to vent my anger and because I ask you to push the claim for my visa as soon as possible. From the moment of the approval until the reunion with my family, it will take several weeks anyhow.... I did not work for the Zionist movement in order to gain benefits, but now I beg you to let me and my family live here.[11]

The forced separation of spouses had serious consequences for both partners, as these examples show. Mansbach suffered severe psychosomatic symptoms due to his worries about his wife in Nazi Germany, who was close to her breaking point. His legal status was not only his problem, but it shaped the fate of his dependent family members. Georg Landauer, even though not technically in charge of immigration permits, personally interceded with the Palestine Office in Berlin on Mansbach's behalf, asking them to speed up proceedings in his case and to send an immigration certificate to Cyprus for Mansbach and his family: "Even though visa cases don't belong in this department, countless individuals turn to me with their requests. In most cases I have to reject them, but the following cases I pass on to you because they seem to be urgent."[12] Because Mansbach was a long-term affiliate of the Zionist movement, he received the help he desired, unlike many others in similar situations. Thus, his case also demonstrates the successful use he made of his affiliation with a crucial network, which was invaluable for the reunification of his family.

British immigration policy also required some parents to separate from their children: parents could not include children over the age of seventeen as dependents on their capitalist (category A) certificate. The only exception was for children with chronic illnesses who were completely dependent on their parents. Ilse B., who immigrated as a fourteen-year-old with her younger sister and her parents, but without her eighteen-year old sister, due to these regulations, described the ramifications: "It was terrible for my mother to leave my older sister behind. . . . For two years, my mother cried daily; it was horrible. We had to board the train, and my mother had to leave her daughter behind, not knowing if she would ever see her again."[13] Children over seventeen who stayed behind in Germany then needed to obtain a labor certificate of their own, because the British authorities perceived them as seeking their own employment, not secured through the family income. This policy became an issue primarily for unmarried daughters. The difficulty for Ilse B.'s parents of leaving their daughter behind must be seen in the light of the prevailing attitude toward unmarried women: because young women were seen as needing protection, it was easier to leave sons behind.

The German Department had to deal with the fallout of this practice in the form of letters of complaint, and in some cases, it interceded with the Immigration Department on behalf of unmarried daughters. In some individual instances, if the family owned several thousand pounds, daughters were allowed to enter as if they were independent capitalist certificate holders. In other cases, Landauer himself advocated for young women who were daughters of veteran Zionists.[14] While not questioning the discrimination against women in general, he argued that these women had received no vocational training and constituted an integral part of the family and household and should therefore be allowed to immigrate with their parents.[15] Those young women who received no such preferential treatment simply had to stay behind. Because labor certificates had long waiting lists, and because the Jewish Agency preferred to allocate the labor certificates to young men rather than young women, it could take years until a family was finally reunited.

It was not only spouses and children, but also elderly parents and other family members who were supposed to follow the main family wage earner. If they could not obtain their own capitalist or labor certificates, there was the option of family reunions through dependent certificates. In general, dependent certificates, to be requested through the Immigration Department, were limited to particular groups. The dependents needed to be wholly financially dependent, and the applicant had to be able to provide for them once in Palestine. Gender, age, and marital status were crucial in the dependent category, as can be seen from the regulations. Dependents had to be under eighteen or over fifty-five, and they could not have their own independent means. Requests could be made for the applicant's wife; parents or grandparents of the applicant and his wife; the applicant's fiancée; the applicant's and/or his wife's sons, grandsons, and nephews only if they were under eighteen or disabled and unable to support themselves. Certificates for the daughters, granddaughters, sisters, or nieces of the applicant and/or his wife could be requested only if they were unmarried, widowed, divorced, or permanently separated from their husbands.[16]

The issue of requesting certificates for their elderly parents was central for many immigrants. In many cases, adult children perceived their own immigration as an advance journey (*Vorabreise*), like husbands immigrating before their wives. They went to check on the conditions of the country, the labor market, and the housing situation, with the intention of reporting back to their elderly parents in Germany and facilitating their subsequent immigration. Parents who could afford it came to visit their children in Palestine as tourists. Heinemann Stern, for example, visited his daughter and stepson in 1938 in Palestine, returned to Nazi Germany, and luckily still managed to emigrate in 1939.[17] There were, however, countless cases in which parents did not have the means to obtain their own capitalist certificates, and their children were unsuccessful in obtaining dependent certificates for them. Letters between family members in Germany and Palestine show them trying to stay in contact as long as possible. But with the outbreak of the war in September of 1939, correspondence with relatives in Germany and Europe became increasingly difficult, and attempts to help parents and other family members escape Nazi Germany became desperate. In other cases, children who would have been able to bring their parents to Palestine were unable to convince them to do so while it was still possible. Fritz Wolf recalled his parents visiting him in Nahariya in 1937 and then, despite his desperate attempts to convince them to stay, returning to Germany:

> Dad could not change the way he was. He wanted to go back.... It was not that he believed that the conditions would become better. But he could not force himself to do it—the leopard could not change his spots. If he had emigrated, he could have kept "only 5000 pounds." For us, that was a fortune, but for my father, merely a gratuity. But more than that: leaving meant

downfall, giving up his life's work; it meant the death of his soul, which could not and no longer wanted to adapt to something else.... Dad wanted to go back. For him, the stay was just a vacation—nothing else. He did not realize then that he was ... returning to death. Maybe he did not want to see it—maybe he wanted to die: or at least to witness the destruction of everything he had created. But Mom, the longer she stayed and the less time was left, the more she wanted to stay, or at least to come back as soon as possible. She saw the end no less clearly, maybe even more clearly. She knew that this could be the last farewell—she wanted the family united, saving what was left to be saved: the business and the money meant nothing to her, but her love for us meant everything. But her place was at Dad's side—she knew that, too.[18]

The story of Fritz Wolf's parents reveals some of the many reasons why German Jews, especially when they were older, sometimes wished to remain in Germany despite the deteriorating political situation.

Nazi policies were unpredictable and included many deceptions. Despite the increasing terror, therefore, it was not possible in the 1930s to predict the deportations and mass murder of the "final solution" or to draw the conclusion that emigration was the only possibility of surviving. This explains why many, especially the elderly, wanted to believe at first, notwithstanding their fear, humiliation, and despair, that things could not get much worse. Even the Jewish organizations concerned with emigration initially thought they would have much more time, and so, rather than hurry the process, worked to ensure that German Jews were well-prepared for emigration.[19] And it was not only men who were skeptical about starting a new life under difficult and completely novel conditions and felt unable to leave their homeland behind. The Zionist Walter Wolff, for example, who wanted to immigrate to Palestine, faced resistance from his wife Ena, who refused to move, with their small children, to such an "underdeveloped country."[20]

Those elderly parents who did immigrate to Palestine, what the German Department called "parent immigration" (*Elternimmigration*), created various challenges for their adult children. Elderly parents, whether they were in Germany or in Palestine, increasingly had to rely on financial support from their children. Surveys conducted by the German Department in the 1930s show that immigrants in Palestine supported their parents back in Germany by sending money as long as that was still possible. The average support for elderly parents came to as much as 20 to 25 percent of their children's monthly income.[21] This need to support parents was one of the reasons for the massive female participation in the labor force: former homemakers took up employment to help support their parents because their husbands' incomes were not sufficient to support the extended families. For those families lucky enough to be reunited in Palestine, accommodation posed another problem. As early as 1933, Georg Landauer addressed the need for middle-class retirement homes for elderly German immigrants in Palestine.[22] He argued that the lack of such homes could thwart the immigration of whole families, especially when the children planned to settle in the countryside and had no way to accommodate their parents. The existing homes for the elderly were seen as inadequate for the German immigrants, and subsequently, more suitable homes were established—many of them still in existence today.[23] While this enterprise turned out to be highly successful, it was initially met with criticism based on specific conceptions of the family. As some interviewees noted, the practice of accommodating elderly parents outside of the family was criticized by Eastern European Yishuv residents, who perceived this as shunting them off.[24]

MARRIAGE FOR ERETZ: MARRIAGE STRATEGIES, MATRIMONIAL ADS, AND "CERTIFICATE MARRIAGES"

Not only married migrants but also singles were affected by the impact of gender on the decision-making process. While a disproportionate number of young men left Germany, young women often faced unique difficulties in convincing their parents to allow them to immigrate alone to a foreign country. In general, "Generation Exodus," as Walter Laqueur has called them, was less connected to German culture than their parents had been and more inclined to leave Germany. For those age twenty-five and under, the emigration process looked very different. By 1939, more than 80 percent of Jews between the ages of eleven and twenty-five had left Germany. Being unable to finish their education in Germany closed professional doors for them and made them eager to learn the professions needed in possible countries of refuge.[25] But while parents and children often had different opinions regarding emigration, parents were more willing to let their sons go than their daughters. This was especially the case for non-Western destinations, such as Palestine, and even more strongly so when it came to the unconventional communal living conditions of the kibbutzim, which fueled parental fears that young single women might go astray. Parents often accepted their sons' choice to retrain but preferred to keep their daughters at home. Thus, many girls received no vocational training. Parents often reasoned that boys would need to establish themselves economically, while daughters would marry, regardless. Jewish community welfare organizations also gave boys preferential treatment, offering them more varieties of training and subsidies, and thus provided more support for emigrating men than for women. In addition, girls were expected to take care of elderly or ill family members in Germany and were more socialized to accept their parents' judgment than boys were.[26] In case of any dispute, according to German law, a father could ultimately decide where his daughter should live until she attained the age of legal majority (twenty-one years).

The disproportionally large emigration of young men resulting from all of the above changed the gender and demographic structure of German Jewry. The imbalance between men and women in emigration became so obvious that the Jüdischer Frauenbund (League of Jewish Women) and Jewish immigration organizations endorsed the practice of young people marrying prior to emigration, in an attempt to make parents let their daughters go.[27] This approach was also informed by the fear that Jewish men abroad would intermarry and the coincident unavailability of partners for the women remaining in Germany. In 1938, the *Jüdische Rundschau* published an article titled "More Female Emigration!" by the immigrant aid organization Hilfsverein der Juden in Deutschland, calling for increased emigration of girls and women from Nazi Germany to all countries. It explicitly encouraged young emigrants to marry before their emigration:

> Primarily, our young emigrants need to understand that, in general, it would be wise for them to commit to their partner, usually through marriage, before emigrating overseas. When two young people go abroad together, they will not only comfort each other, but in many, maybe most, cases, it is also the female partner who will be able to earn a living first, so that marriage before emigration will tend more to ease than to complicate the material struggle for existence.[28]

This was both an appeal to couples who were already together before emigration and a suggestion that singles should actively search for a partner before leaving Germany. The advantages of pre-migration marriages were seen as being both psychological and financial. For German Jews who wanted to leave for Palestine, these points were crucial. Psychological reasons, such as facing the challenges of emigration with a partner of the same cultural and language background, were as important as economic factors, such as the fact that women tended to find jobs more easily than men did. The dowry was also a relevant issue, especially when immigrants intended to establish a business together abroad or needed additional money to reach the necessary 1,000 pounds for a capitalist (category A) certificate.

Given the Mandate regulations, as well as the policy of the Jewish Agency on the allocation of labor certificates, "certificate marriages" were also a way for unmarried women to bypass the restrictions imposed on them. Taking advantage of the Mandate regulations that allowed male certificate holders to bring their spouses was an incentive in all such marriages, but it was seldom the sole or even main reason. Fictitious marriages conducted solely for the sake of the certificate, with no intention of staying together, were only a small subset of "certificate marriages," apparently. Marriages where the clear intention was to separate after immigration are hard to quantify, however, as they were illegal and hardly documented.[29] Even in cases where such pro forma marriages occurred, both partners did not always necessarily perceive it the same way. Yair C., a member of the youth movement Werkleute, was eighteen when he moved to Stuttgart and learned construction work in preparation for his immigration. In the local *Bet Haluz* (pioneer home), he met a young woman who became his girlfriend; the two even met each other's parents. Under the shadow of the pogrom night of 1938, the two then married and immigrated to Palestine on one certificate. Yair was under the impression that he and his girlfriend-turned-wife would stay together in Palestine. For her, however, this marriage was not perceived as a bond for life, and she left him soon after their immigration.[30]

It is important to note that fictitious marriages were opposed by the Jewish immigration apparatus as well as by the Palestine Office.[31] In the Jewish Agency, the possibility of women immigrating through fictitious marriages aroused the fear that prostitutes could enter the country without the oversight of the Immigration Department. Economic and religious factors also mattered in this hostility toward fictitious marriages.[32] The Palestine Office and the German Department made it clear that they shared the objections of the families in Germany to such pro forma marriages. In addition, Georg Landauer warned that filing for divorce in Palestine would be difficult. In a letter to the Palestine Office dated July 1934, the year with the highest rate of immigration from Germany to Palestine, Landauer writes that "a few cases have occurred lately" of certificate holders who had immigrated from Germany and wanted to get divorced shortly after their arrival. Landauer noted that these immigrants were apparently unaware of the difficulties this pursuit would pose for them. Those who had married in civil ceremonies in Germany would need to file there for divorce, too, and they could not do so through the German consul in Palestine.[33] Finally, however, most certificate marriages were intended to establish a family in Palestine.

These marriage strategies differed from those that prevailed in Germany before emigration. After World War I, ideals of romantic love and choosing one's partner oneself had grown stronger among German Jews. Arranged marriages, while still the norm in imperial Germany, declined during the Weimar era, making room for more love matches.[34] Young immigrants-to-be who were born in the imperial period and came of age in Weimar witnessed this change in the marriage strategies of the German-Jewish middle class. However, given the need to leave Nazi Germany, many felt the need to conform after all to marriage norms they had deemed outdated: a convenience instead of companionate marriage based on economic necessity and dowry instead of romantic love and attraction.[35]

Immigrants who came to Palestine as singles and wanted to find a partner had various strategies available to them, depending on their age, preferences, socioeconomic background, and ideas about marriage. One strategy for finding a German partner in Palestine was through personal ads, which appeared throughout the 1930s in the *Jüdische Rundschau* and the *Mitteilungsblatt*. These ads frequently specified a desire for a partner who already held a certificate, with the idea that the two could marry and move to Palestine together, while at the same time expressing the wish to find a partner from the same cultural background. In other words, some actively tried to meet someone before leaving Germany, with the plan of starting a new life together abroad. Others, who were already in Palestine, used ads to search for mates to follow them to Palestine. Both men and women advertised in matrimonial ads, and sometimes other family members advertised on their behalf. These ads make it clear that the requirements for potential partners had changed, as seen here:

> My brother in Palestine seeks a wife from a good family, with qualities that the present age demands. Beauty and capital required. My brother is 45 years old, mid-sized, with a very pleasant appearance and the best possible character. He's a highly skilled merchant, educated, and was successful in his own business in Germany for many years. Now he's been in the country for one year, settled on a *Pardess* [orchard]. In addition, he works as a merchant. Letters will be treated confidentially; please include a photograph.[36]

Mentioning the suitor's successful prior occupation in Germany was crucial here; he apparently did not want to erase his professional history and education and saw it as enhancing his value on the marriage market. Mentioning that he was already a resident of Palestine made it clear that he could provide the immigration certificate for a spouse. His demands for a potential wife are comprehensive and include classic demands like beauty, financial means, and a good upbringing (indicating education and a middle-class background) in addition to "qualities that the present age demands." As these are not detailed, they appear to have constituted a buzzword that readers would understand. Given the discussions surveyed in the chapter on the labor market, this would have meant that he was looking for women who were tough, flexible, steady, and self-sacrificing. Because the man described in this ad worked as an orchard farmer, his wife would also be expected to be able to perform this agricultural work.

The simultaneous demand for old and new characteristics in potential wives is ubiquitous in the ads, as also seen here: "Young farmer, many years in the country, wants to make the acquaintance of a young, beautiful, rich girl, with good character, pioneering spirit, and interest in agriculture—for marriage and founding a large farm in the *Galil* [Galilee]."[37] Here, too, the potential wife is sought as an agricultural coworker; marriage would ensure her immigration certificate because the man is a resident of Palestine, while his being a farmer and "many years in the country" marked him as experienced and hence a promising partner. The list of desired features for his wife is long and thorough: young, beautiful, and rich, but also with a good character, pioneering spirit, and interest in agriculture. The demand for a mixture of requirements from both the old and new worlds is striking: a good family, education, and immaculate appearance go hand in hand with features such as being able to do hard physical labor, being business-minded, eager to work, and flexible.

Women seeking a husband often mentioned the fact that they were already gainfully employed or willing to become so. "Who takes a 23-year-old gal to Eretz? Longtime Zionist, very flexible and modest, seeks a life companion with a certificate or craft, 3000 in cash, linen, and furniture on hand."[38] Men seeking women usually specified that she should also be beautiful—sometimes merely using this adjective, sometimes providing more detail, such as desired hair color, figure, or height. As men were usually the ones providing the immigration certificate, they were in a position to make such demands. Women seeking partners therefore constantly mentioned their beauty in their own ads.

All the different roles a woman should fulfill are also expressed here: "I am seeking a healthy, beautiful life partner, who already lives in Eretz, aged ca. 25 to 32 years, who wants to be a good wife, a capable housewife, and a co-worker on a new, modern agricultural settlement. The farm promises a secure existence and is in an excellent and healthy location. Capital requested for the expansion of the farm."[39] A loving wife, an eager homemaker, and a coworker all at the same time is precisely what the absorption authorities expected German immigrant women to be. The ability and willingness to work hard was often specified, as in this case, where a male immigrant needed a wife because he was widowed with a small child who needed a mother: "Southern German-Jewish merchant (knitwear manufacturer), 40 years old, healthy, widowed, with a 4-year-old son, seeks a hardworking, efficient, beautiful, healthy life companion for the sake of a joint Aliyah, who wants to be a good mother to the boy and happily work on establishing a new existence. A1 immigration certificate already granted."[40] Being physically fit and healthy was of special importance, too. Especially for those immigrants who aimed to establish an agricultural enterprise, age and physical health were crucial factors; this is why phrases like "healthy and strong" were so often used, both as self-descriptions and in requirements for potential partners. Immigrants in their thirties and older, of both sexes, therefore frequently mentioned that they were younger-looking.[41] Business partners were also sought in connection with marriage offers, as when men explicitly sought the daughter of a pharmacist or a physician in order to establish a pharmacy together.[42] Capital was mentioned in most ads, as a requirement or as self-description: both men and women mentioned either that they owned the 1,000 pounds required for the capitalist certificate or that their prospective partner should own this sum. Dowries were mentioned, both by women in their self-descriptions and by men describing their desires, sometimes detailing the wished-for sum. Some immigrants added "Zionist" as a self-description and sought like-minded partners, usually using the Zionist term "comrades," while at the same time looking for capital and a good-looking partner, too: "28-year-old Zionist, employed merchant, knowledge of Hebrew, English, and French, 1.65m, wants to marry a nice, flexible companion, who owns 1000 pounds, for joint immigration to Eretz Israel. Maybe we can meet during my annual summer vacation. Comprehensive letter with full-body picture to."[43]

While most of the advertisers were young and sought young partners, the elderly also tried their luck: "Versatile, hale widow, aged 60, without capital, seeks Palestine emigrant for marriage."[44] Marriage brokers also became involved, arranging for potential partners to get in touch via correspondence. In Palestine, German Jews founded matchmaking companies, such as the Distinguished Palestine Marriage Arrangements (Palästina Ehe-Arrangements vornehmer Art) company run by Henryk Dawidowicz, who noted that he was a former bank representative in Paris, Berlin, and Danzig and advertised his services as "absolutely trustworthy, psychologically sensitive, ... with utmost discretion and according to the best conventions."[45] This description emphasized the exclusivity, norms, and standards of the German immigrants that could continue to be upheld in emigration, with the help of these matchmakers. Other matchmaking entrepreneurs, such as Margarete Bornstein Marital Bliss,[46] joined the existing market of matchmakers active in the Yishuv, but focusing solely on the German-speaking immigrant community.[47] The popularity of matchmaking services for the German Jews can also be seen in the fact that they were often parodied in advertisements placed in Palestine's German-Jewish newspapers. Fortuna, a cookware company founded by a German immigrant, advertised its stove as a fake matchmaking service, because a modern gas cooker was the best way to guarantee a happy marriage (given the issues with the Primus, this advertising campaign does not seem too farfetched).[48] Another company advertised its vegetable oil using mock matrimonial ads, listing features requested of potential marriage candidates: "What else do you want? She is young, beautiful, owns a *Migrash* [parcel of land], and cooks with Izhar oil."[49]

The supply of and demand for German partners in matrimonial ads and matchmaking companies express the common desire to found a family in Palestine with someone of one's own kind. The self-descriptions and requirements for prospective partners in these ads, as well as the many possible reasons for marriage, can also provide insights into ideas about marriage: some women sought partners with a certificate that they could join, because they could not afford the sum for a capitalist visa on their own; some men sought a wife to be an agricultural co-worker. Especially here, spouses were needed: the German Department of the Jewish Agency declared female work an absolute requirement for economic success in the middle-class agricultural settlements.[50] Fritz Wolf, for example, who settled in Nahariya, soon realized that he could not accomplish the necessary workload on his farm alone and needed to hire workers, even though his capital was dwindling away. After a few months in the country, his sister and brother-in-law explained to him that he would have to solve his dilemma through marriage: "Now, of course, a farmer needs to marry.... A farm without a woman—that is impossible. Here you will need a woman who is able to work—not a doll like Alis Baer or a little twerp like Ruth Drucker. The farm stands and falls with the woman."[51] Wolf, his family was convinced, needed not just a woman, but a particular type of woman, in order to succeed financially. According to his sister, his potential wife should be in good health, physically strong, and, in addition, possess a proper dowry. In her mind, a desirable dowry was 5,000 pounds, a very large sum for those years. Wolf was shocked by his sister's advice to find a woman as a coworker, "like a donkey or a cow," and not as a matter of love and of his own choice.[52] In addition, much to his dismay, Wolf was not considered a very good match on the marriage market, a fact that confronted him with the irrelevance, for his "market value" in Palestine, of his former status as a respected lawyer. This exemplifies the challenge many immigrants faced: that of starting from zero, with the achievements of their previous, pre-immigration life now rendered irrelevant.

While immigrants who had arrived as children did not necessarily try to find a partner of German origin when they married, those who arrived at an age to marry often looked for a partner from the same background, their own ethnic community, the most crucial objective being the wish for a shared tradition, language, culture, and background. However, those immigrants who did get married in 1930s Palestine nevertheless often felt a strong discrepancy between their old and new lives. Many complained bitterly about their very modest engagements and weddings.[53] For those who immigrated as young adults, comparisons with the ceremonies they had attended in Germany were painful. Instead of large celebrations, most new immigrants had coffee and cake at a coffeehouse, with only a handful of guests. Fritz Wolf complained that while in Germany, lavish events and generous engagement presents had been common in his family, none of this was possible in Palestine. When he visited his bride-to-be's parents, all they had to offer was a glass of preserved cherries they had brought from Germany and kept for special occasions.[54] Eva W. remembers that she received no formal dowry, because her parents simply could not afford it; instead, she received used items from her mother's household.[55]

MIGRATING MARRIAGES

Facing the challenges of a foreign country along with a spouse was beneficial in many ways. Families were, without a doubt, a tremendous source of emotional, financial, and social support for the new immigrants. However, family dynamics also created conflicts and challenges. Jewish families had already been under tremendous pressure in Nazi Germany. As discussed earlier, slow changes in gender roles over the previous decades had been involuntarily accelerated through Nazi persecution, causing reversals of gender roles between husbands and wives. This process continued in migration, where changing dynamics in the division of labor led to new allocations of tasks within the family, which often called into question old roles and ideas. How did this affect interactions between spouses, as well as their roles as fathers and mothers? The fact that women started to work outside the home, supporting their families financially, as discussed in chapter 4, also had a psychological impact on marriages. In general, research has shown both positive and negative effects of migration on couples. The experience of migration can lead both to greater intimacy between partners and to severe distress. Especially the fact of female migrants joining the labor market and gaining economic power has been described as challenging patriarchal gender roles and potentially generating conflict within migrant couples.[56] In the case of the German-Jewish immigrants to Palestine, while many male immigrants expressed gratitude for the ways in which their former homemaker-wives now provided for them, the changing roles within the family also led to tension. Coming to terms with a new distribution of roles that contradicted the traditional perception of gender assignments was difficult. Martin Feuchtwanger described a discussion with a man who suffered from the fact that after immigration, he could no longer provide for his family. Now, his wife supported the family as a domestic worker, which troubled him. He shared this feeling with a friend, who tried to cheer him up: "Don't be depressed because of that. It's not your fault, because you would prefer to make money and have your wife run the household and care for the children."[57] This statement aimed to reassure the unemployed man that his current inability to support his family was not his fault, because he hadn't wanted this change in gender roles to happen. Female employment, while appreciated as necessary for survival, was seen as abnormal, and the changing gender roles were worrying to at least some of the immigrants. Apparently, it was not only the fact that married women provided for their families, but also that they did so by working as domestic help, that caused unease to immigrants. About his own wife's employment, Feuchtwanger wrote that he was initially opposed to it: "I could not get over my pride. My wife as an *oseret* [domestic worker]?"[58] An interesting new phenomenon was the little businesses that immigrant couples, especially older ones, often tried to establish together, in both formal settings (cafés, shops, guesthouses) and informal ones (offering room and board, selling homemade items). One such kind of joint project was lunch tables (*Mittagstische*), a widespread transitional phenomenon in immigrants' first decade in their new homeland. Lunch and other meals were served in private homes to regular guests, usually other German immigrants who had no place or opportunity to cook and who wanted to eat German food in the company of their own kind. In most cases, the women cooked while their husbands served the food. Other joint projects included pastries or sweets that women baked at home and their husbands delivered to the customers. These endeavors had in common that women produced the goods, while men worked as their assistants. Compared to the situation in Germany, where married women had sometimes worked in their husbands' businesses or doctor's offices, the tables had now turned. Not all men found this easy to accept; Ilse B.'s father, for example, felt ill at ease serving food to guests while his wife cooked.[59] Ernst Loewy, who wanted his parents to join him in Palestine, wrote them about the possibility of opening such a *Mittagstisch* together. In his letters, he assured his apparently worried father that such joint work was acceptable for men in Palestine and that he knew of many cases where husbands served the lunch that their wives prepared.[60] In Martin Feuchtwanger's case, however, conditions were reversed. In the *Mittagstisch* he ran with his wife, he was the cook. For Feuchtwanger, who could not make a living as a publisher, this new career started by chance. At first, he cooked for his wife, a hatter, and her co-workers. Then those co-workers brought friends and, eventually, his private *Mittagstisch*, serving both lunch and dinner at their apartment, had twenty to thirty guests per day. Feuchtwanger was busy all day shopping, cooking, cleaning, and serving, while still trying to contact publishing houses. His wife, who made hats in the same apartment, assisted him on her breaks. Feuchtwanger recalls one of their typical conversations about planning the day:

> —*At 7 am I'll go to the grocery, at 8 am on to the market—meat, vegetables, fruit—then I need to visit two printing houses. Most of the food I'll prepare in the evening, but you need to be in charge of the kitchen from 9 to 11 am because I won't get back till 11.*
> —*Sure, but I also need to attend to customers at that time and prepare a few hats.*[61]

Feuchtwanger may have been a unique case, not only because he was the one running the *Mittagstisch* but also because he did not experience this new work as a step down from his former occupation. He realized that he genuinely enjoyed cooking and felt satisfaction in it. Maybe this was because he was not just helping his wife, as many other men did, but working largely independently.

Work dynamics in immigrant families in Palestine caused not only feelings of unease but, often, also, open conflict, especially when a couple was facing severe financial problems. The new immigrant Simon Grosshut, for example, confided to his mother in Germany the many arguments he had with his wife, Bela. In a March 1938, letter he explained: "Do you think that there is shalom between me and Bela? Not at all. In her eyes, I am 100% responsible for the situation because I missed the opportunity to integrate myself properly into the labor market. She just cannot understand that I did work but was sent away because I am simply too weak."[62] Grosshut mentioned that his wife had to work long hours to support them both; due to her physical exhaustion, she often fell ill. Grosshut felt that his wife blamed him for their terrible economic situation because, due to his physical weakness, he was not able to keep a job. Their marriage suffered from the permanent quarrels. Grosshut continued: "The kind of discussions we often have—I can't even describe them to you, it is so depressing. I would not have believed that after only ten months of marriage, two young people could be this demoralized. Often, we don't exchange a friendly word for days. . . . As I've told you before, I don't know what's going to happen!!!"[63] The fact that Bela Grosshut had to provide for her husband, while he could not find a regular job, strained their relationship to the degree that their marriage was at risk, as Grosshut perceived it. Unsurprisingly, the imbalance between exhausted women, on the one hand, overburdened by gainful occupation, homemaking, and childcare, and unemployed men, on the other, frustrated about their situation, led not only to conflicts but also to separations. Yair C. discussed the divorce of his cousin, a lawyer who had found no job in Palestine, while his wife started to work as a seamstress: "She was skillful, and the whole family income was hers and that, of course, changes everything. When the man is the breadwinner, he is automatically the stronger one, but when the woman earns money herself—and more money than the man—then the situation changes."[64]

It was not just occupational changes, but also the overall impact of immigration that could lead to separation and divorce. Gaby W. understood the breakup of his parents in this framework: "You come to a new *class*, you meet new people. In Berlin, she knew my father, his friends, his colleagues, who all came from more or less the same background. . . . But here everything was very, very different, the people came from different places, and I think that this revolutionized her life."[65] Yair C. also connected his own divorce, shortly after immigration, to the "more liberal life" in Palestine. In his mind, his former wife's desire to untie her German connections was because of all the new and different people she had met in Palestine.

Undoing a marriage, however, was difficult for the immigrants. The legal aspects and requirements for German Jews filing for divorce in Palestine were repeatedly discussed in the newsletters of the Palestine Office in Berlin and in articles in the *Jüdische Rundschau* and *Mitteilungsblatt;* they were also addressed in lectures at the HOG.[66] The amount of attention given to it indicates that this was a topic of concern for immigrants. In Palestine, the Mandate granted the different religious communities autonomy in the realm of personal law. Thus, questions of marital status fell under the jurisdiction of religious courts; civil courts were not responsible for them. For Jews, religious law required a divorce document called a *get* to effectuate the divorce. Those immigrants who were already Palestinian citizens could end their marriages through a religious court, but only if their marriage in Germany had involved a religious ceremony. If they had only had a civil ceremony, they first had to have a religious wedding in Palestine in order to then get a religious divorce, as reported in the *Jüdische Rundschau*.[67] Meta Frank remembered the case of her employer, Lotte Loewenberg, who sought a divorce from her husband. Because Loewenberg had been married in a civil ceremony in Germany, she could not get divorced in Palestine, and had to travel to Germany in 1936 to file for divorce there.[68] These regulations, however, only applied to Palestinian citizens. Jewish foreigners could not be divorced by either civil or religious courts in Palestine, but only by German courts and according to German law, as the *Newsletter of the Palestine Office* informed its readers. And yet, even though it was prohibited, some religious courts did apparently sometimes divorce such couples when both partners turned to them unanimously.[69]

The question of divorces for foreigners was relevant for all new immigrants who were not yet naturalized in Palestine, since legal immigration granted only resident status and did not automatically provide citizenship.

To apply for citizenship, the British legislation demanded a residence in Palestine of at least two years; proof of intention to permanently settle there; mastery of one of the three official languages—Hebrew, Arabic, or English; and an oath of loyalty and abandonment of any other citizenship.[70]

The absorption apparatus observed the disintegration of marriages with discomfort, as the authorities believed, or at least feared, that such disintegrations could be disruptive to the absorption process. A 1936 article by Lotte Hanemann in the *Jüdische Rundschau*, dealing with the legal situation of immigrants seeking a divorce, assumed that "the tendency to dissolve marriages is stronger here, given the psychological tension because of the complete reorientation, than it would be in a stable environment."[71] In general, spouses who left their families posed a problem for the apparatus, as they then often depended on social welfare, becoming "social cases." A 1936 HOG report, for example, mentions Mrs. C., who immigrated in 1935 with her one-year-old child, as dependents of her husband, who had applied for them to join him. As the social worker notes, the husband failed from the very beginning to take care of his wife. After a few months, he left her and the child and for months paid her no alimony. Another man left his family in Palestine and emigrated alone to Australia, leaving his family destitute and dependent on welfare. Most of the immigrants who deserted their spouses were men, but there were also a few documented cases of women who left their families.[72] M., for example, was a forty-two-year-old man who immigrated in 1933 with his wife and child. They opened a laundry shop, but when his wife left him and the child, he could not maintain the business.[73]

The issue went beyond just the German-Jewish immigrant community: welfare authorities in the Yishuv were concerned about a growing number of divorces in the 1930s overall, as a result of massive immigration, housing shortages, and economic hardships. As Tammy Razi has shown, the potential breakdown of families was discussed as a concern, first, in the context of the worry that divorced parents would be unable to take adequate care of their children, possibly leading to neglect, youth crime, and prostitution. In addition, the rise of divorce and the associated deterioration of families was feared to be the expression of a general lack of morality and norms, endangering the healthy upbringing of the next young generation and the stability of the nation itself.[74]

In the case of the immigration from Germany, however, it not just the migration itself and the related economic need that were understood as having a negative influence on cohesive family life. Some reports also mention experiences of persecution and incarceration in Nazi Germany as having had adverse impacts, such as in the following comment by a social worker on a request for a loan:

> Mrs. S. came to the country with two children at the beginning of the year; her husband was in a concentration camp then, and was not released until seven months later. In this time, Mrs. S. managed to survive somehow by working as a domestic aide; her children were housed in the countryside through the social welfare system. The family lost all of its fortune, and the husband is so demoralized by the incarceration and the loss of their capital that he has become a bad influence on his wife, who acquitted herself so well before. Mr. S. is a chauffeur, and if we could manage to let him work in that capacity, that could possibly save the family.[75]

While incarceration in Nazi concentration camps was mentioned by some social workers as a potential factor in family conflicts, however, it must be noted that it was not, at the time, generally discussed as a crucial factor.

It is unclear how many divorces occurred among German Jews in Palestine, because such data was not collected in connection with former nationalities. But while quarrels and conflicts due to the difficult economic situation, the changing gender roles, and the new reality of a foreign country were common, it does not appear that divorces did became a massive phenomenon. In general, the immigrants from Germany displayed a robust cohesion in the long run, expressed in their adherence to their language and culture, loyal membership in their landsmanshaft, and also in their family cohesion. While some immigrants cut ties to their spouses, most couples apparently stayed together despite their difficulties, whether because of traditionalist views on marriage, the fear of being alone in the new country, the difficulty of obtaining a divorce, or because they managed to overcome their conflicts and found ways to come to terms with the changed reality.

PARENTING IN PALESTINE

Immigrating with young children posed additional difficulties for immigrants: from the one-week voyage to Palestine, through the crowded conditions in immigrant hostels and the challenges of finding an apartment, to the problems of finding childcare and being able to provide for the children financially. The all-encompassing changes of immigration also affected concepts of motherhood and fatherhood. Before immigration, German-Jewish middle-class homemakers were primarily responsible for the household and the upbringing of the children and more often than not had household help.

As already noted, amidst the disruption of Jewish family life in Nazi Germany, mothers had been expected to hold the family together, provide emotional comfort and stability, create an atmosphere of normalcy despite the terror surrounding them, and pull themselves together for the sake of the family.[76] Immense expectations were also placed on women in the process of immigration and absorption, in three ways: as mothers, as homemakers, and as contributors to the family income. The social worker Helene Hanna Thon boiled these pressures down to this: "the woman is always the most important element in the house, and needs to convey calm and optimism to her family—if she does not prove equal to this task, she and her whole family will fail."[77] German immigrant women were pressured to live up to this ideal and were also lauded and gushed about as "women of valor." In other debates taking place in the Yishuv at the same time, however, medical manuals intended for Hebrew-speaking women criticized many mothers as problematic—mostly Mizrahi mothers or members of the Old Yishuv, who were seen as inadequate and neglectful of their children, hygiene, and education, but also urban, educated mothers. The latter were criticized, among other things, for being hysterical and overly anxious.[78] As Sachlav Stoler-Liss observes, this discourse placed "motherhood and proper childrearing at the very heart of the Zionist effort to shape a 'new society' and a 'new Jew.' "[79] In internal discussions within the German-Jewish absorption apparatus, however, while parenting advice was given just as unremittingly and ideologically as in the rest of the Yishuv, the dominant note was nevertheless praise for the German-Jewish immigrant mothers. Many immigrants who arrived with their parents as children or adolescents spoke similarly. Asked how her mother had coped with her new responsibilities after immigration, Eva W., who immigrated as a girl, replied: "I do not know! I do not know it to this very day. I have to say, that was the common picture everywhere: that the woman shouldered everything while the men were placed on hold."[80] Given the downward social mobility, the absorbing bodies constructed being a responsible mother as being a mother who sought gainful employment, a new task that contradicted the former social role of a middle-class Jewish mother in Germany. As Nadja Stein observed, the female immigrant carried the heavy "burden of combining motherhood and employment, in a place where climate, living conditions, and low incomes already asked the utmost of her."[81]

One of the most critical aspects of the social work provided by the absorption apparatus was childcare; it was also the most significant item in the social work budget.[82] Already during the very first absorption in the *Batey Olim* (immigration hostels), there was childcare for the children so that parents could concentrate their efforts on finding a job. But it soon became apparent that childcare was in fact a permanent need. The option that men might take care of the children was not discussed, probably because of both the prevailing conservative ideology of childcare and the idea that male unemployment was only temporary. Childcare was the premise for female participation in the labor market. Therefore, childcare facilities for immigrant children were established in cooperation with other institutions. Some new immigrants founded children's homes and made a living from them.[83] Social workers also facilitated the temporary accommodation of children, free of charge, in veteran families on kibbutzim or in the children's village Ben Shemen.[84] For families who had relatives living in the country, that was another possibility for childcare. Rafael T.'s mother, for instance, divorced from his father, had a poorly paid job as a domestic servant and lived in a single room in Tel Aviv. She did not have the money, space, or time to take care of her son, who was therefore raised by his stepmother in a village.[85] Given the importance of female work for the survival of the families, professional childcare facilities were seen as a necessity and promoted to the immigrants in very positive terms: "Most of the children in Palestine go there because the mother is kept so busy, both in her job and with housework, that she has little time left over to play with her children. There [in the childcare facility], they have a wonderful time; . . . they receive everything necessary to make a child's life meaningful and enjoyable."[86] The caretakers' professionalism and loving care were repeatedly praised: "The working mother who can bring her little one to the *Maon* [daycare center] in the early morning, to the loving and knowing arms of the nurses, and can pick the child up in the evening healthy and well-rested, is relieved of grave worry—even more so than if she herself was taking care of her child."[87] On the one hand, this emphasis on the superior quality of care for children outside of their families can be seen as an attempt to put (female) immigrants' minds at ease: given the excellent care, they could pursue their employment without worrying about their children's well-being. On the other hand, this notion should also be understood as part of the discourse of social workers in the Yishuv, which was highly overbearing and critical toward parents regarding their abilities to properly care for their offspring themselves.[88] Professional childcare was regarded as especially favorable for the absorption of immigrant children. In childcare, the children would learn Hebrew and be exposed to Hebrew culture.[89] And yet, in spite of this positive view by the social workers, the families themselves could find it very hard to have to send their small children to daycare facilities because of their economic situation. Martin Feuchtwanger wrote of a friend of his who lived with his family in crowded conditions in a sublet room. They had to share one toilet with twenty people and had to cook in their only room:

> The children would degenerate in such surroundings. This is why our son left us three days ago. The *Aliyat HaNoar* [Youth Aliyah] has accommodated him on a kibbutz. Do you know what it means to parents to lose a son? And we take our little girl to a WIZO childcare facility at 8 am and pick her up at 6 at night. You need to understand how far we have fallen. In Prague, I was an attorney for a large company. . . . We had a five-room apartment, a maid, an electric stove and a refrigerator, our own laundry room. Now we live worse than proletarians in Europe, my wife has become a simple domestic servant, and I run off my feet to find dirty, difficult work.[90]

For this family, the fact that their children were not cared for at home was hard to accept and symbolized their deep social, economic, and cultural fall. Given their financial struggle, however, they had no choice. For such families, the lack of available places in childcare facilities was the main problem. A survey from Haifa, for example, showed that only one-quarter of the children who needed care could be placed in childcare. Childcare remained a permanent challenge for immigrant families.[91] There was never enough funding to provide the appropriate amount of places. Bella Preuss, a social worker for the HOG, constantly negotiated with the German Department over the budget, arguing that they needed childcare because of the immigrants' terrible economic situation: "If we have to close the childcare, the mothers, who mostly provide for their families, will lose their jobs."[92]

Immigration affected family planning, too. Already in Nazi Germany, the worsening situation had impacted the desire among Jews to have children, as Trude Maurer has noted.[93] In Palestine, the necessity for women to take paying jobs also caused changes in family planning, as the apparatus noted. Britschgi-Schimmer, for example, pointed out the relatively high percentage of young marriages without children. She linked this phenomenon to the number of married women who were employed. Her 1936 survey showed that 41.5 percent of employed married women had no children, and 28 percent had only one child.[94] The background for her interest was a decline in birthrate in the Yishuv in the 1930s and 1940s. As Lilach Rosenberg-Friedman argues, this decline was brought about by widespread abortion in those years. There is no way to know exactly how many female immigrants chose to terminate unwanted pregnancies—abortions were illegal in most cases, under the Mandate, and politically undesirable from a Zionist demographic standpoint; they were also a taboo that is hardly touched on either in contemporary ego-documents or in autobiographies and memoirs.[95] But whatever their number, these abortions were often the result of the economic hardship, unemployment and underemployment, and crowded living situations that the new immigrants from Germany encountered.[96]

Another factor was that the climate, along with the female immigrants' changed social reality, including difficult homemaking, additional paid work, little assistance, and often a lack of supportive relatives, made being pregnant and giving birth themselves more taxing in Palestine. Also, the technological and medical state of the hospitals apparently worried some expectant immigrants. The apparatus tried to assuage pregnant women's fears by publishing detailed articles and information. Toni Stern, for example, explained the birthing procedure in a Palestinian hospital in detail in the *Jüdische Rundschau*. She addressed questions such as when expectant women were admitted to the hospital (eight days before the due date for those who did not live near a hospital) and how women in labor should get to the hospital (they should make an agreement with a taxi driver to be on call for them around their due date). She also explained how the maternity wards worked, how long after the delivery a mother was allowed to see her newborn, and what the nurses and physicians would expect of her for her own recovery (daily exercises) and regarding infant care (breastfeeding for at least nine months; strict hygiene regarding baby food, clothes, linen, etc.).[97]

In low-income families, pregnancy and childbirth posed an economic risk factor, as it meant a decrease in income while simultaneously adding child-rearing costs. In January, 1934, in a letter to the Jewish Agency's Immigration Department, Nathan Baruch asked for financial help for his family because he had not found work as an agricultural worker, and his wife, a domestic worker, was pregnant: "My wife will give birth in the middle of May this year and then she will no longer be able to support me with her work. In addition, our daily maintenance costs will, of course, then rise."[98] A female immigrant who lived in Herzliya with her husband wrote to friends in Germany about the hardships she faced during her pregnancy and birth. During her pregnancy, for health reasons, she had stopped working as a domestic, but once her husband lost his job, their financial situation became so severe that she had to start working again shortly after the delivery: "I was not even able to walk, let alone work. Nonetheless, 4 1/2 weeks later, I went back to work as an *oseret* [maid], but I hardly earned anything because I needed to return in between to the child." To be able to make a living, the couple pondered moving to Tel Aviv, to make use of childcare facilities not available in Herzliya: "We could send the child to a daycare center in Tel Aviv, and then I could work full-time as an *oseret*, which would earn me 4 to 5 LP [Palestine pounds]. I would also try to get typing work, which I could do in the evenings. I don't know yet if that will work out, but if not, we really don't know what's going to happen."[99] While motherhood was at the center of the absorption apparatus's debates and considerations, the social meaning of fatherhood also changed in Palestine. Losing their role as a family provider was devastating to many male immigrants, especially given the crucial relevance of the father in Jewish middle-class families before immigration. Nazi persecution had already attacked and, as Marion Kaplan writes, "essentially destroyed the patriarchal structure of the Jewish family."[100] Immigrants who had been subjected to violence and incarceration in Germany were in complicated psychological and physical shape, as the HOG documented, causing problems both for their ability to work and in their family lives.[101] Alisa E.'s father, for instance, had been imprisoned in the Buchenwald concentration camp before the family was able to leave Germany and immigrate to Palestine. As Alisa E. recalls, he changed after his imprisonment and became a nervous man, constantly yelling at his family.[102] Post-immigration downward social mobility also caused a crisis for male immigrants, especially family fathers. Utterly desperate letters to the authorities by family fathers bear witness to this, as we have seen. For some, the contradiction between their old and new roles in the family was so devastating that they tried, or threatened, to commit suicide. In one of these cases, a family father from Haifa wrote to the *Va'ad HaKehilla* (community council) that, because he had not earned money in months, he could not support his family nor pay the rent nor his children's tuition fees, and therefore, he implies, he felt compelled to take his own life.[103]

Inner-family decision-making dynamics also changed due to fathers' diminished roles, as Ilse B.'s story exemplifies. Her father had been a prosperous merchant in Germany and the undisputed head of the family. Realizing that he would need a new profession in Palestine, he brought with him the equipment to establish a cabinetmakers' shop, but unfortunately, soon after arriving in Palestine, the equipment was stolen, which meant that he lost all of his capital. He then failed at starting another business and thereupon lost all initiative, as Ilse B. recalls. The family survived because his wife started a *Mittagstisch*, and Ilse, then fourteen, and her sister also started working to support the family. Initially, the father made all the decisions for the family, such as where and how to live and where to invest the family's capital. However, after his many ill-fated choices in their first months in Palestine, a story of "continuous disasters," as Ilse described it, he ceased to be the family's sole decision-maker. Instead, Ilse, her sister, and her mother started to take charge, and when her father, in despair, wanted to work as a peddler, it was his wife and daughters who prevented that from happening: "One day, my father told us that he wanted to make a hawker's tray and peddle wares, and then the whole family started to cry and said: Anything but that! We could not stand to see him do that."[104] When Ilse's father died, his family saw his death as being directly related to his inability to live up to his pre-immigration successes; in their perception, immigration killed him: "He was shattered, psychologically and physically, in this country. He died all of a sudden at age 61. He had been a respected merchant in Lüneburg. And here, he was nothing."[105]

The lives of these German-Jewish fathers deviated not only from the normative ideal of fatherhood back in pre-Nazi Germany but also from the dominant normative conception of fatherhood in the Yishuv of those years. In the discourse of the time, failing, passive, and unemployed fathers were largely perceived as a Mizrahi, rather than German, phenomenon. The situation of German-Jewish fathers complicated this dichotomy. In addition, as Matan Boord argues, in the hegemonic labor Zionist ideology, normative fathers were envisioned as being absent from home for reasons of work, war, or other national duties, while mothers were present at home to take care of their children.[106] But the newcomers from Germany exhibited the opposite case: an increased presence of fathers at home.

While the above examples illustrate the difficulties fathers had in coping with the loss of their patriarchal role, German-Jewish men could also gain a new role in Palestine: that of a caring and involved father. A 1935 article in the *Jüdische Rundschau* was accompanied by a photo of a man pushing a stroller.

> The Jewish woman in Eretz Israel is often employed. She is also, in most cases, in charge of homemaking, which is more exhausting and takes more time than in Europe, as is known. This is why, in his free hours, the man often helps in the household. Gently and proudly, he pushes his stroller, where the child sleeps under the protective canopy. Pushing the stroller is a beloved specialty of Palestinian husbands.[107]

This statement refers both to the change in roles because of women's gainful employment and to the general enthusiasm for children in the Yishuv, apparently promoting a different role for the father than what the immigrants had previously recognized as normal. This description could also be read as an appeal to immigrant men to follow the lead of this gentle, caring, involved father and assist their wives with homemaking and childcare. Descriptions of stroller-pushing fathers also appear in other sources. A 1937 article in the *Jüdische Rundschau* describes the Gan Binyamin, a park in Haifa, where each afternoon, men would reunite with their wives and children after the workday: "The little children are put into their strollers, and the father pushes the stroller with a smile. That is his privilege in Palestine."[108] This common sight of caring fathers pushing baby strollers through the streets apparently made a huge impression on the immigrants, who declared how happy they were to take over this task. Martin Feuchtwanger, who immigrated in 1939 to Palestine, described the love of fathers for their children as being unique in Palestine: "In all the cities and villages, the Israeli father with his kids is a common sight. His friends accompany him, walk next to the stroller, and participate in the well-being and joy of the kid. The father changes the diapers, he bathes his baby, he gives him the bottle."[109] Feuchtwanger himself became a father when he was well into his sixties and described how he enjoyed these activities.

Fritz Wolf, who lived in Nahariya, expressed a similar pride in being the one who carried his baby girl through the village, as well as the changing mode of parenting, as he, too, now changed diapers and cared in other ways for his infant child. In a song called "Ringel Reihen Tanz der 1. Väter" (Ring-around-the-rosy of the first fathers), Wolf memorialized this changing role of the fathers in Nahariya:

> *We play ring-around-the-rosy*
> *Today we want to be merry and bright*
> *The kids make lots of pee and poop*
> *We are the first fathers of the Moshava*
> *We are the first fathers of the Moshava*
> ....
> *We play ring-around-the-rosy*
> *When our tiny children cry*
> *We push the stroller and rock the rocking horse*
> *Only breastmilk God did not grant us*
> *Only breastmilk God did not give us.*[110]

This visible new role for fathers reflects the Zionist idealization of children as representing the future of the state-in-the-making. The new immigrants found it fascinating to observe this pride in fatherhood. While it is hard to estimate how this actually translated into shared care-work, apparently, many became fond of this new role of active and involved fatherhood, compared to the distant role fathers played in Germany. The children enjoyed it as well. Yohanan B. described how happy he was to spend more time with his father in Palestine. In Germany, he had only seen him when they said good night in the *Herrenzimmer* (the study of the man of the house), but post-immigration, they had much more contact, and their relationship became more intense. On the other hand, he now saw his mother much less. While she had been his primary caretaker in Germany, he did not see her much in the early years in Palestine, as she had to work twelve-hour shifts as a private nurse.[111]

CHILDREN AND ADOLESCENTS IN MIGRATION

Age is a crucial factor in immigration. Children and adolescents experienced the process differently from their parents. Those young immigrants who had not finished their education before immigration, in particular, had less connection to German society, culture, and language. Therefore, although they too had been subjected to anti-Semitism, they did not, as a rule, experience the emigration as an uprooting in the same way their parents did.[112] Children immigrating with their parents also tended to be less aware of the difficulties of the migration process; some even experienced it as an adventure. Those who had been active in Zionist youth movements in Germany felt, in addition, that they were part of a revolutionary movement of building and constructing a new society. Generally speaking, while children, like adults, had to deal with adapting to a different language, culture, and society, they coped with the situation much more easily. They learned Hebrew faster and, through schools and youth movements, became integrated into society, sometimes also meeting later life partners from different ethnic backgrounds.

Youngsters often found it easier to deal with the informal character of the society, which their parents were more likely to experience as chaotic.

Young immigrants commonly took things more lightly, making it easier for them to deal with difficulties. Ruth R., for example, who immigrated in 1933, as a twenty-one-year-old, on a labor certificate, remembers how improvised and informal things were, but she did not experience this as negative. She had neither a family in Palestine nor money for a hotel. Still, she eventually met friends from Germany on the streets of Haifa, and they invited her to dinner and spontaneously organized a place for her to sleep.[113] Yohanan B., formerly Hans, who immigrated with his parents as a child, mentioned how much easier and more intuitive cultural adaptation was for him than for his parents: "Children understood better than their parents how to behave in a culturally correct way." At home, for example, Yohanan behaved as his parents expected him to: he spoke German, dressed according to German middle-class norms, and showed respect to his parents. Outside, however, he quickly adapted to the Yishuv culture in his behavior, looks, and language. He Hebraized his name, and when asked for his father's first name, he provided the name Avraham instead of Adolf to avoid stigmatization.[114] Unlike

FIGURE 12. A little girl looking at a storybook on the train from Berlin to Marseille; Berlin, September 1, 1936. Photographer: Herbert Sonnenfeld. Source: Jewish Museum Berlin, FOT 88/500/106/007, purchased with funds provided by the Stiftung Deutsche Klassenlotterie Berlin. Reprinted with permission.

their parents, youngsters were willing and eager to immediately adapt to their Palestinian peers. While older immigrants tended to be critical of the local "Levantine" youth, whom they perceived as impolite, noisy, rude, and untidy, most immigrant children looked up to the Sabras (the native-borns) and tried to emulate them, even though they too were subjected to mocking and hostility from the local children.[115] Gaby W. proudly recalls how he turned from a polite, obedient boy into a naughty, rowdy young man in Palestine by following the example of the local youth.[116]

Many children experienced the different and less formal life in Palestine as liberating, not only from anti-Semitic hostility but also from the strict middle-class conventions they had been used to in Germany. Helga Kressel, for example, was thrilled with the simple clothes and the Middle Eastern climate: "The best thing was the clothing. Boys and girls ran around in short trousers, shirts, and sandals. No one wore socks in the summer. Also, you didn't always wear your sandals—you just walked barefoot. I couldn't imagine anything better than that."[117] Ruth M. recalls how much more fun it was to run around half-naked at the beach with her brother than to have to go for walks in Breslau's parks with her nanny, dressed elegantly and uncomfortably and constantly instructed on how to behave.[118] Many girls particularly appreciated the change from skirts and dresses to the ubiquitous short trousers; it was "pure joy," as Miriam S. recalls.[119] The relationship between boys and girls in Palestine was also experienced as very different. While children in Germany had attended separate schools by gender, engaged in gendered hobbies, and generally had different prospects in life, in Palestine, many girls felt much more liberated. They attended coed schools and went to youth movement activities and sports venues along with the boys. Ilse B. recalls: "The girls behaved just like the boys . . . very cheeky . . . totally different [than in Germany]; they felt freer and equal to the boys, there was no difference."[120]

Miriam R. remembers that she stopped accepting her parents' authority and maintained socialist political attitudes against their will: "I cannot imagine that we would have enjoyed that amount of freedom in Germany. . . . Regarding discipline and such things . . . everything was much freer here."[121] However, while parents might accept the behavioral changes to a certain degree, they often did not completely change their more traditionalist views.

Eva W. remembers that when it came to education, it was understood that her parents, who could only pay for higher education for one child, would choose her brother. As a result, she had to leave school at the age of thirteen to earn money to augment the family income: "That's how it was back then, even though my parents were not like that normally; it wasn't that they preferred boys, but reality dictated these kinds of things."[122] While it was difficult for parents to make such decisions, since education had been at the center of their world view before migration, once they were under economic pressure girls were expected to step aside and give boys the advantage. This echoes the debates within the Jewish community in Nazi Germany, when girls and women had also been expected to step aside.[123]

As a result of immigration, children received not only more freedom but also more responsibility, for example in the household. A letter from a boy who had recently immigrated to Palestine, published in the children's supplement of the *Jüdische Rundschau*, explains: "It is very important to tell you that I had a nanny in Germany, but here, of course, I do not. Here I help my mother, I pump water for the garden, and I dry the dishes; sometimes I prepare eggs and tea."[124] Many children also needed to support their families financially; some were even forced to quit school as a result. Miriam R. had to start working to pay for her tuition fees. Two years before the school-leaving examination, her parents explained to her that this was no longer sufficient and that she would have to work full-time to earn her own living.[125] Jacob M. left school at fourteen and started working as an errand boy in a factory because of his family's difficult economic situation.[126] The HOG and the German Department also discussed the phenomenon of children who not only helped their parents financially but were the family's sole breadwinners. A 1936 HOG report describes the case of a family whose business idea had failed and who now depended on the income of the sixteen-year-old-son, who worked as a tile setter, and the fourteen-year-old daughter, who worked in a factory.[127] It was hard for parents to cope with needing their children to support them. In the middle class, children had been perceived as innocent and needing protection; child labor was taboo. The middle class of the Yishuv also understood a "sheltered childhood as a hallmark of Western civilization."[128] In Yishuv society, it was mostly Mizrahi parents who were criticized for having their children work instead of sending them to school.

In the case of Mizrahi parents, this was interpreted as expressing a lack of proper parenting.[129] When German-Jewish children worked to support their families, however, there was hardly any criticism expressed. Instead, it was perceived as a temporary necessity.

Leaving aside these perceptions from the outside, losing their place in the middle class also meant a seismic shift in how immigrant parents and children understood their relationship with each other. In the agricultural villages, for example, it was taken for granted that children would help in the daily work in the fields and with the animals. Helga Kressel, who lived with her parents in the agricultural village of Ramot HaShavim, wrote: "It was not an easy life; there was little money and what was asked of us, because there was simply no other way, seems almost cruel today. Regarding this, I can say for sure that we felt neither poor nor exploited. A lot of my peers worked, too, and it was 'trendy' and 'in' to behave like responsible adults."[130] The fact that their income was needed to secure the survival of the family caused a feeling of independence among youngsters and could undermine the authority of the parents.[131] Children suddenly felt all grown-up and no longer waited for their parents' permission, and parents felt they could no longer tell their children how to behave because of the children's contributions to the family income. Ilse B. states: "Back in Lüneburg, I had respect for my parents and did not dare talk back to them, but here . . . I kind of lost that respect for my parents."[132] Some children were ambivalent about this changed dynamic in their relationships with their parents, though. While some children enjoyed the new freedom, others felt left alone with their worries and unable to turn to their parents for help, as the parents were too absorbed in everyday worries. In addition, their parents' lack of Hebrew hindered them from helping with homework or advocating for their children at school, for example in conflicts with teachers. Uri S., who grew up in Sde Warburg, recalls that the freedom he enjoyed through lack of parental control could also become dangerous. He and the other children of the village played games so wild that they often seriously injured themselves; tragically, one child even died in such an incident.[133]

Malka Schmuckler, who lived with her parents in another middle-class settlement, complained about receiving no emotional support from her parents whatsoever. They did not even realize that she had started to be active in the Haganah (the Zionist paramilitary organization) and was therefore often up all night: "My parents were so overloaded with work that they simply had no time for that. That had grave consequences for me. In school, I tried less and less to keep up. In the afternoons, I needed to work in the fields and in the house, and the evenings I spent secretly with my comrades."[134] Other German children, too, missed out on education and nurture. As Schmuckler put it, they were "birds who fell out of the warm nest, not yet ready to spread their wings, and they had to learn how to fly on their own."[135] Comments like this one hint at the fact that despite the common statements by children and adolescents that everything was relatively easy for them, immigration also took its toll on them.[136]

Lacking parental monitoring was also relevant when it came to flirting and dating. At first, girls and young women were delighted by the surplus of men in the Yishuv: "There were more boys than girls everywhere. So it was never a problem to go out for a date; if one of them didn't want to, you took the next one. That was no problem at all. Very comfortable, because there were so many. That was a very comfortable time."[137] Ilse B. recalls: "There was one girl for ten boys, and you could go out every night with another boy, without any promises, and it was all modest, you did not do anything."[138] Palestine was therefore called "The promised land for girls who want to get married." Letters from Palestine emphasized the fact that it was easy for single women to integrate themselves into society because of the many parties and social events one could attend.[139] Yair C. observed that in Palestine, German-Jewish girls could have a free sexual life for the first time in their lives:

> They could act out sexually here—there was no father here, no mother, and they could enjoy life. . . . In Germany, a young girl lived with her parents until marriage. . . . They helped their mothers or learned stitching and the like, and the mothers watched out for them. . . . My sister was in the youth movement HaBonim, and when she came home late, my father would walk up and down and wait until she was home. And if she wasn't home before 10 in the evening, he would send me out to search for her. . . . Then Father would ask her: Why do you come home so late? Who are you hanging around with? But once she came here, there was no father and no mother and no one, and the boys were freer, too.[140]

With regard to sexual encounters, this sudden freedom could evoke ambivalent feelings. Those who immigrated without their parents, in particular, could experience this sudden liberation as dramatic. Gretel M., for example, notes: "I grew up in an absolutely Prussian way, under my mother's thumb. And then suddenly for the first time in my life I could do whatever I wanted, and of course, I did everything wrong. People really enjoyed that—but also in a wrong way. There were those who went out with everybody, others only with some. But you were suddenly without your parents, free."[141] Gretel M. added that on the kibbutz where she lived, the married veteran residents actively pursued sexual relations with the new female immigrants, often bordering on sexual harassment: "There were no moral rules in that regard; everybody did what they wanted to do."[142] Many female immigrants complained that they had to face the new liberties without any prior sexual education, mentioning that they had no clue about birth control or sexual practices in general.[143]

The matter of unattended youngsters who lacked parental guidance was also discussed from a social welfare perspective, both in reports by social workers and in newspaper articles. As mentioned earlier, the social workers would place immigrant children in Palestinian families or organize their accommodation on kibbutzim when their parents could not care for them. In a report about the children placed in Palestinian families, the social worker Siddy Wronsky describes the following case. The sisters Hannah and Ruth A. immigrated with their parents in 1933. Their father died of typhoid shortly after their arrival, and their mother was left alone with five young children, whom she tried to support by working as a domestic servant. Wronsky writes: "The two older girls were in danger of going astray because they were left to their own devices all day long, being unable to attend school because a shortage of school accommodation had arisen due to the spate of immigration of that period." The girls were therefore placed with a family in Nahalal. While the older girl had no problems adjusting and made herself popular, Wronsky notes, "the younger, a nervous child, had suffered keenly from the scurrilous ditties she had been forced to listen to in Germany.... She found it very hard to feel at home in a Palestinian village."[144]

The example above reflects the fact that children, too, were affected by anti-Semitism, and that for some, it was hard to recover. But it also exemplifies the contemporary therapeutic discourse in the Yishuv about "problematic" children: children from Ashkenazi groups were overdiagnosed as neurotic, while Mizrahi children were more likely to be labeled as retarded. As Tammy Razi argues, this discourse expressed two tendencies in the society of the Yishuv: first, the perception of Mizrahim as inferior, and second, a "pathologization of social and economic problems, thus obscuring the harsh realities of immigration."[145] In this discourse, special emphasis was placed on nervousness and melancholy due to the language difficulties of immigrant children.

It is also worth noting that the language Wronsky uses links not attending school with "going astray," or possible transgressive sexual behavior. This was seen as a danger only for girls, as already mentioned. Social workers looked at boys and girls differently, as seen for example in the following article about "parents' worries in Palestine." The author describes the case of Micha, a young boy from Germany. His worried mother is quoted as saying:

> Unrecognizable, I am telling you! In Berlin, the boy was so well-bred, polite, attentive, tactful, an ideal child; it was a joy to look at him and observe him. Come out here on the balcony for a minute! Do you see over there, ... yes, the one with the wild hair and the blue shirt—that is little Micha. That's right! What do you say; he is yelling and beating—now he is rolling on the ground. Micha, come up here right now! ... The child has completely run wild here in the last three months! How about that?

The author then comments:

> The situation—in short—is something like this: Most of the parents of Micha's classmates work; the father and mother are both away from home for most of the day. The children are left to themselves in the afternoons; roaming around, they organize gangs and play pretty wild games. Micha, who was dressed more elegantly than they were, stayed on the sidelines at the beginning, and he was mocked a lot. "The new guy isn't allowed to play with us; we aren't good enough for him!" For a while, you can just watch that happening; for a certain period, you can hover between the duty to be well-mannered and restrained and the desire to be unruly and unrestrained like everybody else. A real boy, however—and luckily, Micha is a real boy—does not hover for long; he takes off his suit and jumps right into the turmoil. Enough with politeness! The mama's boy turns into a first-class rowdy![146]

The author, a social worker, suggests that the mother not get so upset but instead take better care of the boy: show an interest in him, have him help with running errands and the like, and most importantly, keep him busy by sending him to a youth movement. The article goes on to say that this is the fear and the dilemma of all parents: that their children, in an attempt to become a part of the new society, will throw away all of their education, politeness, punctuality, and tidiness.

While the initial conditions were similar in the cases of Micha and of the two sisters in Nahalal—no parental oversight, children left to their own devices—Micha's case was discussed differently. For boys, it seems, it was more accepted, even applauded, to become wild and to leave behind their conservative behavior, which was seen as unmanly, unfitting for Palestine. Micha's transition from a well-behaved child into a "real boy" was seen as a positive development rather than a threat. The two girls, however, were seen as being in danger of going astray and, as a result, were accommodated in the countryside and placed under the further oversight of social workers.

Some immigrants saw the lack of oversight over the immigrant children as indicating a general problem within the immigrating group. Martin Hauser expressed his fears over the moral state of the young immigrants in a letter to a friend in September of 1935:

> *Just as there is a misconceived feeling of "freedom" in marriages, there is also a similar conception in the realm of education, where one lets the children have free rein, and hence they go from one extreme to the other. The children grow up without parenting—because the parents are working—lacking knowledge, lacking respect for the elderly, maturing too early and therefore lacking shame or decency, all of these lacks being attributes that the parents do not nurture, partly because both are tired from their work but mainly because of their own ignorance, their own immaturity, and the parenting of their children with the misguided goal of letting the children grow up "free."*[47]

In the wake of the turmoil that immigration had caused, there was anxiety—among the immigrants, within the apparatus, and in the receiving society more broadly—over moral decay in the immigrating group. Signs of such decay were perceived in connection with sexuality, as well as in questions of hygiene, homemaking, dressing, and, as seen here, in "libertinism" in family life, whether evidenced by overly liberal parenting or in divorce. A loss of control, it was feared, could put the inner cohesion of the community at risk. In general, the question of freedom was an important one in the Yishuv in these years, especially in its biggest city, Tel Aviv, which became a major hub for the immigrants from Germany as well. Accusations of too-liberal behavior included unruly behavior, improper dress, free love, smoking in the streets, immodest behavior by couples, and prostitution.[148] Meir Dizengoff, the mayor of Tel Aviv, also voiced the opinion that even the European immigrants joined in this behavior, behaving as if they were free from "all the precepts of decorum" that they had held onto in Europe but now abandoned in their new homeland.[149]

Children had a unique position in this anxiety. Observing their children and their important place in the immigration process was, on the one hand, a source of pride for parents and for the immigrating group in general. Children stood for survival and continuation, as well as for the promise of entrenchment in the new country. On the other hand, parents also perceived the changing relations with their children as painful, bemoaning their loss of authority. They were afraid that their children would become rude, wild, loud, disobedient Levantines, without a proper knowledge of German. As Marion Kaplan stated, Jews had made family a central value and symbol in the nineteenth century, necessary for achieving bourgeois respectability. Education and cultivation had been perceived as essential in this endeavor.[150] But Nazi rule and emigration radically transformed this vision of family life.

The ambivalent attitude toward the development of their children was characteristic of the more general ambivalence many of the German immigrants felt toward their new homeland. As one immigrant put it:

> Older immigrants from Europe sometimes complain about the fact that children and adolescents here are cheeky and arrogant and show no respect for adults, that the relationship between teachers and students is too casual, that there is a lack of authority and discipline.... In the world they came from, the stronger one rules and the weaker must obey unconditionally. The wife had to serve her husband submissively.... The children received a strict upbringing from their parents and their teachers. This world has sunk. A new world is born. This is nowhere as clear as it is in Palestine.[151]

CONCLUSION

Immigration shook up the immigrants' lives in every possible way, including in their family relationships. While some enjoyed this new freedom, including with regard to family life, others bemoaned the "overly liberal life" in Palestine with respect to its effect on marriages and children. These concerns expressed a deep fear of disintegration, of losing the feeling of security and order in the most intimate aspect of one's life: partners and children. The anxiety over the instability of the immigrant family was shared by the absorbing bodies in the Yishuv. They saw family cohesion as necessary for the immigrants' economic survival and to prevent a crisis for the host society. Stable families were required to serve as the building block of the nation, in this understanding. The discourse on families in the 1930s Yishuv, as research has shown, was riddled with contradictions, however, because it included attempts to both strengthen the family and minimize its role.[152]

One decisive point about the discourse on the allegedly dysfunctional families among the German immigrants is the fact that many of the participants in these debates—social workers, medical professionals, welfare department members, activists, and others—were themselves either immigrants from Germany or had been trained there. Thus, when the marriages and parenting of German immigrants were critiqued, it was an internal discussion of sorts, unlike the discussions by these same professionals about Jewish immigrants from Muslim countries. Nevertheless, the tone of the criticism was harsh, as the professionals who were immigrants from Germany themselves identified strongly with the Zionist endeavor. While the main point in the absorbing bodies' anxiety over dysfunctional families was their potential threat to the nation-building project, that anxiety also drew on notions of traditional Jewish, as well as German bourgeois, family norms.[153]

It is crucial to point out that a potential breakdown of norms and values was feared not only by the absorbing authorities but also by the immigrants themselves. The migration process caused multiple conflicts and had far-reaching consequences for family dynamics. The very shifts in roles between spouses and between children and parents that enabled the immigrants to survive economically (including female labor and child labor) also stripped them of their bourgeois identity. The context of these experiences was relationships with family members who had been left behind. Nazi politics ripped families apart through emigration—and many of those family members would never meet again. At the time, it was impossible to foresee the deportations and mass murder of the "final solution." However, as is the case with other emigration waves caused by the flight from persecution, it is naturally the heartfelt wish of the emigrants to leave together with their loved ones. But given the difficulties in finding countries of refuge, members of German-Jewish families were soon scattered all over the world. A 1934 article in the *Jüdische Rundschau* entitled "Dissolution and New Bonds" observed: "The upheaval to which German Jewry has been subjected is expressed in one crucial characteristic: the dissolution of the family. There is hardly any [family] in which no one has left and gone into the world."[154]

This background further added to the anxiety over the dissolution of families in the new homeland. Many years later, when German-Jewish immigrants wrote their memoirs, one of their main motivations, as Guy Miron and others have pointed out, was to honor the legacy of their family and transmit the values of the lost world to their children and grandchildren.[155]

When immigrating with a family, it was not only the individual who had to cope with difficulties, but a group of people tied together through family bonds and a shared past in another country. Immigration had far-reaching consequences for families, as it changed the relationships between spouses as well as between parents and their children. Gender relations within a family unit were subjected to manifold challenges through the immigration process, from the decision to immigrate, through the journey itself, to the reorganization of daily life in Palestine. Responsibilities within the family that had been distributed according to the gender of the family members changed through the process of immigration, as did those that were related to the roles of parents on the one hand and children on the other. This process, as I have shown, was very ambivalent. Different family members could experience it as new freedom or as disintegration, as independence or as emotional neglect, as a promising new future or as the definitive loss of the old life.

Conclusion

GENDER ROLES ARE NOT ESSENTIAL or natural, but subject to historical change. Under normal conditions, that change can take many years, but immigration tends to propel such processes as well as causing immediate and radical transformations. For those German Jews who escaped Nazi Germany and found refuge in Mandatory Palestine, this book has argued, gender was at the core of the transformations in their professional, social, and cultural lives. This telling of the story of the "German Aliyah" as gender history has demonstrated that the migration was shaped by gendered policies and ideologies and experienced by men and women in a gendered form. Gender relations were changed through this immigration, leading to new models of family life, responsibilities, and self-perceptions.

The experiences were not uniform, though. In intersection with gender, factors such as occupation, marital status, and age were crucial for the outcome of the immigration. However, several common topics emerged within the diverse experiences of the group of immigrants that implicate gender in specific and important ways: from access to networks and work options, through relationships with spouses and expectations of potential partners, to changing conceptions of masculinity and femininity. This book has presented both transformations that were perceived as negative, such as the cases of frustrated veteran Zionists, and transformations that were perceived as positive, for instance, new fatherhood roles or attempts to emulate new masculinities. It has also shown how life in Palestine appeared especially attractive to female adolescents who were suddenly free of parental control, while for adult women who had to carry the burden of a double workday, menial jobs did not provide much empowerment. Thus, gender came into play in diverse ways, and gender roles and relations underwent manifold transitions after the immigrants' arrival in Palestine.

Gender structured how immigration was controlled and monitored through the specific regulations of both the British Mandate and the Jewish Agency. It was a central element in the policies of the absorbing apparatus in Palestine, too, in both discourse and practice. As this book has demonstrated, the discussions and activities of the apparatus evaluated and addressed men and women differently and allocated them different positions in the integration process. While the apparatus, acting as the backbone of the absorption process, aimed to prevent a social crisis and facilitate the successful integration of the mass immigration wave, it expressed a paternalistic view of the new immigrants, especially of women. Normative doctrines prevailing within the absorbing apparatus and the immigrant community aimed to leave gender relations intact as much as possible, despite the necessary changes. While women took on new roles—and were in fact urged to take them on—they were not supposed to destroy social barriers in the process. Inequality between men and women, in opportunities, power, and access to resources, continued to exist.

A discussion of the place of the immigrants in Yishuv society through 1948 and their subsequent place in the state of Israel exceeds the scope of this book. In choosing the 1930s as its focus, this study was able to concentrate on the rocky and challenging period of absorption and the many struggles and problems of adaptation to the conditions in the new country. Documents from the 1930s present a very different view of the immigrants than the image of well-to-do immigrants found in much of the research literature or the image of the Yekkes in today's popular culture. Thus, the picture presented in this book contradicts the conventional perception, in large part due to my focus here on the initial absorption. A wider scope that included the 1940s and, especially, the 1950s and later decades would likely change this picture. A much longer period would also need to be examined to answer the question of whether the changes in gender relations were temporary or permanent. The first decade after the founding of the State of Israel and the beginning of individual reparation payments by the Federal Republic of Germany would be of particular interest for such further study. This research might analyze how financial reparations transformed the socioeconomic status of the German Jews in the 1950s and how that in turn affected gender relations and their place in Israeli society. Analyzing a much longer period might also change the perception of the immigrants' Jewish identity and religiosity: in the sources used in this research, religion is conspicuously absent. This can be explained both by the high level of secularism in this group as well as by how hard the group had to struggle for its existence. When using sources conducted in hindsight, which express searching for a narrative and meaning, this picture changes. Miron writes about the tendency in autobiographies to strengthen the Jewish aspect of one's life in Germany in hindsight, as a result of the authors adoption of the Zionist narrative as well as their reaction to the Holocaust.[1]

Another consequence of the time frame chosen here is that this book has only marginally engaged with the Holocaust. The majority of the immigrants portrayed in this book came to Palestine before 1936 and thus were not subjected to the open violence and terror that began after the pogrom night in 1938. Until 1939, they were still in contact with family members who had been left behind, and while the immigrants were increasingly desperate to help those family members leave Germany, they could not know what would eventually happen to them. Given the time frame under study here, this book neither includes survivors who arrived in the Yishuv after the end of the war nor reflects on the immigrants' eventual painful realization that their loved ones who remained behind had been murdered. And yet despite these caveats, the history of these immigrants is also part of the history of the Holocaust, because if they had not found refuge in Palestine, they would likely have shared the fate of the German Jews murdered in the Shoah, including those who fled to countries that were later conquered by the Nazis.

Lastly, this book is based mainly on German-Jewish sources. Therefore, it presents how the immigrants saw themselves, how they were perceived by absorbing bodies that also consisted mostly of German Jews, and how they understood and reacted to the criticisms with which they were confronted. While much has been written about how the Yishuv's veteran residents of Eastern European and Russian origin saw the German immigrants, future research would be enriched by further exploring the image of the immigrants in the eyes of other groups in the society of Mandatory Palestine as well: the British, Arabs, and Mizrahim.

The main ideas of this book can be applied beyond the geographical scope of Mandatory Palestine. As discussed in the introduction, slow changes in gender roles with German Jewry that had been occurring over several decades were involuntarily accelerated through the Nazi persecution. These already shifted gender relations were then brought to all countries of refuge and affected adjustments and integrations therein. In addition to Palestine, German Jews found refuge in countries as diverse as the United States, Great Britain, various South American states such as Brazil and Argentina, South Africa, Australia, and the International Zone of Shanghai. In all these countries of refuge, the immigrants faced manifold challenges and a complicated process of adjusting and integrating into their host countries. They needed to learn a new language, become acclimatized to a new climate and culture, find a source of income and a place to stay, and often learn a new occupation. The conditions for integration differed depending on the country of refuge and the individual background of the immigrants. Those who emigrated to the United States or England moved to countries perceived as Western and therefore culturally relatively similar. But those who emigrated to the Middle East, South America, or Shanghai were confronted with what they perceived as extreme conditions: tropical or desert climates, unknown diseases, unfamiliar food, underdeveloped economies, poor housing, a lack of sanitary conditions, and insufficient healthcare. However, even those who fled to Western countries faced a difficult economic situation due to the worldwide Great Depression, along with ambivalent attitudes in the host society. In many countries, the immigrants were subjected to apprehension, hostility, and anti-Semitism. Only a few immigrants could continue with their careers uninterrupted and enjoy a swift economic and social integration, the famous physicist Albert Einstein being possibly the most prominent example. Most had to make do with what Wolfgang Benz called the "exile of the little people": menial jobs, poverty, and crowded housing.[2]

With the outbreak of World War II, the situation worsened. Those immigrants who had sought shelter in countries attacked by Germany and the Axis powers were faced with war, and those in countries that were conquered were deported and murdered. Almost a hundred thousand German Jews had fled to countries that were later invaded by the Nazis, and eventually, thirty thousand of these were killed. Even Tel Aviv and Haifa were attacked by Italian warplanes in 1940; and in 1941, there was growing fear of a possible German invasion of Palestine by Erwin Rommel and the Africa Corps of the Axis. In Shanghai, German Jews had to live in a ghetto established by the Japanese military after 1943. In the countries of the Allied Powers, the United States, and England, German-Jewish immigrants were classified as enemy aliens and in certain cases even arrested. These various political conditions had gendered consequences, as well. To name just one example, in Great Britain, female immigrants were in greater danger by far of being arrested than men, and eventually more women than men were registered as enemy aliens.[3]

The shock of being exiled from Germany and having to deal with a harsh new reality posed economic, social, and psychological challenges for all immigrants—problems that had a gendered dimension. Men in general had greater problems finding a job in the host countries, not only due to the economic situation but also, as has been argued, because they were less willing to work in badly paid jobs than their wives were.[4] They often underwent vocational retraining to lay the foundation for a later, better career while their wives worked in menial jobs to provide for the family in the meantime. In all countries of refuge, immigrant women took upon themselves a triple burden: they became breadwinners; at the same time they remained responsible for housekeeping and childcare; and they were responsible as well for providing emotional support for their families, given the continued patriarchal expectations of families and communities. The majority of German-Jewish women had been homemakers before emigration; now they needed to take up work outside the home for the first time in their lives. The number one job for female immigrants was working as a maid—as it remains to this day. Female professionals, such as physicians, meanwhile, faced sexist discrimination on the job market and at work, while also being expected to continue to handle the household at home.

Thus, German-Jewish women and men in all countries of exile faced gendered crisis and role reversals. The manifestations of this experience differed, however, due to the range of gender relations and ideals of masculinity and femininity in the respective countries. This book has engaged with this discussion of female immigrants and their characterization as "women of valor" in the Palestinian case. In so doing, it has contested the assumption that it was easier for women than for men to cope with the outcomes of their immigration, an assumption that seems to rest on essentialist characterizations of both women and men. The conclusions of this book are applicable to other countries of refuge as well: the possibilities for expressing themselves and making their voices heard, and hence for being documented in the historical records, were different for men and for women, and the respective absorbing bodies in the various countries responded differently to such expressions when they came from men versus when they came from women, based on normative gendered ideologies.

What, then, is specific to the migration of German Jews to Mandatory Palestine, compared with these other countries of refuge? First of all, Palestine was not a sovereign state. Thus, there were two main governmental actors that needed to be taken into consideration in this case, the British and the Yishuv. Each had its own policies and agendas that can be seen in gendered migration policies. While immigration is always a selective process, in Palestine, a pioneering country, this selection process was different in terms of gender than it was in the immigration to the United States and the United Kingdom. As a result, the latter two received more female than male migrants, while in Palestine, there were more male immigrants. A further difference was that Palestine was considered a less-developed country with a non-Western character and different geographical and climatic conditions, and the adaptation required to migrate there was therefore perceived to be more radical than it was for the main countries of absorption. This may have produced an even greater strain on gender relations, given the necessary adaptations for homemaking and to the labor market. These conditions were more comparable to those in the Dominican Republic and Shanghai, but in those places, first of all, only relatively small groups of German-Jewish arrived to begin with, and secondly, most never intended to stay.

Moreover, the immigrants to Palestine arrived while the Yishuv was in an intensive period of nation building, calling for the transformation of its residents into new men and women and requiring that they participate in the project of creating a new society. This led to much more rigorous demands on its new immigrants from the host society than was the case in other countries, also in terms of gender. The immigrants found themselves in the middle of an ongoing ideological struggle over the very boundaries of this state-in-the-making. Central to this definition was the construction of the boundary between Jews and non-Jews, a process in which women were seen as crucial. These claims were conveyed to the newcomers through the unique setting of an official absorption apparatus that itself consisted of immigrants, while also being part of the authorities of the receiving society.

In proportion to its population, the Yishuv absorbed more German-Jewish immigrants than any other country in the world. This made processes such as ethnic neighborhood formation more visible, and the prospect of a social crisis in this group more threatening, and placed the immigrants and their actions more firmly in the spotlight than in other countries. The size of the group in proportion to the receiving society also gave rise to a strong and well-connected immigrant community with a wish for continuity. The situation in Palestine was therefore unique in a variety of ways: it absorbed proportionally more German immigrants than any other country; it entailed the most difficult socioeconomic and climatic conditions of the main countries of absorption; and it turned into the longest-lasting diaspora of German Jewry, with the most visible legacy to this day.[5]

Migration is a normal part of the human experience. Even involuntary and forced migration movements like that of the German Jews to Palestine are, historically speaking, not an odd phenomenon. Especially in the twentieth century, migration was an experience undergone by millions of people. The twenty-first century could see migration become an even bigger phenomenon. Migration can disrupt patriarchal structures and enable the renegotiating of gender relations; however, it can also lead to the reinforcement of traditional gender roles. In general, when we look at migration through a gendered lens, there are several patterns that can frequently be found: changing gender roles; renegotiations of gender relations; relational strains and family dissolution; gendered acculturation dissonance; greater constraints on female than on male mobility; and hypersurveillance of girls, both through families and communities.[6]

The remarks that this book makes about German Jews in Palestine also apply more broadly to other migration movements, both historic and modern. Restrictive migration policies, for example, often affect men and women differently, and absorption policies can either mitigate or perpetuate the resulting power imbalances. Discourses about new immigrants often rest on gendered assumptions to which migrants react in different ways—sometimes accepting and internalizing them, sometimes also ignoring or resisting them. Thinking about the impact of gender on the specific historical migration to Palestine can help us think more broadly about the timely issue of large migration movements.

Methodologically as well, this book makes suggestions that go beyond the scope of this study. In researching migration, we choose among a variety of hierarchical viewpoints: taking a micro versus macro perspective (in other words, individual immigrants or the immigration wave); looking at the center (desirable immigrants in the eyes of the absorbing society) versus the margins (unwanted immigrants and marginalized groups); studying immigrants versus emigrants. Bringing together different perspectives can provide us a broader and more in-depth understanding of the complexity of the migration process, its (historic) actors, and their decisions. The micro perspective can shed light on the macro, for example when we examine the reactions of individual immigrants who protest against certain immigration policies. By the same token, looking at the margins can shed new light on the center, such as when we look at how newcomers react to the discourse of the veteran society that criticizes and "others" those newcomers. Creating a dialogue between different source groups, interpreting and linking them with each other, can enhance the validity and significance of the research of migration by drawing on the different perspectives present in the source groups. And lastly, there is the crucial question of how immigrants are remembered, both in the society they left—or were expelled from—and in the society they joined. The evaluation of immigrants according to the ultimate success of their integration is a timely issue. As Leo Lucassen notes, there is a tendency to idealize historic immigrants while discussing today's immigrants mainly as a cause of trouble, even apocalypse.[7] The German Jews in Palestine are a very apt example. While today, they serve as a metaphor for everything considered Western, liberal, and progressive in Israeli society and are hailed for their manifold contributions, at the time they arrived, they were heavily criticized for endangering Yishuv society economically, culturally, and morally.

Ultimately, bringing gender into the study of migration means bringing to the fore this crucial axis of social relations at all stages of the migration process. Looking at migration through a gendered lens enables us to understand the category of gender in the process of its very construction and reconstruction. This is imperative, given that in the ways that debates about migration today are structured and experienced, gender is as crucial as it was in the 1930s for those German Jews who found refuge in Mandatory Palestine.

Notes

Introduction

1. Leni Grünstein, "Als wir einst ins Land herkamen," Bet Yitzhak 1940. Bet Yitzhak Archive, Leni Grünstein Collection, Box 5, File 4. All translations of written sources and interviews into English are by the author, unless otherwise noted. A *turiah* is an agricultural tool, comparable to a hoe.

2. Scott, "Gender."

3. See Green, "Changing Paradigms"; Green and Reynolds, "Four Ages of Migration Studies"; Nawyn, "Gender and Migration"; Donato and Gabaccia, *Gender and International Migration*.

4. Calavita, "Gender, Migration, and Law"; Piper, "Gendering the Politics of Migration."

5. Dwork and van Pelt, *Flight from the Reich*, xiii.

6. See Benz, *Das Exil*. For an overview of the emigration of German Jews, see Stiftung Jüdisches Museum Berlin and Stiftung Haus der Geschichte der Bundesrepublik Deutschland, *Heimat und Exil*.

7. Halamish, "Immigration Is Israel's History."

8. Shuval, "The Mythology of 'Uniqueness'"; Alroey, *An Unpromising Land*; Lavsky, *The Creation of the German-Jewish Diaspora*.

9. Halamish, "Palestine as a Destination," 123.

10. Lavsky, *The Creation of the German-Jewish Diaspora*, 2–6. See also see Niederland, *Yehudey Germania*.

11. See the contributions in Tramer, *In zwei Welten*; Feilchenfeld, Michaelis, and Pinner,

Haavara-Transfer nach Palästina; Turnowsky-Pinner, *Die zweite Generation*; Luft, *Heimkehr ins Unbekannte*.

12. See for example Niederland, "Deutsche Ärzte-Emigration"; Jütte, *Die Emigration der deutschsprachigen "Wissenschaft des Judentums*.

13. Miron, *Mi "sham" le "kan" beGuf rishon*; Schlör, *Endlich im gelobten Land?*; Zimmermann and Hotam, *Zweimal Heimat*, 10–13; Brunner, *Deutsche(s) in Pälastina und Israel*; Siegemund, *Deutsche und Zentraleuropäische Juden*.

14. Yonay, "Gay German Jews and the Arrival of 'Homosexuality' to Mandatory Palestine."

15. See for example Erel, *Kaleidoskop Israel*.

16. Miron, *Mi "sham" le "kan" beGuf rishon*, 297.

17. Lavsky, *The Creation of the German-Jewish Diaspora*, 10.

18. Sela-Sheffy, "Integration through Distinction"; Sela-Sheffy, "High Status Immigration Group."

19. Wassermann, "Das Deutsche in Erez Israel."

20. For interview collections, see for example Betten and Du-Nour, *Wir sind die letzten*. For autobiography-based research, see for example Kreppel, *Deutsch, Jüdisch, Israelisch*.

21. Siegemund, "'Die Jeckes,'" 22.

22. Kaplan, *The Making of the Jewish Middle Class*.

23. See Freidenreich, "Die jüdische 'Neue Frau.'"

24. See, e.g., Meyer and Brenner, *Deutsch-jüdische Geschichte in der Neuzeit*; Zimmermann, *Die deutschen Juden 1914–1945*; Dahm and Benz, *Die Juden in Deutschland 1933–1945*; Paucker, Gilchrist, and Suchy, *Die Juden im nationalsozialistischen Deutschland*.

25. Kaplan, *Between Dignity and Despair*, 8–10. See also Ofer, "The Contribution of Gender"; Koonz, "Courage and Choice"; Thalmann, "Jüdische Frauen"; Huebel, *Fighter, Worker, and Family Man*.

26. Miron, *Lehiot Yehudi beGermania ha Nazit*, 1–12.

27. Quack, *Between Sorrow and Strength*; Quack, *Zuflucht Amerika*; Quack, "Changing Gender Roles"; Kushner, "Fremde Arbeit"; Levine, *Class, Networks, and Identity*; Kaplan, *Dominican Haven*; Luscher, *Frauen in der Emigration*; Grossmann, "'Neue Frauen' im Exil"; Miron, "Introduction," 44–54.

28. Quack, "Introduction," 9. See the same notion in other contributions to Quack's edited volume *Between Sorrow and Strength*, for example Gay, "Epilogue: The First Sex"; Kranzler, "Women in the Shanghai Jewish Refugee Community," 133; Kaplan, "Jewish Women in Nazi Germany."

29. For a study on masculinities, see Gerson, "Family Matters."

30. Miron, "From Bourgeois Germany to Palestine"; Miron, *Mi "sham" le "kan" beGuf rishon*, 256–63; Yosef, "Mi 'Yekkiot' le Zioniot"; Yosef and Miron, "Burganut ve Zionut."

31. Farges, "'Muscle' Yekkes?"; Farges, "Multiple Masculinities"; Farges, "'Generation Palmach'?"

32. Shilo, *Nashim bonot Uma*; Halpern, "Jewish Social Workers"; Davidi, *Bonot Aretz Hadasha*.

33. See Barkai, "Selbsthilfe im Dilemma." See also Jünger, *Jahre der Ungewissheit*.

34. Kaplan, *Between Dignity and Despair*, 63–65; Kaplan, "Jewish Women in Nazi Germany," 34–48.

35. Kaplan, *Between Dignity and Despair*, 59, 67; see also Barkai, "Jüdisches Leben unter der Verfolgung."

36. Schüler-Springorum, *Geschlecht und Differenz*, 121–22.

37. Kaplan, "Jewish Women in Nazi Germany," 41–42.

38. Halperin, *Babel in Zion*.

39. Shilo, "The Double or Multiple Image." See also the various chapters in Bernstein, *Pioneers and Homemakers* as well as in Kark, Shilo, and Hasan-Rokem, *Jewish Women in Pre-State Israel*.

40. Halamish, "Palestine as a Destination."

41. Halamish, "Palestine as a Destination," 125.

42. Halamish, "Aflayat Nashim beTkufat haMandat"; Halamish, *BeMirutz Kaful Neged haSman*, 178–85.

43. Bernstein, "Daughters of the Nation."

44. Department of Statistics of the Jewish Agency for Palestine, Jewish Immigration into Palestine from Germany during 1933–1938. Bulletin No. 3, February 1939, CZA S7/787; Kaplan, "Jewish Women in Nazi Germany," 42.

45. On the history and development of the German Department and the HOG, see Gelber, *Moledet Hadasha*, 222–316.

46. Cherniavsky, *BeOr Shineyhem*, 27–28.

47. Feilchenfeld, Michaelis, and Pinner, *Haavara-Transfer*; Barkai, "German Interests"; Nicosia, "Haavara, Hachschara und Aliyah-beth." See also Segev, *The Seventh Million*, 19–20.

48. For a description of this experience, see for example Heller, *Dr. Seligmanns Auswanderung*.

49. On the use of memoirs in German-Jewish gender history, see the debate between Marion Kaplan and Miriam Gebhardt: Kaplan, "Weaving Women's Words"; Gebhardt, "Der Fall Clara Geißmar." See also Gebhardt, *Das Familiengedächtnis*.

50. Miron, *Mi "sham" le "kan" beGuf rishon*, 54.

51. See for example Portelli, "What Makes Oral History Different." See also Niethammer, *Lebenserfahrung und kollektives Gedächtnis*.

Chapter 1

1. Vera Rosenbaum-London, "Hausfrauenbrief aus Palästina," *Jüdische Rundschau*, November 3, 1933, 751.

2. Advertisements for N. Israel and others can be found in Palästina-Amt, *Alijah*, 75–78.

3. Kaplan, *Between Dignity and Despair*, 133. Judith Gerson also mentions this as a reason why male autobiographers hardly mention the logistical work: Gerson, "Family Matters," 222.

4. *Informations-Rundschreiben des Palästina-Amtes Berlin*, May 19, 1936, 252–53.

5. See "Brief an das Palästina-Amt Berlin, Abt. für Veröffentlichungen," November 7, 1933, CZA, S7/27/2-106; "Ratschläge für Einwanderer. Was nimmt man mit?" *Jüdische Rundschau*, no. 86, October 27, 1933, 706.

6. M. Bergner-Teichner, "Brief aus Palästina," *Jung Wizo: Monatsschrift* 8 (1936), 9/10, 18.

7. Yissakhar Ben-Yaacov described how his parents sold their belongings in an auction prior to emigration, using that money to buy new clothes that were suitable for the climate in Palestine. See Ben-Yaacov, *Leben für Israel*, 28. See also Stern, *In bewegter Zeit*, 10, 130; Mühsam, *Mein Weg zu mir*, 169.

8. *Informations-Rundschreiben des Palästina-Amtes Berlin*, May 19, 1936, 251. Emigrants from Germany were only allowed to take 10 reichsmark with them in cash, an amount they had usually used up by the time they arrived in Palestine.

9. Miron, *Lehiot Yehudi beGermania ha Nazit*, 121–28.

10. Interview with Yohanan B.

11. See interview with Yohanan B.; Fritz Wolf, "Das Zwischenreich 1958/59," Tefen/Galilee, GF 0113/2, 375; Interview with Miriam R., May 29, 2011.

12. Albert Baer, "Palästina-Bilderbogen: Erste Folge," *Jüdische Rundschau*, December 22, 1933, 994. See also Helene Hanna Thon, "Umzugstage in Palästina," *Jüdische Rundschau*, May 4, 1934, 5.

13. Shifman and Katz, "'Just Call Me Adonai.'"

14. See for example Hans Wallach, "Was sind 'Jeckes'?" *Jüdische Rundschau*, June 22, 1937, 8.

15. Other options included a journey by train via Istanbul and Beirut or a journey by plane or by car. There were, however, only a few immigrants who arrived in those ways. See Palästina-Amt, *Alijah*, 89.

16. Jonas, *Memoirs*, 75. Those who escaped Germany in a hurry to avoid incarceration could not even say good-bye, as Martin Hauser writes (Hauser, *Wege jüdischer Selbstbehauptung*, 51.). See also Meta Frank, who remembered the last words her mother told her on the platform: "May G'd give you the strength to endure your new life" (Frank, *Schalom, meine Heimat*, 33).

17. Ben-Yaacov, *Leben für Israel*, 33.

18. See for example Feuchtwanger, *Zukunft*, 173; Stern, *Warum hassen sie uns?*, 313. See also Mühsam, *Ich bin ein Mensch gewesen*, 170.

19. Herlitz, *Mein Weg nach Jerusalem*, 154.

20. See for example Margarete Sallis, "Meine beiden 40 Jahre, Netanya 1975," Leo Baeck Institute Archives New York, ME 550. See also Schlör, "Solange wir auf dem Schiff waren."

21. Justus Klimann, April 24, 1936, letter from aboard the ship *Tel Aviv* on the way from Trieste to Haifa (Archive Kfar Shmaryahu, Klimann Family Collection, no file reference).

Klimann was later one of the founders of the middle-class German-Jewish settlement Kfar Shmaryahu.

22. See Schlör, "Solange wir auf dem Schiff waren." Schlör's thought-provoking articles on the subject have recently led to further research. See, for example, the various contributions in Schlör, "Die Schiffsreise als Übergangserfahrung."

23. Ben-Yaacov, *Leben für Israel*, 37. For a description of spending the trip in steerage, see Aloni, *Zypressen zerbrechen nicht*, 5–20.

24. Siegel, "Die Jungfernfahrt der 'Tel Aviv.'"

25. See Schlör, "Solange wir auf dem Schiff waren." Palästina-Amt, *Alijah* also included many tourism-oriented comments about the various possible routes for the journey to Palestine. See also Sallis, "Meine beiden 40 Jahre," 168.

26. Stern, *Warum hassen sie uns?*, 255.

27. See Frieda Weinreich, "Fürsorgerin in Jaffa. Aus der Praxis des Hafendienstes bei der Landung," *Jüdische Rundschau*, July 24, 1934, 4; Frank, *Schalom, meine Heimat*, 34.

28. Hitahdut Oley Germania, *Bordmerkblatt*.

29. Yoav Gelber argues that the questions addressed in this information sheet, such as about the average prices for taxis, public transfers, telephones, were different from those asked by immigrants of earlier immigration waves as well as from those asked by most other immigrants of the Fifth Aliyah: Gelber, "Oley Germania beHaifa."

30. See Sallis, "Meine beiden 40 Jahre," 167; interview with Miriam S. See also Wolff and Wolff, *Das eigene Leben erzählen*, 115.

31. Aloni, *Zypressen zerbrechen nicht*, 13.

32. Interview with Miriam S. See also interview with Hilde S.; Ben-Yaacov, *Leben für Israel*, 38; Aloni, *Zypressen zerbrechen nicht*, 89.

33. Hauser, *Wege jüdischer Selbstbehauptung*, 56.

34. Stern, *Warum hassen sie uns?*, 253–54.

35. See Frank, *Schalom, meine Heimat*, 34, 253; Granach, *Where Is Home?*, 59. See also Godenschweger, Vilmar, and Michaeli, *Die rettende Kraft der Utopie*, 70.

36. Tergit, *Im Schnellzug nach Haifa*, 11–12.

37. Lotte Pinkus, "99 Shanim haRishonot. Sipura shel Lotte Pinkus, Kibbutz Baram," no year, Tefen/Galilee, GF 0335, 24–25.

38. Hans Bernkopf, "Brief an die Eltern," August 3, 1934, Tefen/Galilee, GF 0093/5.

39. Shlomit (Irna) Mueller, "Dereh Ha adasha sheli: Pardess Chana," 1998, Tefen/Galilee, GF 0290/1, 5.

40. Tergit, *Im Schnellzug nach Haifa*, 13.

41. Tergit, *Im Schnellzug nach Haifa*, 13.

42. Wolf, "Israelbuch für Anfänger," Tefen/Galilee, GF 0112/23, 40.

43. See Alianov-Rautenberg, "From Cravat to Khaki."

44. Herbert Wolff, "Erste Erlebnisse: Erster Tag in Palästina," *Jüdische Rundschau*, July 4, 1933, 303.

45. Granach, *Where Is Home?*, 60.

46. Ben-Yaacov, *Leben für Israel*, 38.

47. With the beginning of the Arab Unrest, the Jaffa port was closed to Jews and thus, from 1936 on, most of the immigrants immigrated via Haifa.

48. Interview with Rafael and Ulli T., January 11, 2010. Ulli is referring to Hugo Herrmann's book *Palästina, wie es wirklich ist*. In many interviews, people reported that the sight of the Arabs had caused a strong wish to return to Germany; see for example also interview with Ilse B., November 1, 2009.

49. See, for example, the quote from Jacob Renka in Wetzel, "Auswanderung aus Deutschland"; interview with Hugo M.

50. Alroey, *An Unpromising Land*, 156–58; Cherniavsky, *BeOr Shineyhem*, 73–74.

51. Hitahdut Oley Germania, *Bordmerkblatt*, 13–17. On the examinations, see Katvan, "Hakamat 'haMisrad haRefui.'"

52. See Palästina-Amt, *Alijah*, 37; "Protocol of the Palestine Office in Berlin," November 3, 1935, CZA, S7/150.

53. See Immigration Department of the Palestine Zionist Executive, "Instructions for the Medical Examination of Immigrants."

54. The HOG complained repeatedly about such cases; see, for example, letter from the HOG to the Palestine Office in Berlin, February 10, 1935, CZA, S7/149/5; letter from the HOG to the Palestine Office in Berlin, August 19, 1934, CZA, S7/66/1. See also letter from the HOG to Werner Senator, December 29, 1935, CZA, S7/281/3 about a man at the Bet Olim (immigrant hostel) in Haifa who suffered from epileptic attacks whenever he undertook physical work.

55. German Department, "Report on Jewish Immigration from Germany to Palestine for the years 1933 and 1934," CZA, S7/148; Georg Landauer to Palestine Office Berlin, August 19, 1934, CZA, S7/66/1.

56. See for example the letter from the German Department to Martin Rosenblüth in London, March 7, 1935, CZA, S7/1494; German Department to Palestine Office in Berlin, September 7, 1934, CZA, S7/70/4; Palestine Office Berlin to H. Neumann, March 15, 1935, CZA, S7/149/4.

57. On the experience of vaccinations, see Ben-Yaacov, *Leben für Israel*, 39.

58. Gelber argues that German Jews were the only ones with this problem: Gelber, *Moledet Hadasha*, 245; Ben-Yaacov, *Leben für Israel*, 39. See also Stern, *Warum hassen sie uns?*, 257. If an immigrant family had a *Lift* arriving separately, they had to declare it upon their arrival at customs and it then had to arrive no more than ninety days after their disembarkation. Otherwise, the immigrants would have to pay customs on their items. On problems with receiving the *Lifts*, see Mühsam, *Ich bin ein Mensch gewesen*, 173.

59. This service consisted initially of volunteers; after much debate, the HOG's welcomers eventually received payment for their work in the harbor. Gelber, *Moledet Hadasha*, 227–29.

60. Max Kober to Georg Landauer, February 13, 1934, CZA, S7/70/2. Max Kober (1894–1981) had been the cofounder of the Herzl-Club in Breslau.

61. See for example interview with Ruth B.; Hauser, *Wege jüdischer Selbstbehauptung,* 51, 53, 58–60.

62. Hugo Schachtel to the German Department, October 30, 1934, CZA, copy, S7/108–18. Hugo Schachtel (1876–1949) had been the founder and chairman of the Jewish community and the local Zionist organization in Breslau and was a member of the executive committee of the Zionist Organization in Germany. He immigrated to Haifa in 1933.

63. For similar letters see also CZA, S7/21–83 and S7/21–92.

64. Department of Statistics of the Jewish Agency for Palestine, "Jewish Immigration into Palestine from Germany During 1933–1938. Bulletin No. 3," February 1939, CZA S7/787.

65. Stella Rosenkranz, "Die Einordnung jugendlicher Einwanderinnen," *Jüdische Rundschau,* March 6, 1934, 5–6.

66. "Fürsorge für die alleinstehende Einwanderin," *Jüdische Rundschau,* June 9, 1936, 13.

67. See for example "Report on the Activities of the Hitachduth Olej Germania Haifa," December 1933, CZA S7/26/1; Britschgi-Schimmer, "Probleme der deutschen Mädchen-Alijah," *WIZO Pioniere und Helfer,* February/March, 1935, 17–19.

68. Bernstein, *Daughters of the Nation,* 287–311.

69. Henrietta Szold to Landauer, February 28, 1934, CZA, S7/22–16; Gusta Strumpf to Arthur Ruppin, December 14, 1934, CZA, S7/210/3–23.

70. Landauer to Mahlakat haAliyah, March 12, 1934, CZA, S7/95; "Report on the Case of the Bornstein Family, March 1934," CZA, S7/95; Henrietta Szold to Georg Landauer, February 20, 1934, CZA, S7/95; Lerman to Becher, 1934, CZA, S7/95.

71. See Bernstein, "Gender, Nationalism and Colonial Policy."

72. Georg Landauer to Yizhak Greenboim, February 15, 1934, CZA, S7/70/2. See also Landauer to Executive of the Jewish Agency, London, March 5, 1934, CZA, S7/22–10, in which he asks directly how to deal with Goldschmidt's letter.

73. Henrietta Szold to Georg Landauer, February 28, 1934, CZA, S7/22–16.

74. Frieda Weinreich, "Fürsorgerin in Jaffa. Aus der Praxis des Hafendienstes bei der Landung," *Jüdische Rundschau,* July 24, 1934, 4.

75. Haim Barlas to Henrietta Szold and Georg Landauer, May 16, 1934, CZA, S7/70/2.

76. David Beharel to Yitzhak Greenboim, May 24, 1934, CZA, S7/70/2.

77. Henrietta Szold to Frieda Weinreich, May 24, 1934, CZA, S7/70/2–26.

78. The German Department approved various loans for concrete endeavors but also rejected many of these requests. See CZA, S7/210.

79. Gusta Strumpf to German Department, April 30, 1934, CZA, S7/95.

80. Britschgi-Schimmer, "Probleme der deutschen Mädchen-Alijah," *WIZO Pioniere und Helfer,* February/March, 1935, 19.

81. Interview with Gretel M., November 25, 2010. See also D.-C., "Diary 1914–1938," Tefen/Galilee GF 0184/1.

82. Aloni, *Zypressen zerbrechen nicht,* 90, 91, 104, 117.

83. Landau, "Erste Stationen im Lande." See also the many advertisements in the *Jüdische Rundschau, Mitteilungsblatt,* and *Bordmerkblatt.*

84. "Die Tätigkeit der Hitachduth Olej Germania Gruppe Haifa, Dezember 1933," CZA, S7/26/1.

85. "Die Wizo und das Hilfswerk," *WIZO Pioniere und Helfer*, no. 12 (1933/1934): 13; "Report on Jewish Immigration from Germany to Palestine for the years 1933 and 1934," CZA, S7/148.

86. See also the account of the *Bet Olim* in Tel Aviv in Feuchtwanger, *Zukunft*, 199.

87. Frank, *Schalom, meine Heimat*, 35.

88. Wormann, "Kulturelle Probleme," 285.

89. HOG Haifa to Georg Landauer, April 19, 1934, CZA, S7/95; "Zeltlager auf dem Har Hacarmel," *Mitteilungsblatt*, October 1934, II, 10; Martin Scheftelowitz, "Gute 77 Jahre: Erlebte Tatsachen 1907–1984," Leo Baeck Institute Archives New York, Memoirs Collection, ME 239.

90. Lecture in "Merkas Le'Avodah Sozialith," February 2, 1943, CZA, S7/2078; Levy, *10 Jahre Einwanderer-Fürsorgestelle*, 3.

91. Manfred Geis, "Sozialer Frauendienst in Tel Aviv," *Jüdische Rundschau*, December 24, 1937, p. 10; Cohn, *10 Jahre neue Alijah*, 66–67; Scheftelowitz, "Gute 77 Jahre," 29; Bella Preuss to Landauer, April 4, 1937, CZA, S7/494-171.

92. Berlowitz, "Hausbesuche," *WIZO-Pressedienst aus Erez Israel*, November, 1936, 8. See also "Eingliederung der Frau in die zionistische Bewegung. Ein Vortrag Kurt Blumenfelds über die Frauenarbeit," *Jüdische Rundschau*, no. 38, May 10, 1935, 9.

93. Albert Baer, "Altes und neues Haifa. Das Einwandererheim der HOG," *Jüdische Rundschau*, April 15, 1936, 15.

94. See for example CZA, S7/16-17-18. See also ads for children's homes in the *Bordmerkblatt*, the *Jüdische Rundschau*, and the *Mitteilungsblatt*.

95. Gelber, *Moledet Hadasha*, 247.

96. Interview with Beate D., April 14, 2012.

97. Baer, "Altes und neues Haifa," 15; Heinz Wydra, "Wie macht man den Umzug?" *Jüdische Rundschau*, October 27, 1933, 706. Then, when a family's *Lift* finally arrived, new hassles often began, over broken or wet furniture, with harbor officials and shipping agents.

98. Interview with Ilse B., November 1, 2009.

99. Miron, *Lehiot Yehudi beGermania ha Nazit*, 107–14.

100. Albert Baer, "Deutsche Juden in Palästina. Illusionen der Einwanderer," *Jüdische Rundschau*, November 10, 1933, 785.

101. See Scheftelowitz, "Gute 77 Jahre," 29; Baer, "Deutsche Juden in Palästina," 785.

102. Elias Auerbach, "Rückkehr nach Haifa. Erste Eindrücke," *Jüdische Rundschau*, December 1, 1933, 882.

103. Erich Kraemer, "Zum Artikel 'Missverstandene nationale Disziplin': Antwort an meine Kritiker," *Mitteilungsblatt*, May 1937, II, 12–13, here 13.

104. Baer, "Deutsche Juden in Palästina," 785.

105. Nanny Margulies-Auerbach, "Die Frau in der Alijah aus Deutschland," *Jüdische Rundschau*, March 6, 1934.

106. Helman, "Hues of Adjustment."
107. Levy, *10 Jahre Einwanderer-Fürsorgestelle*.
108. Lavsky, *The Creation of the German-Jewish Diaspora*, 87–90.
109. Interview with Ruth B.
110. Trezib and Sonder, "The Rassco"; Gelber, *Moledet Hadasha*, 357–84; Amikam, *Nirim Rishonim*.
111. Helman, *Young Tel Aviv*, 121–24.
112. Granach, *Where Is Home?*, 97–100.
113. Interview with Ruth R.
114. Hitahdut Oley Germania, *Bordmerkblatt*.
115. Interview with Hugo M.
116. Interview with Eva W., June 7, 2010.
117. See Scheftelowitz, "Gute 77 Jahre," 33.
118. Halperin, *Babel in Zion*, 33–34.
119. Halperin, *Babel in Zion*, 45–59. See also Volovici, *German as a Jewish Problem*, 203–7.
120. Knox and Pinch, *Urban Social Geography*, 337.
121. Knox and Pinch, *Urban Social Geography*, 171–79.
122. Lowenstein, "Women's Role."
123. Herlitz, *Mein Weg nach Jerusalem*, 190–91. See also "Gruppen-Dankesbrief anlässlich der Glückwünsche zu seinem 60. Geburtstag, Juli 1936," CZA, S7/305.
124. See Schwarz-Gardos, *Von Wien nach Tel Aviv*, 141; Wormann, "German Jews," 90.
125. Manfred Geis, "Sozialer Frauendienst in Tel Aviv," *Jüdische Rundschau*, December 24, 1937, 10; Cohn, *10 Jahre neue Alijah*, 66; Scheftelowitz, "Gute 77 Jahre," 29; Bella Preuss to Georg Landauer, April 4, 1937, CZA, S7/494–171. In the 1940s, separate female groups were founded within the HOG: *Mitteilungsblatt*, February 28, 1947, 10; *Mitteilungsblatt*, May 17, 1946.
126. Jonas, *Memoirs*, 83–85. "Pil" stood for the friends Hans Jacob Polotsky, Jonas himself, and Hans Lewy. The fellow Zionists who joined them later, in addition to Sholem, included Georg Lichtheim and Hans Sambursky.

Chapter 2

1. Hans Bernkopf to his parents and Lotte, August 8, 1934. Archives of the German-Speaking Jewry Heritage Museum in Tefen/Galilee, GF 0093/5, 2. All translations of written sources and interviews into English are by the author, unless otherwise noted.
2. Helman, *Young Tel Aviv*, 150.
3. For interactions between Arabs and "Oriental" Jews, see Jacobson and Naor, *Oriental Neighbors*.
4. Bernstein, "Contested Contact."
5. Both terms are problematic: *Oriental Jews* carries derogatory implications, while *Mizrahim* is anachronistic. On the complex debate regarding the use of these terms, see for example Shohat, "Invention"; Raz-Krakotzkin, "Zionist Return"; Jacobson and Naor, *Oriental Neighbors*, 6–9.

6. Kalmar and Penslar, "Orientalism and the Jews: An Introduction."

7. See Saß, *Berliner Luftmenschen*. See also Brinkmann, *Migration und Transnationalität*, 61–91.

8. Aschheim, *Brothers*, 58. See also Aschheim, *Beyond the Border*; Aschheim, "Reflections."

9. Kalmar and Penslar, "Orientalism and the Jews: An Introduction," xxxviii.

10. Cherniavsky, *BeOr Shineyhem*, 76–79.

11. Shifman and Katz, "'Just Call Me Adonai.'"

12. See for example Sznaider, "Between Past and No Future," 29–49; Stachel, "HaAliyah," 191–210.

13. Fritz Loewenstein, "Sprechsaal: Emigranten und Olim," *Mitteilungsblatt*, November 1934, II, 9–10.

14. See for example Hotam, "Emigrierte Erinnerung"; Wormann, "Kulturelle Probleme"; Volkmann, *Neuorientierung*, 306–8.

15. Halperin, *Babel*, 26.

16. Feuchtwanger, *Zukunft*, 341. German Jews often pointed out in return that most of Yishuv society spoke not proper Hebrew but Yiddish. See also Volovici, *German as a Jewish Problem*, 203–7.

17. See for example "Kritik an der deutschen Alijah," *Jüdische Rundschau*, October 20, 1933, 669; "Von einer Palästinareise," *Kinder-Rundschau*, no. 13, July 24, 1936.

18. Rubin, "'Turning Goyim.'"

19. Helman, *Young Tel Aviv*, 91–99, 153–57. See also Schlör, "How to Cook."

20. Contemporary articles also referred to this conflict as having been imported from Europe: for example Georg Blumenthal, "Sprechsaal 2," *Mitteilungsblatt*, October 1934, II, 3–4; E. P., "Die Kinder haben Europa vergessen," *Jüdische Rundschau*, March 4, 1938, 14.

21. Else Bodenheimer-Biram to Georg Landauer, November 14, 1933, CZA, S7/1/1–110. Spinneys was a British import supermarket chain.

22. Tom Lewy (*Bühnen*, 166) shows this for theater plays with stereotypical Yekke characters in the Ohel Theater in the 1930s.

23. See for example Kloetzel, "Schabbat in Jerusalem. Leserbrief." *Jüdische Rundschau*, September 8, 1936, 12.

24. Helene Hanna Thon, "Freiheit und 'Freiheit': Erlebnisse mit neuen Einwanderern," *Jüdische Rundschau*, May 10, 1934, 12.

25. Halperin, *Babel*, 32–34.

26. Interview with Eva W.

27. Interview with Eva W.

28. Interview with Ilse B., November 8, 2009.

29. Interview with Avraham M., July 21, 2010.

30. Georg Goldstein to *Va'ad HaKehilla* Haifa, November 1, 1937, Haifa City Archive, 00236/9.

31. Walter Blumenthal, "Die Vorgeschichte der Kupat Milve Ha Oleh," unpublished manuscript, 7, quoted in Viest, *Identität*, 53.

32. Martin Scheftelowitz, "Gute 77 Jahre: Erlebte Tatsachen 1907–1984," Leo Baeck Institute Archives New York, ME 239, 23.

33. Erich Badrian, "Bericht für Bundesbrüder über Prozess in Haifa gg. ehem: Leitung der Autobus-Kooperative," 1937, CZA, S7/801.

34. See for example Nanny Margulies-Auerbach, "Der neue Jischuw und Tozereth Haarez," *WIZO Pioniere und Helfer* 10, no. 4 (June 1936): 9.

35. See for example Stern, "'He Walked through the Fields.'"

36. Moshe Yaakov Ben-Gavriel (1891–1965), born Eugen Hoeflich in Vienna, author and novelist, proponent of pan-Semitism and *Brith Shalom*, immigrated first in 1915, returned to Vienna, then immigrated again in 1927. Remarkably, Ben-Gavriel, himself of Austrian origin and only in Palestine since 1927, presented himself in his letter as a "veteran Palestinian." The harsh critiques of their German brethren by Ben-Gavriel and others were surely partly motivated by the desire to establish themselves as old-timers.

37. Moshe Yaakov Ben-Gavriel, "Ein Wort an die Einwanderer aus Deutschland," *Jüdische Rundschau*, September 12, 1933, 51.

38. Cherniavsky, *BeOr Shineyhem*, 77–79.

39. Albert Baer, "Die andere Seite: Eine Antwort," *Jüdische Rundschau*, October 27, 1933, 707.

40. H. Katz, "Sprechsaal," *Mitteilungsblatt*, October 1934 (2), 2–3. He was referring to Moshe Yaakov Ben-Gavriel, "Gedanken- oder Taktlosigkeit," *Mitteilungsblatt*, September 1934, 4.

41. Interview with Miriam L.; interview with Eva W., June 7, 2010, for example.

42. Helman, *Coat of Many Colors*, 21–50.

43. Cherniavsky, *BeOr Shineyhem*, 57.

44. Helman, *Young Tel Aviv*, 134.

45. Stern, "'He Walked through the Fields'"; Shilo, "The Double or Multiple Image."

46. On the feminist theory of objectification see Nussbaum, "Objectification."

47. Scheftelowitz, "Gute 77 Jahre," Leo Baeck Institute Archives New York, 36; Feuchtwanger, *Zukunft*, 209.

48. Interview with Ruth L., June 17, 2010. See also Gerda Luft (*Chronik eines Lebens*, 26) who described how in Germany, her mother wouldn't let her play with the neighbors' children because they were all from Eastern Europe.

49. Stachel, "HaAliyah," 206–10.

50. Granach, *Where Is Home?*, 66.

51. W. Sachs to his friend Leo (copy), March 20, 1934, CZA, S7/80.

52. Miron, *Mi "sham" le "kan" beGuf rishon*, 132–35.

53. Interview with Ruth M.

54. Interview with Eva W., June 14, 2010.

55. Interview with Eva W., June 14, 2010; interview with Miriam L.; interview with Gretel M., November 25, 2010.
56. Tergit, *Im Schnellzug nach Haifa*, 64.
57. See Freidenreich, "Die jüdische 'Neue Frau.'" For the discussion in the Yishuv, see Stern, "'He Walked through the Fields.'"
58. Interview with Beate D., March 17, 2012.
59. Interview with Ilse B., November 8, 2009.
60. Gelber, "Central European Immigration," 329. See also Miron, *Mi "sham" le "kan" beGuf rishon*, 136–37. Conflicts and differences between Ostjuden and Westjuden were relevant in other countries of refuge, too: see for example Berghahn, *Continental Britons*, 228–30.
61. Conversation with Dr. Ishay Geva, May 10, 2015.
62. Ilsar, *Leben in Wandlungen*, 49.
63. Ilsar, *Leben in Wandlungen*. See also interview with Jacob M., July 14, 2010, for similar experiences, as well as Ben-Yaacov, *Leben für Israel*, 15, about his grandparents' worries that his father might marry an Ostjudin, "an unthinkable step into a mixed marriage."
64. Interview with Gretel M., November 25, 2010.
65. Helene Hanna Thon, "The Jewish Mothers of Germany," CZA, A 217/19.
66. Ruth Meier, *Mitteilungsblatt Yakinton* (251(, April 2012, Dalet.
67. Gertz, *Statistical Handbook*, 60; Poliak, *The Jews of Palestine*, 19–27.
68. Smooha, "The Mass Immigrations," 4.
69. Kalmar and Penslar, "Orientalism and the Jews: An Introduction," xxxviii. See also Helman, *Young Tel Aviv*, 134–36; Khazzoom, *Shifting Ethnic Boundaries*, 8–9.
70. See for example the article on Yemenite theatre in the *Jüdische Rundschau*, June 28, 1938; Chemjo Winawer, "Von Jemenitischen Gesängen," *Jüdische Rundschau*, December 13, 1935.
71. Shilo, *Nashim bonot Uma*. See also Halpern, "Jewish Social Workers."
72. Hirsch, "We Are Here to Bring the West," 590; Hirsch, "'Interpreters of Occident.'"
73. Radai, "Yozey Arzot ha-Islam."
74. Gerda Luft, "Tel-Awiw: Zwei Städte," *Jüdische Rundschau*, May 14, 1937.
75. Luft, "Tel-Awiw."
76. See the discussion of similar descriptions in Hirsch, "We Are Here to Bring the West."
77. Luft, "Tel-Awiw."
78. See Konrad, *Wurzeln jüdischer Sozialarbeit*.
79. Nadja Stein, "Comments on a WIZO Movie," CZA, A 217/13.
80. See for example *Palästinablatt*, no. 20, March 11, 1938, 1; Nadja Stein, "Die Jugendfürsorge der Stadt Tel Aviv," CZA, A217/18; "WIZO Broschüre über Palästinaarbeit," CZA, A217/22; see also Konrad, *Wurzeln jüdischer Sozialarbeit*, 202–6.
81. Luft, "Tel-Awiw." See also, for many very similar pictures, Hirsch, "Interpreters of Occident."

82. Esther Smoira, "Frauen-Arbeit: Aufgaben der 'Histadruth Naschim Zionioth,'" *Jüdische Rundschau*, November 3, 1936, 11.

83. Interview with Ruth M.

84. Gerda Luft, "Wieviel kostet ein Haushalt in Palästina?" *Jüdische Rundschau*, April 28, 1933, 169.

85. "WIZO-Pressedienst aus Erez Israel (Deutsche Ausgabe)," volume 2, no. 7, April 1937, CZA, A 217/19.

86. Cheskel Zwi Kloetzel (1891–1951), a German-Jewish journalist and writer.

87. C. Z. Kloetzel, "Jerusalemer Gestalten: Meine Osereth," *Jüdische Rundschau*, July 1, 1938, 12.

88. On the Orientalist discourse on effeminacy, see for example Peleg, "Re-Orientalizing the Jew."

89. Feuchtwanger, *Zukunft*, 257–58.

90. Interview with Miriam S.

91. She is comparing "mixed marriages" with Mizrahim to interfaith marriages between Jews and Gentiles. Conversation with Gitta B. See also interview with Eva W., June 7, 2010.

92. Interview with Alisa E.

93. Hitahdut Oley Germania Jerusalem to presidium of the Hitahdut Oley Germania Tel Aviv, November 21, 1937, CZA, S7/690–59.

94. Cherniavsky, *BeOr Shineyhem*, 59–60.

95. For a concise overview, see Almog, *The Sabra*, 185.

96. The historian Anja Siegemund, who has researched German Zionism and its approach to the Arab question in pre-state Palestine, argues that *Verständigung* is the key term in their discussions. The centrality within the German Zionist movement of the search for a solution to the conflict with the Arabs, she suggests, justifies the neologism of *Verständigungszionismus*: Siegemund, "German Zionists of *Verständigung*."

97. Lavsky, *Before Catastrophe*, 34–36.

98. On the political organization see Gelber, *Moledet Hadasha*, especially 476–545. See also Getter, "HaHitargenut."

99. Hauser, *Wege jüdischer Selbstbehauptung*, 56.

100. See Palästina-Amt, *Alijah*, 173.

101. Fritz Wolf, "Israelbuch für Anfänger," Archives of the German-Speaking Jewry Heritage Museum in Tefen/Galilee, GF 0112/23, 45. On sexualized perceptions of Arabs reflected in contemporary Hebrew literature on the harem, see Peleg, *Orientalism*, 92–93, 120–21.

102. See for example interview with Ruth L., June 17, 2010; interview with Eva W., June 7, 2010; "Letter to Alfred," April 9, 1933, CZA, S7/21–121.

103. "Picture of Mrs. Klimann," Kfar Shmaryahu 1930s, Kfar Shmaryahu Archive, Klimann Family Collection.

104. Interview with Ilse B., November 1, 2009.

105. Miron, *Mi "sham" le "kan" beGuf rishon*, 139–43.

106. Gerda Luft, "Interviews," 1971/72, CZA, A504/37; interview with Eva W., June 7, 2010.

107. Feuchtwanger, *Zukunft*, 211–12.

108. Tergit, *Im Schnellzug nach Haifa*, 22–24.

109. Jacobson and Naor, *Oriental Neighbors*, 119.

110. M. Kopeljuk, "Die Araber in Palästina, Sitten und Ethik," *Jüdische Rundschau*, March 24, 1936, 10.

111. Erez, "'Ahava ve Koz ba,'" 93–96.

112. See for example Helene Hanna Thon, "Unpolitisches zur Araberfrage," *Jüdische Rundschau*, November 14, 1933, 802; Robert Beer, "Palästinensische Wanderungen: Frühlingsfahrt nach Um-Kejss," *Jüdische Rundschau*, March 24, 1936, 10; Moshe Yaakov Ben-Gavriel, "Als Warnung," *Jüdische Rundschau*, March 19, 1937, 12.

113. Thon, "Unpolitisches zur Araberfrage."

114. Thon, "Unpolitisches zur Araberfrage."

115. See Helman, *Young Tel Aviv*, 36–38, 114; Bernstein, "Contested Contact," 215; Segev, *Es war einmal*, 192–93.

116. Bernstein, "Contested Contact," 232.

117. Ernst Alexander-Katz, "Streng Vertraulich! An die Sozialhilfestelle des Jüdischen Gemeindeausschuss Haifa," June 2, 1934, CZA, S7/22-16.

118. Erez, "'Ahava ve Koz ba,'" iv–vi.

119. This section is based on my article: Alianov-Rautenberg, "Kindred Spirits."

120. Sherman, *Mandate Days*, 157; Halamish, "The Yishuv."

121. On the government sector, see Bernstein, *Constructing Boundaries*, 34–35. Jewish-British relations in private encounters, leisure time, and everyday life in Mandatory Palestine have remained under-studied. For an exception, see Lazar, *ha-Mandatorim*. On interactions in the realm of education, see Elboim-Dror, "British Educational Policies," as well as Halperin, "The Battle over Jewish Students." On the social history of the British in Palestine, see Krik, "Colonial Lives in Palestine."

122. Bar-Yosef, "Bonding with the British"; Dubnov, "On Vertical Alliances."

123. Sherman, *Mandate Days*, 27–29, 45. See also Krämer, *Geschichte Palästinas*, 203–5.

124. Abbady, *Benenu le-ven ha-Anglim*.

125. Golani and Reich, "Bein shelihot li-menudot."

126. On the HOG labor exchange, see Levy, *10 Jahre Einwanderer-Fürsorgestelle*.

127. Gelber, *Moledet Hadasha*, 472–75.

128. Conversation with Dan Exiner, Haifa Rowing Club.

129. For an account of sport in the Yishuv in general, see Kaufman, "Jewish Sports in the Diaspora." On German-Jewish immigrants and sport see Ashkenazy, "German Jewish Athletes."

130. Golani and Reich, "Bein shelihot li-menudot," 328.

131. Interview with Ruth M.

132. Eisenberg, *Meine Gäste*; Letter from Hedwig Grossmann to Rudi Lehmann (1940), Archives of the German-Speaking Jewry Heritage Museum in Tefen/Galilee, GF 0390/23; Chotjewitz, *Die mit Tränen säen*; interview with Rafael T., January 11, 2010.

133. Kreppel, *Nahariyya und die deutsche Einwanderung*, 230–31; Oppenheimer, *Nahariya*, 110.

134. Granach, *Where Is Home?*, 74.

135. Tergit, *Im Schnellzug nach Haifa*, 40–44. See also "Brief aus Palästina," *Jung Wizo: Monatsschrift*, May/June 1936, 18. Lotte Cohn wrote about the sartorial influence the British already had in the Yishuv in the 1920s: Cohn, *Die Zwanziger Jahre*, 34.

136. On dress culture in the Yishuv see Helman, *Coat of Many Colors*.

137. Interview with Ruth M.

138. Hedwig Grossmann to Rudi Lehmann, 1940, Archives of the German-Speaking Jewry Heritage Museum in Tefen/Galilee, GF 0390/23.

139. Interview with Rafael T., January 11, 2010.

140. Interview with Alisa E.

141. Bernstein, "Gender, Nationalism and Colonial Policy," 91.

142. Interview with Miriam R., May 29, 2011.

143. See Helman, *Young Tel Aviv*, 127.

144. Interview with Avraham M., July 29, 2010.

145. Else Bodenheimer-Biram to Georg Landauer, November 14, 1933, CZA, S7/1/1–110.

146. Interview with Ruth M.

147. Sherman, *Mandate Days*, 34; Golani and Reich, "Bein shelihot li-menudot," 342.

148. Golani and Reich, "Bein shelihot li-menudot," 344–46. See also Segev, *Es war einmal*, 534–35.

149. Bernstein, "Gender, Nationalism and Colonial Policy."

150. Bar-Yosef, "Bonding with the British," 22.

151. Interview with Rafael T., January 11, 2010.

152. Interview with Hilde S.

153. Bar-Yosef, "Bonding with the British."

154. For a discussion of Jewish students in English schools, including the Haifa English High School for Girls mentioned here, see Halperin, "The Battle over Jewish Students."

155. Interview with Ruth B.

156. Segev, *Es war einmal*, 534–35.

157. See also the comments on this issue in Golani and Reich, "Bein shelihot li-menudot," 325–26.

158. Georg Landauer, "Wir sind der Westen im Osten," *Mitteilungsblatt*, May 16, 1952, 1. See also Georg Landauer, "Gegen den Levantinismus," *Mitteilungsblatt*, January 7, 1955, 1.

Chapter 3

1. "Arbeits- und Berufsberatung in Palästina," in *Informations-Rundschreiben des Palästina-Amtes Berlin* 1936, 263–68 (here 264).

2. "Mitteilungen des Merkas der H.O.G. und der Ortsgruppe Tel Aviv," *Mitteilungsblatt*, December 1934, II, 12–13.

3. Department of Statistics of the Jewish Agency for Palestine, Jewish Immigration into Palestine from Germany during 1933–1938, "Bulletin No. 3," February 1939, CZA, S7/787.

4. Barkai, "Bevölkerungsrückgang," 40–43.

5. Lavsky, *The Creation of the German-Jewish Diaspora*, 31, 81.

6. Hitachduth Olej Germania Tel Aviv, "Aus den Erfahrungen unserer täglichen Arbeit: Berufsumschichtung bei den Einwanderern aus Deutschland," *Mitteilungsblatt*, September 1935, 20. See also HOG to Palestine Office Berlin, November 16, 1934, CZA, S7/149/5.

7. Hitachduth Olej Germania, "Ein Jahr Hilfsarbeit fuer Einwanderer aus Deutschland," *Jüdische Rundschau*, June 8, 1934, 5.

8. Beling, *Gesellschaftliche Eingliederung*, 34.

9. Britschgi-Schimmer, *Umschichtung*, 16.

10. See for example "Nicht zur Veröffentlichung! Beachtenswerte Mitteilungen der Arbeitsberatungsstelle der Jung-Wizo in Tel Aviv," June 1937, CZA, A 217/19; "Bericht der HOG Haifa für die Monate Oktober–November–Dezember 1934," *Mitteilungsblatt*, January 1935, I, 12–13; "Die Tätigkeit der HOG Haifa," December 1933, CZA, Bericht, S7/26/1; "Statistische Erhebungen über die deutschen Olim in Haifa," December 1936, CZA, S90/877/1. See also "Hitachduth Olej Germania: Machleketh Hamoschawoth," September 20, 1934, CZA, S7/26/1.

11. "Bericht HOG Haifa über 40 Sozialfälle," February 27, 1935, CZA, L13/33.

12. Pinner, *Ansiedlung von 675 Familien*.

13. Britschgi-Schimmer, *Umschichtung*; and see also her draft for this report in CZA, S7/402–026; Oppenheimer, *Zur wirtschaftlichen Einordnung*.

14. Britschgi-Schimmer, *Umschichtung*, 63.

15. Britschgi-Schimmer, *Umschichtung*, 16.

16. See also "Zahlen über deutsche Juden in Haifa," *Mitteilungsblatt*, August 1937, I, 9–10, here 9; "HOG Haifa, Sozial-Enquete," July 1936, CZA, S7/494–278; "Lebenshaltung in Palästina," November 1933, CZA, A 217/18.

17. Britschgi-Schimmer, *Umschichtung*, 15.

18. Oppenheimer, *Zur wirtschaftlichen Einordnung*, 85.

19. Britschgi-Schimmer later conducted a follow-up study: Ina Britschgi-Schimmer, "Die Umschichtung und das berufliche Schicksal der deutschen Einwanderer in gewerblichen Berufen," Jerusalem 1940, CZA, S90/1054. This survey, commissioned by the Jewish Agency, examined the immigrants who underwent occupational change to take industrial jobs in Haifa and Jerusalem.

20. See for example "Bauarbeiter werden vorbereitet: Ein wichtiges Gebiet der Berufsumschichtung für Palästina," *Jüdische Rundschau*, March 28, 1934, 12.

21. L. Peritz, "Schicksal der Juden aus Deutschland: Einige Typen," *Jüdische Rundschau*, January 25, 1938. Typologies like this were a common stylistic device; see also Erich Gottgetreu, "Sie kamen aus Deutschland: Palästina privat/ Fünf von Fünfhunderttausend," *Jüdische Welt-Rundschau* 1, August 4, 1939, 9.

22. "Die Tätigkeit der HOG Haifa," December 1933, CZA, S7/26/1.

23. See for example Jochanan Lewinson, "Weg der Heimkehr," *Jüdische Rundschau*, May 28, 1935, 7.

24. Gerda Luft, "Die Palästina-Einwanderung von 1933," *Jüdische Rundschau*, May 19, 1933, 1–2. See also Palästina-Amt Berlin, "Arbeiterzertifikate (Kategorie C)," in *Informations-Rundschreiben des Palästina-Amtes Berlin* 1935, 129–133, here 132; Fritz Loewenstein, "Berufsaussichten in Palästina: Erfahrungen mit der deutschen Alijah," *Jüdische Rundschau*, December 1, 1933, 881.

25. "Briefe aus Palästina," *Jung Wizo: Monatsschrift* 6, nos. 4–5 (1934): 15–18, here 18.

26. "Der Mittelstandssiedler auf dem Lande," *Jüdische Rundschau*, May 1, 1936, 12.

27. "Rundbrief zur Frage der Einwanderung und Einordnung der deutschen Juden in Erez Israel," May 26, 1936, CZA, S7/219, 4.

28. "Bericht über eine Sozial-Enquete der HOG, Haifa," July 1936, CZA, S7/494–278; Samson to Georg Landauer, April 23, 1937, CZA, S7/445.

29. Oppenheimer, *Zur wirtschaftlichen Einordnung*, 28.

30. Jenny Radt, "Einordnungs-Schwierigkeiten," *Jüdische Rundschau*, July 2, 1937, 10.

31. See also, for example, Majer, "Ärzte der Kupat-Cholim: Nähere Informationen für Interessenten," *Jüdische Rundschau*, November 8, 1935.

32. See Gerda Luft, "Eier und Gemüse: Das Dorf deutscher Juden 'Ramot Haschawim,'" *Jüdische Rundschau*, March 15, 1935; Gerda Luft, "Der Siedler aus Deutschland: Psychologisches zu diesem Thema," *Jüdische Rundschau*, January 14, 1938.

33. A. L., "Juden aus Deutschland siedeln: Als Siedler in Herzliah," *Jüdische Rundschau*, 19, March 8, 1938, 6.

34. J. Bar Tikva, "Jüdische Akademiker in der Landwirtschaft: Der Herr Doktor als Taglöhner," *Jüdische Rundschau*, July 21, 1939, 8.

35. Frieda Weinreich, "Arbeitsuchende Frauen: Aus der Praxis der Arbeitsvermittlung der Hitachduth Olej Germania Tel-Awiw," *Jüdische Rundschau*, March 26, 1937, 20.

36. Frieda Weinreich, "Vom Arbeitsmarkt in Palästina," *WIZO Revue* 1 (1937/1938): 16–17.

37. Nadja Stein, "Frauen im Beruf," 1934, CZA, A 217/18.

38. Gerhard Holdheim, "Zur Psychologie der deutschen Alijah," *Jüdische Rundschau*, July 27, 1934, 5.

39. See, for example, Nanny Margulies-Auerbach, "Die Frau in der Alijah aus Deutschland," *Jüdische Rundschau*, March 6, 1934, 5; "Eingliederung der Frau in die zionistische Bewegung: Ein Vortrag Kurt Blumenfelds über die Frauenarbeit," *Jüdische Rundschau*, May 10, 1935, 9.

40. See for example "Erez Israel—das Jugend-Paradies," *Jüdische Rundschau*, February

2, 1934, 5; Arthur Eloesser, "Palästina-Reise: Die Jugend," *Jüdische Rundschau*, June 15, 1934, 4; H. Schachtel, "Das Eier-Dorf: Eine Siedlung von Juden aus Deutschland," *Jüdische Rundschau*, March 2, 1936, 14; Jacob, "Wie wir Hafenarbeiter wurden," *Mitteilungsblatt*, no. 19, July 1938, II, 10; "Baumeisterinnen und Bauarbeiterinnen in Erez Israel," CZA, A 217/18; "Arbeiterinnen beim Chausseebau," *Jüdische Rundschau*, November 10, 1936, 10.

41. Frieda Weinreich, "Vom Arbeitsmarkt in Palästina," *WIZO Revue* 1 (1937/1938): 14–16, here 15.

42. Helene Hanna Thon, "Frauenberufe in Palästina: Ein typisches Gespräch aus der Jerusalemer Beratungsstelle fuer Einwanderer," *Jüdische Rundschau,* June 16, 1933, 260.

43. Cohn, *10 Jahre Neue Alijah*, 66.

44. Levy, *10 Jahre Einwanderer-Fürsorgestelle*, 4; Gelber, *Moledet Hadasha*, 262.

45. See for example, for Haifa, "HaTipul BaAliyah HaGermanit beshana 1934," Haifa City Archive, 00236/9.

46. "Statistik der Besucher der Sprechstunde fuer Arbeitsbeschaffung in den Wochen vom 16.-31.Oktober 1933," November 1, 1933, CZA, S7/27/2–78; Hitachduth Olej Germania Haifa, "Bericht der HOG Tel Aviv: An unsere Mitglieder!," *Mitteilungsblatt*, August 1934, II, 6–7.

47. Frieda Weinreich analyzed the 1,000 job seekers who who were first-time clients at the Tel Aviv HOG from January to May of 1937: Frieda Weinreich, "Aufgaben und Ergebnisse der Arbeitsvermittlung der H.O.G.," *Mitteilungsblatt*, Juni 1937, II, 6–7.

48. "Arbeits- und Berufsberatung in Palästina," *Informations-Rundschreiben des Palästina-Amtes Berlin* 34, June 29, 1936, 264.

49. Weinreich, "Aufgaben und Ergebnisse."

50. Hitachduth Olej Germania Jerusalem, "Bericht der HOG Jerusalem," *Mitteilungsblatt*, February 1934, 5–6; "Aus der Arbeit der HOG Jerusalem," *Mitteilungsblatt*, June 1937, I, 13; Hitachduth Olej Germania Tel Aviv, "Arbeitsnachweis HOG Tel-Aviv," *Mitteilungsblatt*, May 1937, I, 15.

51. "Die Ausbildungsarbeit der WIZO," *Jüdische Rundschau*, April 26, 1938, 7; Hitachduth Olej Germania, "Aus der Arbeit der HOGOA. Haifa," *Mitteilungsblatt*, October 1939, 10.

52. Grete Turnowsky-Pinner, "Zur Soziologie der deutschen Einwanderung in Palästina, Ende 1933," CZA, Memorandum, S7/11-122-128. Margarete ("Grete") Turnowsky-Pinner (1894–1982), born in Kosten/Posen, was a sociologist, social welfare worker, and author. In 1933, she analyzed data provided by 431 German immigrants who used the services of the HOG in Jerusalem.

53. Hedi Schur, "Nicht zur Veröffentlichung! Beachtenswerte Mitteilungen der Arbeitsberatungsstelle der Jung-Wizo in Tel Aviv, Juni 1937," CZA, A 217/19.

54. See Nadja Stein, "Frauen im Beruf," 1934, CZA, A 217/18; Frieda Weinreich, "Vom Arbeitsmarkt in Palästina," *WIZO Revue* 1 (1937/1938), 14–16.

55. For this discussion, see Bernstein, "On Rhetoric and Commitment."

56. E. Goldstein, "Doppelverdienste. Leserbrief," *Mitteilungsblatt*, October 1939, 8. See also Levy, *10 Jahre Einwanderer-Fürsorgestelle*, 3.

57. "Ergebnis einer Besprechung mit Frl. Weinreich von der H.O.G. und Herrn Dr. Voss vom K.J.V. vom 27.4.1937," April 28, 1937, CZA, S7/452.

58. "Arhion HaKLali le Misrah HaKarov to Georg Landauer," May 7, 1936, CZA, S7/303; Frieda Weinreich to Georg Landauer, August 12, 1936, CZA, S7/591.

59. Martin Scheftelowitz, "Gute 77 Jahre: Erlebte Tatsachen 1907–1984. Leo Baeck Institute Archives New York, Memoirs Collection, ME 239, 30.

60. See "Die Tätigkeit der HOG Haifa," December 1933, CZA, Bericht, S7/26/1; "HOG to Fritz Loewenstein," November 7, 1933, CZA, S7/95; "Lishkat haAvoda Haifa to HOG," November 15, 1933, CZA, S7/95; German Department, "Report on Jewish Immigration from Germany to Palestine for the Years 1933 and 1934," CZA S7/148; Abteilung für die Ansiedlung deutscher Juden, "Bericht über Stand der Einwanderung und finanzielle Unterstützung," October 1934, CZA, S7/148; "Rundbrief zur Frage der Einwanderung und Einordnung der deutschen Juden in Erez Israel," May 2, 1936, CZA, S7/219.

61. "Die Tätigkeit der HOG Haifa," December 1933, CZA, Bericht, S7/26/1; "Frauenarbeit in Palästina," CZA, A217/22; "Die Wizo und das Hilfswerk," *WIZO Pioniere und Helfer* (December/January 1933/1934), 2; Fritz Naftali, "Ausbildungsschulen für Mädchen," *Mitteilungsblatt*, September 1934, 5–6.

62. "HaTipul BaAliyah HaGermanit beshana 1934," Haifa City Archive, 00236/9.

63. Britschgi-Schimmer, *Umschichtung*, 63.

64. "Entwurf von Richtlinien fuer die Verteilung der LP 3000 konstruktiver Darlehen fuer die Liquidierung sozialer Fälle," January 4, 1936, CZA, S7/494-102.

65. "Anhang zum Bericht über eine Sozial-Enquete der HOG Haifa: Aus unserer Sprechstunde," 1936, CZA, S7/494-289.

66. See Pfefferman and De Vries, "Gendering Access," 581.

67. "The Women behind the WIZO Shops: The Original Stories of the Immigrant Women Who Have Become the Home-Industry Workers for the WIZO Shops," May 1946, CZA, A217/19.

68. See loan recommendation documents, CZA, S7/494-69; S7/494-27; S7/360-2. See also similar documents in CZA, S7/360 and S7/494-69.

69. Pfefferman and De Vries, "Gendering Access," 587.

70. See for example HOG to Georg Landauer, January 18, 1934, CZA, S7/82.

71. German Department, "Report on Jewish Immigration from Germany to Palestine for the Years 1933 and 1934," CZA, S7/148.

72. "Bericht über eine Sozial-Enquete der HOG Haifa," July 1936, CZA, S7/494-278; "Aus der Arbeit der H.O.G.," *Mitteilungsblatt*, n.o. 6, December 1938, 14–15; "Vortrag im 'Merkas Le'Avodah Sozialith,'" February 2, 1943, CZA, S7/2078.

73. Scheftelowitz ("Gute 77 Jahre," 22) called this "suffering *Ha'avara*."

74. Frieda Weinreich to Georg Landauer, August 12, 1936, CZA, S7/591.

75. HOG to Georg Landauer, August 8, 1933, CZA, S7/65/2.

76. Samson to Georg Landauer, April 23, 1937, CZA, S7/445.

77. Julius Reisapfel to HOG, 1934 (copy), CZA, S7/166.

78. Bella Preuss to Georg Landauer, August 18, 1936, CZA, S7/304.

79. Hauser, *Wege jüdischer Selbstbehauptung*, 56–59.

80. See for example Cherniavsky, *BeOr Shineyhem*, 70–72.

81. Britschgi-Schimmer, *Umschichtung*, 70.

82. Albert Baer, "Palästinensischer Bilderbogen: Von Chauffeuren und Berufsumschichtung," *Jüdische Rundschau*, March 9, 1934, 6; conversation with Uri and Atara Rosenfelder.

83. Feuchtwanger, *Zukunft*, 202.

84. Gerda Luft, "Interviews," 1971–72, CZA, A 504/37. Luft prepared her book *Heimkehr ins Unbekannte* by interviewing immigrants in 1971 and 1972 about their integration and encountered many former *osrot*.

85. Frank, *Schalom, meine Heimat*, 45–49.

86. Aloni, *Zypressen zerbrechen nicht*, 52.

87. Interview with Gretel M., November 25, 2010.

88. Interview with Ilse S.

89. Interview with Ilse B., November 1, 2009.

90. Aloni, "Erste Begegnungen," 34. She is referring to herself in the third person here.

91. Interview with Beate D., April 7, 2012; J. Majer, "Ärzte der Kupat-Cholim: Nähere Informationen für Interessenten," *Jüdische Rundschau*, November 8, 1935.

92. Tergit, *Im Schnellzug nach Haifa*, 8.

93. See Halamish, *BeMirutz kaful neged haSman*, 178–85.

94. Hana Majofis to GD, March 26, 1939, CZA, S7/2075.

95. M. Kreutzberger to Tanne (HOG Haifa), April 9, 1939, CZA, S7/2075.

96. Hana Majofis to Georg Landauer, June 25, 1939, CZA, S7/2075.

97. Ina Britschgi-Schimmer to Arthur Ruppin, January 15, 1936, CZA, S7/302; Britschgi-Schimmer to Arthur Ruppin, February 4, 1936, CZA, S7/302.

98. Gerda Luft to Werner Senator, February 14, 1936, CZA, S7/302.

99. Werner Senator to Julius Rosenfeld, January 30, 1936, CZA, S7/302.

100. Landsberg to Georg Landauer, January 8, 1936, CZA, S7/304; see also Heinreich Margulies to Alfred Landsberg, October 29, 1935, CZA, S7/304.

101. Hilde Oppenheimer to Arthur Ruppin, May 18, 1936, CZA, A107/61-2-3.

102. Hana Majofis to Georg Landauer, May 15, 1943, CZA, S7/2075.

103. Kurt Beer to Georg Landauer, November 21, 1937, CZA, S7/446. The Hebrew term *poel* is used for "worker" instead of the German word *Arbeiter*.

104. Kurt Beer to Keren Hayesod, May 9, 1936, CZA, S7/302.

105. Shlomo Juengster to Moshe Brachman, 1937, CZA, S7/446 (copy).

106. Hans Falkenstein to Georg Landauer, January 26, 1938, CZA, S7/801.

107. Gustav Kahn to Werner Senator, February 28, 1938, CZA, S7/801.

108. See for example Gustav Cohen to the German Department, February 4, 1936, CZA, S7/304. Cohen was not able to cope with the physical work on the kibbutz and suffered a nervous breakdown.

109. The *Jüdische Rundschau* published letters of complaint about age discrimination;

see Harry Friedlaender, "Die brennende Auswanderungsfrage," *Jüdische Rundschau*, November 15, 1935, 16: "Menschen suchen Lebensraum," *Jüdische Rundschau*, November 26, 1935, 2. See also Meyer, "From a Zero to a Hero."

110. See also for example J. Tschernoff to Georg Landauer, August 5, 1935, CZA, S7/101/2; Martin Auerbach to Jewish Agency for Palestine, July 22, 1935, CZA, S7/101/2. Both ask for help in getting a job by mentioning their Zionist work in Germany.

111. See for example Alexander Bloch to Georg Landauer, December 28, 1933, CZA, S7/82; Rudolf Reich to Georg Landauer, November 9, 1937, CZA, S7/563; Laupheimer to Rosenblueth, November 3, 1933, CZA, S7/79/2; Tanne to Georg Landauer, November 9, 1937, CZA, S7/563.

112. Leni Grünstein Collection, no date (probably early 1940s), Bet Yitzhak Archive, Box 5, File 6. To be sung to the melody of the traditional German song "Es klappert die Mühle." "Outside work" (*Aussenarbeit* in German) refers to *Avodat Huz*, paid work outside of the communal agricultural village, in this case.

113. "Als Siedler in Erez Israel: Aus Privatbriefen," *Jüdische Rundschau*, November 30, 1937, 6.

114. Scheftelowitz, "Gute 77 Jahre," 25–26.

115. Feuchtwanger, *Zukunft*, 200–201.

116. Lehmann, *Nahariya*, 125; Erel, *Neue Wurzeln*, 63. See also Quack, "Changing Gender Roles and Emigration," and the contributions in Quack, *Between Sorrow and Strength*.

117. Interview with Ruth L., July 15, 2010. See also Bella Preuss to Georg Landauer, August 18, 1936, CZA, S7/304; David Tanne to Georg Landauer, February 14, 1937, CZA, S7/446.

118. Interview with Yohanan B.

119. Kaplan, *Between Dignity and Despair*.

120. Schüler-Springorum, *Geschlecht und Differenz*, 118–19.

121. Hilde Nesselroth to Werner Senator, October 15, 1938, CZA, S7/803.

122. "Anonymous Haluza [female pioneer] from Herzliya," February 26, 1935, CZA, S7/168/1 (copy).

123. Georg Landauer to Hans Friedenthal, April 16, 1935, CZA, S7/168/1.

124. See Kaplan, *Between Dignity and Despair*, 63–65.

125. Feuchtwanger, *Zukunft*, 236.

126. Oppenheimer, *Zur wirtschaftlichen Einordnung*, 14–15.

127. For a discussion of female professionals in Mandatory Palestine, see Shilo, *Nashim bonot Uma*. See also Davidi, *Bonot Aretz Hadasha*.

128. Bernstein, "The Women Workers' Movement," especially 466–70. See also Stern, "Rebels of Unimportance."

129. Gelber, *Moledet Hadasha*, 606–8.

Chapter 4

1. Gerda Luft, "Die andere Seite der Medaille," *Jüdische Rundschau*, December 14, 1934, 2. All translations of written sources and interviews into English are by the author, unless otherwise noted. See also Nanny Margulies-Auerbach, "Die Frau in der Alijah aus Deutschland," *Jüdische Rundschau*, March 6, 1934, 5.

2. Department of Statistics of the Jewish Agency for Palestine, "Jewish Immigration into Palestine from Germany during 1933–1938," Bulletin No. 3, February 1939, CZA, S7/787.

3. On the double day, see for example Beaujot and Jiu, "Models of Time Use."

4. Reagin, *Sweeping the German Nation*, 3–12.

5. Palästina-Amt, *Alijah*. This compilation was explicitly promoted as an important read for homemakers; see for example "Palästina-Hinweise: Was muss die Hausfrau zu ihrer Übersiedlung nach Palästina wissen?" *Jüdische Rundschau*, November 7, 1933, 774. See also the material I mentioned in chapter 2.

6. Interview with Eva W., June 7, 2010.

7. Interview with Ruth L., June 17, 2010.

8. Palästina-Amt, *Alijah*, 167; Gerda Luft, "Wieviel kostet ein Haushalt in Palästina?" *Jüdische Rundschau*, April 28, 1933, 169; Moses Beilinson, "Haushaltskosten in Palästina," *Jüdische Rundschau*, May 30, 1933.

9. See, for example, interview with Ruth L., July 15, 2010; Hans Bernkopf to his parents and Lotte, August 22, 1934, Archives of the German-Speaking Jewry Heritage Museum in Tefen/Galilee, GF 0093/5.

10. Interview with Miriam R., June 19, 2011.

11. See for example Letter to Alfred, April 9, 1933, CZA, S7/21–121; interview with Ruth L., June 17, 2010.

12. Interview with Eva W., June 14, 2010; interview with Beate D., April 7, 2012; Gerda Luft, Interviews 1971/72, CZA, A 504/37; Tergit, *Im Schnellzug nach Haifa*, 35. See also Helman, "Cleanliness and Squalor."

13. Gerda Luft, Interviews, 1971/72, CZA, A 504/37.

14. See also Rautenberg-Alianov, "Alte und neue Rollen."

15. A. Abrahams, "Sprechsaal," *Mitteilungsblatt*, November 1934, II, 12–13.

16. See Hitachduth Olej Germania, "Aus der täglichen Arbeit der HOG. Tozereth Haarez," *Mitteilungsblatt*, November 1935, II, 6–7; Helene Hanna Thon, "Luxusberufe," *Jüdische Rundschau*, November 24, 1933, 849.

17. Albert Baer, "Kleine Haifaer Chronik," *Jüdische Rundschau*, February 18, 1936, 10.

18. Martin Scheftelowitz, "Gute 77 Jahre: Erlebte Tatsachen 1907–1984," Leo Baeck Institute Archives New York—Memoirs Collection, ME 239, p. 23.

19. Hella Schleuderer, "Die Hausfrau in Palästina," *Jüdische Rundschau*, September 8, 1933, 496.

20. Irene S., "Briefe aus Palästina, Tel Aviv, December 5, 1934," *Jung Wizo: Monatsschrift* 7, 3/4 (1934–1935): 16–17; interview with Miriam R., May 29, 2011; Leonie Landsberg to

NOTES TO CHAPTER 4

her parents, April 22, 1934, Archives of the German-Speaking Jewry Heritage Museum in Tefen/Galilee, GF 0047/42.

21. Werner Bloch, "Tel-Awiwer Notizbuch. Sorgen der Hausfrauen," *Jüdische Rundschau*, January 29, 1937, 13.

22. Quoted in Shifman and Katz, "'Just Call Me Adonai.'"

23. Bericht über eine Sozial-Enquete der HOG, Haifa, July 1936, CZA, S7/494–278.

24. "Bericht HOG Haifa über 40 Sozialfälle," February 27, 1935, CZA, L13/33.

25. Interview with Eva W., June 7, 2010.

26. Interview with Jacob M., July 22, 2010.

27. Ben-Yaacov, *Leben für Israel*, 42.

28. Frank, *Schalom, meine Heimat*, 36.

29. Feuchtwanger, *Zukunft*, 272.

30. Interview with Yair C., December 5, 2009.

31. Interview with Yair C., February 17, 2010.

32. Interview with Ilse B., November 1, 2009.

33. Miron, *Lehiot Yehudi beGermania ha Nazit*, 107–15.

34. M. F. to Alfred, April 9, 1933, CZA, S721-121-27. See also Chotjewitz, *Die mit Tränen säen*, 211.

35. Gerda Luft, "Krankheitsverhütung. Zur sanitären Lage im Sommer," *Jüdische Rundschau*, July 12, 1935.

36. Heller, "Was und wie?" This brochure was recommended constantly; see Dr. Erna Meyer, "Hauswirtschaftliche Ratschläge für die neueingewanderte Hausfrau," *Mitteilungsblatt*, August 1936, I, 12–14.

37. See for example Hans Bernkopf to his parents and Lotte, August 22, 1934, Archives of the German-Speaking Jewry Heritage Museum in Tefen/Galilee, GF 0093/5.

38. See for example the remarks in Lowenthal and Oppenheimer, *Philo-Atlas*.

39. Dr. E. Bodenheimer-Biram to Dr. Landauer (in German), November 14, 1933, CZA, S7/1/1–110. For a different perception of this issue, see Yosef and Miron, "Burganut veZionut," 223–24.

40. Britschgi-Schimmer, *Umschichtung*, 72.

41. Wolf, "Israel Buch für Anfänger," Archives of the German-Speaking Jewry Heritage Museum in Tefen/Galilee, GF 0112/23, 45.

42. For an in-depth analysis of Fritz Wolf and his gendered immigration experience, see Alianov-Rautenberg, "From Cravat to Khaki."

43. Wolf, "Israel Buch für Anfänger," Archives of the German-Speaking Jewry Heritage Museum in Tefen/Galilee, GF 0112/23, 47.

44. Wolf, "Die grosse Parnosse," Archives of the German-Speaking Jewry Heritage Museum in Tefen/Galilee, GF 0113/28, 9.

45. "Hitachduth Olej Germania, Die HOG im Dienste der Hausfrauen," *Mitteilungsblatt*, January 1937, 17.

46. "Die Tätigkeit der Hitachduth Olej Germania Gruppe Haifa, Dezember 1933," CZA, S7/26/1.

47. Berlowitz, "Hausbesuche," *WIZO-Pressedienst aus Erez Israel*, November, 1936, 9.

48. Nadja Stein, "Hauswirtschaftliche Fortbildungsarbeit durch die WIZO," 1934, CZA, A 217/18.

49. Berlowitz, "Hausbesuche," 9, 10.

50. Frieda Weinreich, "Sozial-Probleme: Einwanderer-Fürsorge in Tel-Awiw," *Jüdische Rundschau*, April 21, 1936, 10; Volkmann, *Neuorientierung*, 205; "WIZO-Pressedienst aus Erez Israel (Deutsche Ausgabe)," January 1937, 3; "WIZO-Pressedienst aus Erez Israel (Deutsche Ausgabe)," 1938, 1–2. See also "WIZO-Broschüre über Palästinaarbeit," CZA, A217/22; "Der Auskunftsdienst für Touristen und Neueingewanderte, Veranstaltungshinweise 1933," CZA, A217/22; "Frauenarbeit in Palästina, 1933," CZA, A217/22; "Hauswirtschaftliche Fortbildungsarbeit durch die WIZO, 1934," CZA, A 217/18.

51. Helene Hanna Thon, "Freiheit und 'Freiheit': Erlebnisse mit neuen Einwanderern," *Jüdische Rundschau*, May 10, 1934, 10.

52. Reagin, *Sweeping the German Nation*, 22–24, 36–47.

53. Tene, "'Kah nevashel.'"

54. Halperin, *Babel*, 26–27.

55. Kanowitz, "Das Kind in gesunden und kranken Tagen," Hitahdut Oley Germania, ed. *Krankheiten und Hygiene in Palästina: Sonderheft des Mitteilungsblatts in Verbindung mit der Kupath Cholim*, 1935, 8.

56. Sahavy, *Haushaltslexikon*, I:31.

57. Shemen, "Die tüchtige Hausfrau" (advertisement), *Mitteilungsblatt*, July 1937, II, cover.

58. Assis, "Ratschläge für die Hausfrau Nr. 2. Ein Wort zum Thema Kinder-Ernährung" (advertisement), *Mitteilungsblatt*, Dezember 1935, I, 4.

59. Matok, "Was ist 'Matok'?" (advertisement), *Mitteilungsblatt*, January 1936, I, 8.

60. Schemen, "Menschen hat man oft belogen: Doch den Magen nie betrogen!" (advertisement), *Mitteilungsblatt*, November 1935, I, 7.

61. Tene, "'Kah nevashel,'" 102–6.

62. Stoler-Liss, "'Mothers Birth the Nation,'" 104.

63. B. G., "Koche palästinensich! Ein Kapitel für die Hausfrauen—Praxis," *Jüdische Rundschau*, February 13, 1934, 6. See also "Nicht nur die Liebe, auch die Einordnung geht durch den Magen," CZA, A217/13.

64. For the following remarks, see also Rautenberg-Alianov, "Schlagsahne oder 'Shemen'-Öl?"

65. See for example Meyer, *Der neue Haushalt*. See also Wimmer, "Abstraktion durch Anschaulichkeit."

66. See for example WIZO, "Histadruth Naschim Zionioth—HNZ (Palästina-Federation der WIZO), Februar/März-Programm," in *Mitteilungsblatt*, February 1935, II, cover; "Die Wizo auf der Tel Aviver Messe," 1934. CZA, A 217/18; "Veranstaltungsankündigungen für Clubabende in deutscher Sprache," CZA, A 217/22.

67. Meyer, *Wie kocht man?*

68. Nadja Stein and Erna Meyer, in *WIZO Pioniere und Helfer* 10, no. 4 (1936): 8–9, here 9.

69. See *Mitteilungsblatt*, December 1936, I, 16.

70. Nanny Margulies-Auerbach, "Wie koche ich in Palästina?" *Jüdische Rundschau*, June 19, 1936, 16.

71. Theodor Zlocisti, "Wie kocht man in Erez-Israel? Zum neuen Wizo-Kochbuch (Herausgegeben von Dr. Erna Meyer unter Mitarbeit von Milka Saphir)," *Mitteilungsblatt*, Dezember 1936, II, 10–11.

72. Meyer, *Wie kocht man?*, 7.

73. Heti Horwitz-Schiller, "Die Ernährungslage in Palästina. Ergebnisse einer Studienfahrt," *Jüdische Rundschau*, June 25, 1937, 10.

74. See for example Erna Meyer, "Wir kaufen Tozereth Haaretz," *Mitteilungsblatt*, August 1935, II, 19–23.

75. "Protokoll der Vorstandssitzung des Verbandes Jüdischer Frauen für Palästina-Arbeit vom 10. April 1930," April 24, 1930, CZA, Protokoll, A 217/17. Meyer, who had planned model kitchens for the rationalization of homemaking back in Germany, also created a WIZO model kitchen that was efficiently and hygienically furnished: Gerda Luft, "'Grosse Tage' der Levante-Messe: Und was man dort lernen kann," *Jüdische Rundschau*, June 8, 1934, 4. For an analysis of the rationalization of the household, see Nolan, "'Housework Made Easy.'"

76. Erna Meyer, "Wichtig für Hausfrauen," *Jüdische Rundschau*, June 28, 1938, 7.

77. Meyer, "Hauswirtschaftliche Ratschläge."

78. Meyer, *Wie kocht man?*, 19.

79. Meyer, *Wie kocht man?*, 23.

80. Meyer, "Hauswirtschaftliche Ratschläge."

81. Erna Meyer, "Hauswirtschaftliche Ratschläge für die neueingewanderte Hausfrau: Festtagsbäckerei mit wenig Geld," *Mitteilungsblatt*, November 1936, II, 21–22.

82. Meyer, "Hauswirtschaftliche Ratschläge: Festtagsbäckerei."

83. Meyer, *Küchenzettel in Krisenzeiten*, 9.

84. Nadja Stein, "Nicht nur die Liebe, auch die Einordnung geht durch den Magen," CZA, A217/13.

85. Tene, "'Kah nevashel,'" 95–96.

86. Sahavy, *Haushaltslexikon*.

87. Sahavy, *Haushaltslexikon*, I:3.

88. Sahavy, *Haushaltslexikon*, 2:25.

89. Sahavy, *Haushaltslexikon*, I:49.

90. Sahavy, *Haushaltslexikon*, I:18, I:20, I:30.

91. Sahavy, *Haushaltslexikon*, 3:35.

92. Assis, "Ratschläge für die Hausfrau Nr. 1: An die Hausfrauen der deutschen Alijah" (advertisement), *Mitteilungsblatt*, November 1935, I, 1.

93. Heti Horwitz-Schiller, "Die Ernährungslage in Palästina: Ergebnisse einer Sudienfahrt," *Jüdische Rundschau*, June 25, 1937, 10.

94. Manfred Scheuer, "Diary, summer of 1938," quoted in Armbruster, *Willkommen im gelobten Land?*, 51.

95. Interview with Ruth L., June 17, 2010.

96. Interview with Lieselotte R.; conversation with Yona Pintus Decker; and interview with Hannah W.

97. "Mittagstisch E. Koch, Tel Aviv. Deutsche Küche" (advertisement), *Mitteilungsblatt*, March 1933, 5.

98. Feuchtwanger, *Zukunft*, 233; interview with Ilse B., November 1, 2009; interview with Uri S.

99. Cafe Lorenz, "Neueröffnung," *Mitteilungsblatt*, December 1933, 11.

100. Scheftelowitz, "Gute 77 Jahre," 27. According to J. Adler ("Marktprobleme Palästinas," *Jüdische Rundschau*, March 23, 1934); 750 of the 900 tons of butter consumed annually were imported.

101. Interview with Eva W., June 7, 2010; interview with Ruth L., June 17, 2010.

102. Interview with Eva W., June 7, 2010.

103. W. K., "Kaleidoskop," *Jüdische Rundschau*, March 8, 1935.

104. *Mitteilungsblatt*, July 1936, I, cover.

105. Zerline Berney, "Cookbook," Würzburg, Ramataim, and Sde Ya'akov, 1932–1940s. The cookbook is in the possession of Berney's son, Jacob Barnai, Tel Aviv. I am grateful to him for providing me with a digital copy of his mother's recipe collection, as well as biographical information on his mother.

106. Fritz Levinson Estate, June 11, 1946. In the possession of Esther Yiftah El, née Levinson, Kibbutz Matzuba. Conversation with Esther Yiftah El.

Chapter 5

1. Shlomit (Irna) Mueller, *Dereh Ha adasha sheli*, Pardess Chana 1998, Tefen/Galilee, GF 0290/1, 5.

2. These characteristics of family migration are true not only for German Jews migrating to Mandatory Palestine, but for family migration in general, both past and present, as research has shown, see Guerry and Thébaud, "Editorial"; Rapaport and Doucerain, "Shared Immigration Process."

3. For the following remarks, see also Alianov-Rautenberg, "Migration und Marginalität."

4. See, for example, Dr. Ascher to Kramer (ZVfD), December 12, 1933, CZA, S7/22–169.

5. Gelber (*Moledet Hadasha*, 56–60) attributes this discrepancy to the fact that wives arrived later than their husbands. This is doubtful, though, especially given the gender-based discrimination in the allocation of certificates. In addition, a husband and wife would appear on the same capitalist certificate, even when the wife immigrated later. Also, wives following their husbands usually arrived a few months, not years, after their husbands.

6. Kaplan, *Between Dignity and Despair*, 8.

7. See, for example, Werner Senator to Laupheimer, April 17, 1934, CZA, S7/79/2.

8. *Informations-Rundschreiben des Palästina-Amtes Berlin*, no. 6, January 29, 1934; see also *Informations-Rundschreiben des Palästina-Amtes Berlin*, no. 1, October 23, 1933; *Informations-Rundschreiben des Palästina-Amtes Berlin*, no. 4, November 9, 1933.

9. For a list of legalization recommendations, see for example Moshe Carmeli to Landauer, October 26, 1934, CZA, S7/149.

10. Interview with Miriam R., May 29, 2011.

11. Erwin Mansbach to Georg Landauer, October 8, 1933, CZA, S7/65/2.

12. Landauer to Kimmel/Palestine Office Berlin, October 18, 1933, CZA, S7/65/2.

13. Interview with Ilse B., November 8, 2009.

14. Georg Landauer to Aron Barth, October 3, 1933, CZA, S7/74/2.

15. Georg Landauer to Immigration Department, October 3, 1933, CZA, S7/74/2.

16. *Informations-Rundschreiben des Palästina-Amtes Berlin*, no. 6, January 29, 1934.

17. Stern, *Warum hassen sie uns?*, 129.

18. Fritz Wolf, "Das Zwischenreich," Nahariya 1958/59, Tefen/Galilee, GF 0113/2, 217.

19. See Barkai, "Selbsthilfe im Dilemma." See also also Jünger, *Jahre der Ungewissheit*.

20. Wolff and Wolff, *Das eigene Leben erzählen*, 81.

21. Britschgi-Schimmer, *Umschichtung*, 66–67.

22. Georg Landauer to Palestine Office Berlin, December 15, 1933, CZA, S7/94.

23. See also Davidi, "Caring for Parents."

24. Interview with Eva W., June 7, 2010.

25. See Laqueur, *Geboren in Deutschland*, xi–xv; Angress, "Jüdische Jugend."

26. Kaplan, "Jewish Women in Nazi Germany," 41–42; Benz, *Flucht aus Deutschland*, 127.

27. Kaplan, *Between Dignity and Despair*, 40.

28. Hilfsverein der Juden in Deutschland, "Mehr Frauenauswanderung!," *Jüdische Rundschau*, January 21, 1938, 4.

29. On fictitious marriages as a way to enter Palestine, and the reactions of different institutions in the Yishuv, see Bernstein, "Nissuim Fiktivim." Fictitious marriages in the case of the German Jews are mentioned, for example, in Godenschweger, Vilmar, and Michaeli, *Die rettende Kraft der Utopie*, 70; Martin Scheftelowitz, "Gute 77 Jahre: Erlebte Tatsachen 1907–1984," Leo Baeck Institute Archives New York, Memoirs Collection, ME 239, 36–37. See also Segev, *Es war einmal*, 410.

30. Interview with Yair C., December 5, 2009.

31. Bernstein, "Nissuim Fiktivim," 20–26.

32. Bernstein, "Nissuim Fiktivim," 26–28; Halamish, *BeMirutz kaful neged haSman*, 183–85.

33. Georg Landauer to Palestine Office Berlin, July 20, 1934, CZA, S7/66/1.

34. Kaplan, "As Germans and Jews in Imperial Germany."

35. Maurer, "Family Life," 284–85. For a discussion of marriage strategies of the same years in Mandatory Palestine, see Boord, "Creating the Labor-Zionist Family."

36. Matrimonial ad, *Jüdische Rundschau*, July 6, 1934, 13.
37. Matrimonial ad, *Mitteilungsblatt*, September 1935 (cover).
38. Matrimonial ad, *Mitteilungsblatt*, July 1937 (cover).
39. Matrimonial ad, *Mitteilungsblatt*, January 1936, 6.
40. Matrimonial ad, *Jüdische Rundschau*, July 6, 1934, 13.
41. Matrimonial ad, *Jüdische Rundschau*, May 31, 1935, 7.
42. Matrimonial ad, *Mitteilungsblatt*, September 1935, 14.
43. Matrimonial ad, *Jüdische Rundschau*, July 6, 1934, 13.
44. Matrimonial ad, *Jüdische Rundschau*, July 19, 1935, 9.
45. Palästina Ehe-Arrangements vornehmer Art, advertisement, *Jüdische Rundschau*, June 4, 1935, 12.
46. Advertisement, *Jüdische Rundschau*, August 6, 1937, 9.
47. On matchmaking in the Yishuv press, see Yaal, "The Modern Matchmaker."
48. Fortuna "marriage ad," *Mitteilungsblatt*, November 1937, II, 2.
49. Advertisement, *Blumenthal's Neueste Nachrichten*, July 23, 1936.
50. See, for example, Palästina-Amt, *Alijah*, 155.
51. Wolf, "Israel Buch für Anfänger," Tefen/Galilee, GF 0112/23, 61. See for this and the following remarks Alianov-Rautenberg, "From Cravat to Khaki."
52. Wolf, "Zwischenreich," Tefen/Galilee, GF 0113/2, 192.
53. Interview with Ruth R.; interview with Yair C., December 5, 2009; Wolf, "Zwischenreich," Tefen/Galilee, GF 0113/2, 210.
54. Wolf, "Zwischenreich," Tefen/Galilee, GF 0113/2, 375–76.
55. Interview with Eva W., June 7, 2010.
56. Rapaport and Doucerain, "Shared Immigration Process"; Hyman, Guruge, and Mason, "The Impact of Migration."
57. Feuchtwanger, *Zukunft*, 227.
58. Feuchtwanger, *Zukunft*, 235.
59. Interview with Ilse B., November 1, 2009. See also interview with Miriam L.
60. Loewy, *Jugend in Palästina*, 164.
61. Feuchtwanger, *Zukunft*, 269.
62. Simon Grosshut to his mother, March, 1938, CZA, S7/591 (copy).
63. Simon Grosshut to his mother, March, 1938, CZA, S7/591 (copy).
64. Interview with Yair C., December 5, 2009.
65. Interview with Gaby W., February 25, 2010.
66. See for example "Neue Rechtskurse der HOG," *Mitteilungsblatt*, October 1938, II, 13; Lotte Hanemann, "Lücken im Personenstandsrecht," *Jüdische Rundschau*, February 4, 1936; Werner Fraustaedter, "Ehescheidung von Ausländern in Palästina," *Mitteilungsblatt*, June 1937, I, 9–10; *Juristischer Informationsdienst des Palästina-Amtes Berlin* 55 (1938): 346.
67. Fritz Loewenstein, "Umschau. Rechtsleben, Ehescheidungsrecht," *Jüdische Rundschau*, May 28, 1937, 13.

68. Frank, *Schalom, meine Heimat*, 75.
69. *Juristischer Informationsdienst des Palästina-Amtes Berlin* 22 (1937): 417–19.
70. Gelber, *Moledet Hadasha*, 237.
71. Hanemann, "Lücken im Personenstandsrecht."
72. "Anhang zum Bericht über eine Sozial-Enquete der HOG Haifa: Aus unserer Sprechstunde," 1936, CZA, S7/494-289. For similar cases, see, for example, Moshe Brachmann to GD, October 19, 1937, CZA, S7/802.
73. "Anhang zum Bericht über eine Sozial-Enquete der HOG Haifa: Aus unserer Sprechstunde," 1936, CZA, S7/494-289.
74. Razi, "The Family."
75. "Anhang zum Bericht über eine Sozial-Enquete der HOG Haifa: Aus unserer Sprechstunde," 1936, CZA, S7/494289.
76. Kaplan, *Between Dignity and Despair*, 8–10.
77. Bertha Badt-Strauss, "Die jüdische Frau im Alltag Palästinas: Ein Vortragsabend von Helene Hanna Thon," *Jüdische Rundschau*, September 13, 1935.
78. Stoler-Liss, "Mothers Birth the Nation."
79. Stoler-Liss, "Mothers Birth the Nation," 106.
80. Interview with Eva W., June 7, 2010.
81. Nadja Stein, "Vorwort zum Wizo-Film," no date, CZA, A217/13.
82. See, for example, HOG Tel Aviv, November 21, 1937, CZA, S7/690-59-62.
83. See for example advertisement for Ada Kober-Cahen's children's home in the *Jüdische Rundschau*, December 8, 1936, 20.
84. See "Das Tageskinderheim für Einwandererkinder aus Deutschland," *Mitteilungsblatt*, January 1937, 16; "10 Jahre Einwanderer-Fürsorgestelle Tel Aviv," 1943, CZA, S7/2078; Bella Preuss to Georg Landauer, October 20, 1936, CZA, S7/443; "Placement of Jewish Children in Families in Palestine: Report of the Social Service Department of the General Council (*Va'ad leumi*) of the Jewish Community of Palestine," January 5, 1938, CZA, S7/690; "Richtlinien und Entwurf für ein Arbeitsprogramm für die Palästina-Einwanderung der deutschen Juden," January 1936, CZA, S 7/216; "Die Jugendfürsorge der Stadt Tel Aviv," 1935, CZA, A217/18; "Report by G. M.," CZA, S7/16. See also the many ads in the *Bordmerkblatt*, the *Jüdische Rundschau*, and the *Mitteilungsblatt* for children's homes. On childcare, see also Konrad, *Wurzeln jüdischer Sozialarbeit*, 172, 184, 198.
85. Interview with Rafael and Ulli T., January 11, 2010.
86. Toni Stern, "Baby- und Kinderpflege in Palästina," *Jüdische Rundschau*, October 7, 1938, 12.
87. Nadja Stein, "Vorwort zum Wizo-Film," no date, CZA, A217/13.
88. Razi, "The Family," 407–9.
89. Sandbank and Wormann, *Chinuch*, 15.
90. Feuchtwanger, *Zukunft*, 227–28.
91. "Bericht HOG Haifa über 40 Sozialfälle," February 27, 1935, CZA, L13/33; Gerda

Luft, "Die andere Seite der Medaille," *Jüdische Rundschau*, December 14, 1934, 1–2; "Richtlinien und Entwurf für ein Arbeitsprogramm für die Palästina-Einwanderung der deutschen Juden," 1936, CZA, S7/216-2-1.

92. Bella Preuss to Landauer, October, 1937, CZA, S7/690–4.

93. Maurer, "Family Life."

94. Britschgi-Schimmer, *Umschichtung*, 8.

95. For an exception, see Proskauer, *Wege und Umwege*, 86–87.

96. See Rosenberg-Friedman, "Abortion in the Yishuv." See also Kozma, "Sexology in the Yishuv."

97. Toni Stern, "Baby- und Kinderpflege in Palästina," *Jüdische Rundschau*, October 7, 1938.

98. Nathan Baruch to Mahlakat ha Aliyah, January 17, 1934, CZA, S7/79/2.

99. "Anonymous Haluza [female pioneer] from Herzliya," February 26, 1935, CZA, S7/168/1 (copy).

100. Kaplan, *Between Dignity and Despair*, 59.

101. Levy, *10 Jahre Einwanderer-Fürsorgestelle*.

102. Interview with Alisa E.

103. Georg Goldstein to *Va'ad HaKehilla* Haifa, November 1, 1937, Haifa City Archive, 00236/9.

104. Interview with Ilse B., November 1, 2009.

105. Interview with Ilse B., November 1, 2009.

106. Boord, "Fatherhood."

107. Gidal, "Aus der Welt des palästinensischen Kindes," *Jüdische Rundschau*, September 27, 1935.

108. G. Neumann, "Im Park von Haifa," *Jüdische Rundschau*, June 11, 1937, 13.

109. Feuchtwanger, *Zukunft*, 344.

110. Fritz Wolf, "Die grosse Parnosse," Nahariya 1940, Tefen/Galilee, GF 0113/28, 3. See also Wolf's lullaby, "Naharier Wiegelied," 1937, Tefen/Galilee, GF 0113/52. For an in-depth discussion of his experiences, see Alianov-Rautenberg, "From Cravat to Khaki."

111. Interview with Yohanan B.

112. See for example Laqueur, *Geboren in Deutschland*; Angress, "Jüdische Jugend." See also Wolf, *Schliesslich waren wir alle jung*.

113. Interview with Ruth R. On this attitude of taking things easily, see also Wolf, *Schliesslich waren wir alle jung*.

114. Interview with Yohanan B.

115. Anselm Bing, "Zur Problematik des jüdischen Kindes in Palästina: Die Stellung der jüdischen Kinder aus Deutschland," *Jüdische Rundschau*, April 13, 1934; Oskar Neumann, "Der neue Mensch," *Jüdische Rundschau*, October 31, 1933, 734; Hugo Schachtel to Georg Landauer, July 15, 1934, CZA, S7/67/1. See also Helman, *Young Tel Aviv*, 36–38.

116. Interview with Gaby W., February 25, 2010.

117. Kressel, *Von der Mosel ins Heilige Land*.

118. Interview with Ruth M.
119. Interview with Miriam S.
120. Interview with Ilse B., November 1, 2009.
121. Interview with Miriam R., May 29, 2011.
122. Interview with Eva W., June 7, 2010.
123. Schüler-Springorum, *Geschlecht und Differenz*, 115.
124. Ben Reich, "Leserbrief aus Palästina," *Kinder-Rundschau* 8 (1936), 2.
125. Interview with Miriam R., May 29, 2011.
126. Interview with Jacob M., July 14, 2010.
127. "Anhang zum Bericht über eine Sozial-Enquete der HOG Haifa: Aus unserer Sprechstunde," 1936, CZA, S7/494–289.
128. Shoham, "'Small Sales Agents,'" 93.
129. Razi, "Immigration and Its Discontents," 347. See also Razi, *Forsaken Children*.
130. Kressel, *Von der Mosel ins Heilige Land*, 34.
131. See for example Gerda Luft, "Interviews," 1971/72, CZA, A 504/37.
132. Interview with Ilse B., November 1, 2009.
133. Interview with Uri S.
134. Schmuckler, *Gast im eigenen Land*, 23–24.
135. Schmuckler, *Gast im eigenen Land*, 23–24.
136. See Razi, "Immigration and Its Discontents," 351.
137. Interview with Ruth M.
138. Interview with Ilse B., November 1, 2009.
139. "Nach der Einwanderung: Ein Privatbrief aus Palästina," *Jüdische Rundschau*, August 15, 1933, 431.
140. Interview with Yair C., December 5, 2009.
141. Interview with Gretel M., December 31, 2010.
142. Interview with Gretel M., December 31, 2010.
143. See, for example, interview with Beate D., April 7, 2012.
144. Siddy Wronsky, "Placement of Jewish Children in Families in Palestine," January 5, 1938, CZA, S7/690. Wronsky (1883–1947) was the director of the welfare archives in Berlin, edited the *Deutsche Zeitschrift für Wohlfahrtspflege* (German Journal of Social Welfare), taught at the Alice Salomon School of social work, and was a member of the board of Germany's Central Jewish Welfare Organization. She immigrated to Palestine in 1934 and began teaching social work in Jerusalem. See Wieler, "Destination Social Work."
145. Razi, "Immigration and Its Discontents," 340.
146. Anselm Bing, "'Vollständig verwahrlost . . .' Elternsorgen in Palästina," *Jüdische Rundschau*, April 6, 1937, 10.
147. Martin Hauser to a friend, September 19, 1935, in Hauser, *Wege jüdischer Selbstbehauptung*, 67.
148. Anat Helman, *Young Tel Aviv*, 35–7.
149. Quoted in Helman, *Young Tel Aviv*, 36.

150. Marion Kaplan, "As Germans and Jews in Imperial Germany," 182. See also Reagin, *Sweeping the German Nation*, 22–24.

151. Feuchtwanger, *Zukunft*, 267.

152. Razi, "The Family," 407–9.

153. Razi, "The Family," 407–9.

154. See for example Elfriede Bergel-Gronemann, "Auflösung und neue Bindung," *Jüdische Rundschau,* February 13, 1934, 5.

155. See Miron, "From Bourgeois Germany to Palestine"; Gerson, "Family Matters." See also Yosef, "From Yekke to Zionist."

Conclusion

1. Miron, Mi "sham" le "kan" beGuf rishon, 113–15.

2. Benz, *Das Exil*.

3. Kushner, "Fremde Arbeit."

4. Quack, *Between Sorrow and Strength*.

5. Lavsky, *The Creation of the German-Jewish Diaspora*.

6. Donato et al., "A Glass Half Full?"; Donato and Gabaccia, *Gender and International Migration*.

7. Lucassen, "Beyond the Apocalypse."

Bibliography

Archival Sources
Bet Yitzhak Archive
    Leni Grünstein Collection
CZA: Central Zionist Archives, Jerusalem
    A 217 Nadja Stein Collection
    A 504 Gerda Luft Collection
    S7 Central Bureau for the Settlement of German Jews in Palestine
Haifa City Archive
Kfar Shmaryahu Archive
    Klimann Family Collection
Leo Baeck Institute Archives New York
    Memoirs Collection
Tefen/Galilee: Archives of the German-Speaking Jewry Heritage Museum in Tefen/Galilee
    GF Collection

Private Estates and Collections
Archives of the Haifa Rowing Club (Dan Exiner)
Fritz Levinson Estate (Esther Yiftah El, née Levinson, Kibbutz Matzuba)
Zerline Berney Estate (Jacob Barnai, Tel Aviv)

Oral History Interviews
Interview with Alisa E., May 18, 2011
Interview with Avraham M., July 21, 2010; July 29, 2010
Interview with Beate D., March 17, 2012; April 7, 2012; April 14, 2012
Interview with Eva W., June 7, 2010; June 14, 2010
Interview with Gaby W., February 25, 2010; March 7, 2010
Interview with Gretel M., November 25, 2010; December 31, 2010
Interview with Hannah W., September 3, 2012
Interview with Hilde S., June 2, 2011
Interview with Hugo M., November 30, 2009
Interview with Ilse B., November 1, 2009; November 8, 2009
Interview with Ilse S., June 29, 2010
Interview with Jacob M., June 14, 2010; July 22, 2010
Interview with Lieselotte R., September 3, 2012
Interview with Miriam L., December 13, 2010
Interview with Miriam R., May 29, 2011; June 2, 2011; June 19, 2011
Interview with Miriam S., July 13, 2010
Interview with Rafael and Ulli T., January 11, 2010; February 18, 2010
Interview with Ruth B., December 2, 2009
Interview with Ruth L., June 17, 2010, July 15, 2010
Interview with Ruth M., June 18, 2012
Interview with Ruth R., December 5, 2009
Interview with Uri S., September 3, 2012
Interview with Yair C., December 5, 2009; February 17, 2010
Interview with Yohanan B., December 2, 2009

Conversations with Second-Generation Immigrants
Conversation with Dan Exiner, president of the Haifa Rowing Club, October 18, 2015
Conversation with Esther Yiftah El, September 23, 2011
Conversation with Gitta B., November 1, 2009
Conversation with Dr. Ishay Geva, May 10, 2015
Conversation with Uri and Atara Rosenfelder, May 10, 2010
Conversation with Yona Pintus Decker, September 3, 2012

Periodicals and Newsletters
Informations-Rundschreiben des Palästina-Amtes Berlin
Jüdische Rundschau
Jüdische Welt Rundschau
Juristischer Informationsdienst des Palästina-Amtes Berlin
Jung Wizo: Monatsschrift
Mitteilungsblatt

Mitteilungsblatt Yakinton
WIZO Pioniere und Helfer
WIZO-Pressedienst aus Erez Israel
WIZO Revue

Published Primary Sources
Autobiographies, Memoirs, Diaries

Aloni, Jenny. "Erste Begegnungen im Lande." In *Kaleidoskop Israel: Deutschsprachige Einwanderer in Israel erzählen*, edited by Shlomo Erel, 34–45. Klagenfurt: Alekto, 1994.

Aloni, Jenny. *Zypressen zerbrechen nicht*. Vol. 2 of *Gesammelte Werke in Einzelausgaben*. Paderborn: Schöningh, 1990.

Ben-Yaacov, Yissakhar. *Leben für Israel: Erinnerungen eines Diplomaten*. Hamburg: Hoffmann und Campe, 2007.

Eisenberg, Lotte. *Meine Gäste, Tiberias und ich*. Jerusalem: Rubin Mass, 1979.

Feuchtwanger, Martin. *Zukunft ist ein blindes Spiel: Erinnerungen*. Munich: Langen Müller, 1989.

Frank, Meta. *Schalom, meine Heimat: Lebenserinnerungen einer hessischen Jüdin 1914–1994*. Hofgeismar: Verein für hessische Geschichte und Landeskunde, 1994.

Granach, Gad. *Where Is Home? Stories from the Life of a German-Jewish Émigré*. Los Angeles: Atara Press, 2009.

Hauser, Martin. *Wege jüdischer Selbstbehauptung: Tagebuchaufzeichnungen 1929–1967*. Bonn: Bundeszentrale für Politische Bildung, 1992.

Heller, Alfred. *Dr. Seligmanns Auswanderung: Der schwierige Weg nach Israel*. Munich: C. H. Beck, 1990.

Herlitz, Georg. *Mein Weg nach Jerusalem: Erinnerungen eines zionistischen Beamten*. Jerusalem: R. Mass, 1964.

Ilsar, Yehiel. *Leben in Wandlungen: Erinnerungen eines Neunzigjährigen*. Paderborn: Mentis, 2004.

Jonas, Hans. *Memoirs*. Edited by Christian Wiese. Waltham, MA: Brandeis University Press, 2008.

Kressel, Helga. *Von der Mosel ins Heilige Land: Jugenderinnerungen einer Emigrantin*. Trier: Spee, 1993.

Landau, Lola. "Erste Stationen im Lande." In *Kaleidoskop Israel: Deutschsprachige Einwanderer in Israel erzählen*, edited by Shlomo Erel, 22–33. Klagenfurt: Alekto, 1994.

Loewy, Ernst. *Jugend in Palästina: Briefe an die Eltern, 1935–1938*, edited by Brita Eckert. Berlin: Metropol, 1997.

Luft, Gerda. *Chronik eines Lebens für Israel*. Stuttgart: Edition Erdmann in K. Thienemanns Verlag, 1983.

Mueller, Shlomit (Irna). *Dereh Ha adasha sheli*. Pardess Chana: self-published, 1998.

Mühsam, Paul. *Ich bin ein Mensch gewesen: Lebenserinnerungen*. Berlin: Gerlingen Bleicher, 1989.

Mühsam, Paul. *Mein Weg zu mir: Aus Tagebüchern.* Konstanz: Hartung-Gorre Verlag, 1992.
Schmuckler, Malka. *Gast im eigenen Land: Emigration und Rückkehr einer deutschen Jüdin.* Cologne: Verlag Wissenschaft und Politik, 1983.
Schwarz-Gardos, Alice. *Von Wien nach Tel Aviv: Lebensweg einer Journalistin.* Gerlingen: Bleicher, 1991.
Stern, Arthur. *In bewegter Zeit: Erinnerungen und Gedanken eines jüdischen Nervenarztes.* Jerusalem: R. Mass, 1968.
Stern, Heinemann. *Warum hassen sie uns eigentlich? Jüdisches Leben zwischen den Kriegen: Erinnerungen,* edited and with commentary by Hans Chanoch Meyer. Düsseldorf: Droste, 1970.
Tergit, Gabriele. *Im Schnellzug nach Haifa.* Edited by Jens Brüning. Frankfurt am Main: Fischer, 1998.
Wolf, Anni. *Schliesslich waren wir alle jung und lebenslustig.* Erinnerungen: Von Berlin nach Israel. Berlin: Mackensen, 1993.
Wolff, Walter, and Moshe Wolff. *Das eigene Leben erzählen: Geschichte und Biografie von Hamburger Juden aus zwei Generationen.* Edited by Linde Apel. Göttingen: Wallstein Verlag, 2014.

Other Contemporary Publications

Abbady, Yizhak. *Benenu le-ven ha-Anglim: nisayon le-nituah ma'arekhet ha-yehasim she-ben Anglim le-Yehudim u-ven Yehudim le-Anglim.* Jerusalem: Kiryat Sefer, 1947.
Britschgi-Schimmer, Ina. *Die Umschichtung der jüdischen Einwanderer aus Deutschland zu städtischen Berufen in Palästina: eine Untersuchung.* Jerusalem: Central Bureau for the Settlement of German Jews, 1936.
Cohn, Benno, ed. *10 Jahre neue Alijah.* Tel Aviv: Alija Chadaschaa, 1943.
Cohn, Lotte. *Die Zwanziger Jahre in Erez Israel: Ein Bilderbuch ohne Bilder.* Tel Aviv: L. Cohn, 1965.
Gertz, Aaron, ed. *Statistical Handbook of Jewish Palestine.* Jerusalem: Jewish Agency for Palestine, Department of Statistics, 1947.
Heller, Harry. "Was und wie soll der Neueinwanderer essen?" Krankheiten und Hygiene in Palästina. *Sonderheft des Mitteilungsblatts in Verbindung mit der Kupath Cholim* 4 (1935): 1–2.
Herrmann, Hugo. *Palästina wie es wirklich ist.* Vienna: Fiba-Verlag, 1934.
Hitahdut Oley Germania, ed. *Bordmerkblatt für die Ankunft in Palästina,* 5th ed. Tel Aviv: Hitahdut Oley Germania, 1935.
Hitahdut Oley Germania, ed. Krankheiten und Hygiene in Palästina. *Sonderheft des Mitteilungsblatts in Verbindung mit der Kupath Cholim,* 1935.
Immigration Department of the Palestine Zionist Executive. "Instructions for the Medical Examination of Immigrants," compiled by the Health Council of the Palestine Zionist Executive. Jerusalem, 1926.
Levy, Ernst. *10 Jahre Einwanderer-Fürsorgestelle.* Tel Aviv: Hitahdut Oley Germania, 1943.

Lowenthal, Ernst G., and Hans Oppenheimer. *Philo-Atlas: Handbuch für die jüdische Auswanderung.* Berlin: Philo GmbH jüdischer Buchverlag, 1938.

Meyer, Erna. *Küchenzettel in Krisenzeiten: Zeitgemässe Rezepte und Menüzusammenstellungen.* Tel Aviv: Goldstein, 1940.

Meyer, Erna, with Milka Saphir. *Wie kocht man in Erez Israel? Wizo Kochbuch.* Tel Aviv: WIZO, 1936.

Meyer, Erna. *Der neue Haushalt. Ein Wegweiser zu wirtschaftlicher Hausführung.* Stuttgart: Franckh, 1926.

Oppenheimer, Hilde. *Zur wirtschaftlichen Einordnung der deutschen kapitalistischen Alijah.* Jerusalem [no publisher identified], 1935.

Palästina-Amt der Jewish Agency for Palestine, ed. *Alijah: Informationen fur Palästina-Auswanderer.* 8th ed. Berlin: Palästina-Amt der Jewish Agency for Palestine, 1936.

Pinner, Ludwig. *Ansiedlung von 675 Familien aus Deutschland in Einzelwirtschaften: eine Enquete des Central Bureau for the Settlement of German Jews, der Jewish Agency for Palestine und der Hitachdut Olej Germania.* Jerusalem [no publisher identified], 1938.

Pirsum Sahavy, ed. *Das Haushaltslexikon für Erez Israel: Wegweiser durch Haushaltsführung, Gesundheitspflege, Erziehung und alle anderen Gebiete des häuslichen Lebens.* 4 vols. Tel Aviv: Sahavy Advertising, 1939/1940.

Poliak, A. N. *The Jews of Palestine at the War's End.* Merhavyah: Hashomer Hatzair, 1945.

Sandbank, Jakob, and Curt Wormann. *Chinuch: Führer durch das hebräische Schul- und Erziehungswesen in Palästina.* Berlin: Palästina-Amt Berlin der Jewish Agency for Palestine, 1937.

Literature

Alianov-Rautenberg, Viola. "From Cravat to Khaki: Gender and Sexuality in the Immigration of Fritz Wolf to Mandate Palestine." *Leo Baeck Institute Yearbook* 66 (2021): 180–96.

Alianov-Rautenberg, Viola. "Kindred Spirits in the Levant? German Jews in British Palestine." *Israel Studies* 26, no. 3 (Fall 2021): 122–36.

Alianov-Rautenberg, Viola. "Migration und Marginalität: Geschlecht als strukturelle Kategorie in der deutsch-jüdischen Einwanderung nach Palästina/Eretz Israel in den 1930er Jahren." *Internationales Jahrbuch Exilforschung* 36 (2018): 105–17.

Almog, Oz. *The Sabra: The Creation of the New Jew.* Berkeley: University of California Press, 2000.

Alroey, Gur. *An Unpromising Land: Jewish Migration to Palestine in the Early Twentieth Century.* Stanford, CA: Stanford University Press, 2014.

Amikam, Bezalel. *Nirim Rishonim: HaHityashvut beAliyah haHamishit.* Jerusalem, 1980.

Angress, Werner T. "Jüdische Jugend zwischen nationalsozialistischer Verfolgung und jüdischer Wiedergeburt." In *Die Juden im nationalsozialistischen Deutschland, 1933–1943*, edited by Arnold Paucker, Sylvia Gilchrist, and Barbara Suchy, 211–21. Tübingen: J. C. B. Mohr, 1986.

Armbruster, Jörg. *Willkommen im gelobten Land? Deutschstämmige Juden in Israel.* Hamburg: Hoffmann und Campe, 2016.
Aschheim, Steven E. *Beyond the Border: The German-Jewish Legacy Abroad.* Princeton, NJ: Princeton University Press, 2007.
Aschheim, Steven E. *Brothers and Strangers: The East European Jew in German and German Jewish Consciousness, 1800–1923.* Madison: University of Wisconsin Press, 1982.
Aschheim, Steven E. "Reflections on Insiders and Outsiders: A General Introduction." In *Insiders and Outsiders: Dilemmas of East European Jewry*, edited by Richard I. Cohen, Jonathan Frankel, and Stefani Hoffman, 1–14. Portland: The Littman Library of Jewish Civilization, 2010.
Ashkenazy, Ofer. "German Jewish Athletes and the Formation of Zionist (Trans-)National Culture." *Jewish Social Studies* 17, no. 3 (2011): 124–55.
Barkai, Avraham. "Bevölkerungsrückgang und wirtschaftliche Stagnation." In *Aufbruch und Zerstörung 1918–1945.* Volume 4 of *Deutsch-jüdische Geschichte in der Neuzeit*, edited by Michael A. Meyer and Michael Brenner, 37–49. Munich: Beck, 2000.
Barkai, Avraham. "German Interests in the Ha'avara-Transfer Agreement 1933–1939." *Leo Baeck Institute Yearbook* 35 (1990): 245–66.
Barkai, Avraham. "Jüdisches Leben unter der Verfolgung." In *Aufbruch und Zerstörung 1918–1945.* Volume 4 of *Deutsch-jüdische Geschichte in der Neuzeit*, edited by Michael A. Meyer and Michael Brenner, 225–48. Munich: Beck, 2000.
Barkai, Avraham. "Selbsthilfe im Dilemma 'Gehen oder Bleiben?'" In *Aufbruch und Zerstörung 1918–1945.* Volume 4 of *Deutsch-jüdische Geschichte in der Neuzeit*, edited by Michael A. Meyer and Michael Brenner, 301–18. Munich: Beck, 2000.
Bar-Yosef, Eitan. "Bonding with the British: Colonial Nostalgia and the Idealization of Mandatory Palestine in Israeli Literature and Culture after 1967." *Jewish Social Studies* 22, no. 3 (2017): 1–37.
Beaujot, Roderic, and Jianiye Jiu. "Models of Time Use in Paid and Unpaid Work." *Journal of Family Issues* 26 (2005): 924–46.
Beling, Eva. *Die gesellschaftliche Eingliederung der deutschen Einwanderer in Israel: Eine soziologische Untersuchung der Einwanderung aus Deutschland zwischen 1933 und 1945.* Frankfurt am Main: Europäische Verlagsanstalt, 1967.
Benz, Wolfgang. *Flucht aus Deutschland: Zum Exil im 20. Jahrhundert.* Munich: Deutscher Taschenbuch Verlag, 2001.
Benz, Wolfgang, ed. *Das Exil der kleinen Leute: Alltagserfahrung deutscher Juden in der Emigration.* Munich: C. H. Beck, 1991.
Berghahn, Marion. *Continental Britons: German-Jewish Refugees from Nazi Germany.* New York: Berghahn, 2007.
Bernstein, Deborah. *Constructing Boundaries: Jewish and Arab Workers in Mandatory Palestine.* Albany: State University of New York Press, 2000.
Bernstein, Deborah. "Contested Contact: Proximity and Social Control in Pre-1948 Jaffa and Tel Aviv." In *Mixed Towns, Trapped Communities: Historical Narratives, Spatial

Dynamics, Gender Relations and Cultural Encounters in Palestinian-Israeli Towns, edited by Daniel Monterescu and Dan Rabinowitz, 215–42. Aldershot: Ashgate, 2007.

Bernstein, Deborah. "Daughters of the Nation: Between the Public and Private Spheres in Pre-State Israel." In *Jewish Women in Historical Perspective*, edited by Judith Reesa Baskin, 287–311. Detroit: Wayne State University Press, 1998.

Bernstein, Deborah. "Gender, Nationalism and Colonial Policy: Prostitution in the Jewish Settlement of Mandate Palestine, 1918–1948." *Women's History Review* 21, no. 1 (2012): 81–100.

Bernstein, Deborah. "Nissuim Fiktivim: Ravakot mehapsot Moza: Eshnav le dilemot mosariot ve le Metah beyn ha prati le ziburi." *Israel* 18/19 (2011): 5–29.

Bernstein, Deborah. "On Rhetoric and Commitment: The Employment of Married Women during the Depression of 1936–1939." *Women's Studies International Forum* 20, no. 5/6 (1997): 593–604.

Bernstein, Deborah. "The Women Workers' Movement in Pre-State Israel, 1919–1939." *Signs: Journal of Women in Culture and Society* 12, no. 3 (1987): 454–70.

Bernstein, Deborah, ed. *Pioneers and Homemakers: Jewish Women in Pre-State Israel*. Albany: State University of New York Press, 1992.

Betten, Anne, and Miryam Du-Nour, eds. *Wir sind die letzten: Fragt uns aus, Gespräche mit den Emigranten der dreißiger Jahre in Israel*. Gerlingen: Bleicher, 1996.

Boord, Matan. "Creating the Labor-Zionist Family: Masculinity, Sexuality, and Marriage in Mandate Palestine." *Jewish Social Studies* 3 (Spring/Summer 2017): 38–67.

Boord, Matan. "Fatherhood in Labour Zionist Children's Literature: Space, Maculinity and Hegemony in Mandate Palestine." *Gender & History* (September 3, 2021). https://doi.org/10.1111/1468-0424.12561

Brinkmann, Tobias. *Migration und Transnationalität*. Paderborn: Ferdinand Schöningh, 2012.

Brunner, José, ed. *Deutsche(s) in Pälastina und Israel: Alltag, Kultur, Politik*. Tel Aviver Jahrbuch für deutsche Geschichte 41. Göttingen: Wallstein, 2013.

Calavita, Kitty. "Gender, Migration, and Law: Crossing Borders and Bridging Disciplines." In "Gender and Migration Revisited," special issue, *International Migration Review* 40, no. 1 (Spring, 2006): 104–32.

Cherniavsky, Irith. *BeOr Shineyhem: Al Aliyatam shel Yehudey Polin lifney haShoah*. Tel Aviv: Resling Publishing, 2015.

Chotjewitz, Peter. *Die mit Tränen säen: Israelisches Reisejournal*. Munich: Verlag AutorenEdition, 1980.

Dahm, Volker, and Wolfgang Benz, eds. *Die Juden in Deutschland, 1933–1945: Leben unter nationalsozialistischer Herrschaft*. Munich: C. H. Beck, 1988.

Davidi, Sigal. *Bonot Aretz Hadasha: Adrihaliot ve Irguney Nashim beTkufat HaMandat*. Raanana: Open University Publishing, 2020.

Davidi, Sigal. "Caring for Parents: Modern Dwellings for Elderly German-Jewish Immigrants in Mandatory Palestine." *Journal of Architecture* 25, no. 3 (2020): 203–29.

Donato, Katharine M., and Donna Gabaccia. *Gender and International Migration.* New York: Russell Sage Foundation, 2016.

Donato, Katharine M., Donna Gabaccia, Jennifer Holdaway, Martin Manalansan IV, and Patricia R. Pessar. "A Glass Half Full? Gender in Migration Studies." In "Gender and Migration Revisited," special issue, *International Migration Review* 40, no. 1 (Spring, 2006): 3–26.

Dubnov, Arie M. "On Vertical Alliances, 'Perfidious Albion,' and the Security Paradigm: Reflections on the Balfour Declaration Centennial and the Winding Road to Israeli Independence." *European Judaism* 52, no. 1 (2019): 67–110.

Dwork, Debórah, and Robert Jan van Pelt. *Flight from the Reich: Refugee Jews, 1933–1946.* New York: W. W. Norton, 2009.

Elboim-Dror, Rachel. "British Educational Policies in Palestine." *Middle Eastern Studies* 36, no. 2 (2000): 28–47.

Erel, Shlomo. *Neue Wurzeln: 50 Jahre Immigration deutschsprachiger Juden in Israel.* Gerlingen: Bleicher Verlag, 1983.

Erel, Shlomo, ed. *Kaleidoskop Israel: Deutschsprachige Einwanderer in Israel erzählen.* Klagenfurt: Alekto, 1994.

Erez, Idith. "'Ahava ve Koz ba.' Ha Memad haMigdari beYahassey Yehudim ve Aravim beAretz Israel haMandatorit: Kishrey Nashim Yehudiot ve Gvarim Aravim." Master's thesis, University of Haifa, Department of Israel Studies, 2019.

Farges, Patrick. "'Generation Palmach'? Junge Männer in der Post-Migration." In *Deutsche und Zentraleuropäische Juden in Palästina und Israel: Kulturtransfers, Lebenswelten, Identitäten—Beispiele aus Haifa*, edited by Anja Siegemund, 360–73. Berlin: Neofelis Verlag, 2016.

Farges, Patrick. "Multiple Masculinities among German Jewish Refugees: A Transnational Comparison between Canada and Palestine/Israel." In *The Holocaust and Masculinities: Critical Inquiries into the Presence and Absence of Men*, edited by Björn Krondorfer and Ovidiu Creangă, 245–66. Albany: State University of New York Press, 2020.

Farges, Patrick. "'Muscle' Yekkes? Multiple German-Jewish Masculinities in Palestine and Israel after 1933." *Central European History* 51 (2018): 466–87.

Feilchenfeld, Werner, Dolf Michaelis, and Ludwig Pinner, eds. *Haavara-Transfer nach Palästina und Einwanderung deutscher Juden 1933–1939.* Tübingen: J. C. B. Mohr (Paul Siebeck), 1972.

Freidenreich, Harriet Pass. "Die jüdische 'Neue Frau' des frühen 20. Jahrhunderts." In *Deutsch-jüdische Geschichte als Geschlechtergeschichte: Studien zum 19. und 20. Jahrhundert*, edited by Kirsten Heinsohn and Stefanie Schüler-Springorum, 123–32. Göttingen: Wallstein, 2006.

Gay, Peter. "Epilogue: The First Sex." In *Between Sorrow and Strength: Women Refugees of the Nazi Period*, edited by Sibylle Quack, 353–65. Cambridge: Cambridge University Press, 1995.

Gebhardt, Miriam. "Der Fall Clara Geißmar, oder von der Verführungskunst weiblicher

Autobiographik." In *Deutsch-jüdische Geschichte als Geschlechtergeschichte: Studien zum 19. und 20. Jahrhundert*, edited by Kirsten Heinsohn and Stefanie Schüler-Springorum, 233–49. Göttingen: Wallstein Verlag, 2006.

Gebhardt, Miriam. *Das Familiengedächtnis: Erinnerung im deutsch-jüdischen Bürgertum 1890 bis 1932.* Stuttgart: F. Steiner, 1999.

Gelber, Yoav. "The Historical Role of the Central European Immigration to Israel." *Leo Baeck Institute Yearbook* (1993): 323–39.

Gelber, Yoav. *Moledet Hadasha: Aliyat Yehudei Merkaz Europa uKlitatam, 1933–1948.* Jerusalem: Yad Izhak Ben-Zvi, 1990.

Gelber, Yoav. "Oley Germania beHaifa beShnot haShloshim veArbaim." *Idan* 12 (1989): 95–110.

Gerson, Judith. "Family Matters: German Jewish Masculinities among Nazi Era Refugees." In *Jewish Masculinities: German Jews, Gender, and History*, edited by Benjamin Maria Baader, Sharon Gillerman, and Paul Frederick Lerner, 210–30. Bloomington: Indiana University Press, 2012.

Getter, Miriam. "HaHitargenut haPolitit haNifredet shel Oley Germania." *HaZionut* 7 (1981): 240–91.

Godenschweger, Walter B., Fritz Vilmar, and Jacob Michaeli, eds. *Die rettende Kraft der Utopie: Deutsche Juden gründen den Kibbuz Hasorea.* Frankfurt am Main: Luchterhand Literaturverlag, 1990.

Golani, Motti, and Daniela Reich. "Bein shelihot li-menudot: Ha-mifgash bein benot ha-yishuv le-vein lovshei ha-madim meha-tsava ha-briti, 1940–1948." *Tsiyon* 73, no. 3 (2008): 325–48.

Green, Nancy L. "Changing Paradigms in Migration Studies: From Men to Women to Gender." *Gender and History* 24, no. 3 (2012): 782–98.

Green, Nancy L., and Siân Reynolds. "Four Ages of Migration Studies." *Clio: Women, Gender, History*, no. 51 (2020): 183–204.

Grossmann, Atina. "'Neue Frauen' im Exil. Deutsche Ärztinnen und die Migration." In *Deutsch-jüdische Geschichte als Geschlechtergeschichte: Studien zum 19. und 20. Jahrhundert*, edited by Kirsten Heinsohn and Stefanie Schüler-Springorum, 133–56. Göttingen: Wallstein Verlag, 2006.

Guerry, Linda, and Françoise Thébaud. "Editorial: Women, Gender, and Migration." Translated by Siân Reynolds. *Clio: Women, Gender, History*, no. 51 (2020): 19–33.

Halamish, Aviva. "Aflayat Nashim beTkufat haMandat. HaUvdot, haSibot, hashlahot." *Divrei haKongress haOlami ha12 le Mada'ey haYahadut, Division E: Contemporary Jewish Society, World Union of Jewish Studies* (2001): 49–57.

Halamish, Aviva. *BeMirutz kaful neged haSman: Mediniut HaAliyah haZionit beShnot haShloshim.* Jerusalem: Yad Izhak Ben-Zvi, 2006.

Halamish, Aviva. "Immigration Is Israel's History, So Far." *Israel Studies* 23, no. 3 (2018): 106–13.

Halamish, Aviva. "Palestine as a Destination for Jewish Immigrants and Refugees from

Nazi Germany." In *Refugees from Nazi Germany and the Liberal European States*, edited by Frank Caestecker and Bob Moore, 122–50. New York: Berghahn Books, 2010.

Halamish, Aviva. "The Yishuv: The Jewish Community in Mandate Palestine." In *Israel Studies: An Anthology,* edited by Mitchell G. Bard and David Nachmias. Jewish Virtual Library Publications, 2009. http://www.jewishvirtuallibrary.org/jsource/isdf/text/halamish.pdf.

Halperin, Liora. *Babel in Zion: Jews, Nationalism, and Language Diversity in Palestine, 1920–1948*. New Haven, CT: Yale University Press, 2014.

Halperin, Liora. "The Battle over Jewish Students in the Christian Missionary Schools of Mandate Palestine." *Middle Eastern Studies* 50, no. 5 (2014): 737–54.

Halpern, Ayana. "Jewish Social Workers in Mandatory Palestine: Between Submission and Subversion under Male Leadership." *Nashim: A Journal of Jewish Women's Studies & Gender Issues,* no. 35 (Fall 2019): 75–96.

Heinsohn, Kirsten and Stefanie Schüler-Springorum, eds. *Deutsch-jüdische Geschichte als Geschlechtergeschichte: Studien zum 19. und 20. Jahrhundert*. Göttingen: Wallstein Verlag, 2006.

Helman, Anat. "Cleanliness and Squalor in Inter-War Tel-Aviv." *Urban History* 31 (2004): 72–99.

Helman, Anat. *A Coat of Many Colors: Dress Culture in the Young State of Israel*. Boston: Academic Studies Press, 2011.

Helman, Anat. "Hues of Adjustment: 'Landsmanshaftn' in Inter-War New York and Tel-Aviv." *Jewish History* 20 (2006): 41–67.

Helman, Anat. *Young Tel Aviv: A Tale of Two Cities*. Waltham, MA: Brandeis University Press, 2010.

Hirsch, Dafna. "'Interpreters of Occident to the Awakening Orient': The Jewish Public Health Nurse in Mandate Palestine." *Comparative Studies in Society and History* 50, no. 1 (2008): 227–55.

Hirsch, Dafna. "We Are Here to Bring the West, Not Only to Ourselves: Zionist Occidentalism and the Discourse of Hygiene in Mandate Palestine." *International Journal of Middle East Studies* 41, no. 4 (2009): 577–94.

Hirshberg, Sigmund-Shmuel, and Gertrud Hirshberg. *Mi Berlin leShanhai: Mihtavim leEretz Israel*. Edited by Guy Miron. Jerusalem: Yad VaShem, 2013.

Hotam, Yotam. "Emigrierte Erinnerung: Zu Sprache, Identität und Konversion deutschjüdischer Emigranten." In *Populäre Konstruktionen von Erinnerung im deutschen Judentum und nach der Emigration*, edited by Yotam Hotam and Joachim Jacob, 173–95. Göttingen: Vandenhoeck & Ruprecht, 2004.

Huebel, Sebastian. *Fighter, Worker, and Family Man: German-Jewish Men and Their Gendered Experience in Nazi-Germany, 1933–1941*. Toronto: University of Toronto Press, 2022.

Hyman, Illene, Sepali Guruge, and Robin Mason. "The Impact of Migration on Marital Relationships: A Study of Ethiopian Immigrants in Toronto." *Journal of Comparative Family Studies* 39, no. 2 (2008): 149–63.

Jacobson, Abigail, and Moshe Naor. *Oriental Neighbors: Middle Eastern Jews and Arabs in Mandatory Palestine.* Waltham, MA: Brandeis University Press, 2016.

Jünger, David. *Jahre der Ungewissheit: Emigrationspläne deutscher Juden 1933–1938.* Göttingen: Vandenhoeck & Ruprecht, 2016.

Jütte, Robert. *Die Emigration der deutschsprachigen "Wissenschaft des Judentums": Die Auswanderung jüdischer Historiker nach Palästina 1933–1945.* Stuttgart: Franz Steiner Verlag, 1991.

Kalmar, Ivan Davidson, and Derek Penslar. "Orientalism and the Jews: An Introduction." In *Orientalism and the Jews*, edited by Ivan Davidson Kalmar and Derek Penslar, xiii–xl. Hanover, MA: Brandeis University Press, 2005.

Kalmar, Ivan Davidson, and Derek Penslar, eds. *Orientalism and the Jews.* Hanover: Brandeis University Press, 2005.

Kaplan, Marion A. "As Germans and Jews in Imperial Germany." In *Jewish Daily Life in Germany, 1618–1945*, edited by Marion A. Kaplan, 182–200. Oxford: Oxford University Press, 2005.

Kaplan, Marion A. *Between Dignity and Despair: Jewish Life in Nazi Germany.* New York: Oxford University Press, 1998.

Kaplan, Marion A. *Dominican Haven: The Jewish Refugee Settlement in Sosúa, 1940–1945.* New York: Museum of Jewish Heritage, 2008.

Kaplan, Marion A. "Jewish Women in Nazi Germany before Emigration." In *Between Sorrow and Strength: Women Refugees of the Nazi Period*, edited by Sibylle Quack, 11–48. Cambridge: Cambridge University Press, 1995.

Kaplan, Marion A. *The Making of the Jewish Middle Class: Women, Family, and Identity in Imperial Germany.* New York: Oxford University Press, 1991.

Kaplan, Marion A. "Weaving Women's Words: Zur Bedeutung von Memoiren für die deutsch-jüdische Frauengeschichte." In *Deutsch-jüdische Geschichte als Geschlechtergeschichte: Studien zum 19. und 20. Jahrhundert*, edited by Kirsten Heinsohn and Stefanie Schüler-Springorum, 250–75. Göttingen: Wallstein Verlag, 2006.

Kark, Ruth, Margalit Shilo, and Galit Hasan-Rokem, eds. *Jewish Women in Pre-State Israel: Life History, Politics, and Culture.* Waltham, MA: Brandeis University Press, 2008.

Katvan, Eyal. "Hakamat 'haMisrad haRefui' ve haManganon haMerkasi leBdikat haOlim leEretz Israel 1934–1939." *Iyunim bitkumat Israel* (2013): 167–92.

Kaufman, Haim. "Jewish Sports in the Diaspora, Yishuv, and Israel: Between Nationalism and Politics." *Israel Studies* 10, no. 2 (2005): 147–67.

Khazzoom, Aziza. *Shifting Ethnic Boundaries and Inequality in Israel: Or, How the Polish Peddler Became a German Intellectual.* Stanford, CA: Stanford University Press, 2008.

Knox, Paul, and Steven Pinch. *Urban Social Geography: An Introduction.* London: Taylor & Francis Group, 2009.

Konrad, Franz-Michael. *Wurzeln jüdischer Sozialarbeit in Palästina: Einflüsse der Sozialarbeit in Deutschland auf die Entstehung moderner Hilfesysteme in Palästina, 1890–1948.* Weinheim: Juventa, 1993.

Koonz, Claudia. "Courage and Choice among German-Jewish Women and Men." In *Die Juden im nationalsozialistischen Deutschland, 1933–1943*, edited by Arnold Paucker, Sylvia Gilchrist, and Barbara Suchy, 283–93. Tübingen: J. C. B. Mohr, 1986.

Kozma, Liat. "Sexology in the Yishuv: The Rise and Decline of Sexual Consultation in Tel Aviv, 1930–1939." *International Journal of Middle East Studies* 42, no. 2 (May 2021): 231–49.

Krämer, Gudrun. *Geschichte Palästinas: Von der osmanischen Eroberung bis zur Gründung des Staates Israel*. Munich: C. H. Beck, 2002.

Kranzler, David. "Women in the Shanghai Jewish Refugee Community." In *Between Sorrow and Strength: Women Refugees of the Nazi Period*, edited by Sibylle Quack, 129–37. Cambridge: Cambridge University Press, 1995.

Kreppel, Klaus. *Nahariyya und die deutsche Einwanderung nach Eretz Israel: die Geschichte seiner Einwohner von 1935 bis 1941*. Tefen: Das Offene Museum, 2010.

Kreppel, Lena. *Deutsch, Jüdisch, Israelisch: Identitätskonstruktionen in autobiographischen und essayistischen Texten von Erich Bloch, Jenny Cramer und Fritz Wolf*. Würzburg: Königshausen & Neumann, 2012.

Krik, Hagit. "Colonial Lives in Palestine, 1920–1948: British Society and Culture in a Mandate Territory." PhD diss., University of Tel Aviv, Department of History, 2017.

Kushner, Tony. "Fremde Arbeit: Jüdische Flüchtlinge als Hausangestellte in Grossbritannien." In *Heimat und Exil: Emigration der deutschen Juden nach 1933*. Companion book to the exhibit "Heimat und Exil," edited by Stiftung Jüdisches Museum Berlin and Stiftung Haus der Geschichte der Bundesrepublik Deutschland, 72–75. Frankfurt am Main: Jüdischer Verlag im Suhrkamp Verlag, 2006.

Laqueur, Walter. *Geboren in Deutschland: Der Exodus der jüdischen Jugend nach 1933*. Berlin: Propyläen Verlag, 2000.

Lavsky, Hagit. *Before Catastrophe: The Distinctive Path of German Zionism*. Detroit: Wayne State University Press, 1996.

Lavsky, Hagit. *The Creation of the German-Jewish Diaspora: Interwar German-Jewish Immigration to Palestine, the USA, and England*. Berlin: De Gruyter, 2017.

Lazar, Hadara. *ha-Mandatorim*. Jerusalem: Keter, 1990.

Lehmann, Erich M., ed. *Nahariya: Ein Beitrag von Juden aus Mitteleuropa zum Aufbau des Landes Israel*. Nahariya: self-published, 1998 (1960).

Levine, Rhonda F. *Class, Networks, and Identity: Replanting Jewish Lives from Nazi Germany to Rural New York*. Lanham, MD: Rowman and Littlefield, 2001.

Lewy, Thomas. *Zwischen allen Bühnen: Die Jeckes und das hebräische Theater 1933–1948*. Berlin: Neofelis Verlag, 2016.

Lowenstein, Steven M. "Women's Role in the German-Jewish Immigrant Community." In *Between Sorrow and Strength: Women Refugees of the Nazi Period*, edited by Sibylle Quack, 171–83. Cambridge: Cambridge University Press, 1995.

Lucassen, Leo. "Beyond the Apocalypse: Reframing Migration History." In *History, His-

torians and the Immigration Debate: Going Back to Where We Came From, edited by Eureka Henrich and Julian M. Simpson, 33–51. Cham: Palgrave Macmillan, 2019.

Luft, Gerda. *Heimkehr ins Unbekannte: Eine Darstellung der Einwanderung von Juden aus Deutschland nach Palästina vom Aufstieg Hitlers zur Macht bis zum Ausbruch des Zweiten Weltkrieges, 1933–1939.* Wuppertal: Hammer, 1977.

Luscher, Sarah. *Frauen in der Emigration—Ihre Rolle im Exil zwischen Anpassung und Selbstbehauptung.* Munich: GRIN Verlag GmbH, 2010.

Maurer, Trude. "Family Life." In *Jewish Daily Life in Germany, 1618–1945*, edited by Marion A. Kaplan, 283–90. Oxford: Oxford University Press, 2005.

Meyer, Michael A., and Michael Brenner, eds. *Deutsch-jüdische Geschichte in der Neuzeit.* Vol. 4, *Aufbruch und Zerstörung, 1918–1945.* Munich: C. H. Beck, 2000.

Meyer, Tamar. "From a Zero to a Hero: Masculinity in Jewish Nationalism." In *Gender Ironies of Nationalism: Sexing the Nation*, edited by Tamar Meyer, 283–307. London: Routledge, 2000.

Miron, Guy. "From Bourgeois Germany to Palestine: Memoirs of German Jewish Women in Israel." *Nashim: A Journal of Jewish Women's Studies & Gender Issues*, no. 17 (2009): 116–40.

Miron, Guy. "Introduction." In Sigmund-Shmuel Hirshberg and Gertrud Hirshberg. *Mi Berlin leShanhai: Mihtavim leEretz Israel*, edited by Guy Miron, 7–70. Jerusalem: Yad VaShem, 2013.

Miron, Guy. *Lehiot Yehudi beGermania ha Nazit: Merhav veZman.* Jerusalem: Magnes, 2021.

Miron, Guy. *Mi "sham" le "kan" beGuf rishon: Yejudey Germania beEretz Israel/Medinat Israel: Todaatam HaAzmit miBa'ad leTfussey haSikaron HaIshi.* Jerusalem: Magnes, 1998.

Nawyn, Stephanie J. "Gender and Migration: Integrating Feminist Theory into Migration Studies." *Sociology Compass* 4, no. 9 (2010): 749–65.

Nicosia, Francis R. "Haavara, Hachschara und Aliyah-beth: Jüdische-zionistische Auswanderung in den Jahren 1938–1941." In *Wer bleibt, opfert seine Jahre, vielleicht sein Leben: Deutsche Juden 1938–1941*, edited by Susanne Heim, Beate Meyer, and Francis R. Nicosia, 134–48. Göttingen: Wallstein Verlag, 2010.

Niederland, Doron. "Deutsche Ärzte-Emigration und gesundheitspolitische Entwicklungen in Eretz Israel, 1933–1945." *Medizinhistorisches Journal* 20 (1985): 149–85.

Niederland, Doron, ed. *Yehudey Germania—mehagrim o plitim? Iyun beTfusey haHagira beyn shtey milhamot haOlam.* Jerusalem: Magnes, 1996.

Niethammer, Lutz, ed. *Lebenserfahrung und kollektives Gedächtnis: Die Praxis der "Oral History."* Frankfurt am Main: Suhrkamp, 1985.

Nolan, Mary. "'Housework Made Easy': The Taylorized Housewife in Weimar Germany's Rationalized Economy." *Feminist Studies* 16, no. 3 (1990): 549–77.

Nussbaum, Martha. "Objectification." *Philosophy and Public Affairs* 24, no. 4 (1995): 249–91.

Ofer, Dalia. "The Contribution of Gender to the Study of the Holocaust." In *Gender and Jewish History*, edited by Marion A. Kaplan and Deborah Dash Moore, 120–35. Bloomington: Indiana University Press, 2011.

Oppenheimer, Mihal, ed. *Nahariya*. Nahariya: Rotary, n.d.

Paucker, Arnold, Sylvia Gilchrist, and Barbara Suchy, eds. *Die Juden im nationalsozialistischen Deutschland, 1933–1943*. Tübingen; J.C.B. Mohr, 1986.

Peleg, Yaron. *Orientalism and the Hebrew Imagination*. Ithaca, NY: Cornell University Press, 2005.

Peleg, Yaron. "Re-Orientalizing the Jew: Zionist and Contemporary Israeli Masculinities." In *Orientalism, Gender, and the Jews*, edited by Ulrike Brunotte, Anna-Dorothea Ludewig, and Axel Stähler, 176–94. Berlin: De Gruyter, 2015.

Pfefferman, Talia, and David De Vries. "Gendering Access to Credit: Business Legitimacy in Mandate Palestine." *Enterprise and Society* 16, no. 3 (2015): 580–610.

Piper, Nicola. "Gendering the Politics of Migration." In "Gender and Migration Revisited," special issue, *International Migration Review* 40, no. 1 (Spring 2006): 133–64.

Portelli, Alessandro. "What Makes Oral History Different." In *The Oral History Reader*, edited by Robert Perks and Alistair Thomson, 48–58. New York: Routledge, 2015.

Proskauer, Erna. *Wege und Umwege: Erinnerungen einer Rechtsanwältin*. Berlin: D. Nishen, 1989.

Quack, Sibylle. "Changing Gender Roles and Emigration: The Example of German Jewish Women and Their Emigration to the United States, 1933–1945." In *People in Transit: German Migrations in Comparative Perspective: 1820–1930*, edited by Dirk Hoerder and Joerg Nagler, 379–97. Cambridge: Cambridge University Press, 1995.

Quack, Sibylle. "Introduction." In *Between Sorrow and Strength: Women Refugees of the Nazi Period*, edited by Sibylle Quack, 1–10. Cambridge: Cambridge University Press, 1995.

Quack, Sibylle. *Zuflucht Amerika: Zur Sozialgeschichte der Emigration deutsch-jüdischer Frauen in die USA 1933–1945*. Bonn: Dietz, 1995.

Quack, Sibylle, ed. *Between Sorrow and Strength: Women Refugees of the Nazi Period*. Cambridge: Cambridge University Press, 1995.

Radai, Itamar. "Yozey Arzot ha-Islam: Dimuyim veTfissot beHevra haYishuvit: HaMikre shel Hanna Helene Thon." *Iyunim* 32 (2019): 216–44.

Rapaport, Maylys, and Marina M. Doucerain. "Shared Immigration Process, Different Perspectives: The Impact of Immigration-Related Gaps on Couple Relationships." *Migration Studies* 9, no. 4 (December 2021): 1626–44.

Rautenberg-Alianov, Viola. "Alte und neue Rollen. Jeckische Hausfrauen zwischen Bürgerlichkeit, Zionismus und Existenzkampf." In *Deutsche und zentraleuropäische Juden in Palästina und Israel*, edited by Anja Siegemund, 202–12. Berlin: Neofelis, 2016.

Rautenberg-Alianov, Viola. "Schlagsahne oder 'Shemen'-Öl? Deutsch-jüdische Hausfrauen und ihre Küche in Palästina, 1936–1940." In *Deutsche(s) in Palästina und Israel: Alltag,*

Kultur, Politik, edited by José Brunner, 82–96. Vol. 41 of *Tel Aviver Jahrbuch für deutsche Geschichte*. Göttingen: Wallstein, 2013.

Razi, Tammy. "The Family Is Worthy of Being Rebuilt: Perceptions of the Jewish Family in Mandate Palestine." *Journal of Family History* 35, no. 4 (2010): 395–415.

Razi, Tammy. *Forsaken Children: The Backyard of Mandate Tel Aviv*. Tel Aviv: Am Oved, 2009. [In Hebrew.]

Razi, Tammy. "Immigration and Its Discontents: Treating Children in the Psycho-Hygiene Clinic in Mandate Tel Aviv." *Journal of Modern Jewish Studies* 11, no. 3 (November 1, 2012): 339–56.

Raz-Krakotzkin, Amnon. "The Zionist Return to the West and the Mizrachi Jewish Perspective." In *Orientalism and the Jews*, edited by Ivan Davidson Kalmar and Derek Penslar, 162–81. Hanover, MA: Brandeis University Press, 2005.

Reagin, Nancy. *Sweeping the German Nation: Domesticity and National Identity in Germany, 1870–1945*. Cambridge: Cambridge University Press, 2007.

Rosenberg-Friedman, Lilach. "Abortion in the Yishuv during the British Mandate Period: A Case Study of the Place of the Individual in a Nationalist Society." *Jewish History* 29, 3/4 (December 2015): 331–59.

Rubin, Adam. "'Turning Goyim into Jews': Aliyah and the Politics of Cultural Anxiety in the Zionist Movement, 1933–1939." *Jewish Quarterly Review* 101, no. 1 (Winter 2011): 71–96.

Saß, Anne-Christin. *Berliner Luftmenschen: Osteuropäisch-jüdische Migranten in der Weimarer Republik*. Göttingen: Wallstein Verlag, 2012.

Schlör, Joachim. *Endlich im gelobten Land? Deutsche Juden unterwegs in eine neue Heimat*. Berlin: Aufbau-Verlag, 2003.

Schlör, Joachim. "How to Cook in Palestine: Kurfürstendamm Meets Rehov Ben Jehuda." In *Longing, Belonging, and the Making of Jewish Consumer Culture*, edited by Gideon Reuveni and Nils Roemer, 163–82. Leiden: Brill, 2010.

Schlör, Joachim. "'Solange wir auf dem Schiff waren, hatten wir ein Zuhause': Reisen als kulturelle Praxis im Migrationsprozess jüdischer Auswanderer." *Voyage: Jahrbuch für Reise- und Tourismusforschung* 10 (2014): 226–46.

Schlör, Joachim, ed. "Die Schiffsreise als Übergangserfahrung in Migrationsprozessen / The Sea Voyage as a Transitory Experience in Migration Processes," special issue, *Mobile Culture Studies: The Journal* 1, no. 1 (2015).

Schüler-Springorum, Stefanie. *Geschlecht und Differenz*. Paderborn: Schöningh, 2014.

Scott, Joan Wallach. "Gender: A Useful Category of Historical Analysis." *American Historical Review* 91, no. 5 (1986): 152–80.

Segev, Tom. *Es war einmal ein Pälestina: Juden und Araber vor der Staatsgründung Israels*. Munich: Siedler Verlag, 2006.

Segev, Tom. *The Seventh Million: The Israelis and the Holocaust*. New York: Hill and Wang, 1994.

Sela-Sheffy, Rakefet. "High Status Immigration Group and Culture Retention: German Jewish Immigrants in British-Ruled Palestine." In *Culture Contacts and the Making of Cultures: Papers in Homage to Itamar Even-Zohar*, edited by Rakefet Sela-Sheffy and Gideon Toury, 79–100. Tel Aviv: Tel Aviv University, Unit of Culture Research, 2011.

Sela-Sheffy, Rakefet. "Integration through Distinction: German-Jewish Immigrants, the Legal Profession and Patterns of Bourgeois Culture in British-Ruled Jewish Palestine." *Journal of Historical Sociology* 19, no. 1 (2006): 34–59.

Sherman, A. J. *Mandate Days: British Lives in Palestine, 1918–1948*. New York: Thames and Hudson, 1998.

Shifman, Limor, and Elihu Katz. "'Just Call Me Adonai': A Case Study of Ethnic Humor and Immigrant Assimilation." *American Sociological Review* 70 (2005): 843–59.

Shilo, Margalit. "The Double or Multiple Image of the New Hebrew Woman." *Nashim: A Journal of Jewish Women's Studies & Gender Issues* 1 (1998): 73–94.

Shilo, Margalit. *Nashim bonot Uma: HaProfesionaliot ha Ivriot, 1918–1948*. Jerusalem: Carmel, 2020.

Shoham, Hizky. "'Small Sales Agents (of Nationalism) inside the House.' Childhood, Consumer Culture, and Nationalism in the Jewish Yishuv of Interwar Palestine." *Journal of the History of Childhood and Youth* 12, no. 1 (Winter 2019): 88–112.

Shohat, Ella. "The Invention of the Mizrahim." *Journal of Palestine Studies* 29, no. 1 (1999): 5–20.

Shuval, Judith T. "The Mythology of 'Uniqueness.'" *International Migration* 36 (1998): 3–26.

Siegel, Björn. "Die Jungfernfahrt der 'Tel Aviv' im Jahre 1935: Eine 'Besinnliche Fahrt ins Land der Juden'?" In *"Ihre Wege sind liebliche Wege und all ihre Pfade Frieden" (Sprüche 3,17). Die Neunte Joseph Carlebach-Konferenz: Wege Joseph Carlebachs: universale Bildung, gelebtes Judentum, Opfergang*, edited by Miriam Gillis-Carlebach and Barbara Vogel, 106–25. Munich: Dölling und Galitz, 2014.

Siegemund, Anja, "German Zionists of *Verständigung* and Their Ideas for Conflict Resolution in Palestine." In *The Legacy of the German-Jewish Religious and Cultural Heritage: A Basis for German-Israeli Dialogue?*, edited by Konrad Adenauer Stiftung, 143–60. Jerusalem: Konrad Adenauer Foundation, 2006.

Siegemund, Anja. "'Die Jeckes'": Ein Klischee und Faszinosum neu verhandelt. Plädoyer für ein vielfarbiges Mosaik. In *Deutsche und Zentraleuropäische Juden in Palästina und Israel: Kulturtransfers, Lebenswelten, Identitäten—Beispiele aus Haifa*, edited by Anja Siegemund, 11–50. Berlin: Neofelis Verlag, 2016.

Siegemund, Anja, ed. *Deutsche und Zentraleuropäische Juden in Palästina und Israel: Kulturtransfers, Lebenswelten, Identitäten—Beispiele aus Haifa*. Berlin: Neofelis Verlag, 2016.

Smooha, Sammy. "The Mass Immigrations to Israel: A Comparison of the Failure of the Mizrahi Immigrants of the 1950s with the Success of the Russian Immigrants of the 1990s." *Journal of Israeli History* 27, no. 1 (2008): 1–27.

Stachel, Gideon. "HaAliyah HaYehudit MiGermania leEretz Israel beShanim 1933–1939 ve mifgasha im haHevra haYishuvit meNekodat mabatam shel haOlim." PhD diss., Hebrew University of Jerusalem, 1995.

Stern, Bat-Sheva Margalit. "'He Walked through the Fields,' But What Did She Do? The 'Hebrew Woman' in Her Own Eyes and in the Eyes of Her Contemporaries." *Journal of Israeli History* 30, no. 2 (2011): 161–87.

Stern, Bat-Sheva Margalit. "Rebels of Unimportance: The 1930s' Textile Strike in Tel Aviv and the Boundaries of Women's Self-Reliance." *Middle Eastern Studies* 38, no. 3 (2002): 171–94.

Stiftung Jüdisches Museum Berlin and Stiftung Haus der Geschichte der Bundesrepublik Deutschland, eds. *Heimat und Exil: Emigration der deutschen Juden nach 1933*. Companion book to the exhibit "Heimat und Exil." Frankfurt am Main: Jüdischer Verlag im Suhrkamp Verlag, 2006.

Stoler-Liss, Sachlav. "'Mothers Birth the Nation': The Social Construction of Zionist Motherhood in Wartime in Israeli Parents' Manuals." In "Women, War, and Peace in Jewish and Middle East Contexts," special issue, *Nashim: A Journal of Jewish Women's Studies & Gender Issues* 6 (Fall 5764/2003): 104–18.

Sznaider, Nusi. "Between Past and No Future: A Study of German Jews in Palestine." Master's thesis, Tel Aviv University, 1984.

Tene, Ofra. "'Kah nevashel' beyt beIsrael: Kriah bsifrey bishul meshnot hashloshim ad shnot hashmonim." In *Beten melea: Mabat aher al ohel veHevra*, edited by Aviad Kleinberg, 92–130. Tel Aviv: Tel Aviv University, 2005.

Thalmann, Rita. "Jüdische Frauen nach dem Pogrom 1938." In *Die Juden im nationalsozialistischen Deutschland, 1933–1943*, edited by Arnold Paucker, Sylvia Gilchrist, and Barbara Suchy, 295–302. Tübingen: J. C. B. Mohr, 1986.

Tramer, Hans, ed. *In zwei Welten: Siegfried Moses zum 75. Geburtstag*. Tel Aviv: Bitaon, 1962.

Trezib, Joachim, and Ines Sonder. "The Rassco and the Settlement of the Fifth Aliyah: Pre-State and Early State Middle Class Settlement and Its Relevance for Public Housing in Eretz-Israel." *Israel Studies* 24 (Spring 2019): 1–23.

Turnowsky-Pinner, Margarete. *Die zweite Generation mitteleuropäischer Siedler in Israel*. Tübingen: Mohr, 1962.

Viest, Agnes. *Identität und Integration dargestellt am Beispiel mitteleuropäischer Einwanderer in Israel*. Frankfurt am Main: Peter Lang, 1977.

Volkmann, Michael. *Neuorientierung in Palästina: Erwachsenenbildung deutschsprachiger jüdischer Einwanderer 1933 bis 1948*. Cologne: Böhlau, 1994.

Volovici, Marc. *German as a Jewish Problem: The Language Politics of Jewish Nationalism*. Stanford, CA: Stanford University Press, 2020.

Wassermann, Henry. "Das Deutsche in Erez Israel (1933–1948). Vorüberlegungen zum bestehenden Abschluss einer Bibliographie deutschsprachiger in Palästina und Israel geschriebener Titel (1933–2005)." In *Stimmen aus Jerusalem: Zur deutschen Sprache und Literatur in Palästina/Israel*, edited by Hermann Zabel, 92–108. Berlin: Lit, 2006.

Wetzel, Juliane. "Auswanderung aus Deutschland." In *Die Juden in Deutschland, 1933–1945: Leben unter nationalsozialistischer Herrschaft*, edited by Volker Dahm and Wolfgang Benz, 413–98. Munich: C. H. Beck, 1988.

Wieler, Joachim. "Destination Social Work: Émigrés in a Women's Profession." In *Between Sorrow and Strength: Women Refugees of the Nazi Period*, edited by Sibylle Quack, 265–82. Cambridge: Cambridge University Press, 1995.

Wimmer, Mario. "Abstraktion durch Anschaulichkeit: Wirtschaftliche Haushalts- und Lebensführung in der Zwischenkriegszeit." *L'homme: Europäische Zeitschrift für Feministische Geschichtswissenschaft* 22, no. 2 (2011):129–42.

Wormann, Curt D. "German Jews in Israel: Their Cultural Situation since 1933." *Leo Baeck Institute Yearbook* 15, no. 1 (1970): 73–103.

Wormann, Curt D. "Kulturelle Probleme und Aufgaben der Juden aus Deutschland in Israel seit 1933." In *In zwei Welten: Siegfried Moses zum 75. Geburtstag*, edited by Hans Tramer, 280–329. Tel Aviv: Bitaon Publishing, 1962.

Yaal, Orit. "The Modern Matchmaker: Yosef Liber's Hebrew Matchmaking Revolution." *Kesher* 52 (2019): 49–62. [In Hebrew.]

Yonay, Yuval. "Gay German Jews and the Arrival of 'Homosexuality' to Mandatory Palestine." In *Queer Jewish Lives between Central Europe and Mandatory Palestine: Biographies and Geographies*, edited by Andreas Kraß, Moshe Sluhovsky, and Yuval Yonay, 131–156. Bielefeld: transcript Verlag, 2022.

Yosef, Dorit. "From Yekke to Zionist: Narrative Strategies in Life Stories of Central European Jewish Women Immigrants to Mandate Palestine." *Journal of Israeli History* 33, no. 2 (2014): 185–208.

Yosef, Dorit. "Mi 'Yekkiot' le Zioniot: Astrategiot narativiot beSipurey Hayim shel nashim yehudiot-germaniot beEretz Israel." *Israel* 22 (2014): 111–32.

Yosef, Dorit, and Guy Miron. "Burganut ve Zionut beHayei haBayt shel Yozot Merkaz Europa beEretz Israel." *Iyunim beTkumat Israel* 28 (2017): 197–24.

Zimmermann, Moshe. *Die deutschen Juden 1914–1945*. Munich: R. Oldenbourg, 1997.

Zimmermann, Moshe, and Yotam Hotam, eds. *Zweimal Heimat: Die Jeckes zwischen Mitteleuropa und Nahost*. Frankfurt am Main: Beerenverlag, 2005.

Index

Page numbers in *italics* refer to illustrations; "n" after a page number indicates the endnote number.

Abbady, Yizhak, 103
absorption, 6, 7–8, 249; absorbing society as ambivalent, 64; absorption policies, 23, 249; gender, German Jews in Mandatory Palestine and, 3, 10, 19, 25; German Jews in Mandatory Palestine, 5, 9–10, 25, 113, 248; initial absorption, 3, 67, 243; labor market and absorbing society, 115, 148–49. *See also* absorption apparatus; German Jews' interactions with others in Mandatory Palestine
absorption apparatus: arrival of German Jews to Mandatory Palestine and, 20, 47, 48–50, 56–58, 60, 62, 67; childcare and, 223–25; cooking, food, meals, and, 179, 184–85, 189; divorce and, 220; education and, 20, 57; family as central concern, 199, 240; gender and, 115, 243, 247, 248; homemaking practices and, 161, 171, 173, 176, 197; housing and, 20, 56–58; immigration policies, 4–5, 16, 17, 67; integration and, 9, 243; labor market and, 114, 115–20, 121, 122, 123, 127, 129, 131, 135, 136, 143–44, 156; motherhood and, 223, 226; paternalistic view of new immigrants, 243; pre-migration of German Jews to Mandatory Palestine and, 30–32, 35; social workers of, 51, 52, 53–54, 55, 56, 58, 144; vocational training and, 20, 131; women and, 67, 243. *See also* British Mandate; HOG; Jewish Agency; Yishuv
agricultural villages/rural areas, 3, 23, 51, 63; child labor, 234; homemaking practices, 175, 183, 196; labor market options in, 116, 117, 118, 119, 121, 122, 124, 125, 126, 142, 152, 234; matrimonial ads and agricultural work, 211–13, 214. *See also* kibbutzim
Albach, Henriette, *139*

301

Aliyah: 1929–1939 "Fifth Aliyah", 17–18, 255n29; *Aliyah* (ascent), 7; "Aliyah Bet"/"Sonder-Hahshara", 22, 37; "Aliyot"/immigration waves, 17; German Aliyah, 5, 18, 29, 35, 57, 80, 91, 117–18, 127, 132, 152, 199, 200, 202, 242; refuge, Aliyah, and migration, 6–8; Youth Aliyah, 22, 224. *See also* German Jews in Mandatory Palestine

Aliyah-Informationen (Aliyah News), 28, 30

Aloni, Jenny, 38, 55, 140, 141–42

anti-Semitism, 11, 83, 109, 230, 232, 236, 245; anti-Semitic stereotypes of Jewish men, 40, 78. *See also* Nazi Germany

Arab Revolt (1936–1939), 22, 59, 95, 115, 125, 256n47

Arabs, 245; Arab children, 97; Arab/Jewish women comparison, 97–98; Arab majority in Mandatory Palestine, 18, 19, 69; Arab produce, 96, 97; Arabs/Jews conflict, 94–95; Arab women, 96, 97, 102, 129, 164; arrival of German Jews to Mandatory Palestine and, 44–45, 47, 51–52, 95, 256n48; British as pro-Arab, 103; courtesy rules toward, 99, 100; fear of Jewish women being raped by Arab men, 99–100, 101; German Jews' encounters with Arabs, 68, 69, 94–102; Jewish women/Arab men interactions, 52–53, 98–101, 107, 108; labor market: Arabs/German Jews relations, 96, 97, 164; Orientalist perception of, 94, 95, 102; othering of, 97, 102; *Verständigung*, 95, 98, 263n96; Western females' dress code in Arab areas, 99

Argentina, 13, 245

arrival of German Jews to Mandatory Palestine, 28, 38, 67, 198; absorption apparatus and, 20, 47, 48–50, 56–58, 60, 62, 67; Arabs, encounters with, 44–45, 47, 51–52, 95, 256n48; arrival shock, 25, 44–45, 48, 57, 67; customs, 47, 48, 256n58; deported/sent back to Germany upon arrival, 47; family reunification, 198–207; first absorption, 28, 47; first steps in Palestine, 56–60; gender and, 67; *Hafendienst* (harbor service), 48, 256n59; Haifa port, 45, 51, 95, 256n47; harbor hyenas, 48; hardships, difficulties, disappointments, 47–61; HOG reception, 48, 50, 52, 56, 57; housing, 20, 51, 56–58; Jaffa port, 45, 51, 95, 256n47; Jewish Agency and, 46, 47, 50, 56; landing and disembarkation, 44–47; luggage, 47–48; physical examination upon arrival, 45–47; reception at the harbor, 47–56, 67; ship social workers, 53–54; Tel Aviv as port city, 51; vaccinations, 47, 56; veteran Zionists, 48–50, 60–61; young women/lone female immigrants, 48, 50–56

Aschheim, Steven, 71

Ashkenazi Jews, 39, 69, 70, 88; Ashkenazi children, 237; inner-Ashkenazi conflict, 71, 111–12

Association of Israelis of Central European Origin, 110

Australia, 13, 191, 220, 245

Badrian, Erich, 78

Baer, Albert, 33, 80

Baer, Ludwig, 196

Baer, Minna, 196

Bar Tikva, J., 124

Baruch, Nathan, 226

Bar-Yosef, Eitan, 109

Beer, Kurt, 145–47

Beharel, David, 54

Ben-Gavriel, Moshe Yaakov, 79–82, 261n36

Ben-Yaacov, Yissakhar, 36, 37, 38, 45, 48, 167, 254n7

Berlowitz, Sara, 58, 174

Berney, Friedrich, 194
Berney, Zerline (née Oppenheimer): "Cookbook", *192–93*, 194–96, 276n105
Bernkopf, Hans, 40, 42, 68–69
Bernstein, Deborah, 69–70
Bet Yitzhak, 1, 2, 152
Blumenthal, Kurt, 95
Bodenheimer-Biram, Else, 73–74, 170
boundaries: boundary construction, 107, 109, 184; boundary construction and female bodies, 112; boundary construction between Jews and non-Jews, 248; boundary-crossing between Jewish women and non-Jewish men, 70, 101–102, 104, 106–109, 112
Brazil, 13, 245
Brith Shalom (Covenant of Peace), 95
British Mandate, 7, 17, 243, 247; anti-British struggle, 103; British Army, German Jews enlisted in, 104; health issues and immigration, 45–46; HOG and, 104; immigration policy and certificates, 18–19, 20, 22, 45–46, 115, 200, 219–20; on prostitution, 52; security issues, 109; Yishuv and, 18, 102–103, 109. *See also* United Kingdom
British people, 103, 245; British cultural influence on German Jews, 106, 108, 109–10; British Mandate soldiers, 52, 68, 69, 103, 104, 105–107, 108; British masculinity, 106; British people/Yishuv relationship, 102–104, 264n121; British women, 104; drinking habit, 107; German Jews' encounters with, 68, 69, 102–11; Jewish women/British men interactions, 104, 106–107, 108–109; *lehitangles*, 107–108; leisure and sports activities, 104–108; Sephardim and, 111. *See also* United Kingdom
Britschgi-Schimmer, Ina, 54, 118, 119–20, 131–32, 137, 143, 144, 171, 225, 268n19

Brod, Max, 65
Buber, Martin, 95

Cherniavsky, Irith, 20, 72, 79
childcare, 134, 218, 222, 226, 229, 247; absorption apparatus and, 223–25; Ben Shemen village, 223; Haifa, 225; men and, 223, 228–30; social work and professional childcare, 58, 223–24; WIZO childcare, 224. *See also* homemaking practices; motherhood
children and adolescents: Arab children, 97; Ashkenazi children, 237; boys/girls relationship, 232; changing relationship with parents, 232, 234–35, 239, 240, 243; child labor, 233–34, 240; clothing, 232; education, 63, 232–33, 239; flirting and dating, 235–36; freedom and responsibility, 233–34, 238, 243; German Jews, hostility suffered at school, 76; German Jews' interactions with others in Mandatory Palestine, 70, 76, 231–32, 235–36; Hebrew and, 61, 76, 224, 230; housework and, 233; immigration law, impact on children 203–204; integration of, 61, 76, 230–32; kibbutzim and, 58, 85, 223, 224, 236; lack of parental oversight over immigrant children, 234–39; migration by, 38, *200*, 230–39, *231*, 240; Mizrahi children, 237; "problematic" children, 237–38; sexual life freedom, 235–36; social work and, 90, 236–38. *See also* childcare; education; family dynamics of German Jews in Mandatory Palestine
class-related issues: German Jews' bourgeois culture, 13, 30, 32, 73, 76, 78–79, 111, 112, 120, 123, 161, 168, 169, 175, 188, 239, 240–41; German Jews' class relations changes, 2–3, 13, 31, 43; German Jews' downward social mobility, 3, 5, 31, 109, 115, 117, 123, 138, 146–50, 156, 157,

class-related issues (*cont.*) 158, 168, 223, 224, 227; German Jews' middle-class identity, 13, 32, 123, 125, 134, 146, 162–63, 185, 187, 232, 233–34; middle-class vs proletarian femininity, 79, 82; women as less status-conscious than men, 156

climate, 225, 245, 247, 248; clothing and, 30, 57, 92; health issues and, 169, 170; homemaking practices and, 160, 162, 166, 169, 174, 182, 223

clothing: Arabs, 97, 98; British people, 106; caftan, 34, 68, 71; children and adolescents, 232; climate and, 30, 57, 92; cravat, 41, 71; identity and, 81; khaki, 30, 32, 41, 81, 106, 198–99; at the kibbutz, 85; *Kleiderkammer* (free clothing store), 57; men, 41, 82, 106, 198–99; Mizrahim, 90; pre-migration of German Jews to Mandatory Palestine and, 30, 32, 254n7; provision for immigrants in need, 57, 66; Western females' dress code in Arab areas, 99; women, 81, 82, 84, 85, 90, 198; Yishuv's informal dress culture, 106

coffeehouses, 63–64, 68–69, 101, 215; British Mandate soldiers at, 105–106, 107

Cohen, Gustav, 270n108

cooking, food, meals: absorption apparatus and, 179, 184–85, 189; advertisements on, 179, 185, 188, 190, 191; Arab produce, 96, 97; bacon/nonkosher food, 73, 74; baking, 118, 165, 166, 194, 195; challenges faced by German Jewish women, 140, 164; classes for women, 58, *139*, 164, 174; cooking, cookbooks, *178*, 179–89, 196–97; discussion/debates about, 179, 184, 190; Eastern European cuisine, 164, 184, 191; electric stoves, 165, 182; German cuisine, 181, 187, 189, 190–91, 194, 217; health issues and, 170, 176–77, 180, 181, 182–83, 184; HOG and, 57; identity, memory and change, 179, 181, 189, 197; immigrants' cuisine, 189–96; ingredients, vegetables and fruits, 164, 174, 181, 182–83, 184, 190, 191, 194–95; journey of German Jews to Mandatory Palestine and, 38; markets and shops, 164; measurement units, 164, 194, 195–96; *Mittelstandsküche* (middle-class soup kitchen), 57; Orientalism, 164; Oriental vs Western eating culture, 184, 191; "Palestine cooking", 58, *139*, 164, 174, 179–85, 188–89; politicization of consuming and cooking, 184; Primus stove, 1, 31, *139*, 140, 160, 165–66, 168, 169, 174, *178*, 182, 183, 194, 214; provision for immigrants in need, 57, 66; recipes, 165–66, 180, 181, 182–83, 185, 187, 188, 191, *192–93*, 194–97; refrigerators, 166–67, 169, 187; Sahavy's *Encyclopedia* on, 187; storing food, 166, 182, 187; *tozeret ha'aretz*, 74, 96, 97, 165, 177, 182, 183, 184, 188, 191; WIZO and, *178*, 180, 275n75; Zionism and, 180–84, 189. *See also* Berney, Zerline; homemaking practices; Meyer, Erna

countries of refuge, 13, 15, 16, 241, 245, 246, 247

culture, 245; British cultural influence on German Jews, 106, 108, 109–10; cultural anxiety, 73; cultural integration, 9–10; German Jews' cultural alienation, 10, 11, 34; German Jews' self-perceived Western-ness, 71, 102, 110–11, 112, 113; New Hebrew culture, 61, 73, 78, 81, 87

dance, *39*, 105; boundary-crossing between Jewish women and non-Jewish male, 101, 104, 106–107; Jewish women/British men interactions, 104, 106–107; Yishuv, 61, 74–75

divorce, 210, 218–21, 239; absorption apparatus and, 220; divorced women, 19, 205,

223; *get* (divorce document), 219. *See also* family dynamics of German Jews in Mandatory Palestine; marriage
Dizengoff, Meir, 239
Dominican Republic, 247–48
Dwork, Debórah, and Robert Jan van Pelt, 6

Eastern European Jews, 245; Eastern European cuisine, 164, 184, 191; Eastern European landlords, conflicts with, 75–76, 168; Eastern European women vs German women, 80–81, 84–85; elderly parents, housing for, 207; German Jews' interactions with, 34, 60, 61, 70, 71–88, 111–12, 163; German Jews' roots in Eastern Europe, 85–87; labor market: Eastern European Jews/German Jews relations, 140–41, 146, 147, 163; Orientalist view on, 71, 83, 84, 85, 87, 111; *protektzia*, 78, 147, 148; Yishuv and, 70, 71, 72, 82, 87. *See also* Polish Jews; Russian Jews
Eckstein, Ludwig, 134–35
economic crisis, 21–22, 115, 128, 129, 131, 134, 138, 147
education: absorption apparatus and, 20, 57; British cultural influence, 109–10; children and adolescents, 232–33, 239; gender discrimination, 233; German Jewish female education and professionalisation, 11; Hebrew school system, 110; HOG and, 57, 61; schools for German children, 63
Einstein, Albert, 246
employment. *See* labor market
Erez, Idith, 102
exile studies, 6

Falkenstein, Hans, 148–50
family dynamics of German Jews in Mandatory Palestine, 26, 198–99, 240–41; anxiety over dysfunctional families/breakdown of norms and values, 239, 240–41; chain migration, 26, 35, 198, 199–207; challenges caused by immigration process, 26, 60, 201–207, 240–41; children and adolescents in migration, 38, *200*, 203–204, 230–39, *231*, 240; complaint letters, 204; dissolution of family, 241; elderly parents/"parent immigration" (*Elternimmigration*), 204, 205–207; family as central concern for absorbing apparatus, 199, 240; family cohesion, 199, 221, 240; family reunification, 198–207; gender roles, changes of, 26, 215–18, 221, 226–27, 228–30, 240; illegal migration, 202–203; immigration law, effects on families, 200–207; incarceration in Nazi concentration camps as factor in family conflicts, 221; marriage strategies, 26, 199, 207–15; migrating marriages, 26, 215–21; migration as family unit, 199, 241; parenting in Palestine, 26, 222–30; parents/children separation, 203–204; separate immigration, 35–36, 47, 198, 199–204, 241; single young people, migration of, 207–15; veteran Zionists, 203, 204; Zionism, 240. *See also* childcare; children and adolescents; divorce; fatherhood; immigration certificates and policies; marriage; motherhood
Farges, Patrick, 14
fatherhood, 226–27, 243; childcare, 223, 228–30; inner-family decision-making dynamics and fathers' diminished roles, 227–28; normative conception of, 228; post-immigration crisis for, 227–28; Zionism and, 228. *See also* family dynamics of German Jews in Mandatory Palestine; men

femininity: bourgeois femininity, 41, 42, 43, 85; female body and, 85, 112; female pioneer (*haluza*), 41, 85; gender/class/female body intersection, 112; gender and migration, 5, 13, 247; journey of German Jews in Mandatory Palestine and, 41–44; labor market and, 155; middle-class vs proletarian femininity, 79, 82; Mizrahi vs German Jewish femininity, 90; Yishuv and, 79, 82, 85; Zionism and, 42. *See also* women

Feuchtwanger, Martin, 93, 97, 138, 153, 156–57, 168, 216–18, 224, 229

Frank, Meta, 56–57, 167, 219, 254n16

galut (diaspora), 32, 62, 121, 181

Gelber, Yoav, 255n29, 256n58, 276n5

gender, 3; gendered crisis, 3, 13, 247; as historical category, 5; as relational category, 4, 5–6, 9, 14–15, 250; as social construction, 4. *See also* femininity; gender and German Jews in Mandatory Palestine; gender and migration; labor market and gender; masculinity; men; women

gender and German Jews in Mandatory Palestine, 5–6, 14, 11–17, 242–43, 247–48; absorption, 3, 10, 19, 25; absorption apparatus and gender, 115, 243, 247, 248; arrival of German Jews to Mandatory Palestine and gender, 67; changes of gender relations/roles, 2–4, 5, 8, 26, 44, 152–53, 161, 215–18, 221, 226–27, 228–30, 240, 242–44; gender/class/female body intersection, 112; gendered criticism, 79–81; gendered policies, 3, 5, 19, 200, 204–205, 242, 243, 247, 276n5; gender identities, 44, 67; gender inequality, 243; "German Aliyah" story as gender history, 242; German Jews' gender relations as modern and emancipated, 91, 92; German Jews' interactions with others in Mandatory Palestine, 10, 25, 70, 74, 78–82, 90–93, 97, 99, 102, 104, 112; research literature on, 14; unequal emigration ratio, 16–17, 19, 200, 208, 247, 276n5. *See also* gender; gender and migration; labor market and gender; men; women

gender and migration, 4–6, 22–23, 25, 26, 248–50; downward social mobility, 3, 13; femininity and masculinity, 5, 13, 247; gender role change/reversal, 5, 13, 242, 247, 249; German Jews, 13, 16, 246–47; labor market participation, 5, 13; migration policies and gender, 4–5, 17, 249; patriarchal structures and, 216, 228, 248. *See also* gender; German Jews in Mandatory Palestine and gender; men; women

"Generation Exodus", 207

German Jews, 11; after 1933, 11–14; bourgeois lifestyle, 13, 30, 32, 73, 76, 78–79, 111, 112, 120, 123, 161, 168, 169, 175, 188, 239, 240–41; consumerism, 73, 112; emigration challenges, 245–46; emigration challenges, gendered dimension of, 246–47; female education and professionalisation, 11; gender roles changes, 12–13, 215, 245; modernization, assimilation, and emancipation of, 11; musical preferences of, 74–75; socioeconomic profile before Nazi rule, 2, 11. *See also* German Jews in Mandatory Palestine; Nazi Germany

German Jews in Mandatory Palestine, 3, 6, 17–25, *77*, 247, 250; absorption, 5, 9–10, 25, 113, 248; advantages of German Jews over other migrant Jews, 20; class relations changes, 2–3, 13, 31, 43; compared with other countries of refuge, 247–48; cultural alienation, 10, 11, 34; downward social mobility, 3, 5, 31, 109, 115, 117, 123, 138, 146–50, 156, 157, 158, 168, 223, 224,

227; fear of moral decay in the immigrating group, 238–39; first years of mass immigration, 21, 25, 27; as immigrants, 7–8, 11; incentives for immigration, 21; integration, identity, and memory, 8–11; lack of integration/separatism, 61–62, 72, 81, 112, 158; leisure and sports activities, 104–105; middle-class identity, 13, 32, 123, 125, 134, 146, 162–63, 185, 187, 232, 233–34; pre-migration life in Germany, 8, 13; refuge, Aliyah, and migration, 6–8; as refugee movement, 7; research literature on, 8–11; reversed power conditions, 83; self-perception of immigrants, 6, 9, 25, 61, 71, 89, 91, 102, 242; standard of living, loss of, 30, 32, 43, 59–60; stereotypical characterization of, 10, 34, 60–67, 78; superiority feelings, 71, 83–84, 88, 90, 94, 97, 102, 112–13. *See also* arrival of German Jews to Mandatory Palestine; family dynamics of German Jews in Mandatory Palestine; gender and German Jews in Mandatory Palestine; German Jews' interactions with others in Mandatory Palestine; homemaking practices; immigration certificates and policies; labor market; Yishuv

German Jews' interactions with others in Mandatory Palestine, 19–20, 24, 68–70, 111–13; apprehension and hostility toward newcomers, 75–76; Arabs, encounters with, 68, 69, 94–102; boundary-crossing between Jews and non-Jewish as "contested contact", 69–70; the British, encounters with, 68, 69, 102–11; children, 70, 76, 231–32, 235–36; criticism of German Jews by other Jews, 72–75, 76–82, 165, 250, 261n36; discrimination, 76, 78, 82, 87, 112; Eastern European Jews, interactions with, 34, 60, 61, 70, 71–88, 111–12, 163; European/non-European Jews ethnic friction, 70, 73–74, 75–76, 260n20; gender and, 10, 25, 70, 74, 78–82, 90–93, 97, 99, 102, 104, 112; German-Jewish gaze on the Ostjuden, 82–88; individual factors affecting interactions, 70, 75, 81; *Levantinism*, 70; *Liftmenschen/Lift* people, 34; Mizrahim, interactions with, 70, 88–94; negative experiences, 63, 75–76; Ostjuden and Yekkes, reencounter of, 71–76; in urban areas, 69; within the Yishuv, 69, 70. *See also* Orientalism; othering; West vs East; Yekkes

Germany: reparation payments to Israel by West Germany, 158, 244; research on German Jews in Mandatory Palestine, 10–11; social workers as German or trained in Germany, 178, 240. *See also* Nazi Germany

Golani, Motti, and Daniela Reich, 108
Goldschmidt, Willy, 52–53
Goldstein, Georg, 76
Grab, Walter, 65
Granach, Gad, 44, 83
Great Depression, 16, 245
Grosshut, Bela, 218
Grosshut, Simon, 218
Grünstein, Leni, 1–2, 3, 13, 26, 151–52

Ha'avara, 134, 143; 1933 *Ha'avara* agreement, 21
Haganah (Zionist paramilitary organization), 107, 235
Hahshara (preparation/training), 40, 43, 125
Haifa: Arabs in, 96; childcare, 225; coffeehouses, 64; German-Jewish ethnic neighborhoods in, 62; Haifa port, 45, 51, 95, 198, 256n47; immigrants settled in, 59; sports clubs, 105; World War II, 246

INDEX

Halamish, Aviva, 7
Halperin, Liora, 64, 73, 75, 176
haluz program, 56
Haluzim. *See* pioneers
Hanemann, Lotte, 220
Hauser, Martin, 39, 95, 136–37, 238, 254n16
health issues: climate and, 169, 170; cooking, food, and, 170, 176–77, 180, 181, 182–83, 184; homemaking practices and, 169–70, 175, 176; illnesses and lack of hygiene, 175; immigration and disqualifying illnesses, 45–47, 256n54; Jewish Agency and, 46–47; labor market, 122–23, 124, 137, 138, 150, 155–56; male German Jewish migrants, illness and collapse of, 13–14, 120, 122, 123, 130, 132, 133, 135, 138, 150, 155, 203, 218, 227, 228, 270n108; physical examination upon arrival, 45–47; vaccinations, 47, 56; vermin, 30, 140, 169, 174, 182; women, 154, 155–56
Hebrew, 149; children and, 61, 76, 224, 230; *Hebräisch für Jedermann* (Hebrew for everyone), 38; lack of, 48, 54, 59, 91, 122, 142, 234; learning Hebrew/Hebrew classes, 20, 58, 62, 162; national obligation to learn Hebrew, 62, 64; as official language, 220; official request to write only in Hebrew, 76; refusal to speak Hebrew, 73. *See also* languages
Helman, Anat, 62, 63, 69, 73, 81
Herlitz, Georg, 36, 65
Herrmann, Hugo: *Palestine As It Really Is* (*Palästina wie es wirklich ist*), 45, 57, 256n48
Hirsch, Dafna, 89, 90
Histadrut (General Organization of Workers in Eretz Israel), 78, 104, 128, 131, 140, 147–48, 163–64
Hitler, Adolf, 2, 73, 78, 82
HOG (Hitahdut Oley Germania/Association of Immigrants from Germany), 19, 20, 56, 94; on Arabs, 98; arrival of German Jews to Mandatory Palestine and, 48, 50, 52, 56, 57; British Mandate and, 104; cooking, food, meals, and, 57; education and, 57, 61; employment services, 128, 129; homemaking practices and, 165, 170, 173–74; housing and, 56, 57, 58, 59; integration and, 62, 65, 114; journey of German Jews to Mandatory Palestine and, 38; labor market and, 114, 115, 117, 122, 123, 125, 127–29, 130, 131, 135, 143, 144; mission: cultural adaptation and integration of new immigrants, 62, 65; pre-migration of German Jews to Mandatory Palestine and, 29–30; Zionism, 20. *See also* Mitteilungsblatt
Holocaust (Shoah), 6, 12, 22, 64, 158, 244, 246; extermination camps, 12, 16; "final solution", 15, 206, 241
homemaking practices (German Jews in Mandatory Palestine), 26, 160–61, 196–97; absorption apparatus and, 161, 171, 173, 176, 197; in agricultural villages/rural areas, 175, 183, 196; assistance, instruction, and control, 162, 163, 173–78; care work/childcare, 142, 156, 161; challenges faced by German Jewish women, 139–40, 160–73; changed practice of, 161, 162, 169; children and housework, 233; cleaning and hygiene, 169–70, 174, 175–78, 179; climatic conditions and, 160, 162, 166, 169, 174, 182, 223; complaint letters, 170–71; crowded housing conditions and, 168, 169, 171, 173; discussion/debates about, 171–72, 177–78, 196; domestic help and, 162–64, 168, 170–72, 173; domesticity, 161, 168, 169, 171, 185; health issues and, 169–70, 175, 176; HOG and, 165, 170, 173–74; homemakers as responsible for the Yishuv, 182, 189; housework, 26, 161,

171, 180, 186, 189, 196, 197, 223; housework, rationalization of, 179, 182, 184, 187, 275n75; men's absence of, 171–73, 184, 197; placement service for domestic workers, 173; shopping, 165, 174; social workers and, 174–75, 177–78; unpaid homemaking, 152, 161; vermin, 30, 140, 169, 174, 182; WIZO and, 174–75, 182; women and, 30, 58, 119, 126, 152, 155, 161–62, 165, 166, 170–72, 175–78, 183, 185–87, 189–90, 197, 246; women's "double workday", 161, 186, 187, 243, 247; women's workload, appreciation of, 170–73, 182, 183–84, 186, 196, 228; Zionism and, 175–78, 182, 189, 197. *See also* childcare; cooking, food, meals; Sahavy, ed.: *The Household Encyclopedia for Erez Israel*

Horwitz-Schiller, Heti, 181, 190

housing: absorption apparatus and, 20, 56–58; arrival of German Jews to Mandatory Palestine and, 20, 51, 56–58; *Batey Olim* (immigration hostels), 56–58, 223; *Bet Haluzot* (home for pioneer women), 54, 56; convalescent homes, 57; crowded conditions, 167–68, 169, 171, 173, 224, 225; Eastern European landlords, conflicts with, 75–76, 168; elderly parents, housing for, 207; high rents, 30, 59–60, 61, 117, 167, 168; HOG and, 56, 57, 58, 59; homelessness, 57; housing agencies private market, 59; housing crisis/lack of, 59, 60, 74, 167, 220; Jewish Agency, 57–58; kibbutzim, 56; in Nazi Germany, 60; one-room accommodation, 167, 169; permanent housing, 58–59; privacy, 169; residential differentiation in neighborhoods, 62–63; subletting, 167–68, 224; temporary housing, 56–58, 134; young women/lone female immigrants, 51, 54

identity: clothing and, 81; cooking, food, meals, and, 179, 181, 189, 197; "domestic identity", 161; gender identities, 41, 44, 67; German Jews' self-perceived Western-ness, 71, 102, 110–11, 112, 113; integration, memory and, 8–11; landsmanshaft and, 62; subjective identity, 4

Ihud (Unity), 95

Ilsar, Yehiel, 86–87

immigration certificates and policies (German Jews in Mandatory Palestine): absorption apparatus and immigration policies, 4–5, 16, 17, 67; British Mandate and, 18–19, 20, 22, 45–46, 115, 200, 219–20; category A certificates (capitalists), 18, 21, 46, 51, 116–17, 134, 200, 201, 203, 209, 276n5; category B certificates (students, persons of religious occupations), 18; category C/labor certificates, 18, 19, 46, 47, 51, 56, 116, 200, 204, 231; category D certificates (dependents), 18, 46, 54, 118, 200, 202, 204–205; citizenship, 219–20; disqualifying illnesses, 45–47, 256n54; gender and, 5, 19, 200, 204–205, 276n5; health certificate, 46; illegal migration, 202; resident status, 219; tourist certificates, 202–203

insurance, 56, 135, 157

integration, 245; absorption apparatus and, 9, 243; children and, 61, 76, 230–32; cultural integration, 9–10; economic integration, 9, 10, 245–46; gender and, 243, 245; German Jews' lack of integration/separatism, 61–62, 72, 81, 112, 158; HOG and, 62, 65, 114; identity, memory and, 8–11; Israel, 9; labor market, integration of German Jews into, 114–15, 116–17, 121, 122–25, 134, 145, 149–51, 158–59; men's lack of integration, 120, 123–24, 127, 145, 149–50, 154, 218; social integration, 9, 10, 245–46; women as sine qua non

class-related issues (*cont.*)
for the integration of their families, 58, 67, 126, 152; women's superiority over men, 126, 153–54; Yishuv's perspective on, 158

Irgun Yozey Merkas Europa (organization of German Jews), 87–88

Israel (state of), 8; "colonial nostalgia", 109; founding of, 87, 102; as immigration country, 9; integration, 9; post-1948 mass immigration of Jews from Arab countries to, 113; pre-state Israel, 6, 7, 17; reparation payments by West Germany, 158, 244

Israeli historiography, 9, 10; migration history, 6–7

Jacobson, Abigail, and Moshe Naor, 98

Jaffa, 45, 51, 95, 256n47

Jerusalem: Arabs in, 96; coffeehouses, 68; German-Jewish ethnic neighborhoods in, 62; horseback-riding, 105, 107–108; immigrants settled in, 59, 80; Kraal Circle, 65; Mizrahim in, 70, 94

Jewish Agency (Palestine Office), 19–20, 28, 96, 200, 243; 1933 *Ha'avara* agreement, 21; arrival of German Jews to Mandatory Palestine and, 46, 47, 50, 56; Berlin Palestine Office, 20, 28, 96, 116, 143, 145, 201, 203; German Department/Jerusalem office, 20, 47, 50, 51, 53, 115, 118, 127–28, 130, 131, 134, 143, 144, 201, 204; health issues and immigration, 46–47; housing and, 57–58; *Informations-Rundschreiben des Palästina-Amtes Berlin* (Newsletter of the Berlin Palestine Office), 28; journey of German Jews to Mandatory Palestine and, 38; labor market and, 115, 118, 127–28, 130, 131, 134, 143, 144; London headquarters, 20, 53; on marriage and divorce, 209–10, 219; pre-migration of German Jews to Mandatory Palestine and, 28, 29–30, 31–32; Zionism, 20

Jonas, Hans, 35, 66, 259n126

journey of German Jews to Mandatory Palestine, 28, 35–44, 67, 254n15; anticipation of change, 42–43, 44, 67; *Bordmerkblatt* (ship bulletin), 38, 255n29; emotional intensity, 36; family separation, 35–36, 47, 198, 199–204, 241; farewell, *15*, 35, 254n16; femininity and, 41–44; HOG and, 38; Jewish Agency and, 38; meals during journey, 38; men/masculinity and, 40–41; sea voyage, *21*, 35, 36–44, *39*, 198, *200*; social life during journey, 38; train journey to port cities, *15*, 35–36, *231*; traumatic experiences during journey, 36; Trieste-Haifa line, 37; women/pregnant women, 37–38, *39*, *200*; Yishuv society, 39–40; Zionism, 42, 44. See also pre-migration of German Jews to Mandatory Palestine

Jüdischer Frauenbund (League of Jewish Women), 208

Jüdische Rundschau (Jewish Review), 23–24, 40; on Arabs, 98, 99, 100, 102; on children and adolescents, 233; on cooking, 180, 184, 190, 191; criticism of German Jews, 72, 74–75, 79–80; on divorce, 219, 220; on fatherhood, 228–29; on homemaking, 160–61, 163, 165, 166, 170, 175; on labor market, 120–21, 122–24, 125, 126, 136, 137, 142; letters published by, 27, 79–80; on *Lifts*, 33; on marriage, 208, 210–11; on migration and dissolution of family, 241; on Mizrahim, 88–90, 91–92; on motherhood, 226; on Yishuv, 61; on young women, 51

Juengster, Shlomo, 147–48

INDEX

Kahn, Gustav, 150
Kalmar, Ivan Davidson, and Derek Penslar, 71, 88
Kanowitz, Siegfried, 176
Kaplan, Marion, 11, 12, 16, 28, 155, 201, 227, 239
Keren HaYesod, 48, 49, 50, 147
kibbutzim, 40, 55; children and childcare, 58, 85, 223, 224, 236; German/Eastern European Jews tensions, 83, 85; housing, 56; labor market and, 56, 118, 270n108; unconventional communal living conditions, 208; women joining a kibbutz, 51, 85, 208
KJV fraternity (*Kartell Jüdischer Verbindungen*/Cartel of Jewish Fraternities), 66, 78, 130
Klimann, Justus, 36, 254–55n21
Kloetzel, C. Z., 92–93
Kober, Max, 48–49
Kopeljuk, Menahem, 98–99
Kressel, Helga, 232, 234
Kupath milveh shel Oley Germania (credit institution), 132
Kupat Holim (public health fund), 170
Kurfürstendamm Ladies, 78–79, 81, 84, 109, 140

labor market, 25–26, 61, 114–15, 156–59; absorbing society and, 115, 148–49; absorption apparatus and, 20, 114, 115–20, 121, 122, 123, 127, 129, 131, 135, 136, 143–44, 156; age and, 116, 118, 121, 122, 124–25, 131, 133, 137, 145, 146, 150–51, 159; Arabs/German Jews relations, 96, 97, 164; arrival of German Jews to Mandatory Palestine, 20, 56; British people/German Jews relations, 104; child labor, 233–34, 240; complaint letters, 145–51, 155–56; discussion/debates about immigrants' situation, 120–27,
136, 146, 152, 159; dual-income couples, 130; Eastern European Jews/German Jews relations, 140–41, 146, 147, 163; employer-employee dynamics, 140–41, 146, 163; ethnic discrimination, 78; evaluation and monitoring of German Jews, 115–20, 159, 268n19; health issues, 122–23, 124, 137, 138, 150, 155–56; HOG and, 114, 115, 117, 122, 123, 125, 127–29, 130, 131, 135, 143, 144; HOG employment services, 128, 129; integration of German Jews into, 114–15, 116–17, 121, 122–25, 134, 145, 149–51, 158–59; Jewish Agency/German Department and, 115, 118, 127–28, 130, 131, 134, 143, 144; job seekers, 114, 126–7, 128–29, 268n47; loss of former status, 115, 117, 123, 138, 146–50, 156, 157, 158; mistreatment and hostility faced by immigrants, 138, 140, 146, 147; Mizrahim/German Jews relations, 91–93; occupational change, 115–18, 122, 123, 124, 136, 138–39, 146–50, 152–53, 157, 218, 268n19; occupational crisis, 115, 120, 123–24; *protektzia*, 78, 147, 148; social changes and, 117–18, 119; support system to immigrants, 127–36; training/vocational training, 116, 117, 118–19, 121–22, 131, 159, 246; veteran Zionists and, 124, 145, 146, 148–49, 151, 156; WIZO and, 129, 131, 133, 139; workplace conflicts: ethnicity, class, and masculinity, 78; World War I, 119; Yishuv economy and, 114–15; Zionism and, 121, 127, 130, 139, 146, 150–51. *See also* labor market and gender; labor market options; unemployment
labor market and gender, 5, 112, 117, 118–20, 121, 127, 128, 130, 159; challenges faced by female domestic workers/caterers, 139–42; challenges faced by men, 145–51; changing gender roles, 152–53;

labor market and gender (*cont.*)
161; female maltreatment by employers, 138, 140; femininity, 155; gender/class/female body intersection, 112; gender discrimination, 143–45, 154, 247; high-ranking positions and gender, 143–44; loans to support small business, 132–34; masculinity, 125, 148, 150, 151; men, 117–18, 119, 120, 121–25, 127, 129, 130, 136–37, 138, 145–51, 157, 246; Nazi Germany and women as labor force, 119, 155, 161; office jobs, 130; salary and gender, 117, 129, 136, 142, 158; veteran Zionists and gender, 130, 134, 142–45, 151; vocational training and gender, 131–32, 136, 154; women, 112, 114, 117, 118–20, 125–27, 128–29, 131, 133–34, 135, 138–42, 157–58, 207, 216, 240, 246; women, married, 118–19, 126, 129–30, 144–45, 151, 152, 161, 225; women as breadwinners, 58, 66–67, 92, 93, 118–19, 126, 130, 133, 148, 150, 151, 161, 186, 216, 228, 230, 246; women and lowest strata of labor market, 136, 158; women of valor/appreciation of working women, 126, 151–56. *See also* labor market

labor market options: in agricultural villages/rural areas, 116, 117, 118, 119, 121, 122, 124, 125, 126, 142, 152, 234; blue-collar work, 117, 146; bus driving, 137–38; catering industry, 117, 138, 141, 142; commercial sector, 116, 117; construction sector, 117, 118, 126, 131, 134, 136–37, 138; domestic work, 78, 80, 91–93, 117, 118, 127, 128–29, 131, 135, 138, 139–42, 163, 173, 216, 226, 236, 246–47; formal sector, 138, 216; industrial sector, 117, 122, 129, 268n19; informal sector, 118, 138, 142, 146, 216; kibbutzim and, 56, 118, 270n108; laundrywomen, 75, 91, 96, 162, 164; liberal professions, 116, 117, 118; *oseret/osrot* (maid/domestic aide), 92, 125, 138–39, 141, 156, 163–64, 191, 216, 226; physical labor, 118, 122–23, 124, 129, 130, 133, 134, 137, 138, 142, 146, 150, 270n108; physicians, 116, 118, 123, 124, 142, 150, 157, 247; skilled work, 118, 129; stone-beating, 141; temporary work, 58, 129, 132, 135, 137, 140, 141, 154, 156, 157; trading sector, 117, 146–47; unskilled work, 117, 118, 120, 121, 122, 129, 131, 158; in urban areas, 117, 118, 119, 122, 134, 136–37, 153. *See also* labor market

Landauer, Georg, 20, 48, 53, 54, 73, 95, 113, 143–44, 145, 148–49, 156, 170, 203, 204, 207, 210

Landsberg, Alfred, 144

landsmanshaft, 61–62, 64, 70, 72, 128, 221; German landsmanshaft, 62, 85. *See also* Yekkes

languages: Arabic, 91, 220; English, 103, 142, 220; German, 62, 63, 64, 72–73, 76, 96, 100, 145, 231; official languages, 220; Yiddish, 71, 260n16. *See also* Hebrew

Laqueur, Walter, 207

Lasker-Schüler, Else, 65

Lavsky, Hagit, 7, 9, 62

Lawrence, T. E.: *Revolt in the Desert*, 96

Lehmann, Hedwig, 107

Levantinism, 70

Levinson, Fritz, 196

Lewy, Hans, 259n126

Lichtheim, Georg, 259n126

Liftmenschen/Lift people, 33–35

Lifts/Liftvans, 29, *29*, 31, 32–35, *33*, 165, 169, 256n58, 258n97

Loevy, Trude, 168, 217–18

Loewenberg, Lotte, 219

Loewy, Ernst, 217

Lowenstein, Steven, 65

INDEX

Lucassen, Leo, 249–50
Luft, Gerda, 89–90, 91, 122, 138, 143, 144, 160–61, 162, 164, 182, 261n48, 270n84
lunch tables. *See Mittagstische*

Majofis, Hana, 143–44, 145
Mansbach, Erwin, 202–203
Margulies-Auerbach, Nanny, 61, 180
marriage: arranged marriages, 210; British/Yekkes mixed marriages, 108; "certificate marriages", 209–10; dowry, 86, 209, 210, 213, 214, 215; engagements and weddings, 215; fictitious marriages, 209–10; financial problems within migrating marriages, 218, 221; gender role reversal within migrating marriages, 216–18, 221, 226–27; interfaith marriages, 263n91; marriage brokers and matchmaking services, 213–14; matrimonial ads, 210–14; migrating marriages, 26, 215–21; migration and marriage strategies, 26, 199, 207–15; Mizrahim/Yekkes mixed marriages, 93–94, 263n91; in Nazi Germany, 210; *Ostjude*/Yekkes mixed marriages, 86–87, 262n63; pre-migration marriages, 208–14. *See also* divorce; family dynamics of German Jews in Mandatory Palestine
masculinity: British masculinity, 106; gender and migration, 5, 13, 247; German Jews' masculinity, 40–41, 78; *Haluzim* (pioneers), 40–41; ideal masculinity, 40–41; journey of German Jews to Mandatory Palestine and, 40–41; labor market and, 125, 148, 150, 151; Mizrahi masculinity, 92; new masculinities, 243; Zionist masculinity, 40. *See also* men
Maurer, Trude, 225
May, Karl, 96

Mayer-Wolf, Oskar, 106
memoir literature/autobiographies, 8, 9, 10, 14, 24, 36, 84, 96–97, 241, 244
men: anti-Semitic stereotypes of Jewish men, 40, 78; clothing, 41, 82, 106, 198–99; German Jewish migrants, illness and collapse of, 13–14, 120, 122, 123, 130, 132, 133, 135, 138, 150, 155, 203, 218, 227, 228, 270n108; homemaking practices, men's absence of, 171–73, 184, 197; as "indecisive, unstable, depressed, and inclined to grumble", 120; integration, lack of, 120, 123–24, 127, 145, 149–50, 154, 218; intellectual circles/networks, 65, 66–67; labor market and, 117–18, 119, 120, 121–25, 127, 129, 130, 136–37, 138, 145–51, 157, 246; large emigration of young men, 208; male-centrism, 67, 143; male pioneers (*haluz*), 40–41, 43; migration and challenges to male prestige, 65; objectification of women by, 82; occupational crisis, 120, 123–25, 127, 134, 138; resistance to change, 120, 121, 122; rural work as alternative for older men, 124; single male immigrants, 55; suicide, 138, 227; unemployment, 3, 13, 64, 117, 119, 120, 121, 123, 125, 128, 130, 134, 141, 142, 149, 156, 173, 216, 223; vocational training, 121–22, 131–32, 246. *See also* fatherhood; gender; gender and migration; German Jews in Mandatory Palestine and gender; labor market and gender; masculinity; patriarchy
methodology, 3–4, 6, 9, 249; future research recommendations, 244, 245; gender as relational category, 5–6, 14–15, 250; "German Aliyah" story as gender history, 242; sources, 3–4, 6, 23, 24–25, 243, 244–45, 249–50; time frame, 3, 5, 244

Meyer, Erna, 195; *How to Cook in Palestine*, *178*, 179–84, 185, 188–89; *Menu in Times of Crisis*, 184; WIZO model kitchen, 275n75. *See also* cooking, food, meals
Meyer family, *29*, *33*
Meyerstein, Charlotte, 133
migration, 248; changes caused by, 4; immigration policies, 4–5, 16, 17. *See also* countries of refuge; gender and migration; German Jews in Mandatory Palestine
Miron, Guy, 9, 13, 14, 24, 60, 84, 96–97, 169, 241, 244
Mittagstische (lunch tables), 132, 138, 141–42, 168, 216–18, 227
Mitteilungsblatt (Bulletin, HOG), 23, 113; on cooking, food, meals, 180, 184, 188, 190; criticism of German Jews, 72, 79–81; on divorce, 219; on homemaking, 165, 170, 176, 177; on labor market, 120–21, 125, 130; letters published by, 27, 79–81; on marriage, 210
Mizrahim (Easterners), 70, 245, 259n5; clothing, 90; German Jews' interactions with, 70, 88–94; labor market: Mizrahim/German Jews relations, 91–93; at liminal zone between European Jews and Arabs, 88; Mizrahi children, 237; Mizrahi masculinity, 92; Mizrahi parents, 177, 222, 233–34; social work and, 89–91, 177; in Tel Aviv, 89–90; women, 90–93, 177, 222. *See also* "Oriental" Jews
Moezet Hapoalot (Women's Workers Council, Histadrut), 131
motherhood: abortion, 225; absorption apparatus and, 223, 226; breastfeeding, 85, 98, 169, 226; childbirth, 38, 226; childcare, 142, 156, 161, 173, 176, 177, 246; family planning/birth control, 225, 236; German-Jewish proper motherhood, 177, 222–23; improper motherhood, 177, 222; pregnancy, 38, 68, 225–26; Zionism and, 222. *See also* childcare; family dynamics of German Jews in Mandatory Palestine; women
Mueller, Irna (Shlomit), 42, 198–99

Nahariya, 63, 106, 107, 171–72, 173, 205, 214, 229; changing role of fathers in, 229–30; *Lifts*, 32, *33*
Nazi Germany: 1935 Nuremberg Laws, 12; 1938 November pogrom, 7, 12, 16, 201, 209, 244; concentration camps, 57, 135, 221, 227; family planning, 225; freedom, lack of, 75; German Jews, changing gender and socioeconomic relations, 12–13, 215, 245; German Jews: discrimination, forced migration, deportation and murder of, 12, 15–16, 206, 227, 241, 244, 246; German Jews, occupational and demographic structure, 115–16; housing in, 60; Jewish men in, 12; Jewish women in, 12, 16, 19, 201, 203; marriage strategies, 210; mass Jewish emigration from, 2, 5, 6, 7, 13–14, 15–16, *15*, 20, 22, 114, 116, 117, 245; policies against Jews, 15, 157, 169, 206; women as labor force, 119, 155, 161; women's mission of protecting families and communities, 155, 201, 222; World War II and halted immigration from, 16, 22. *See also* Holocaust
Nesselroth, Hilde, 155–56
non-European Jews: European/non-European Jews ethnic friction, 70, 73–74, 75–76, 260n20; Ostjuden and Yekkes, 71–76, 82–88; othering of non-Western Jews, 70–71. *See also* Mizrahim; "Oriental" Jews; West vs East

Oppenheimer, Hilde, 118, 120, 123, 144–45
oral history, 8, 10, 11, 36, 154; oral history interviews, 14, 23, 24, 91, 104, 110

Orientalism, 9, 44, 96, 102, 111, 112; Arabs, Orientalist perception of, 94, 95, 102; cooking, food, meals, 164; Eastern European Jews, Orientalist perception of, 71, 83, 84, 85, 87, 111; "internal orientalism", 71, 88; Mizrahim, Orientalist perception of, 88, 91. *See also* German Jews' interactions with others in Mandatory Palestine; West vs East
"Oriental" Jews, 14, 69, 70, 88, 93, 97, 164, 259n5. *See also* Mizrahim
othering: of Arabs, 97, 102; gender and, 102; of German Jews, 111; of non-Western Jews, 70–71. *See also* German Jews' interactions with others in Mandatory Palestine; Orientalism; West vs East
Ottoman Empire, 17, 164

Palestine: as binational state, 95; fight for national independence, 22
Palestine Office. *See* Jewish Agency
pan-Semitism, 261n36
patriarchy, 216, 227, 228, 246, 248. *See also* men
Pfefferman, Talia, and David De Vries, 133–34
Pil Circle, 66, 259n126
Pinkus, Lotte, 41
pioneers (*Haluzim*), 39; Bet Haluzot (home for pioneer women), 54, 56; female pioneer (*haluza*), 41–42, 43–44, 51, 54, 56; male pioneers (*haluz*), 40–41, 43; Zionism and, 43–44
Polish Jews, 20, 61, 71, 72, 83, 84, 94; women, 79, 80, 81. *See also* Eastern European Jews
Polotsky, Hans Jacob, 259n126
Pomeranz, Max, 144
pre-migration of German Jews to Mandatory Palestine, 25, 27–28, 67, 71; absorption apparatus and, 30–32, 35;

clothing, 30, 32, 254n7; furniture, 30–33, 35, 165; HOG and, 29–30; household shipping, 29, 32–33; Jewish Agency and, 28, 29–30, 31–32; kitchenware, 31; *Liftmenschen/Lift* people, 33–35; *Lifts/Liftvans*, 29, *29*, 31, 32–35, *33*, 165, 169; men as decision-makers, 28; packing, 28–31; packing as female work, 28, 31; pre-migration marriages, 208–14
Preuss, Bella, 135, 143, 225
prostitution, 54, 70, 99, 101, 209–10, 220, 239; British Mandate on, 52; Jewish women in port cities, 52, 108; Yishuv on, 52; young German-Jewish women and, 51–53, 55, 108–109
protektzia (nepotism), 78, 147, 148, 165

Radai, Itamar, 89
RASSCO (Rural and Suburban Settlement Company), 63
Razi, Tammy, 220, 237
Reagin, Nancy, 161, 175
Reisapfel, Julius, 135
religion, 244
Rommel, Erwin, 246
Rosenbaum-London, Vera, 27
Rosenberg-Friedman, Lilach, 225
Rubin, Adam, 73
Ruppin, Arthur, 20, 54, 95, 144–45
Russian Jews, 71, 72, 83, 168, 245; women, 79, 80. *See also* Eastern European Jews

Sabbath, 66, 74, 190
Sahavy, ed.: *The Household Encyclopedia for Erez Israel*, 185–89, *186*; compared to Meyer's *How to Cook in Palestine*, 185, 188–89; eclectic character of, 188. *See also* cooking, food, meals; homemaking practices
Sambursky, Hans, 259n126
Schachtel, Hugo, 49–50, 257n62

Scheftelowitz, Martin, 153, 165
Schlör, Joachim, 36
Schmuckler, Malka, 234–35
Schüler-Springorum, Stefanie, 17, 155
Scott, Joan W., 4
secularism, 244
Sela-Sheffy, Rakefet, 10
Sephardim, 39, 70, 88, 111, 184
sexual harassment and rape, 55–56, 107, 236; fear of Jewish women being raped by Arab men, 99–100, 101
Shanghai, 13, 170, 245, 246, 247–48
Sherman, A. J., 103
Shoah. *See* Holocaust
Siegemund, Anja, 11, 263n96
Simons, Ernst, 62
small business: couples setting up small businesses, 138, 216; loans to support small business, 132–34. *See also Mittagstische*
Smoira, Emma Esther, 90
social work: absorption apparatus, social workers of, 51, 52, 53–54, 55, 56, 58, 144; childcare and, 58, 223–24; children and, 90, 236–38; female social workers, 38, 53, 90, 143, 144; homemaking practices and, 174–75, 177–78; labor market and, 130, 134–35; Mizrahim and, 89–91, 177; ship social workers, 53–54; social workers as German or trained in Germany, 178, 240; women as object of social work, 53, 58, 90
South Africa, 13, 245
Stein, Nadja, 90, 174, 180, 184, 223
Stern, Heinemann, 37, 205
Stern, Toni, 225–26
Stoler-Liss, Sachlav, 177, 222
Strumpf, Gusta, 54
synagogues, 12, 61
Szold, Henrietta, 52, 53–54

Tel Aviv, 76; behavior of Jews at beaches, 100; coffeehouses, 63; German-Jewish ethnic neighborhoods in, 62; immigrants settled in, 59, 239; landsmanshaft in, 62; Mizrahim in, 89–90; as port city, 51; World War II and, 246
Tene, Ofra, 176
Tergit, Gabriele, 41, 42–43, 84–85, 98, 106, 142
Thon, Helene Hannah, 74–75, 87, 89, 99–100, 127, 175, 222
tozeret ha'aretz (products of the country), 74, 96, 97, 165, 177, 182, 183, 184, 188, 191
Turnowsky-Pinner, Grete, 129, 182, 268n52
Turnowsky-Pinner, Margarete, 143

unemployment, 115, 117; female unemployment, 141; male unemployment, 3, 13, 64, 117, 119, 120, 121, 123, 125, 128, 130, 134, 141, 142, 149, 156, 173, 216, 223. *See also* labor market
United Kingdom: German-Jewish immigrants classified as enemy aliens, 246; immigration policies, 16, 247; Jewish emigration from Nazi Germany, 7, 13, 16, 245. *See also* British Mandate; British people
United Sates: German-Jewish immigrants classified as enemy aliens, 246; immigration policies, 16, 247; Jewish emigration from Nazi Germany, 2, 7, 13, 16, 245
urban areas, 3, 51, 54, 58–59, 61, 62–63, 69, 117; labor market in, 117, 118, 119, 122, 134, 136–37, 153. *See also* Haifa; Jaffa; Jerusalem; Tel Aviv

Va'ad haKehilla (community council), 57, 76, 227
Verständigung, 95, 98, 263n96

veteran Zionists, 20, 60–61, 243; family dynamics of German Jews in Mandatory Palestine and, 203, 204; female veterans, 50, 143, 145, 204; labor market and, 124, 145, 146, 148–49, 151, 156; labor market, gender and, 130, 134, 142–45, 151; male veterans, 48–50, 66, 142–43

vocational training, 58; absorption apparatus and, 20, 131; gender and, 131–32, 136, 154; *kvuzot*, 131; labor market and, 116, 117, 118–19, 121–22, 131–32, 136, 154, 159, 246; loans received while in training, 131; men, 121–22, 131–32, 246; women, 56, 119, 131–32, 139, *139*, 140, 154, 204, 208

Weinreich, Frieda, 38, 53–54, 126, 130, 134–35, 144, 268n47
Weizmann, Chaim, 20
Weltsch, Robert, 95, 98
Werner Senator, David, 20, 144, 150, 155–56
West vs East, 61, 70; British and German Jews vs "Orientals" and Eastern Europeans, 110–11; German Jews' self-perceived Western-ness, 71, 102, 110–11, 112, 113; mixed marriages, 86–87, 93–94, 108, 262n63, 263n91; order vs chaos, 61, 89; "Oriental" Jews vs Western Jews, 88–89; Oriental vs Western eating culture, 184, 191; *Ostjude* vs *Westjude*/Yekkes, 71–88, 106, 141, 262n60; "othering" of non-Western Jews, 70–71; Westernization of the Yishuv, 112, 184. *See also* German Jews' interactions with others in Mandatory Palestine; Orientalism; othering

WIZO (Women's International Zionist Organization), 56, 90; childcare, 224; cooking, food, meals and, *178*, 180, 275n75; homemaking practices and, 174–75, 182; *Jung Wizo: Monatsschrift* (monthly magazine), 30; labor market and, 129, 131, 133, 139

Wolf, Fritz, 43–44, 96, 171–73, 205–206, 214–15, 229
Wolff, Herbert, 44
Wolff, Walter, 206

women: absorption apparatus and, 67, 243; as brave, tough, determined, and devoted, 126, 152; as breadwinners, 58, 66–67, 92, 93, 118–19, 126, 130, 133, 148, 150, 151, 161, 186, 216, 228, 230, 246; clothing, 81, 82, 84, 85, 90, 198; as disadvantaged immigrants, 19; "double workday", 161, 186, 187, 243, 247; education and professionalisation, 11; expectations as mothers, homemakers, and contributors to the family income, 222; female complaints, 154, 155–56; female pioneer (*haluza*), 41–42, 43–44, 51, 54, 56; female social workers, 38, 53, 90, 143, 144; as gatekeepers, 67, 82, 102; health issues, 154, 155–56; homemaking and, 30, 58, 119, 126, 152, 155, 161–62, 165, 166, 170–72, 175–78, 183, 185–87, 189–90, 197, 246; homemaking workload, appreciation of, 170–73, 182, 183–84, 186, 196, 228; informal networks of, 65–66; integration and adaptation, superiority compared to men, 126, 153–54; journey of German Jews to Mandatory Palestine, 37–38, *39*, *200*; kibbutzim and, 51, 85, 208; male objectification of, 82; as most important element in the house, 222; New Hebrew Woman (*Ivria Hadasha*), 82; as object of social work, 53, 58, 90; paradigm of women being able to cope better than men in Jewish migration, 15, 247; pre-migration packing as female work, 28, 31; as sine qua

women (*cont.*)
  non for integration of their families, 58, 67, 126, 152; as transgressors, 108, 109; unemployment, 141; vocational training, 56, 119, 131–32, 139, *139*, 140, 154, 204, 208; "women of valor", 126, 151–56, 196, 222, 223, 247; World War I and, 119; World War II and, 246; young women/lone female immigrants, 48, 50–56, 204, 235–36. *See also* cooking, food, meals; femininity; gender; gender and migration; German Jews in Mandatory Palestine and gender; homemaking practices; labor market and gender; motherhood; women (ethnic/national groups)
  women (ethnic/national groups): Arab/Jewish women comparison, 97–98; Arab women, 96, 97, 102, 129, 164; boundary-crossing between Jewish women and non-Jewish men, 70, 101–102, 104, 106–109, 112; British women, 104; Eastern European women vs German women, 80–81, 84–85; German Jewish migrants, 14, 16–17; German Jewish women, criticism by other Jews, 74, 78–82; German-Jewish women classified as enemy aliens, 246; German Jewish women as Kurfürstendamm Ladies, 78–79, 81, 84, 109, 140; Jewish women/Arab men interactions, 52–53, 98–101, 107, 108; Jewish women/British men interactions, 104, 106–107, 108–109; Jewish women in Nazi Germany, 12, 16, 19, 119, 155, 161, 201, 203, 222; Mizrahi/German Jewish women comparison, 90–91; Mizrahi women, 90–93, 177, 222; Polish Jewish women, 79, 80, 81; Russian Jewish women, 79, 80. *See also* women
World War I, 11, 17, 71, 86, 119, 210

World War II, 16, 22, 115, 246
Wormann, Curt, 57, 62
Wronsky, Siddy, 236–37, 281n144

Yakinton (monthly magazine), 87
Yekkes (German-Jewish subculture), 34, 60–67, 69, 78; being bullied as "Yekkish", 75, 76; coffeehouses and, 63–64; criticism of, 81; male intellectual circles/networks, 65, 66–67; reencounter of Ostjuden and, 71–76. *See also* German Jews' interactions with others in Mandatory Palestine; landsmanshaft
Yerida (descent), 7
Yishuv, 5, 247; Ashkenazi Jews and, 71; birthrate decline in, 225; British Mandate and, 18, 102–103, 109; British people/Yishuv relationship, 102–104, 264n121; cultural anxiety, 73; disappointment at, 61; Eastern European Jews and, 70, 71, 72, 82, 87; economy, 114–15; femininity and, 79, 82, 85; gender inequality, 18; German Jews as large ethnic group in, 72, 248; Hebrew culture, 18; Hebrew language, 18; homemakers as responsible for the Yishuv, 182, 189; informal dress culture, 106; on integration, 158; journey of German Jews to Mandatory Palestine and, 39–40; nation-building period, 6, 18, 52, 69, 108, 248; New Yishuv, 17; Old Yishuv, 88, 111, 177, 184, 222; "Oriental" Jews as minority in, 88; policing and social control by, 75; on prostitution, 52; socialism, 18; superiority feelings in, 94; Westernization of, 112, 184; women in, 18, 119
Yosef, Dorit, 14

Zionism, 9; cooking, food, meals and, 180–84, 189; family dynamics of German

Jews in Mandatory Palestine and, 240; fatherhood and, 228; femininity and, 42; German Zionism, 257n62, 263n96; HOG and, 20; homemaking practices and, 175–78, 182, 189, 197; immigration and, 7, 17, 20, 244; Jewish Agency and, 20; journey of German Jews to Mandatory Palestine and, 42, 44; labor market and, 121, 127, 130, 139, 146, 150–51; motherhood and, 222; "normalization" of the Jewish people, 78, 121; pioneers and, 43–44; Westernization of the Yishuv as main objective of, 112; Zionist agenda of founding a new society, 32; Zionist masculinity, 40; Zionist organizations, 19, 28, 38, 124, 143. *See also* veteran Zionists

Zionist Federation of Germany (Zionistische Vereinigung für Deutschland), 20, 23. *See also Jüdische Rundschau*

Zlocisti, Theodor, 180

Zweig, Arnold, 95

STANFORD STUDIES IN JEWISH HISTORY AND CULTURE

David Biale and Sarah Abrevaya Stein, Editors

This series features novel approaches to examining the Jewish past in the form of innovative work that brings the field into productive dialogue with the newest scholarly concepts and methods. Open to a range of disciplinary and interdisciplinary approaches, from history to cultural studies, this series publishes exceptional scholarship balanced by an accessible tone, illustrating histories of difference and addressing issues of current urgency. Books in this list push the boundaries of Jewish Studies and speak compellingly to a wide audience of scholars and students.

Susan Rubin Suleiman, *Daughter of History: Traces of an Immigrant Girlhood*
2023

Sandra Fox, *The Jews of Summer: Summer Camp and Jewish Culture in Postwar America*
2023

David Biale, *Jewish Culture Between Canon and Heresy*
2023

Alan Verskin, *Diary of a Black Jewish Messiah: The Sixteenth-Century Journey of David Reubeni through Africa, the Middle East, and Europe*
2023

Aomar Boum, Illustrated by Nadjib Berber, *Undesirables: A Holocaust Journey to North Africa*
2023

Dina Porat, *Nakam: The Holocaust Survivors Who Sought Full-Scale Revenge*
2023

Christian Bailey, *German Jews in Love: A History*
2023

Matthias B. Lehmann, *The Baron: Maurice de Hirsch and the Jewish Nineteenth Century*
2022

Liora R. Halperin, *The Oldest Guard: Forging the Zionist Settler Past*
2021

Samuel J. Spinner, *Jewish Primitivism*
2021

Sonia Gollance, *It Could Lead to Dancing: Mixed-Sex Dancing and Jewish Modernity*
2021

Julia Elsky, *Writing Occupation: Jewish Émigré Voices in Wartime France*
2020

Alma Rachel Heckman, *The Sultan's Communists:
Moroccan Jews and the Politics of Belonging*
2020

Golan Y. Moskowitz, *Wild Visionary: Maurice Sendak in Queer Jewish Context*
2020

Devi Mays, *Forging Ties, Forging Passports: Migration and the Modern Sephardi Diaspora*
2020

Clémence Boulouque, *Another Modernity: Elia Benamozegh's Jewish Universalism*
2020

Dalia Kandiyoti, *The Converso's Return: Conversion and Sephardi
History in Contemporary Literature and Culture*
2020

Natan M. Meir, *Stepchildren of the Shtetl: The Destitute, Disabled,
and Mad of Jewish Eastern Europe, 1800-1939*
2020

Marc Volovici, *German as a Jewish Problem: The Language Politics of Jewish Nationalism*
2020

Dina Danon, *The Jews of Ottoman Izmir: A Modern History*
2019

Omri Asscher, *Reading Israel, Reading America: The Politics of Translation between Jews*
2019

Yael Zerubavel, *Desert in the Promised Land*
2018

Sunny S. Yudkoff, *Tubercular Capital: Illness and the Conditions of Modern Jewish Writing*
2018

Sarah Wobick-Segev, *Homes Away from Home: Jewish Belonging
in Twentieth-Century Paris, Berlin, and St. Petersburg*
2018

For a complete listing of titles in this series, visit the
Stanford University Press website, www.sup.org.